akuen ALICE™

Volume 4

Tachibana Higuchi

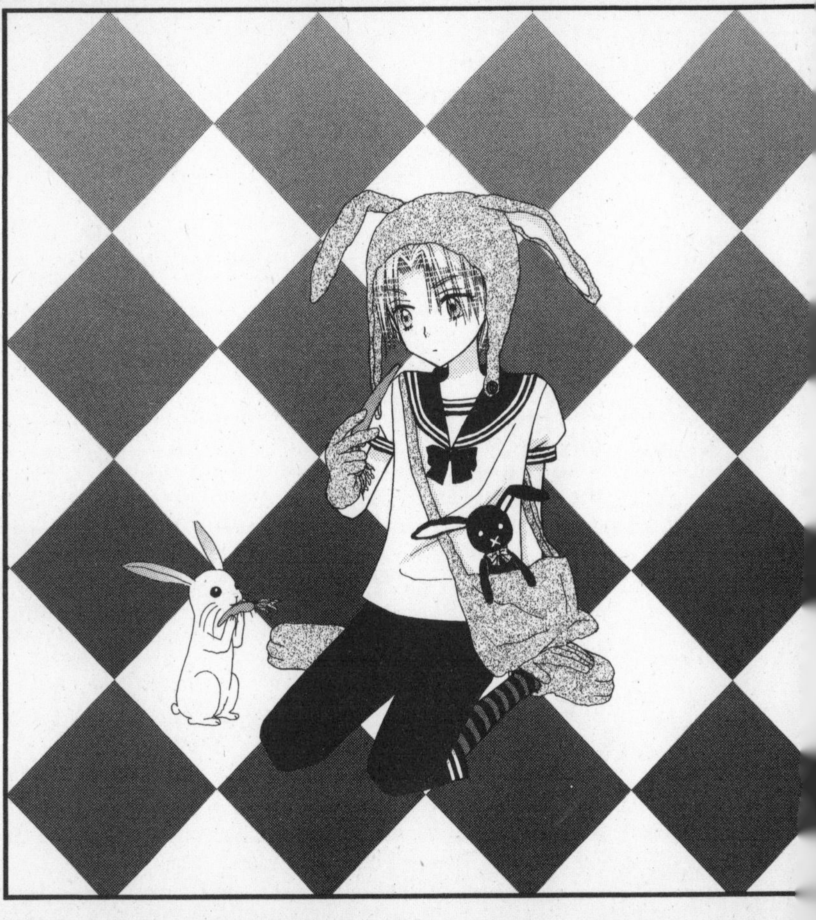

Gakuen Alice

Contents

Gakuen ALICE

Volume 4

Created by Tachibana Higuchi

HAMBURG // LONDON // LOS ANGELES // TOKYO

Gakuen Alice Volume 4
Created by Tachibana Higuchi

Translation - Haruko Furukawa
English Adaptation - Jennifer Keating
Retouch and Lettering - Star Print Brokers
Production Artist - Michael Paolilli
Graphic Designer - James Lee

Editor - Lillian Diaz-Przybyl
Digital Imaging Manager - Chris Buford
Pre-Production Supervisor - Vicente Rivera, Jr.
Production Specialist - Lucas Rivera
Managing Editor - Vy Nguyen
Art Director - Al-Insan Lashley
Editor-in-Chief - Rob Tokar
Publisher - Mike Kiley
President and C.O.O. - John Parker
C.E.O. and Chief Creative Officer - Stu Levy

A  Manga

TOKYOPOP and  are trademarks or registered trademarks of TOKYOPOP Inc.

TOKYOPOP Inc.
5900 Wilshire Blvd. Suite 2000
Los Angeles, CA 90036

E-mail: info@TOKYOPOP.com
Come visit us online at www.TOKYOPOP.com

ISBN: 978-1-4278-0322-1

First TOKYOPOP printing: September 2008
10 9 8 7 6 5 4 3 2 1
Printed in the USA

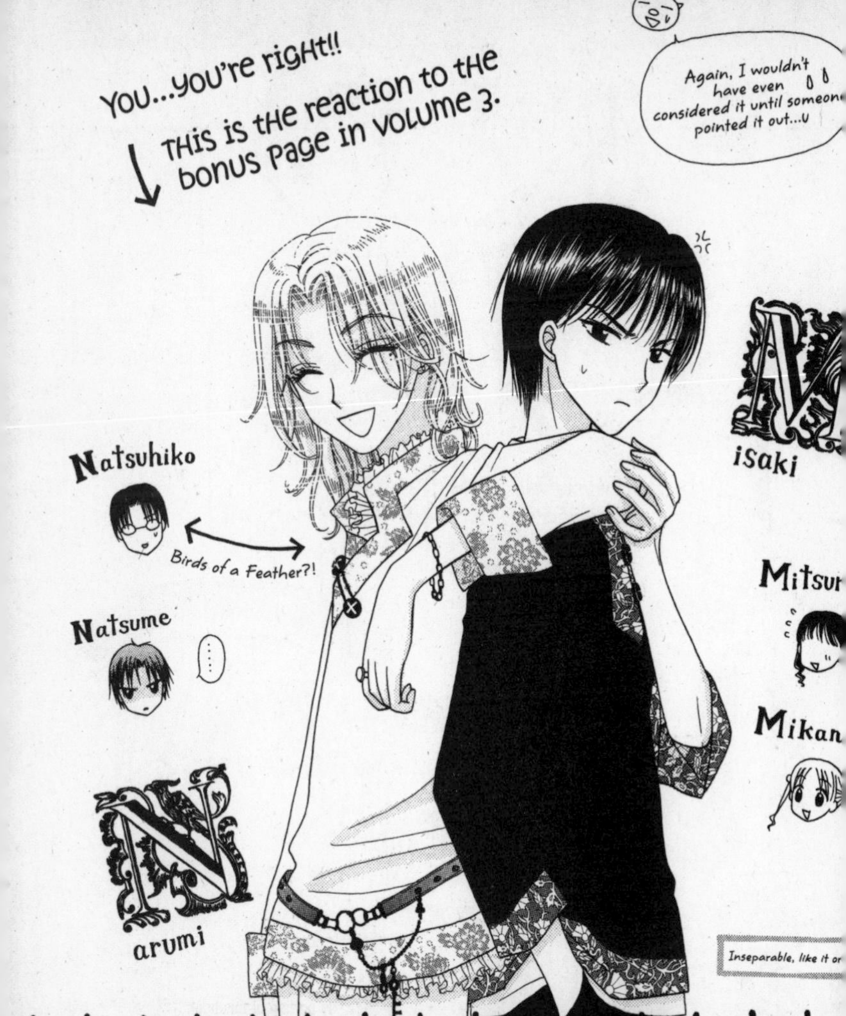
YOU...YOU'RE RIGHT!!
THIS IS THE REACTION TO THE BONUS PAGE IN VOLUME 3.
Again, I wouldn't have even considered it until someon
pointed it out...
Natsuhiko
Birds of a Feather?!
Natsume
.....
isaki
Mitsu
Mikan
arumi
Inseparable, like it or

Readers are reading into everything... Thanks. Yes, Narumi's "N" can also stand for narcissistic. I don't think that Misaki-sensei's "M" stands for masochistic though. But he is sort of like a victim character.

I mean,

Again, if you haven't read my former series "A Portrait of M and N", you must have no idea what I'm talking about. Sorry!

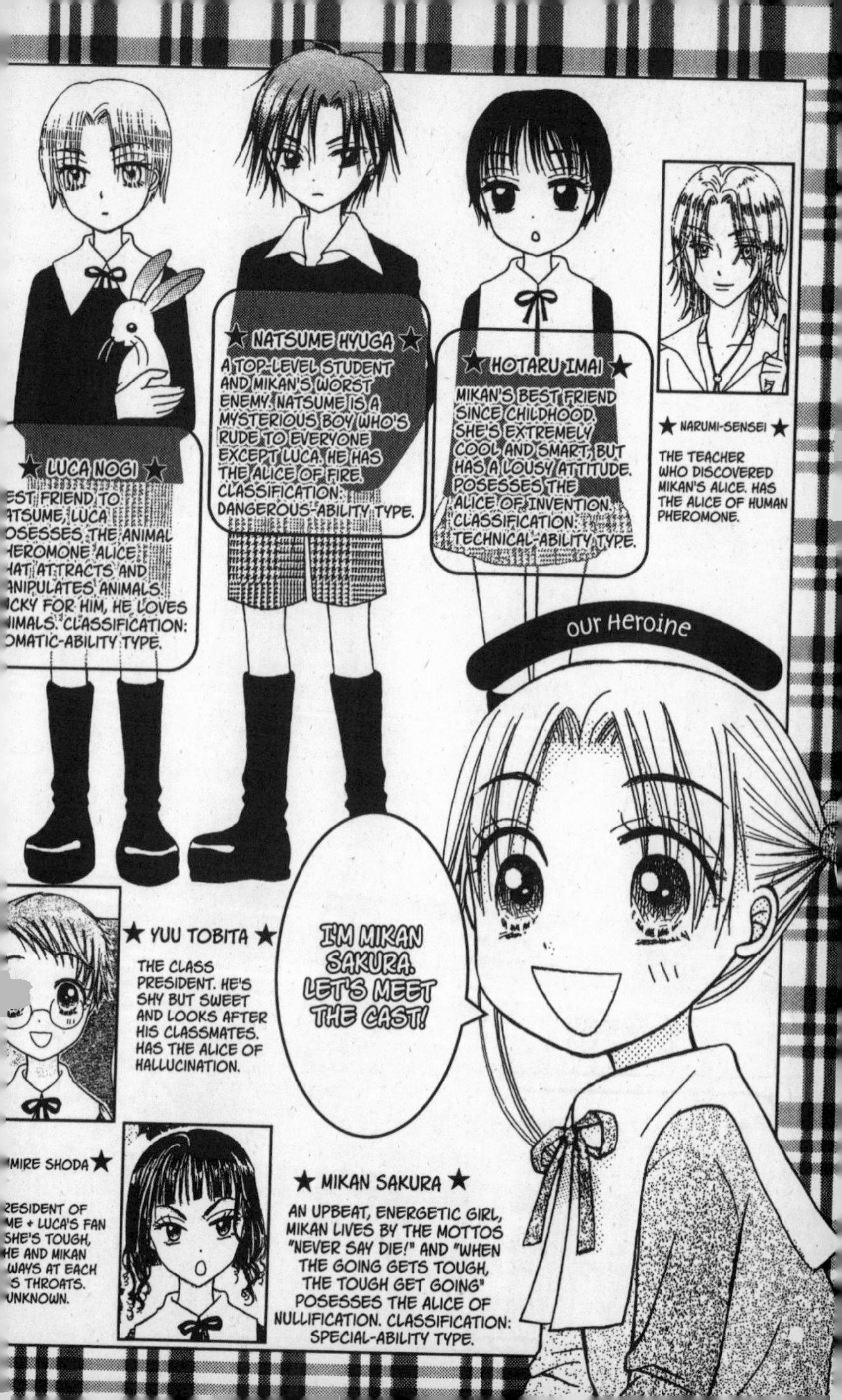

★ NARUMI-SENSEI ★
THE TEACHER WHO DISCOVERED MIKAN'S ALICE. HAS THE ALICE OF HUMAN PHEROMONE.
★ HOTARU IMAI ★
MIKAN'S BEST FRIEND SINCE CHILDHOOD. SHE'S EXTREMELY COOL AND SMART, BUT HAS A LOUSY ATTITUDE. POSESSES THE ALICE OF INVENTION. CLASSIFICATION: TECHNICAL-ABILITY TYPE.
★ NATSUME HYUGA ★
A TOP-LEVEL STUDENT AND MIKAN'S WORST ENEMY. NATSUME IS A MYSTERIOUS BOY WHO'S RUDE TO EVERYONE EXCEPT LUCA. HE HAS THE ALICE OF FIRE. CLASSIFICATION: DANGEROUS-ABILITY TYPE.
★ LUCA NOGI ★
EST FRIEND TO ATSUME, LUCA OSESSES THE ANIMAL HEROMONE ALICE HAT ATTRACTS AND ANIPULATES ANIMALS. JCKY FOR HIM, HE LOVES NIMALS. CLASSIFICATION: OMATIC-ABILITY TYPE.
OUR Heroine
I'M MIKAN SAKURA. LET'S MEET THE CAST!
★ YUU TOBITA ★
THE CLASS PRESIDENT. HE'S SHY BUT SWEET AND LOOKS AFTER HIS CLASSMATES. HAS THE ALICE OF HALLUCINATION.
★ MIKAN SAKURA ★
AN UPBEAT, ENERGETIC GIRL, MIKAN LIVES BY THE MOTTOS "NEVER SAY DIE!" AND "WHEN THE GOING GETS TOUGH, THE TOUGH GET GOING" POSESSES THE ALICE OF NULLIFICATION. CLASSIFICATION: SPECIAL-ABILITY TYPE.
MIRE SHODA ★
RESIDENT OF ME + LUCA'S FAN SHE'S TOUGH, HE AND MIKAN WAYS AT EACH S THROATS. UNKNOWN.

Story & Character Introduction

ALICE ★ MAP

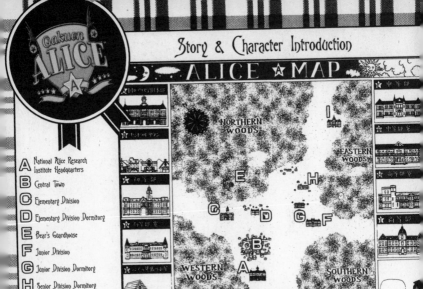

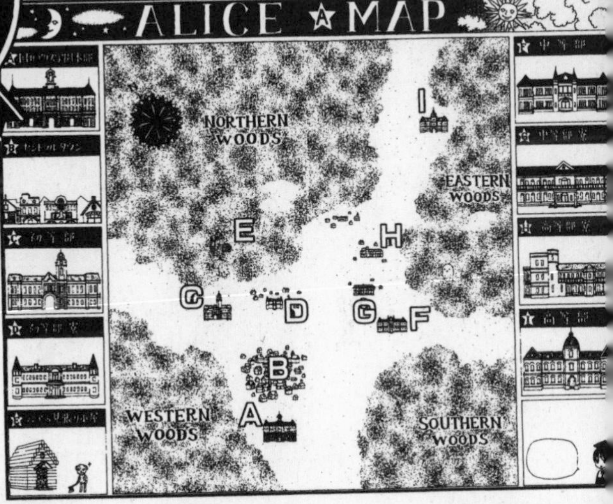
NORTHERN WOODS
EASTERN WOODS
WESTERN WOODS
SOUTHERN WOODS
A
B
C
D
E
F
G
H
I

- A National Alice Research Institute Headquarters
- B Central Town
- C Elementary Division
- D Elementary Division Dormitory
- E Bear's Guardhouse
- F Junior Division
- G Junior Division Dormitory
- H Senior Division Dormitory
- I Senior Division

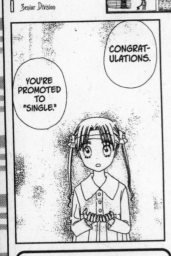

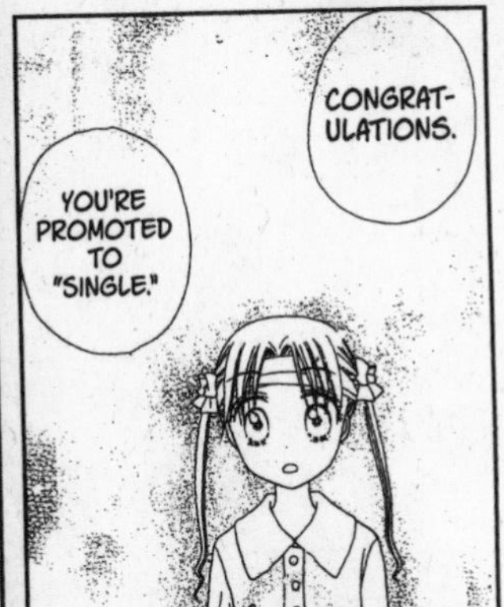
CONGRAT-ULATIONS.
YOU'RE PROMOTED TO "SINGLE."

STORY THUS FAR:

★ CHILDHOOD FRIENDS MIKAN AND HOTARU WERE BROUGHT UP IN A SMALL VILLAGE. WHEN HOTARU TRANSFERRED TO THE ALICE ACADEMY FOR PEOPLE WITH MYSTERIOUS POWERS (OR 'ALICES'), MIKAN FOLLOWED HER! HER SCHOOL LIFE'S ROCKY SOMETIMES, BUT SHE'S TRYING HARD TO LIVE BY HER MOTTOS: "NEVER SAY DIE!" AND "WHEN THE GOING GETS TOUGH, THE TOUGH GET GOING!"

★ AS THE ALICE FESTIVAL NEARS, REO, THE INTERNATIONAL STAR AND ALICE ALUMNUS, PAYS A VISIT TO THE ACADEMY. MIKAN AND SUMIRE ACCIDENTALLY WITNESS HIM KIDNAPPING NATSUME FROM THE HOSPITAL AND GIVE CHASE. NOT ONLY DO THEY SUCCESSFULLY RESCUE NATSUME, BUT MIKAN ALSO GETS PROMOTED TO SINGLE STATUS AS A REWARD. THE ALICE FESTIVAL IS FAST APPROACHING, AND MIKAN CAN'T WAIT TO TAKE PART IN IT!

WHAT IS ALICE ACADEMY?

THE ULTIMATE TALENT SCHOOL THAT ADMITS ONLY SPECIAL PRODIGIES WHO POSESS MYSTERIOUS POWERS CALLED "ALICES." AN EXTREMELY STRICT SCHOOL, THE ACADEMY RESTRICTS STUDENT CONTACT WITH THE OUTSIDE WORLD--INCLUDING THEIR OWN PARENTS!

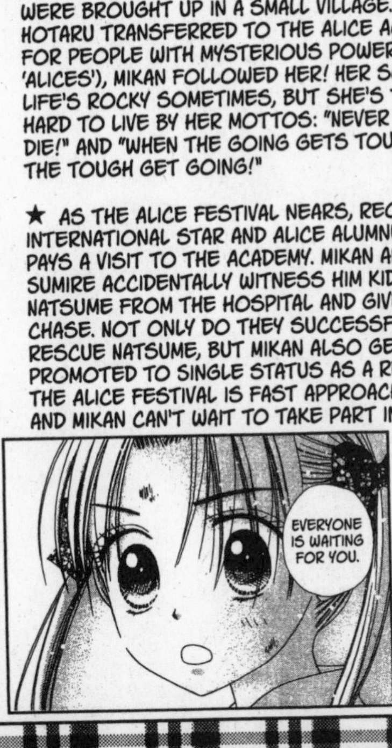
EVERYONE IS WAITING FOR YOU.

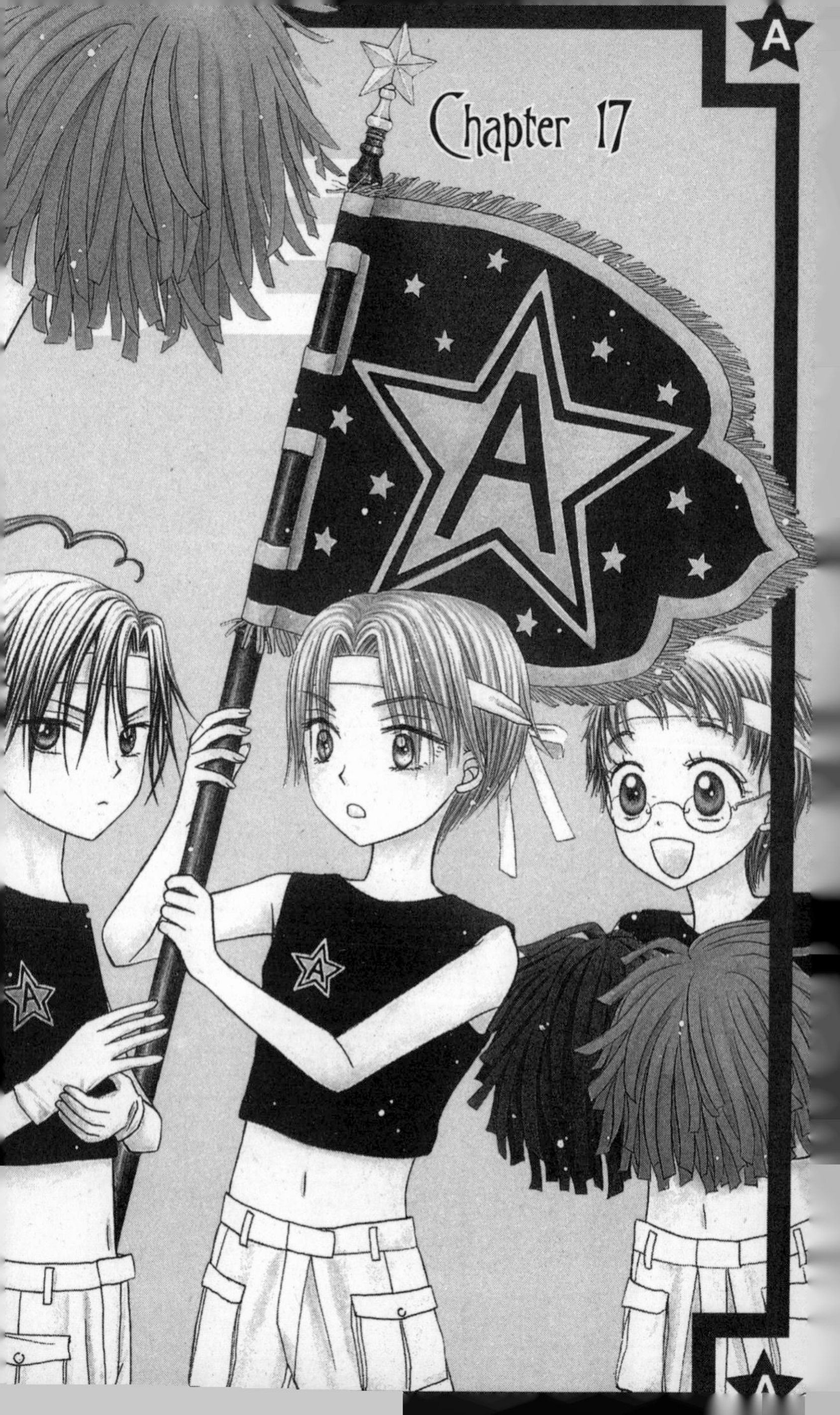
Chapter 17

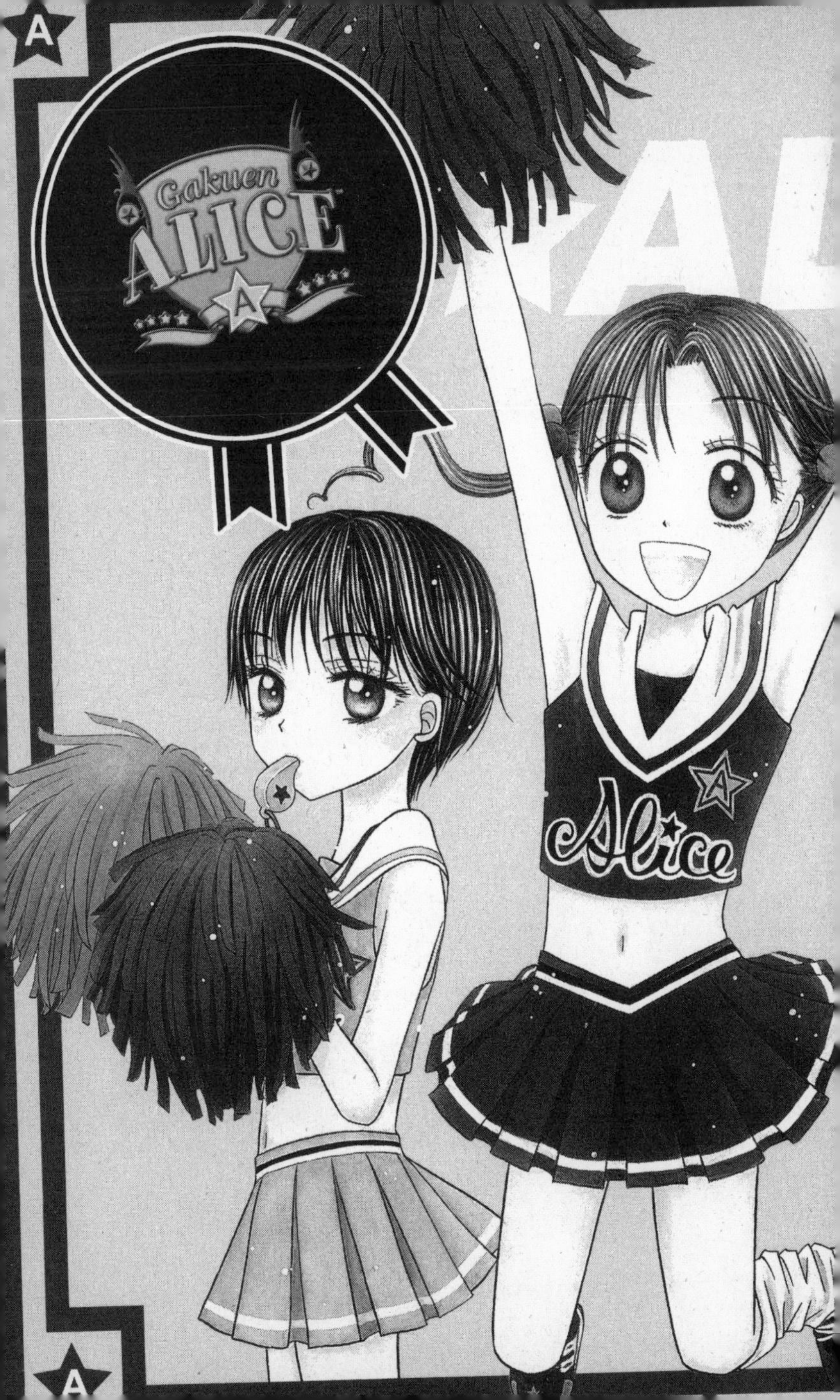
Gakuen
ALICE
Alice

Frequently Asked Questions

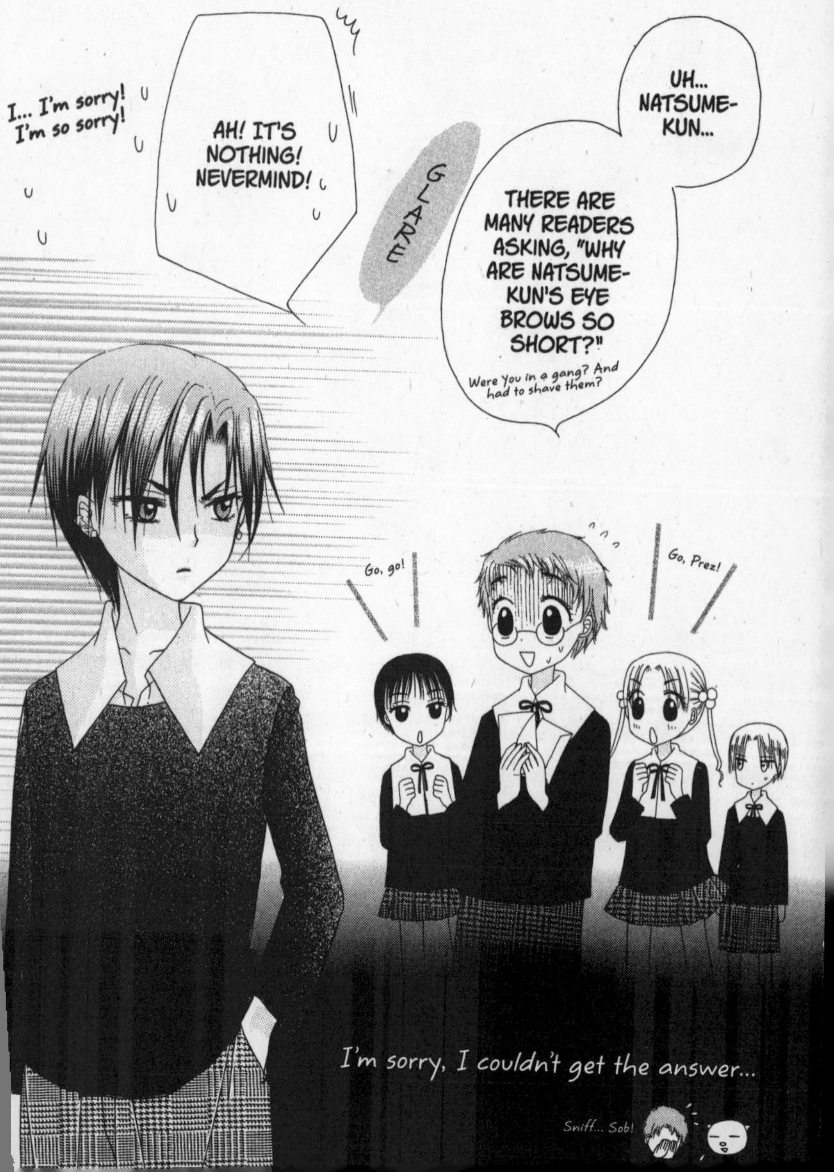
UH... NATSUME-KUN...
THERE ARE MANY READERS ASKING, "WHY ARE NATSUME-KUN'S EYE BROWS SO SHORT?"
Were you in a gang? And had to shave them?
GLARE
AH! IT'S NOTHING! NEVERMIND!
I... I'm sorry! I'm so sorry!
Go, Prez!
Go, go!
I'm sorry, I couldn't get the answer...
Sniff... Sob!

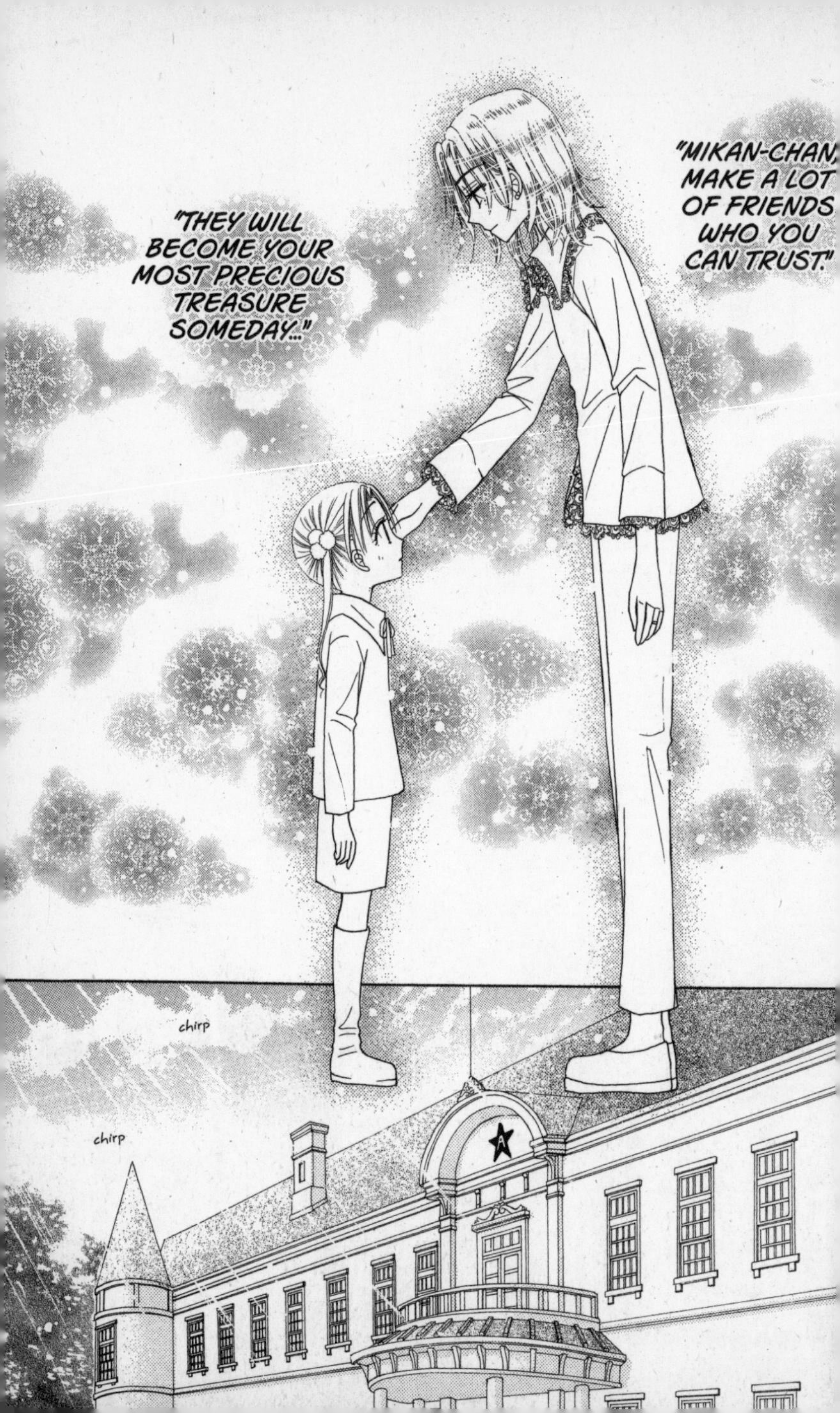
"MIKAN-CHAN, MAKE A LOT OF FRIENDS WHO YOU CAN TRUST."
"THEY WILL BECOME YOUR MOST PRECIOUS TREASURE SOMEDAY..."
chirp
chirp

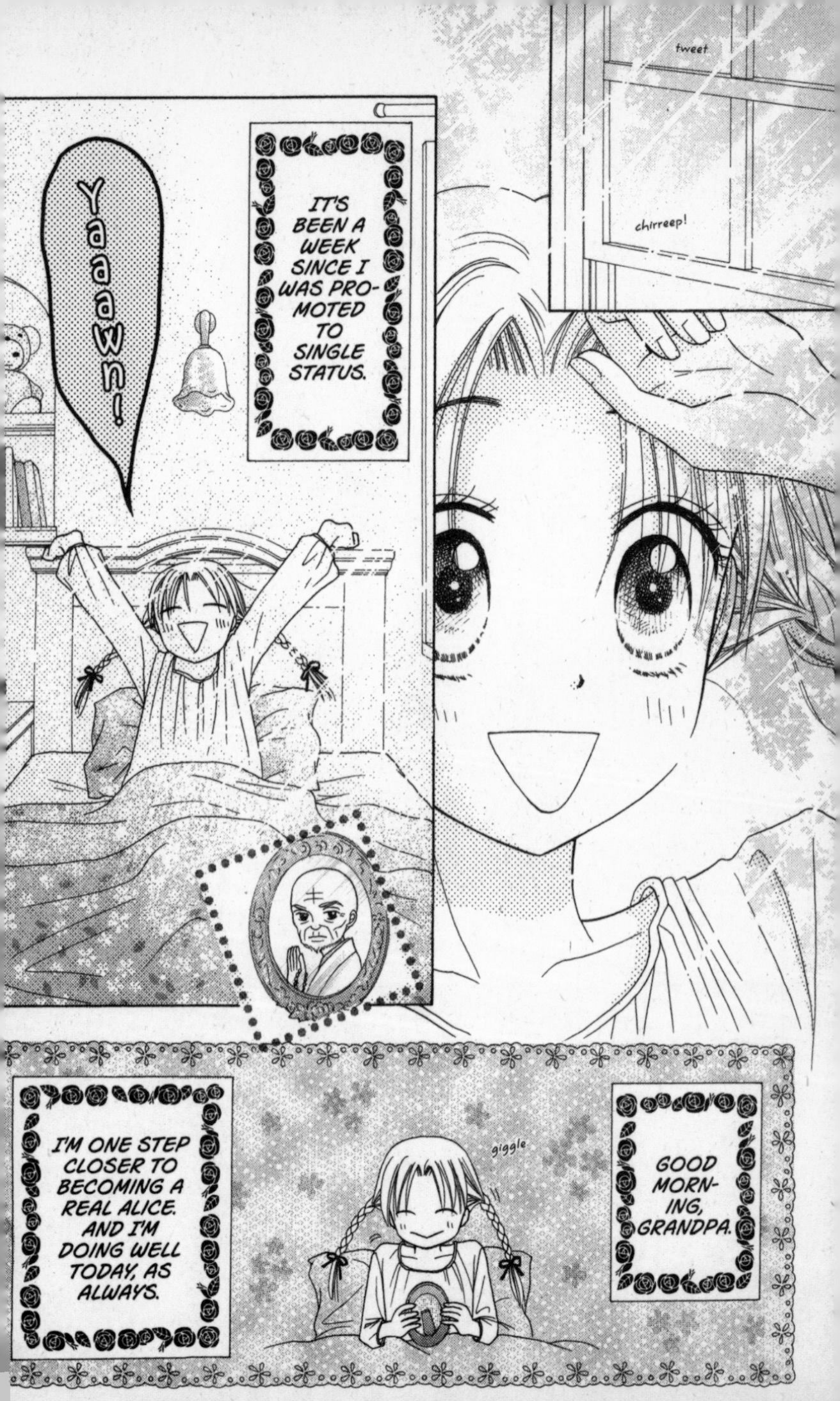
tweet
chirreep!
IT'S BEEN A WEEK SINCE I WAS PRO-MOTED TO SINGLE STATUS.
Yaaawn!
GOOD MORN-ING, GRANDPA.
giggle
I'M ONE STEP CLOSER TO BECOMING A REAL ALICE. AND I'M DOING WELL TODAY, AS ALWAYS.

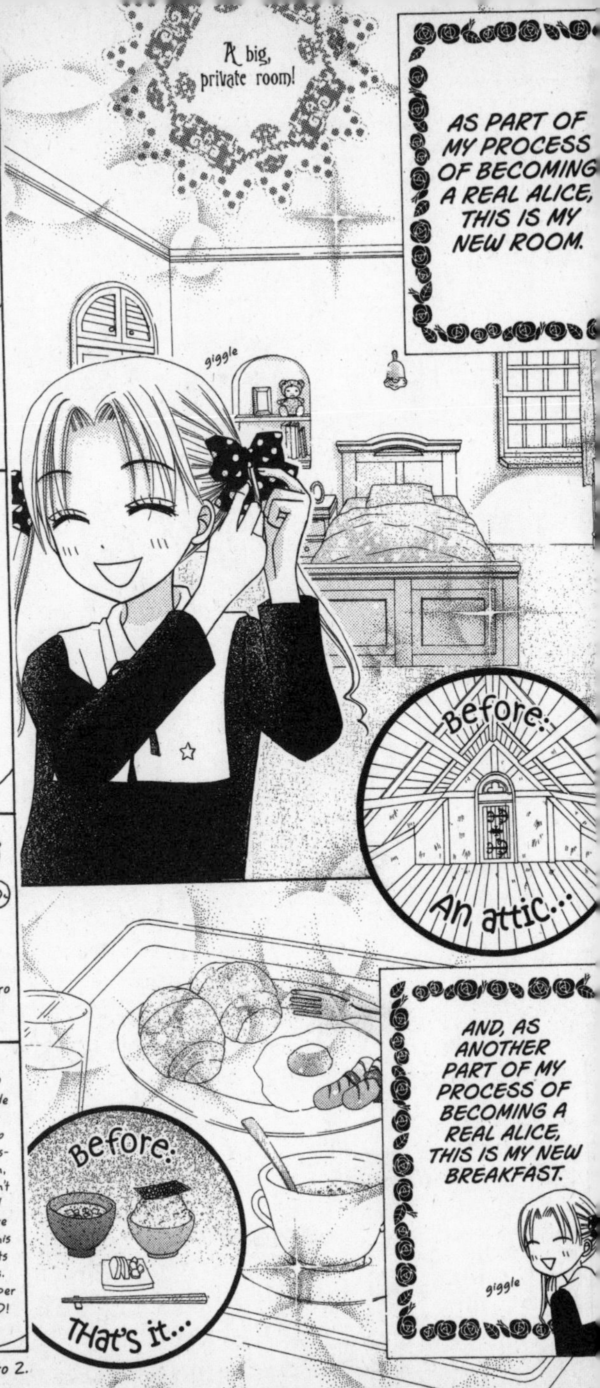
AS PART OF MY PROCESS OF BECOMING A REAL ALICE, THIS IS MY NEW ROOM.
A big, private room!
giggle
Before:
An attic...
AND, AS ANOTHER PART OF MY PROCESS OF BECOMING A REAL ALICE, THIS IS MY NEW BREAKFAST.
giggle
Before:
That's it...

Read at your own discretion.

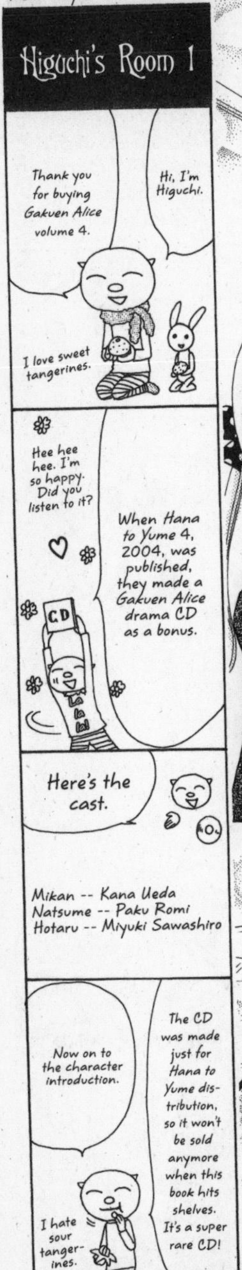
Higuchi's Room 1
Hi, I'm Higuchi.
Thank you for buying Gakuen Alice volume 4.
I love sweet tangerines.
When Hana to Yume 4, 2004, was published, they made a Gakuen Alice drama CD as a bonus.
Hee hee hee. I'm so happy. Did you listen to it?
CD
La la la!
Here's the cast.
Mikan -- Kana Ueda
Natsume -- Paku Romi
Hotaru -- Miyuki Sawashiro
The CD was made just for Hana to Yume distribution, so it won't be sold anymore when this book hits shelves. It's a super rare CD!
Now on to the character introduction.
I hate sour tangerines.

Go to 2.

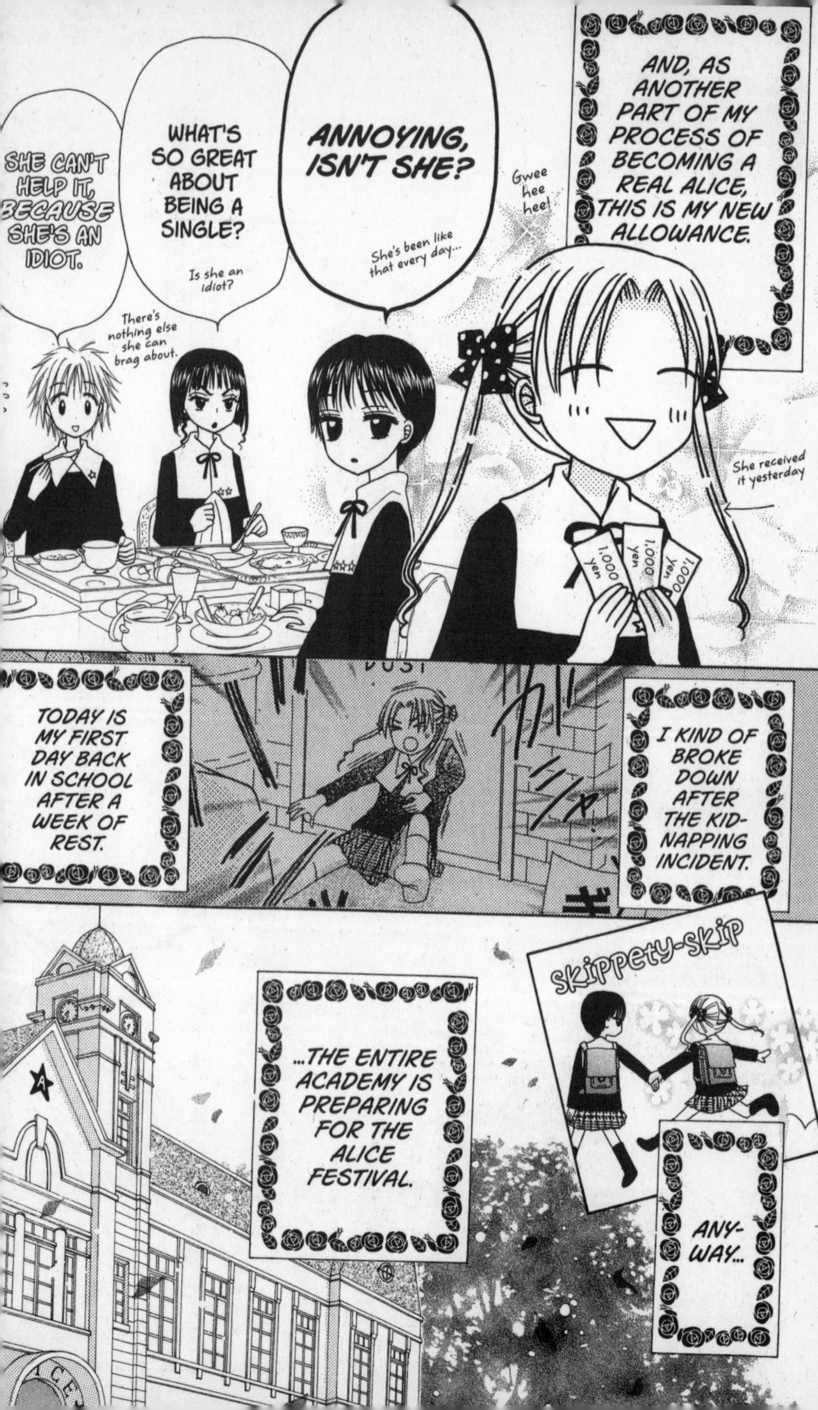
AND, AS ANOTHER PART OF MY PROCESS OF BECOMING A REAL ALICE, THIS IS MY NEW ALLOWANCE.
Gwee hee hee!
She received it yesterday
1,000 yen
1,000 yen
1,000 yen
ANNOYING, ISN'T SHE?
She's been like that every day...
WHAT'S SO GREAT ABOUT BEING A SINGLE?
Is she an idiot?
SHE CAN'T HELP IT, BECAUSE SHE'S AN IDIOT.
There's nothing else she can brag about.
I KIND OF BROKE DOWN AFTER THE KID-NAPPING INCIDENT.
TODAY IS MY FIRST DAY BACK IN SCHOOL AFTER A WEEK OF REST.
SKIPPETY-SKIP
ANY-WAY...
...THE ENTIRE ACADEMY IS PREPARING FOR THE ALICE FESTIVAL.

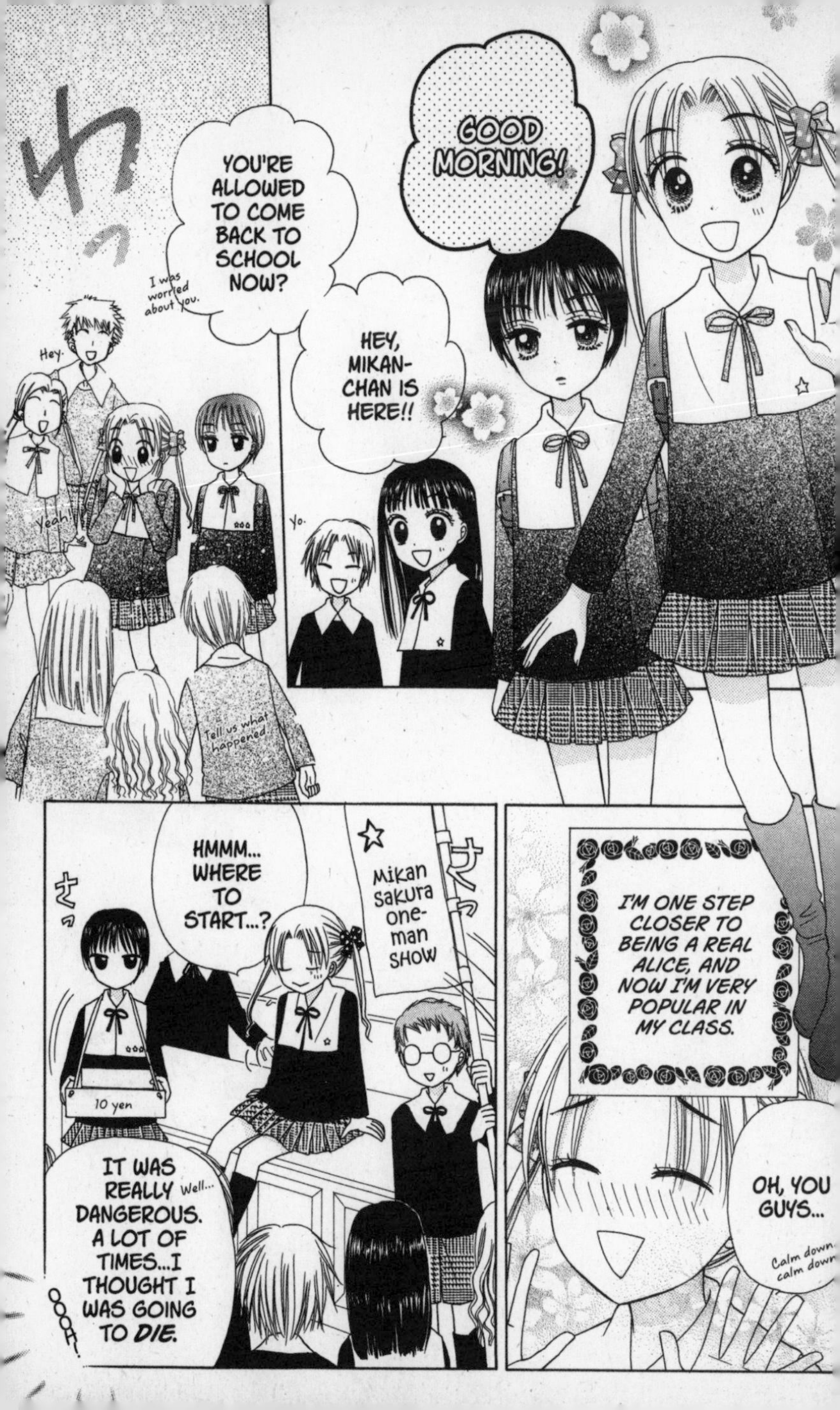
GOOD MORNING!
HEY, MIKAN-CHAN IS HERE!!
Yo.
わっ
YOU'RE ALLOWED TO COME BACK TO SCHOOL NOW?
I was worried about you.
Hey.
Yeah!
Tell us what happened
I'M ONE STEP CLOSER TO BEING A REAL ALICE, AND NOW I'M VERY POPULAR IN MY CLASS.
OH, YOU GUYS...
Calm down calm down
さっ
Mikan Sakura one-man show
HMMM... WHERE TO START...?
さっ
10 yen
Well...
IT WAS REALLY DANGEROUS. A LOT OF TIMES...I THOUGHT I WAS GOING TO *DIE*.
OOOH!

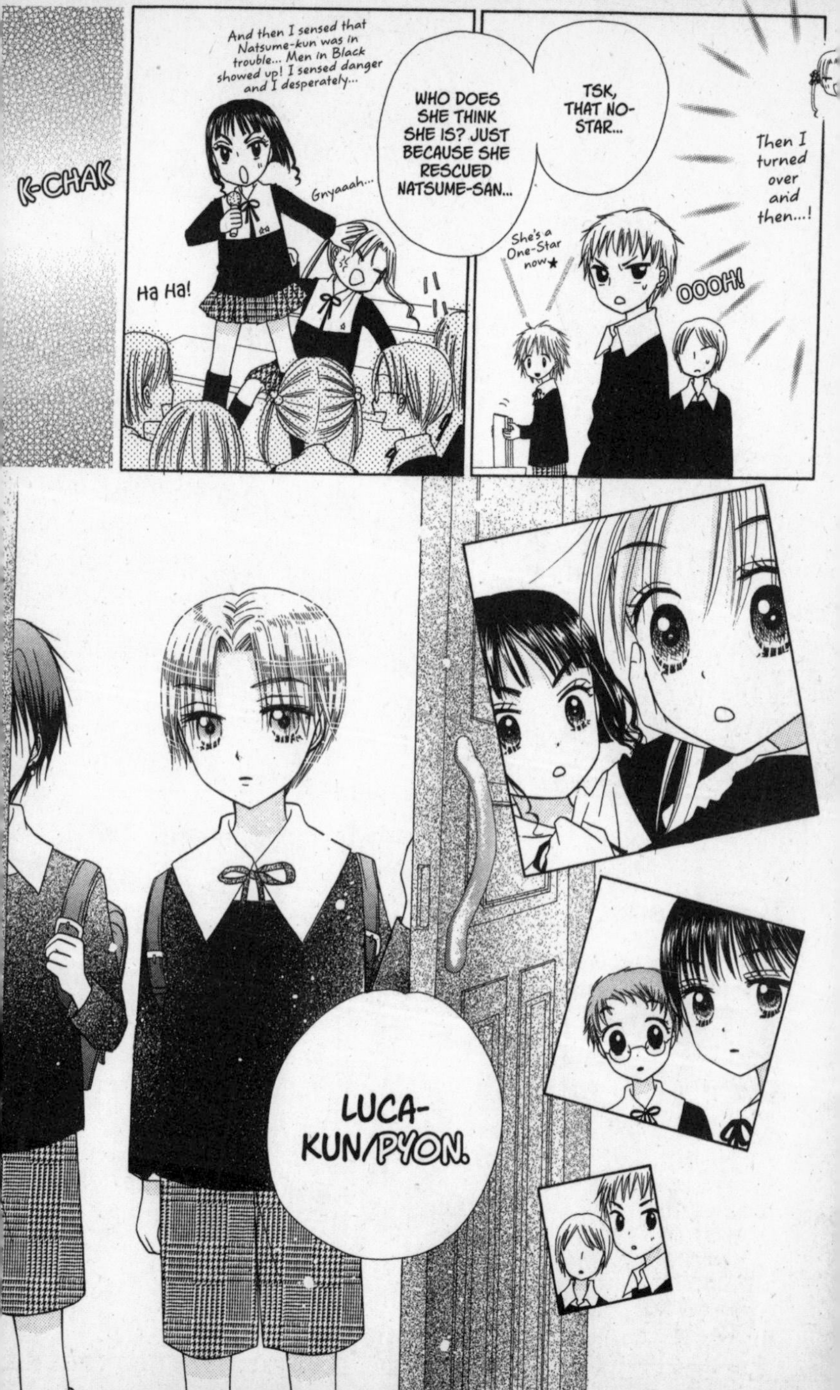

Then I turned over and then...!
OOOH!
She's a One-Star now★
TSK, THAT NO-STAR...
WHO DOES SHE THINK SHE IS? JUST BECAUSE SHE RESCUED NATSUME-SAN...
And then I sensed that Natsume-kun was in trouble... Men in Black showed up! I sensed danger and I desperately...
Gnyaaah...
Ha Ha!
K-CHAK
LUCA-KUN/PYON.

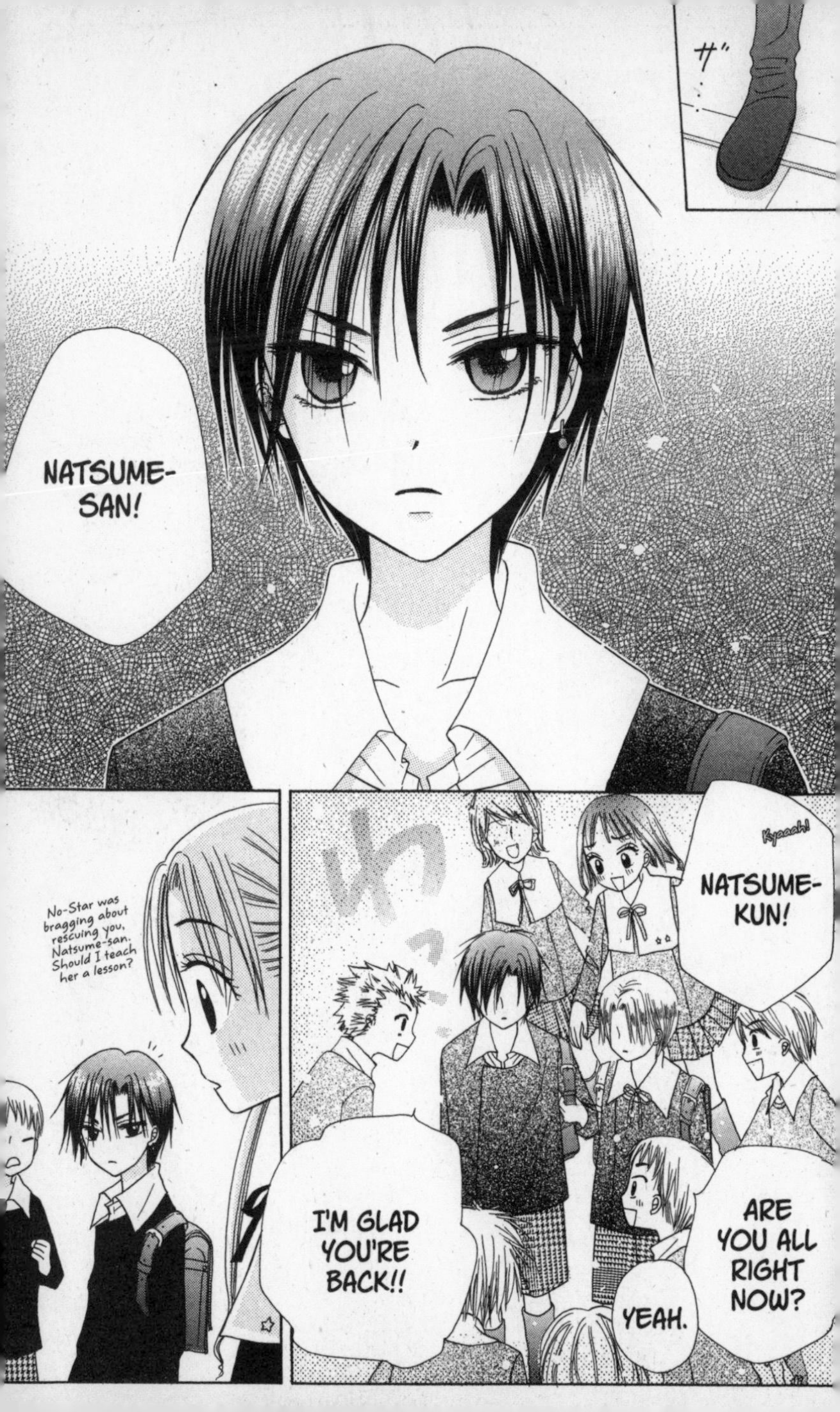
ザ
NATSUME-SAN!
Kyaaah!
NATSUME-KUN!
わっ
ARE YOU ALL RIGHT NOW?
YEAH.
I'M GLAD YOU'RE BACK!!
No-Star was bragging about rescuing you, Natsume-san. Should I teach her a lesson?

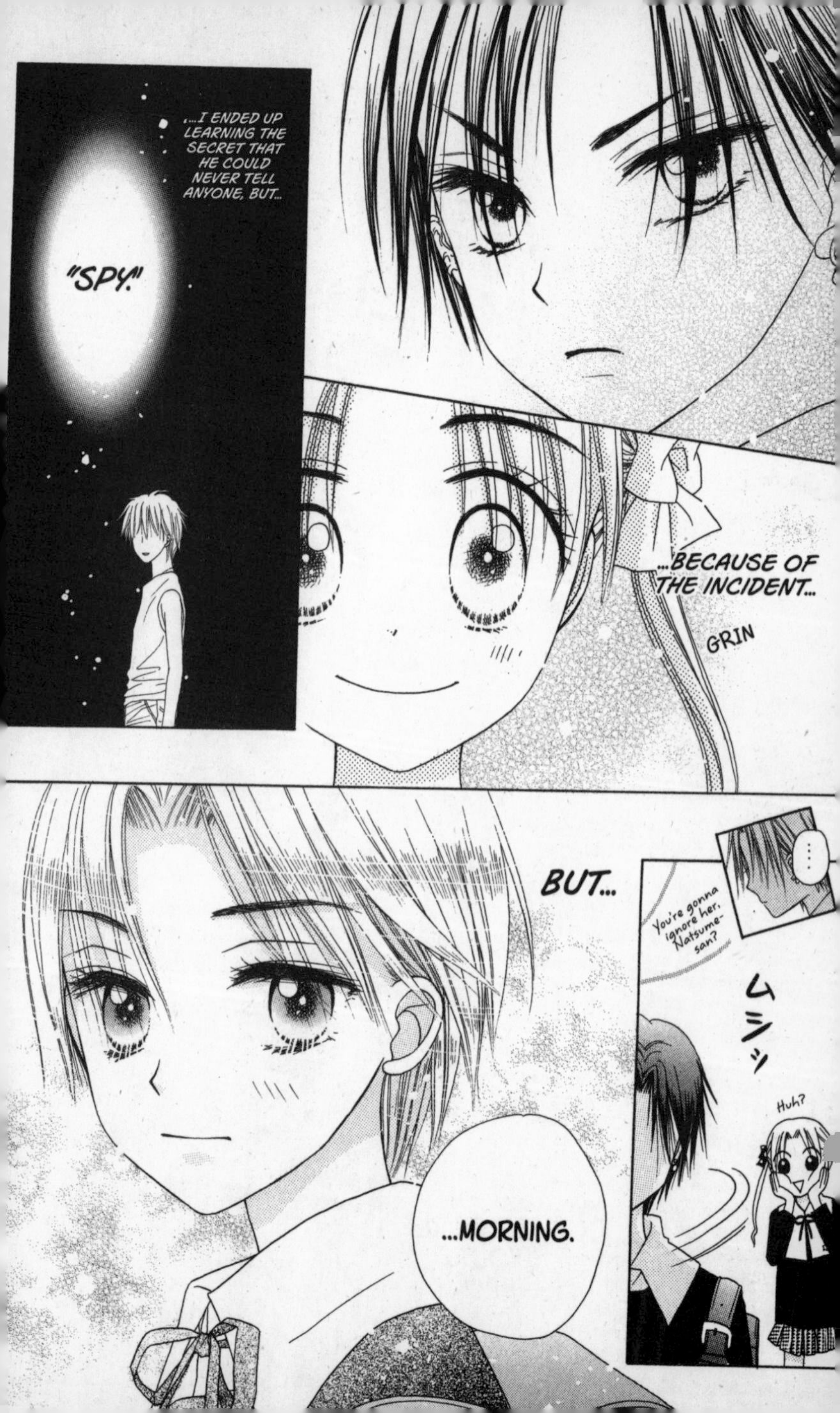
...BECAUSE OF THE INCIDENT...
GRIN
...I ENDED UP LEARNING THE SECRET THAT HE COULD NEVER TELL ANYONE, BUT...
"SPY."
....
You're gonna ignore her, Natsume-san?
ムシッ
Huh?
BUT...
...MORNING.

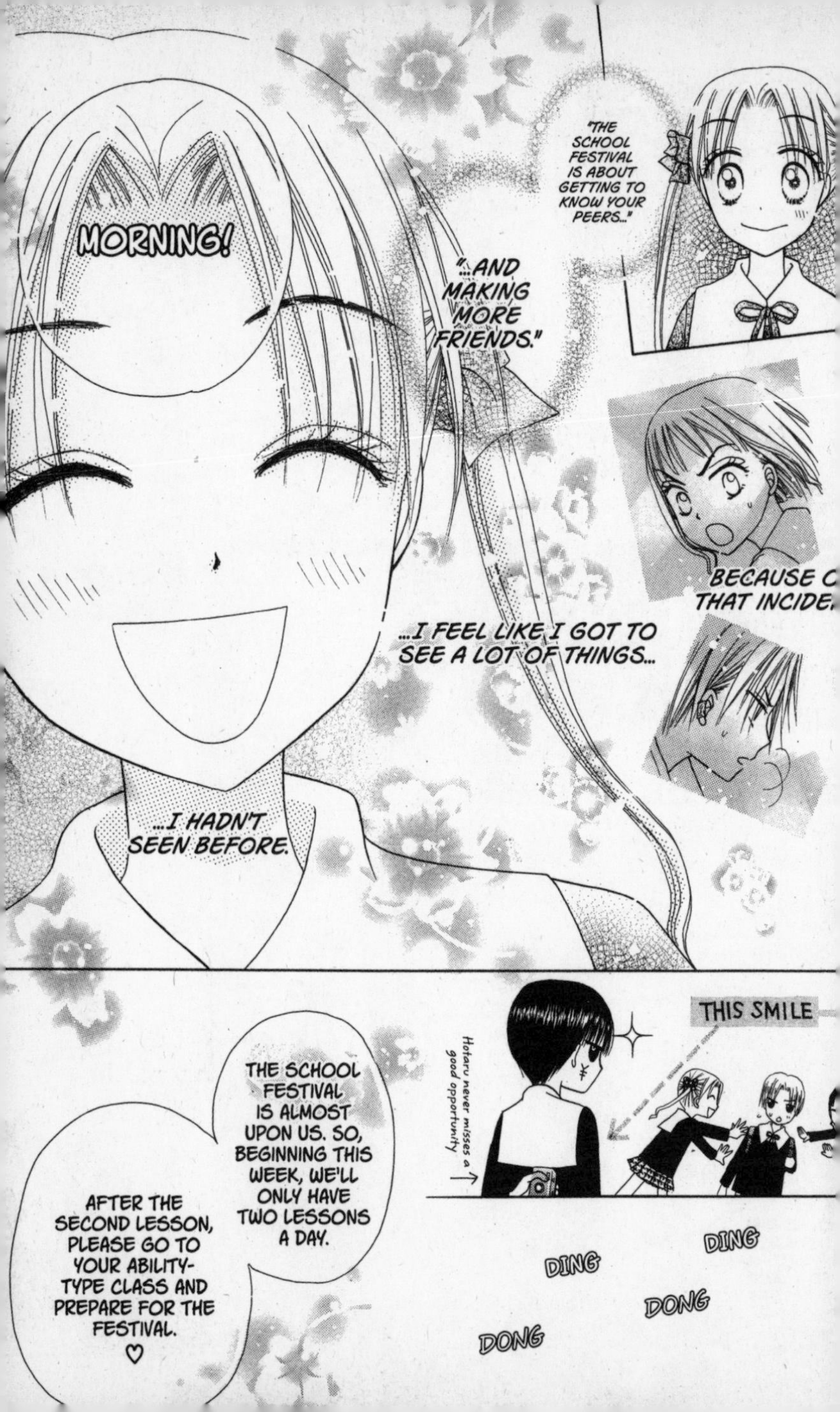
"THE SCHOOL FESTIVAL IS ABOUT GETTING TO KNOW YOUR PEERS..."
"...AND MAKING MORE FRIENDS."
BECAUSE C
THAT INCIDE
...I FEEL LIKE I GOT TO SEE A LOT OF THINGS...
...I HADN'T SEEN BEFORE.
MORNING!
THIS SMILE
Hotaru never misses a good opportunity
THE SCHOOL FESTIVAL IS ALMOST UPON US. SO, BEGINNING THIS WEEK, WE'LL ONLY HAVE TWO LESSONS A DAY.
AFTER THE SECOND LESSON, PLEASE GO TO YOUR ABILITY-TYPE CLASS AND PREPARE FOR THE FESTIVAL. ♡
DING
DING
DONG
DONG

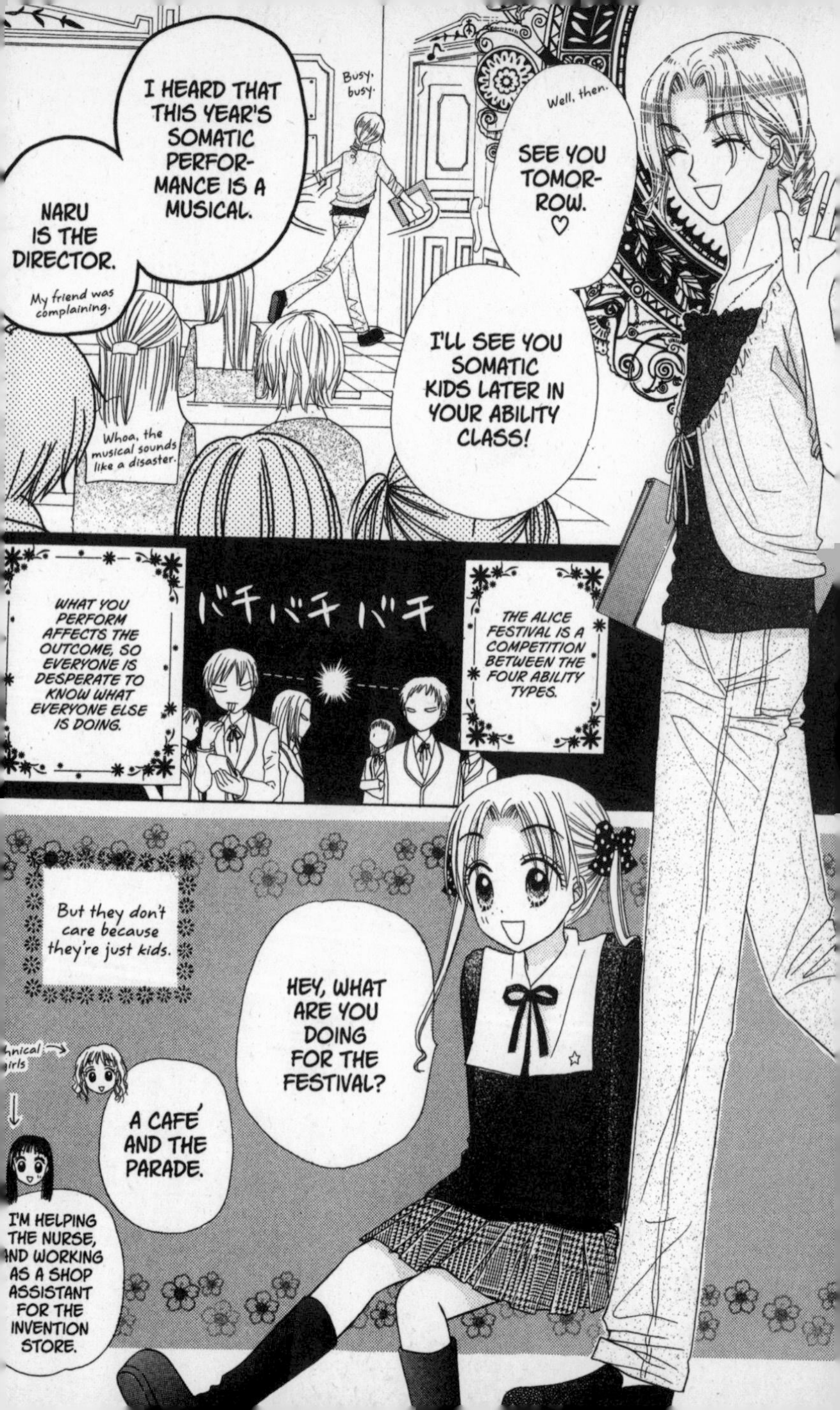
Well, then.
SEE YOU TOMORROW. ♡
I'LL SEE YOU SOMATIC KIDS LATER IN YOUR ABILITY CLASS!
Busy, busy.
I HEARD THAT THIS YEAR'S SOMATIC PERFORMANCE IS A MUSICAL.
NARU IS THE DIRECTOR.
My friend was complaining.
Whoa, the musical sounds like a disaster.
THE ALICE FESTIVAL IS A COMPETITION BETWEEN THE FOUR ABILITY TYPES.
バチバチバチ
WHAT YOU PERFORM AFFECTS THE OUTCOME, SO EVERYONE IS DESPERATE TO KNOW WHAT EVERYONE ELSE IS DOING.
But they don't care because they're just kids.
HEY, WHAT ARE YOU DOING FOR THE FESTIVAL?
hnical girls
A CAFÉ AND THE PARADE.
I'M HELPING THE NURSE, AND WORKING AS A SHOP ASSISTANT FOR THE INVENTION STORE.

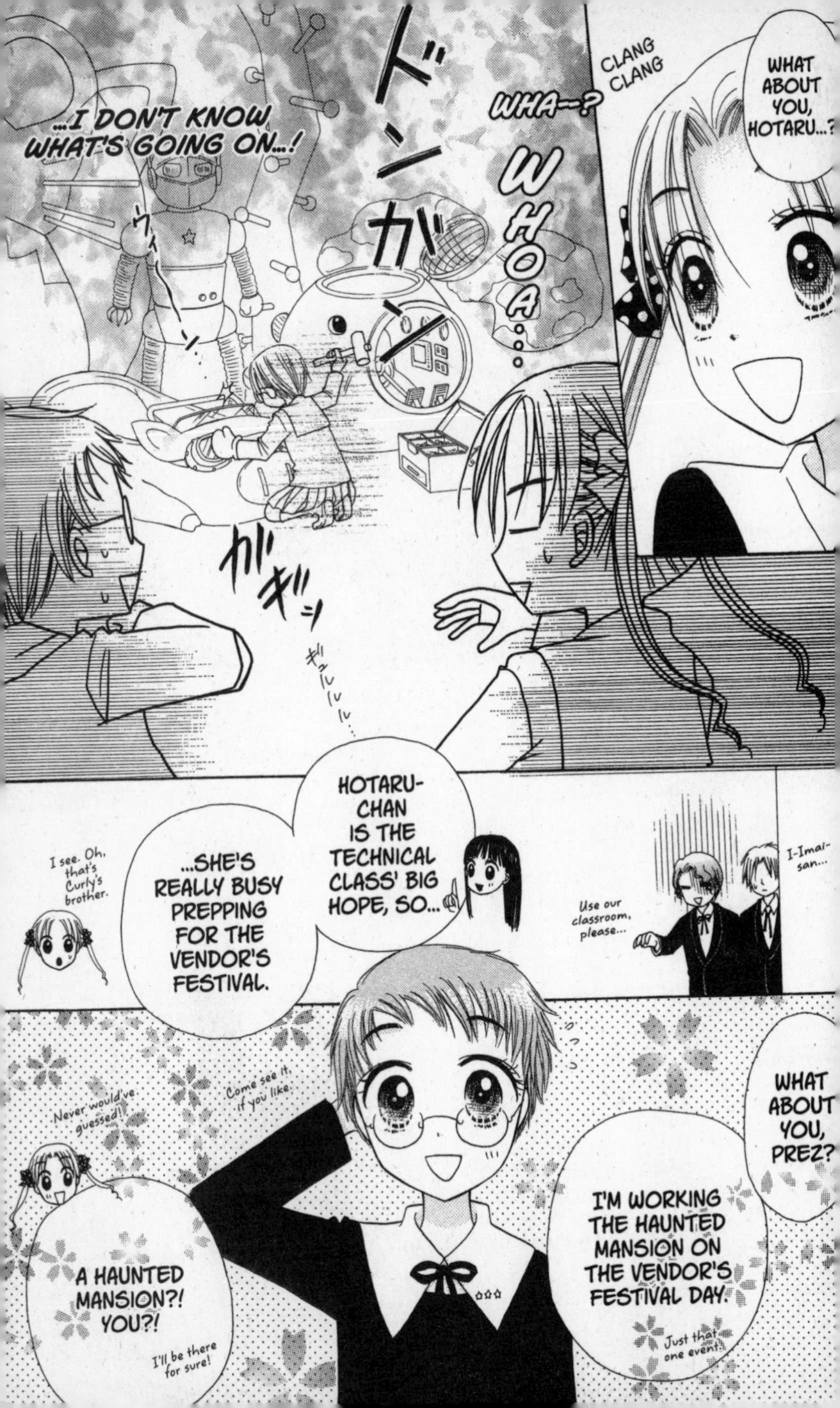
WHAT ABOUT YOU, HOTARU...?
CLANG CLANG
WHA--?
WHOA...
...I DON'T KNOW WHAT'S GOING ON...!
I-Imai-san...
Use our classroom, please...
HOTARU-CHAN IS THE TECHNICAL CLASS' BIG HOPE, SO...
...SHE'S REALLY BUSY PREPPING FOR THE VENDOR'S FESTIVAL.
I see. Oh, that's Curly's brother.
WHAT ABOUT YOU, PREZ?
I'M WORKING THE HAUNTED MANSION ON THE VENDOR'S FESTIVAL DAY.
Just that one event.
Come see it, if you like.
Never would've guessed!
A HAUNTED MANSION?! YOU?!
I'll be there for sure!

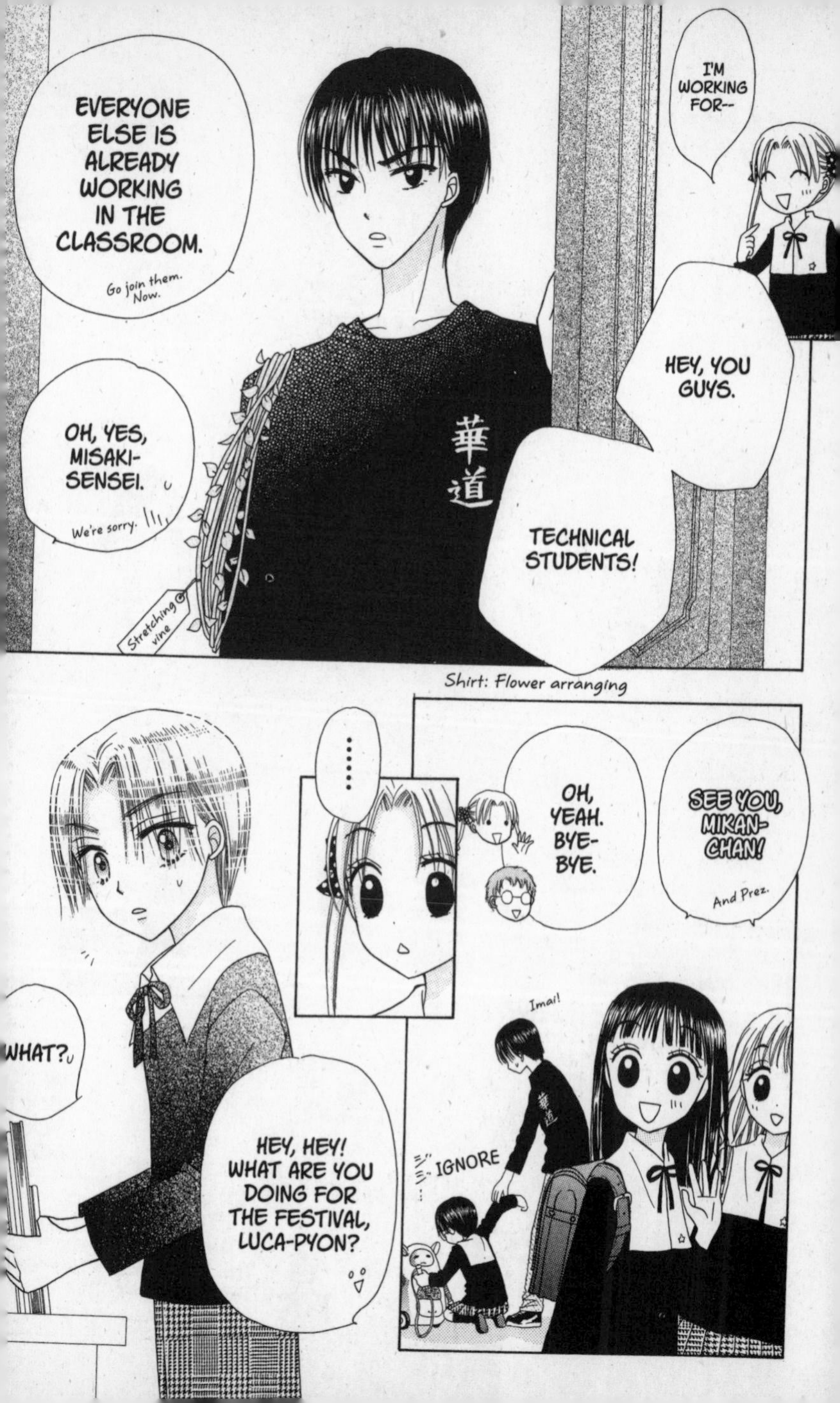
I'M WORKING FOR--
HEY, YOU GUYS.
TECHNICAL STUDENTS!
華道
EVERYONE ELSE IS ALREADY WORKING IN THE CLASSROOM.
Go join them. Now.
OH, YES, MISAKI-SENSEI.
We're sorry.
Stretching vine
Shirt: Flower arranging
SEE YOU, MIKAN-CHAN!
And Prez.
OH, YEAH. BYE-BYE.
Imai!
IGNORE
......
WHAT?
HEY, HEY! WHAT ARE YOU DOING FOR THE FESTIVAL, LUCA-PYON?

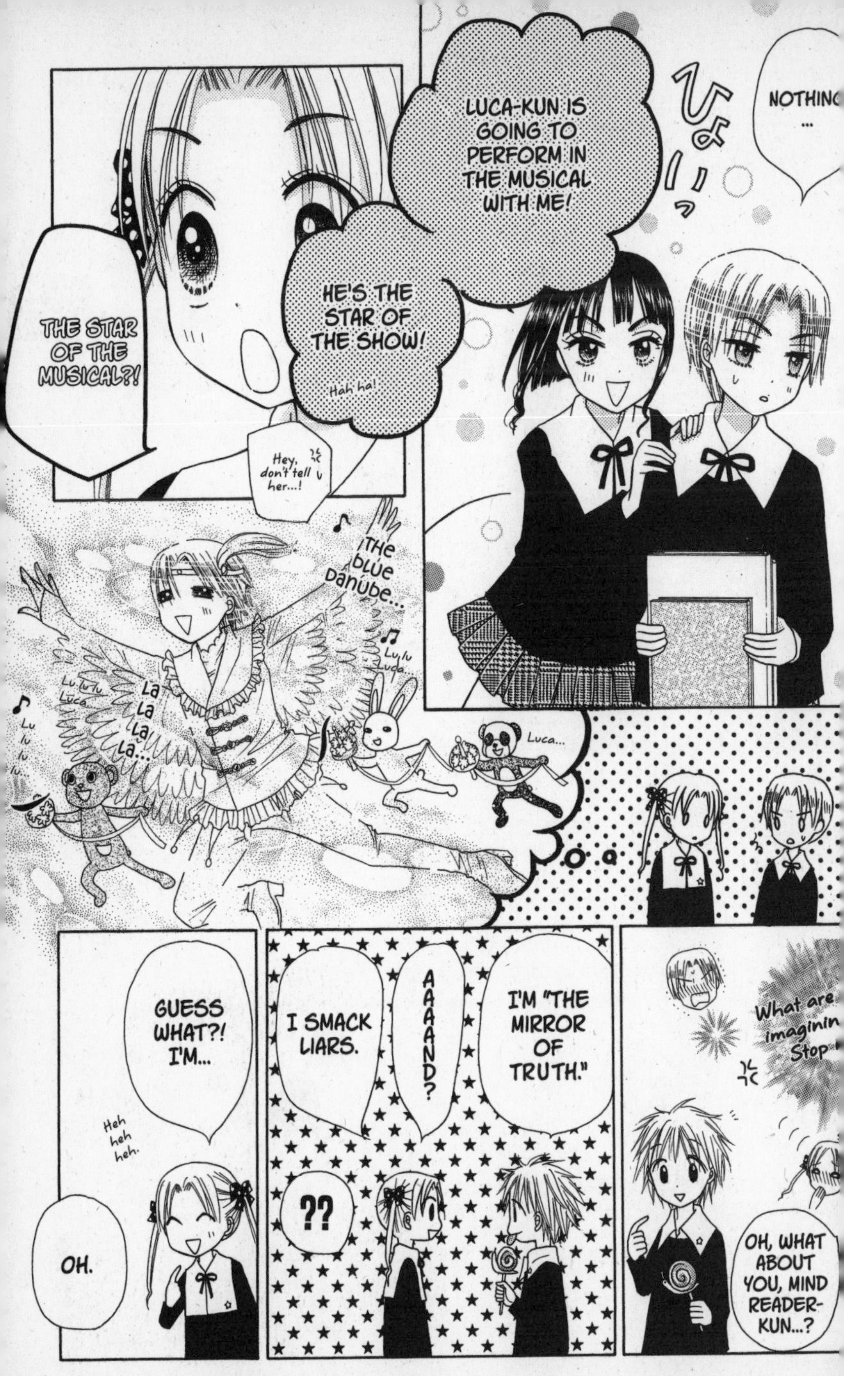
NOTHING ...
LUCA-KUN IS GOING TO PERFORM IN THE MUSICAL WITH ME!
HE'S THE STAR OF THE SHOW!
Hah ha!
THE STAR OF THE MUSICAL?!
Hey, don't tell her...!
The blue Danube...
Lu lu Luca...
Luca...
La La La La...
Lu lu Luca
Lu lu lu lu...
What are imaginin Stop
OH, WHAT ABOUT YOU, MIND READER-KUN...?
I'M "THE MIRROR OF TRUTH."
AAAAND?
I SMACK LIARS.
??
GUESS WHAT?! I'M...
Heh heh heh.
OH.

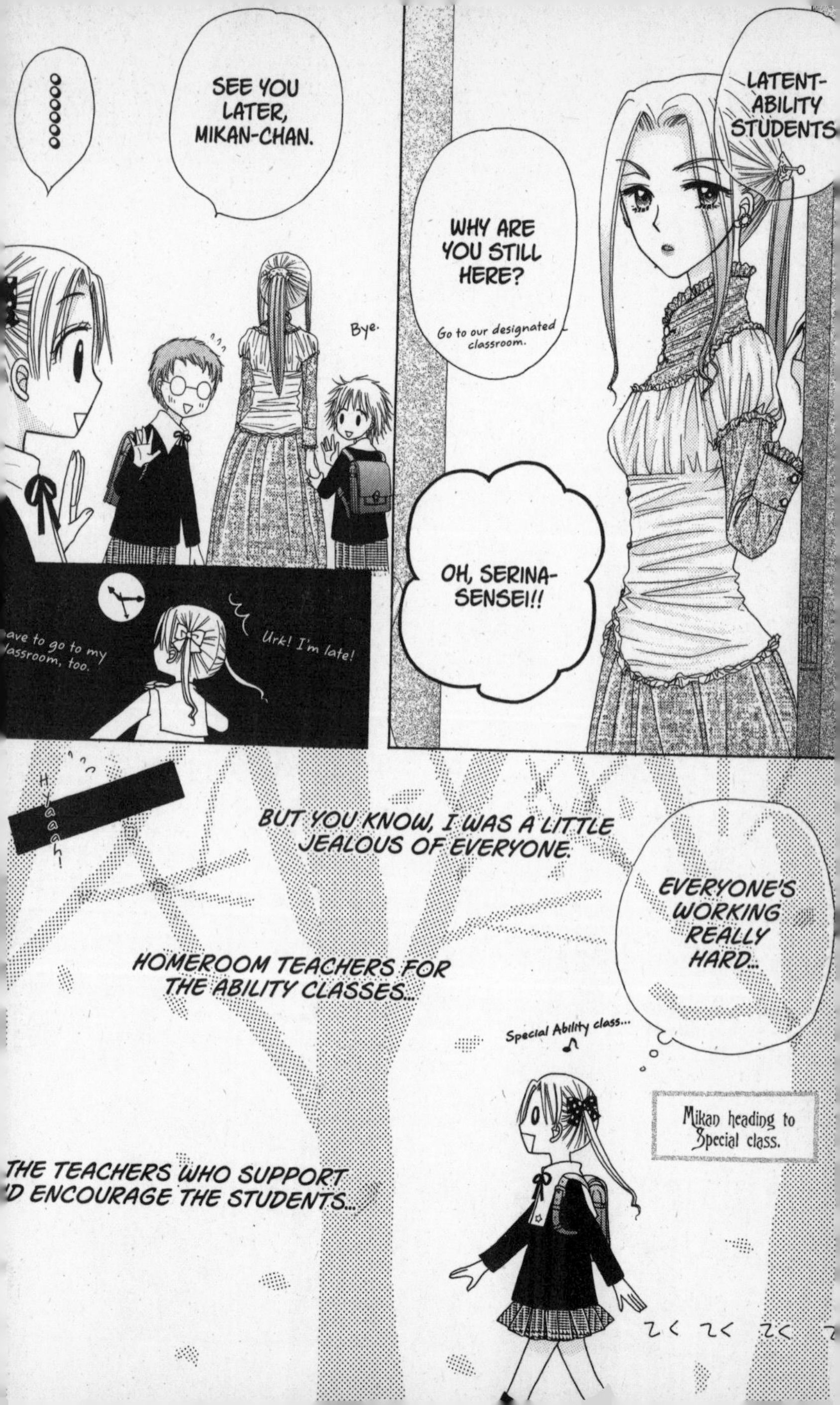

LATENT-ABILITY STUDENTS
WHY ARE YOU STILL HERE?
Go to our designated classroom.
OH, SERINA-SENSEI!!
SEE YOU LATER, MIKAN-CHAN.
......
Bye.
Urk! I'm late!
ave to go to my lassroom, too.
EVERYONE'S WORKING REALLY HARD...
BUT YOU KNOW, I WAS A LITTLE JEALOUS OF EVERYONE.
Special Ability class...
Mikan heading to Special class.
HOMEROOM TEACHERS FOR THE ABILITY CLASSES...
Hyaaah!
THE TEACHERS WHO SUPPORT 'D ENCOURAGE THE STUDENTS...

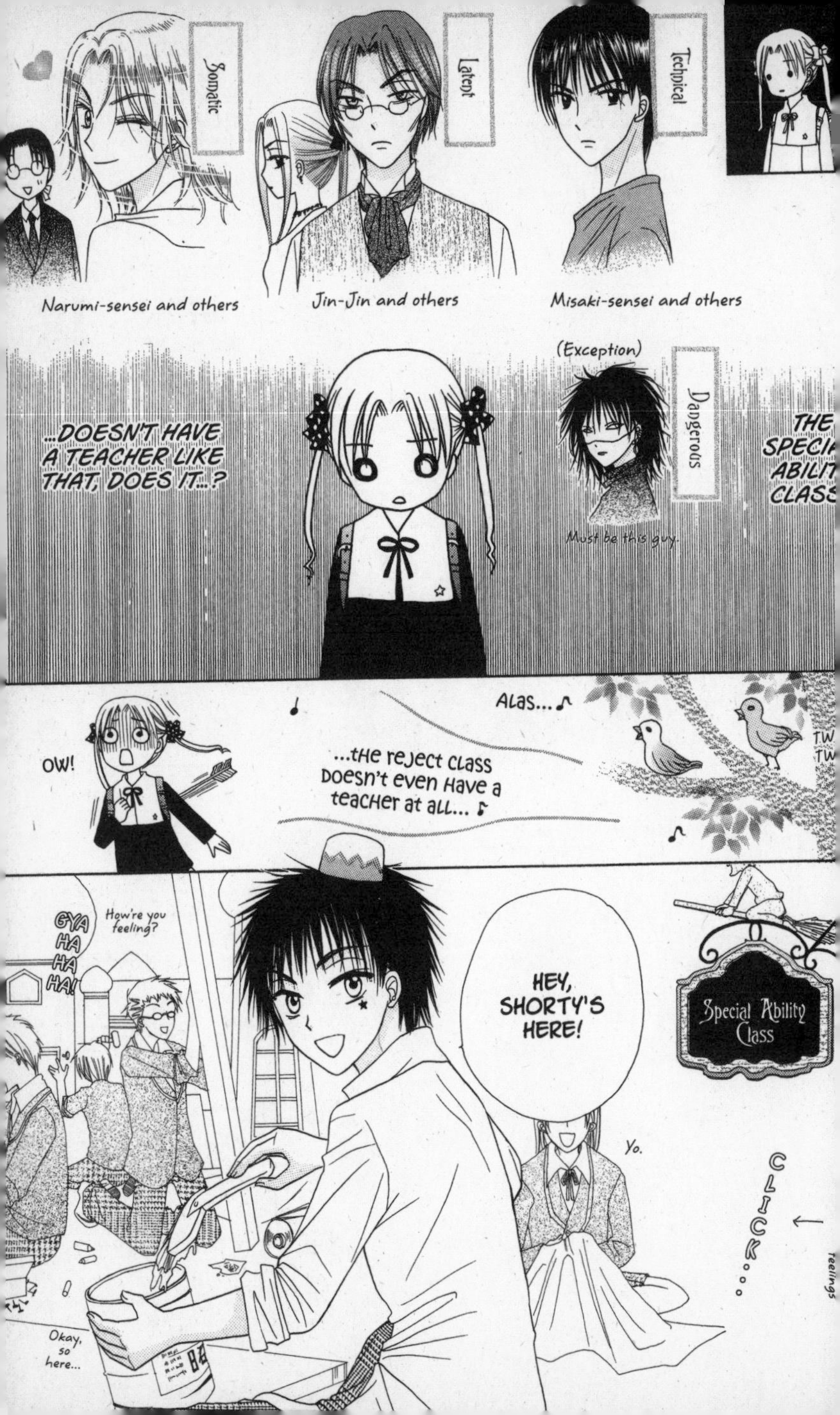
Technical
Misaki-sensei and others
Latent
Jin-Jin and others
Somatic
Narumi-sensei and others
THE SPECIAL ABILITY CLASS
(Exception)
Dangerous
Must be this guy.
...DOESN'T HAVE A TEACHER LIKE THAT, DOES IT...?
TW TW
Alas...
...the reject class doesn't even have a teacher at all...
OW!
CLICK...
Special Ability Class
Yo.
HEY, SHORTY'S HERE!
How're you feeling?
GYA HA HA HA!
Okay, so here...

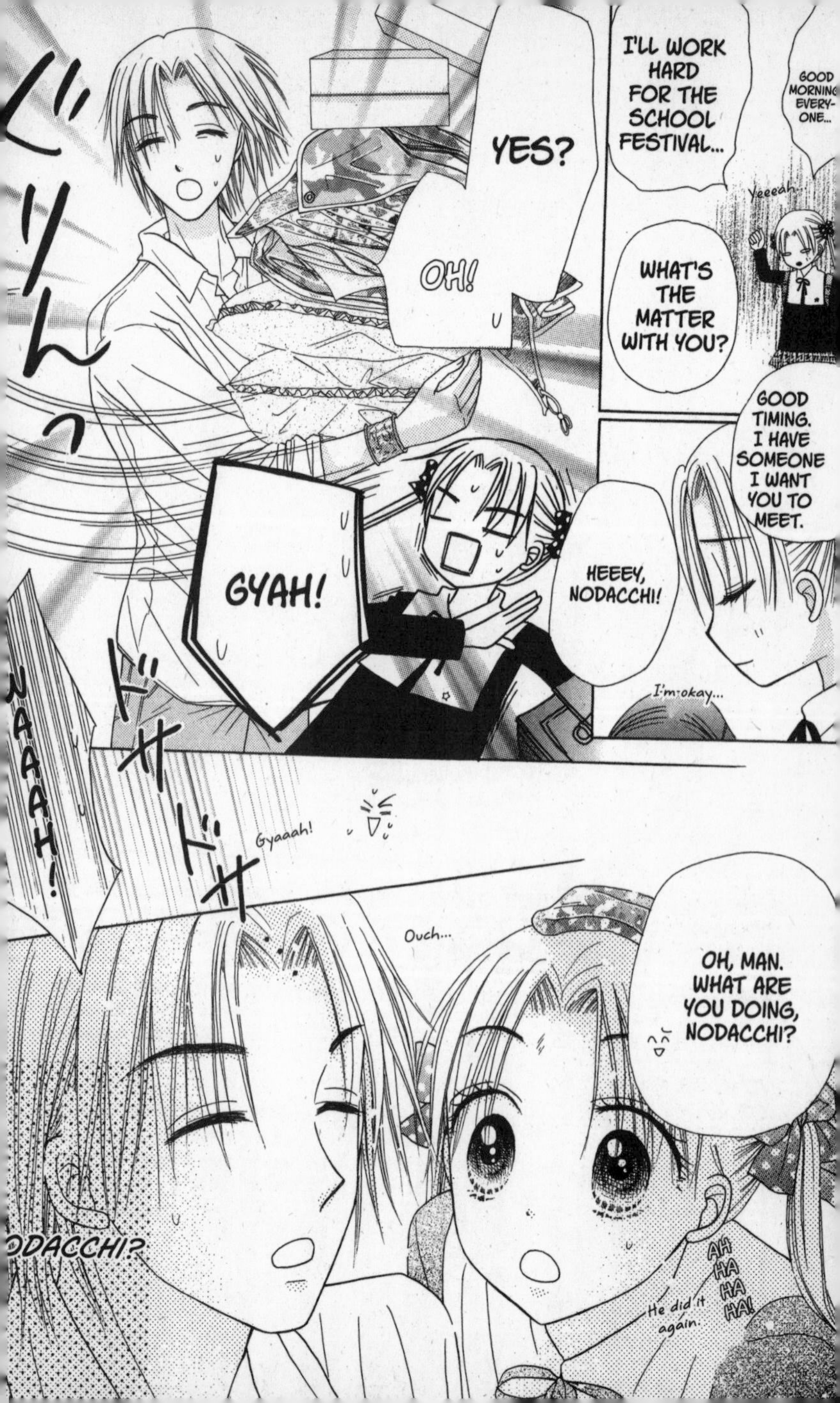
GOOD MORNING EVERY-ONE...
I'LL WORK HARD FOR THE SCHOOL FESTIVAL...
Yeeeah...
WHAT'S THE MATTER WITH YOU?
GOOD TIMING. I HAVE SOMEONE I WANT YOU TO MEET.
HEEEY, NODACCHI!
I'm okay...
YES?
OH!
ぐりん～っ
GYAH!
ドサッ ドサッ
WAAAAH!
Gyaaah!
OH, MAN. WHAT ARE YOU DOING, NODACCHI?
Ouch...
ODACCHI?
AH HA HA HA!
He did it again.

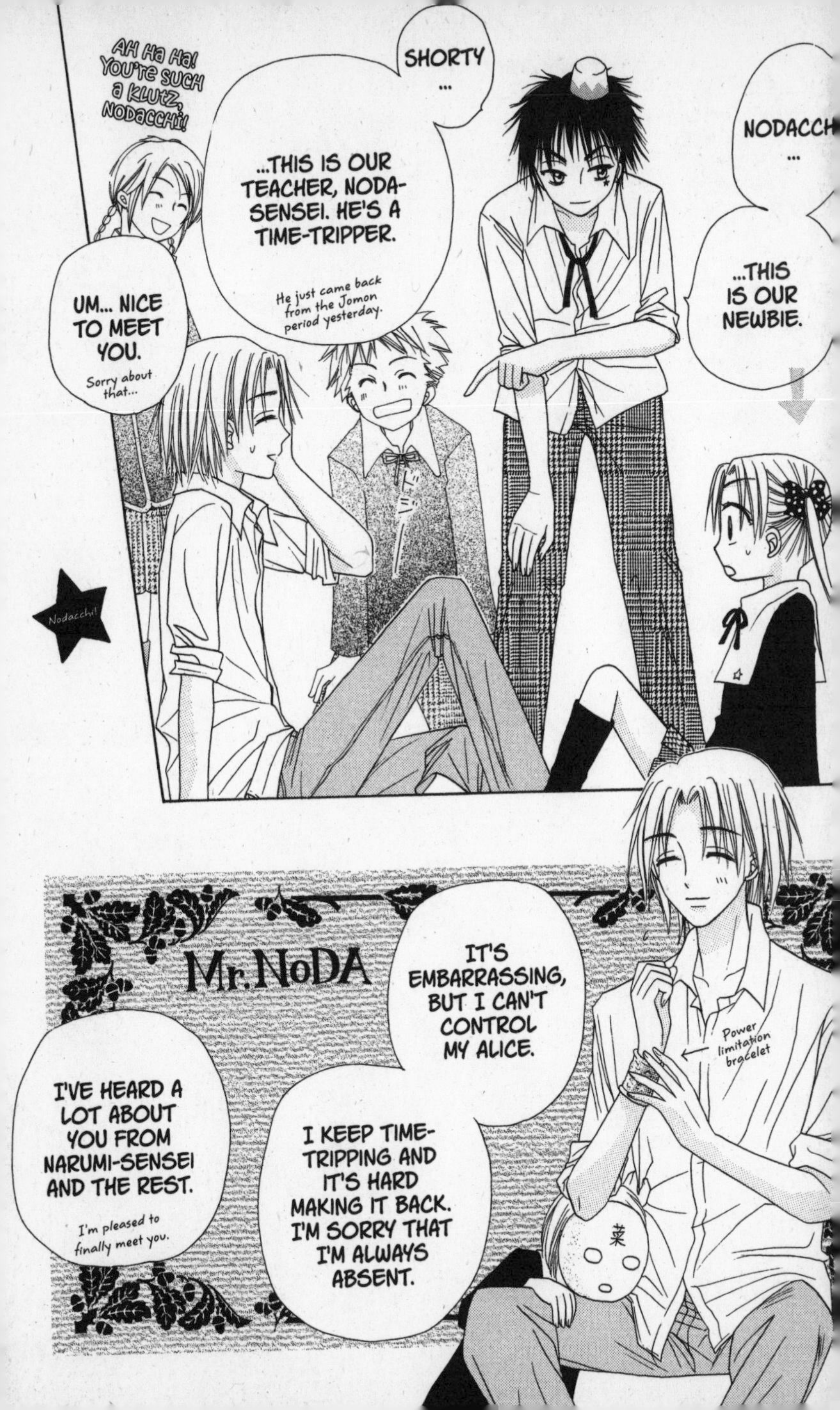
NODACCH ...
...THIS IS OUR NEWBIE.
SHORTY ...
...THIS IS OUR TEACHER, NODA-SENSEI. HE'S A TIME-TRIPPER.
He just came back from the Jomon period yesterday.
AH HA HA! YOU'RE SUCH A KLUTZ, NODACCHI!
UM... NICE TO MEET YOU.
Sorry about that...
Nodacchi!
Mr. NoDA
IT'S EMBARRASSING, BUT I CAN'T CONTROL MY ALICE.
Power limitation bracelet
I KEEP TIME-TRIPPING AND IT'S HARD MAKING IT BACK. I'M SORRY THAT I'M ALWAYS ABSENT.
I'VE HEARD A LOT ABOUT YOU FROM NARUMI-SENSEI AND THE REST.
I'm pleased to finally meet you.

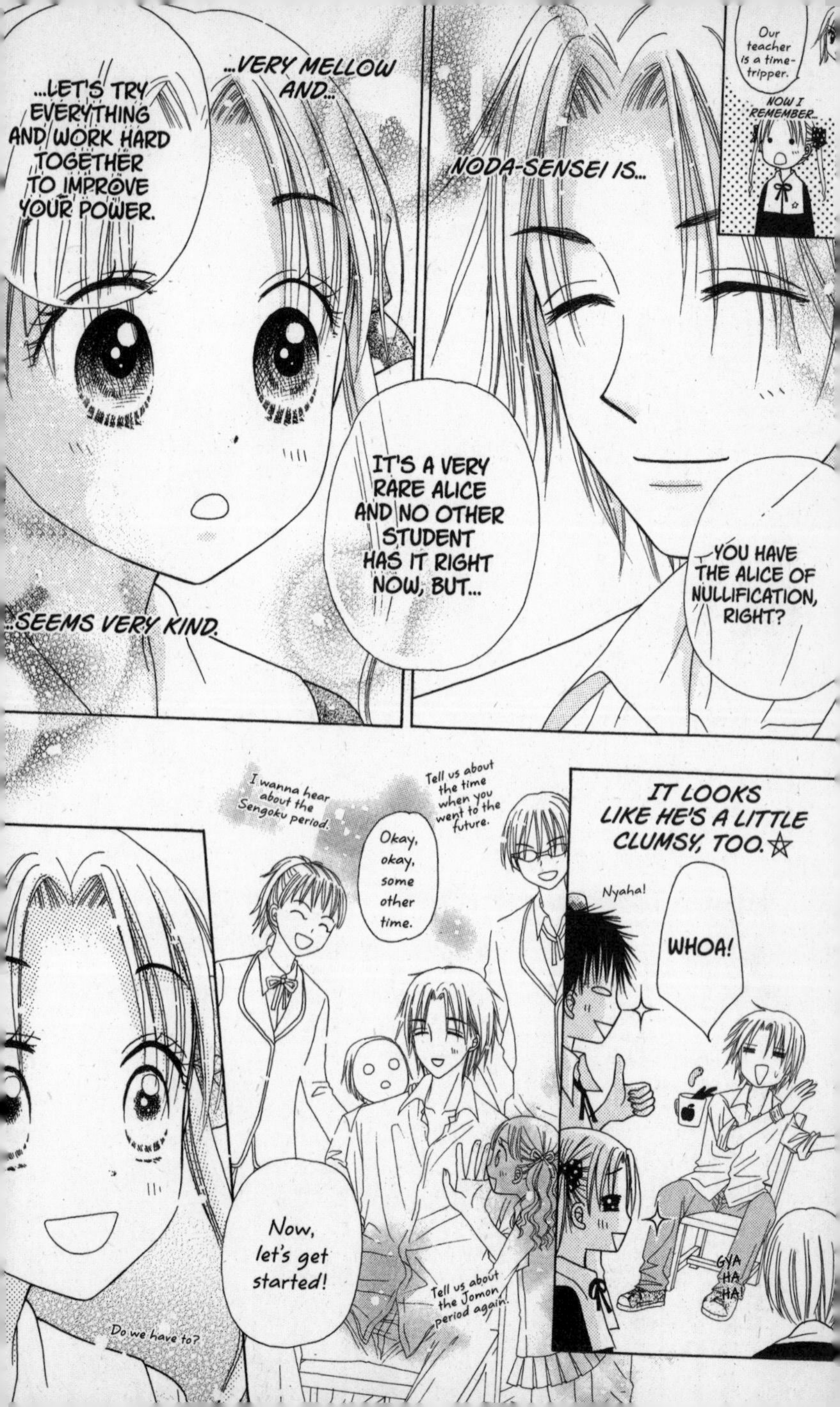

Our teacher is a time-tripper.
NOW I REMEMBER...
NODA-SENSEI IS...
YOU HAVE THE ALICE OF NULLIFICATION, RIGHT?
IT'S A VERY RARE ALICE AND NO OTHER STUDENT HAS IT RIGHT NOW, BUT...
...VERY MELLOW AND...
...LET'S TRY EVERYTHING AND WORK HARD TOGETHER TO IMPROVE YOUR POWER.
...SEEMS VERY KIND.
IT LOOKS LIKE HE'S A LITTLE CLUMSY, TOO.☆
Nyaha!
WHOA!
GYA HA HA!
Tell us about the time when you went to the future.
I wanna hear about the Sengoku period.
Okay, okay, some other time.
Tell us about the Jomon period again.
Now, let's get started!
Do we have to?

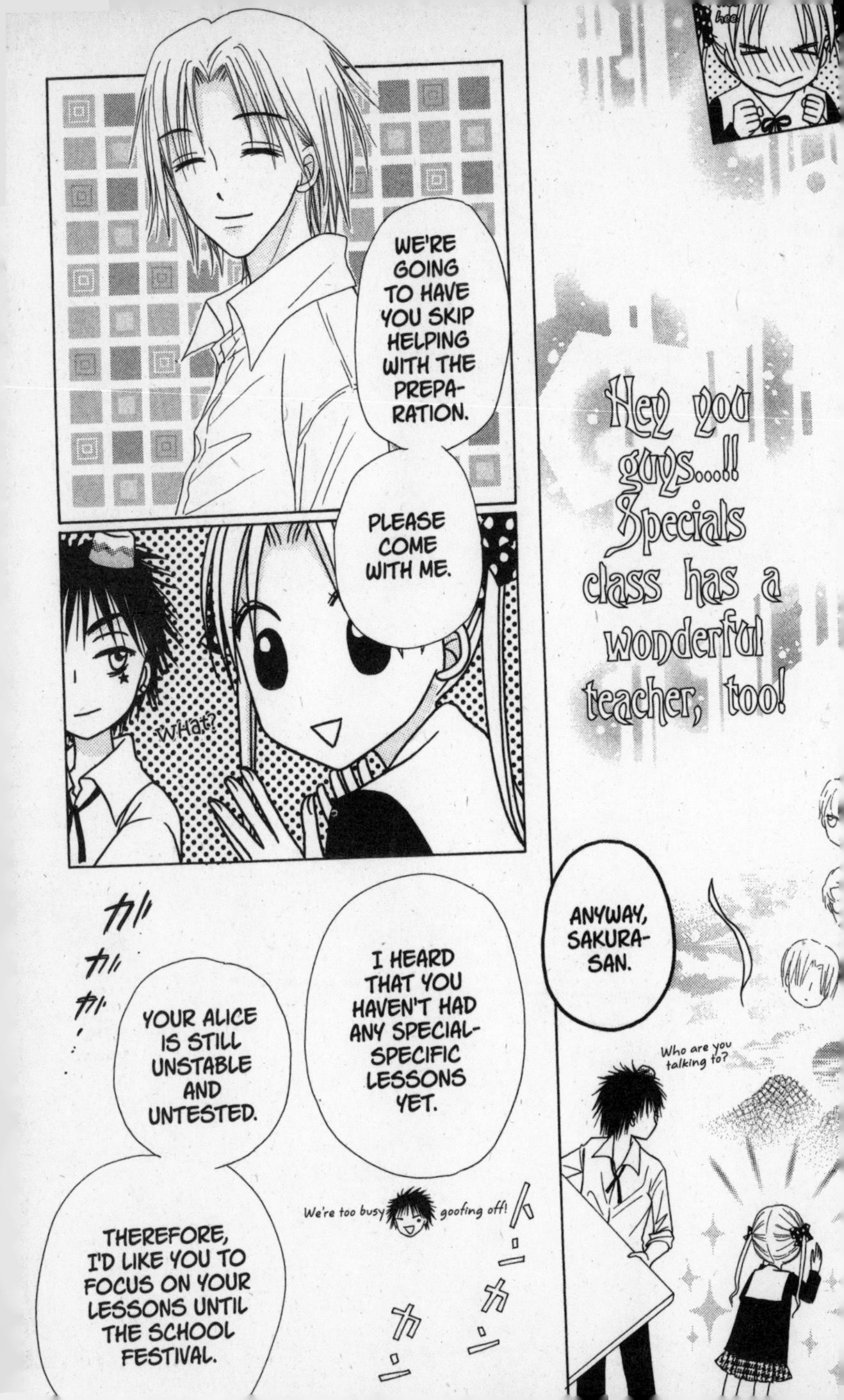
hee!
Hey you guys...!! Specials class has a wonderful teacher, too!
ANYWAY, SAKURA-SAN.
Who are you talking to?
WE'RE GOING TO HAVE YOU SKIP HELPING WITH THE PREPARATION.
PLEASE COME WITH ME.
WHAT?
I HEARD THAT YOU HAVEN'T HAD ANY SPECIAL-SPECIFIC LESSONS YET.
YOUR ALICE IS STILL UNSTABLE AND UNTESTED.
THEREFORE, I'D LIKE YOU TO FOCUS ON YOUR LESSONS UNTIL THE SCHOOL FESTIVAL.
We're too busy goofing off!

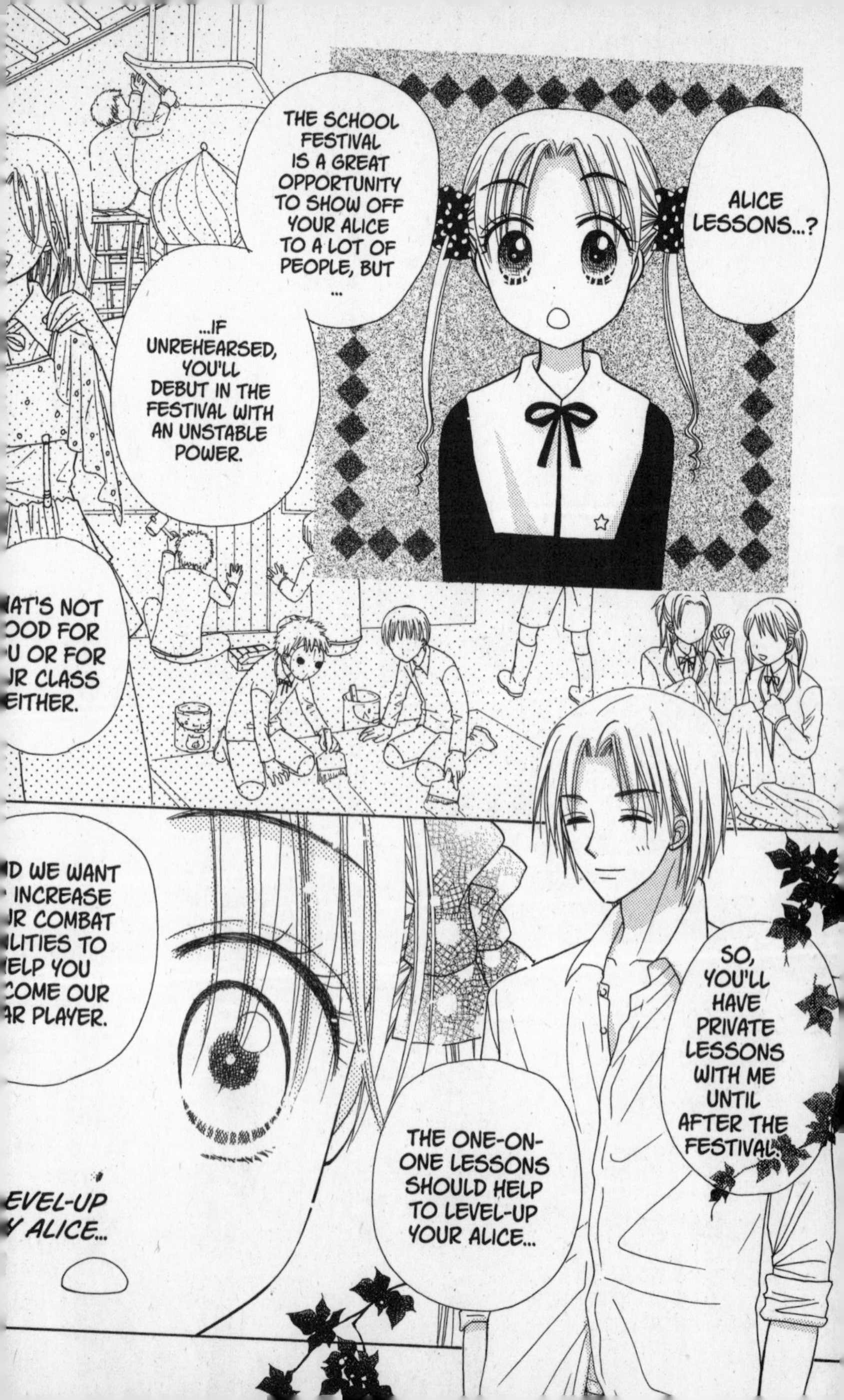
ALICE LESSONS...?
THE SCHOOL FESTIVAL IS A GREAT OPPORTUNITY TO SHOW OFF YOUR ALICE TO A LOT OF PEOPLE, BUT ...
...IF UNREHEARSED, YOU'LL DEBUT IN THE FESTIVAL WITH AN UNSTABLE POWER.
HAT'S NOT OOD FOR U OR FOR UR CLASS EITHER.
SO, YOU'LL HAVE PRIVATE LESSONS WITH ME UNTIL AFTER THE FESTIVAL.
D WE WANT INCREASE UR COMBAT LITIES TO ELP YOU COME OUR AR PLAYER.
THE ONE-ON-ONE LESSONS SHOULD HELP TO LEVEL-UP YOUR ALICE...
EVEL-UP Y ALICE...

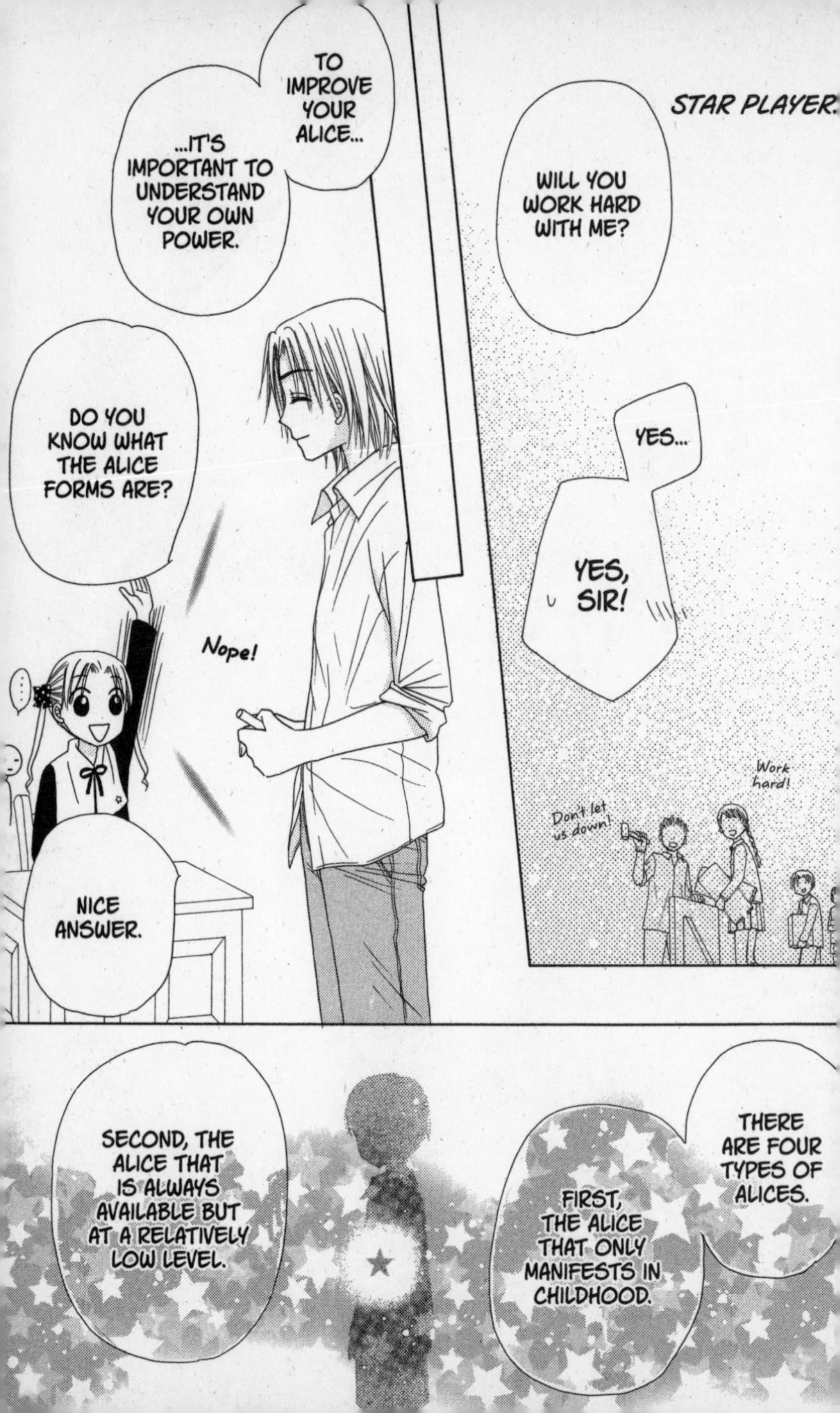
STAR PLAYER.
WILL YOU WORK HARD WITH ME?
YES...
YES, SIR!
Work hard!
Don't let us down!
TO IMPROVE YOUR ALICE...
...IT'S IMPORTANT TO UNDERSTAND YOUR OWN POWER.
DO YOU KNOW WHAT THE ALICE FORMS ARE?
Nope!
NICE ANSWER.
THERE ARE FOUR TYPES OF ALICES.
FIRST, THE ALICE THAT ONLY MANIFESTS IN CHILDHOOD.
SECOND, THE ALICE THAT IS ALWAYS AVAILABLE BUT AT A RELATIVELY LOW LEVEL.

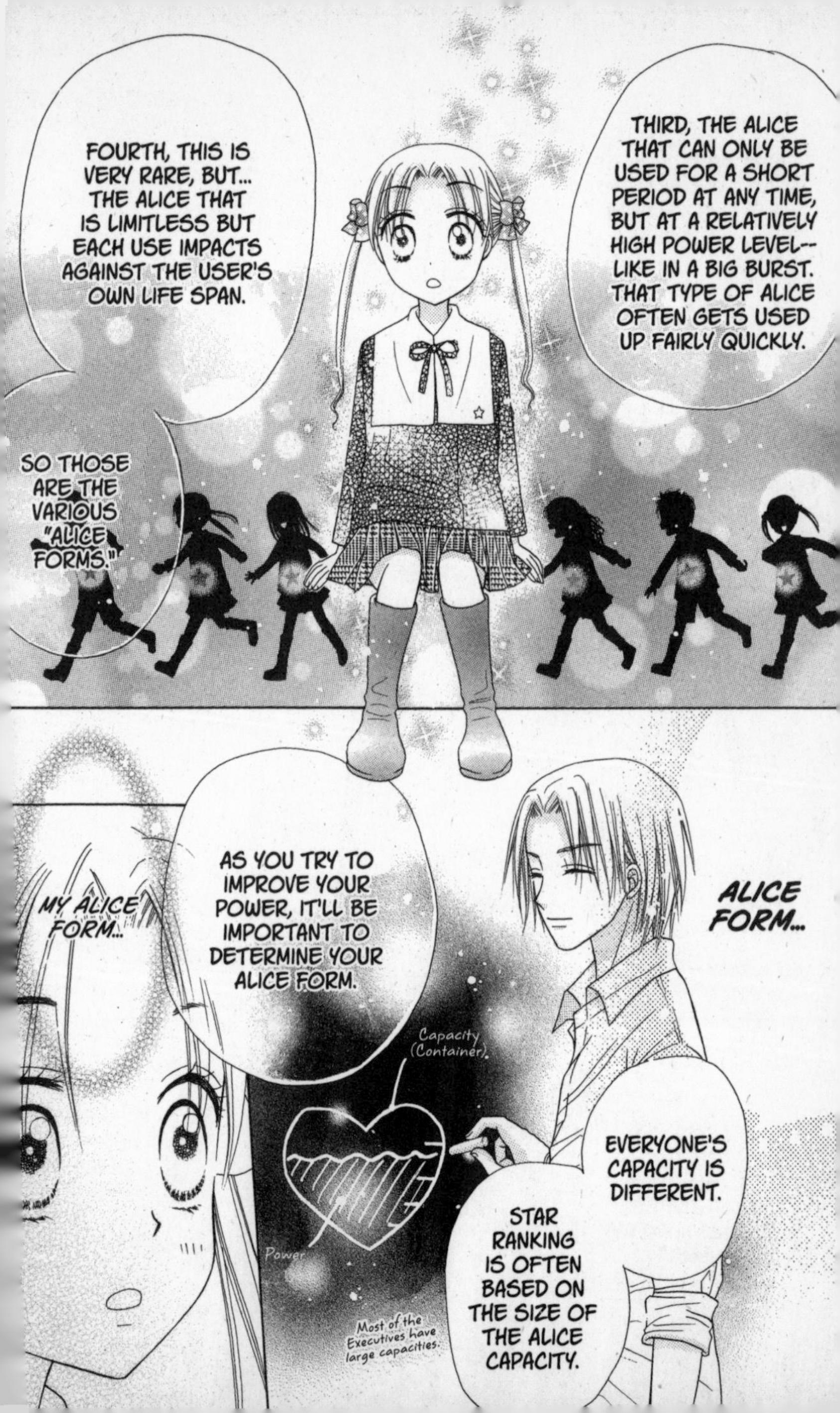
THIRD, THE ALICE THAT CAN ONLY BE USED FOR A SHORT PERIOD AT ANY TIME, BUT AT A RELATIVELY HIGH POWER LEVEL-- LIKE IN A BIG BURST. THAT TYPE OF ALICE OFTEN GETS USED UP FAIRLY QUICKLY.
FOURTH, THIS IS VERY RARE, BUT... THE ALICE THAT IS LIMITLESS BUT EACH USE IMPACTS AGAINST THE USER'S OWN LIFE SPAN.
SO THOSE ARE THE VARIOUS "ALICE FORMS."
ALICE FORM...
AS YOU TRY TO IMPROVE YOUR POWER, IT'LL BE IMPORTANT TO DETERMINE YOUR ALICE FORM.
MY ALICE FORM...
Capacity (Container)
EVERYONE'S CAPACITY IS DIFFERENT.
STAR RANKING IS OFTEN BASED ON THE SIZE OF THE ALICE CAPACITY.
Power
Most of the Executives have large capacities.

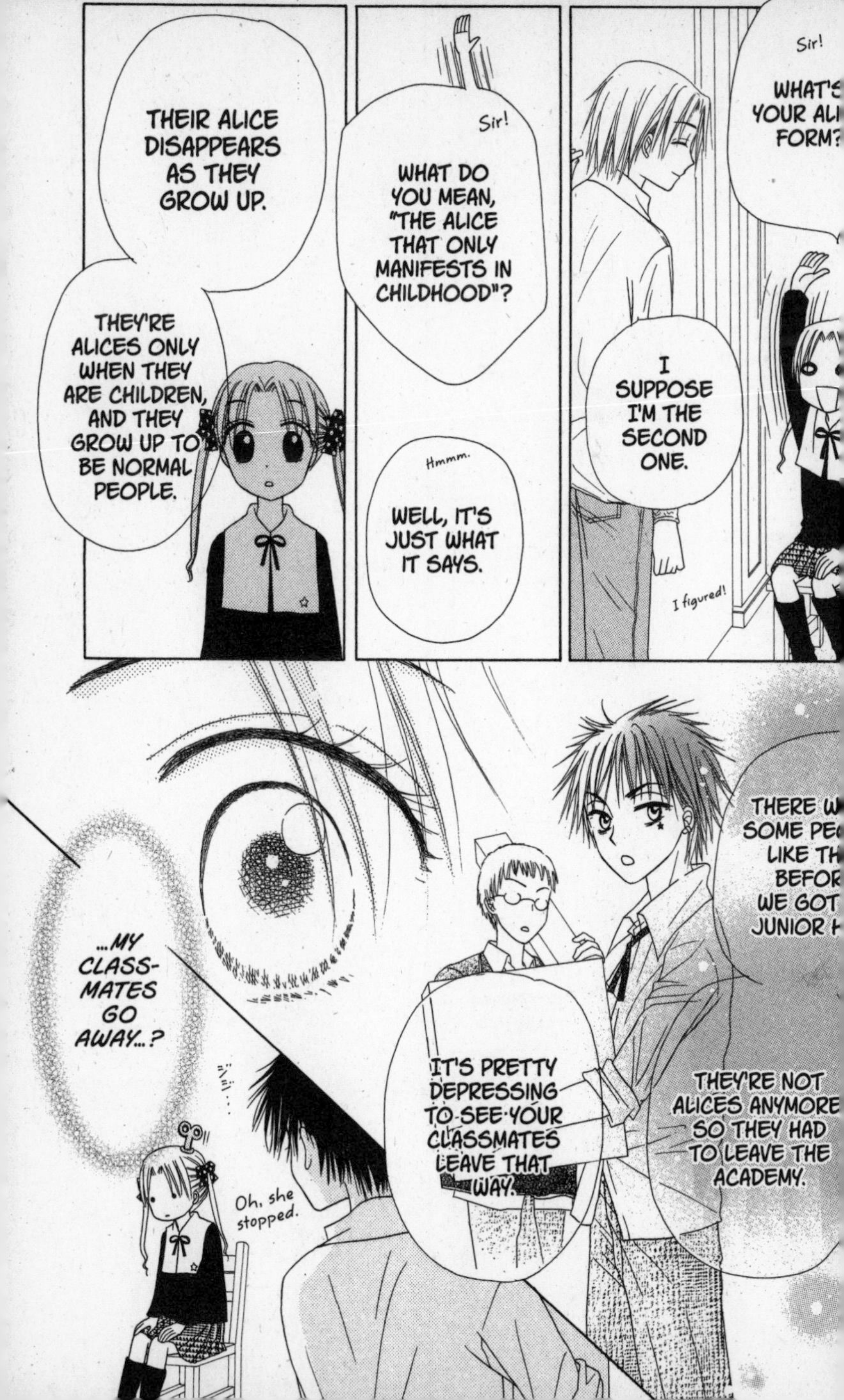
Sir!
WHAT'S YOUR ALI FORM?
I SUPPOSE I'M THE SECOND ONE.
I figured!
Sir!
WHAT DO YOU MEAN, "THE ALICE THAT ONLY MANIFESTS IN CHILDHOOD"?
Hmmm.
WELL, IT'S JUST WHAT IT SAYS.
THEIR ALICE DISAPPEARS AS THEY GROW UP.
THEY'RE ALICES ONLY WHEN THEY ARE CHILDREN, AND THEY GROW UP TO BE NORMAL PEOPLE.
THERE W SOME PE LIKE TH BEFOR WE GOT JUNIOR H
THEY'RE NOT ALICES ANYMORE SO THEY HAD TO LEAVE THE ACADEMY.
IT'S PRETTY DEPRESSING TO SEE YOUR CLASSMATES LEAVE THAT WAY.
...MY CLASSMATES GO AWAY...?
Oh, she stopped.

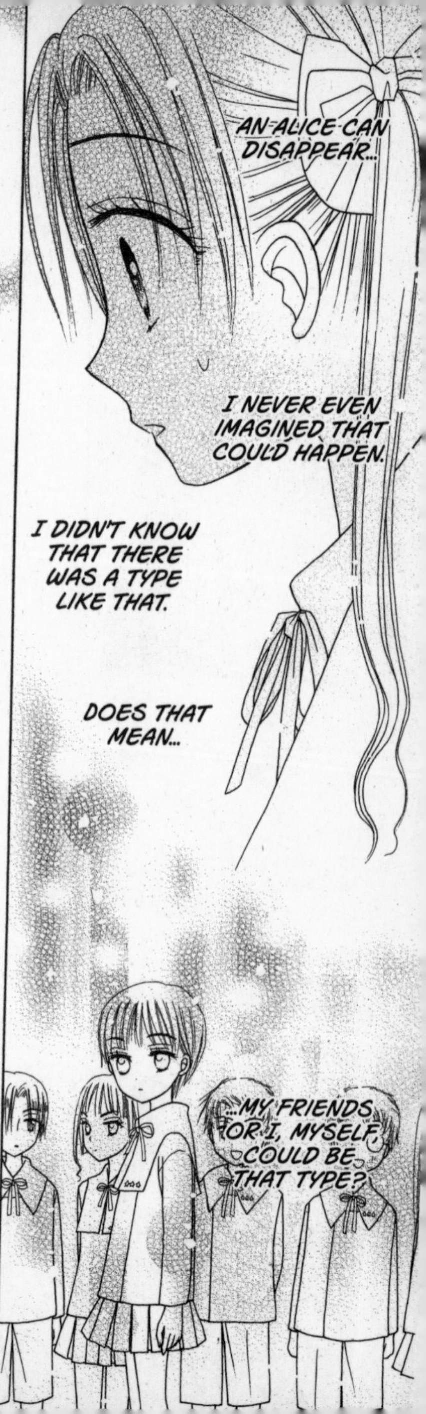
AN ALICE CAN DISAPPEAR...
I NEVER EVEN IMAGINED THAT COULD HAPPEN.
I DIDN'T KNOW THAT THERE WAS A TYPE LIKE THAT.
DOES THAT MEAN...
...MY FRIENDS OR I, MYSELF, COULD BE THAT TYPE?
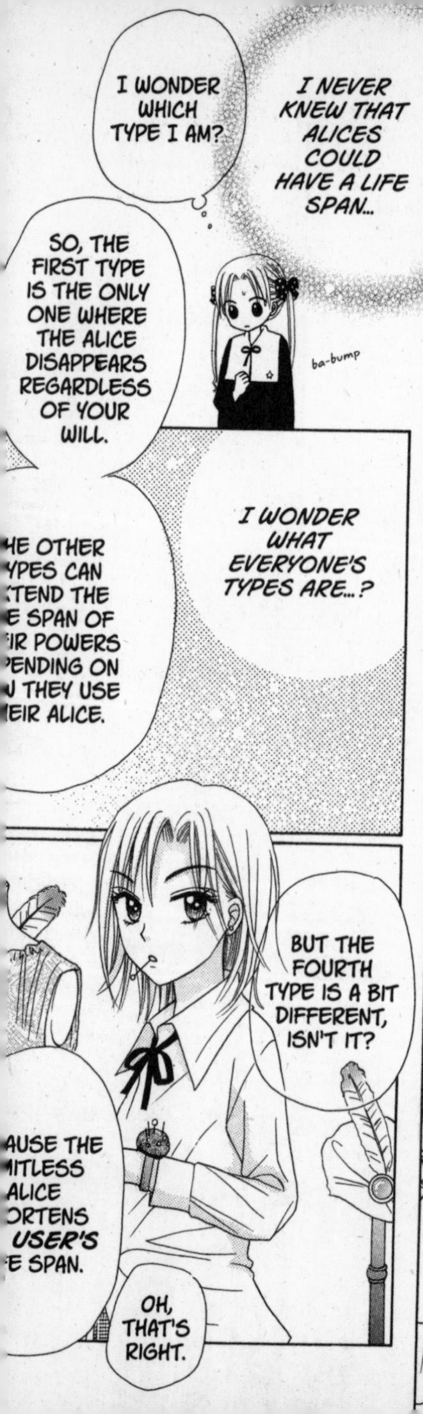
I NEVER KNEW THAT ALICES COULD HAVE A LIFE SPAN...
I WONDER WHICH TYPE I AM?
SO, THE FIRST TYPE IS THE ONLY ONE WHERE THE ALICE DISAPPEARS REGARDLESS OF YOUR WILL.
ba-bump
I WONDER WHAT EVERYONE'S TYPES ARE...?
HE OTHER YPES CAN TEND THE E SPAN OF IR POWERS PENDING ON THEY USE EIR ALICE.
BUT THE FOURTH TYPE IS A BIT DIFFERENT, ISN'T IT?
AUSE THE IMITLESS ALICE ORTENS USER'S E SPAN.
OH, THAT'S RIGHT.

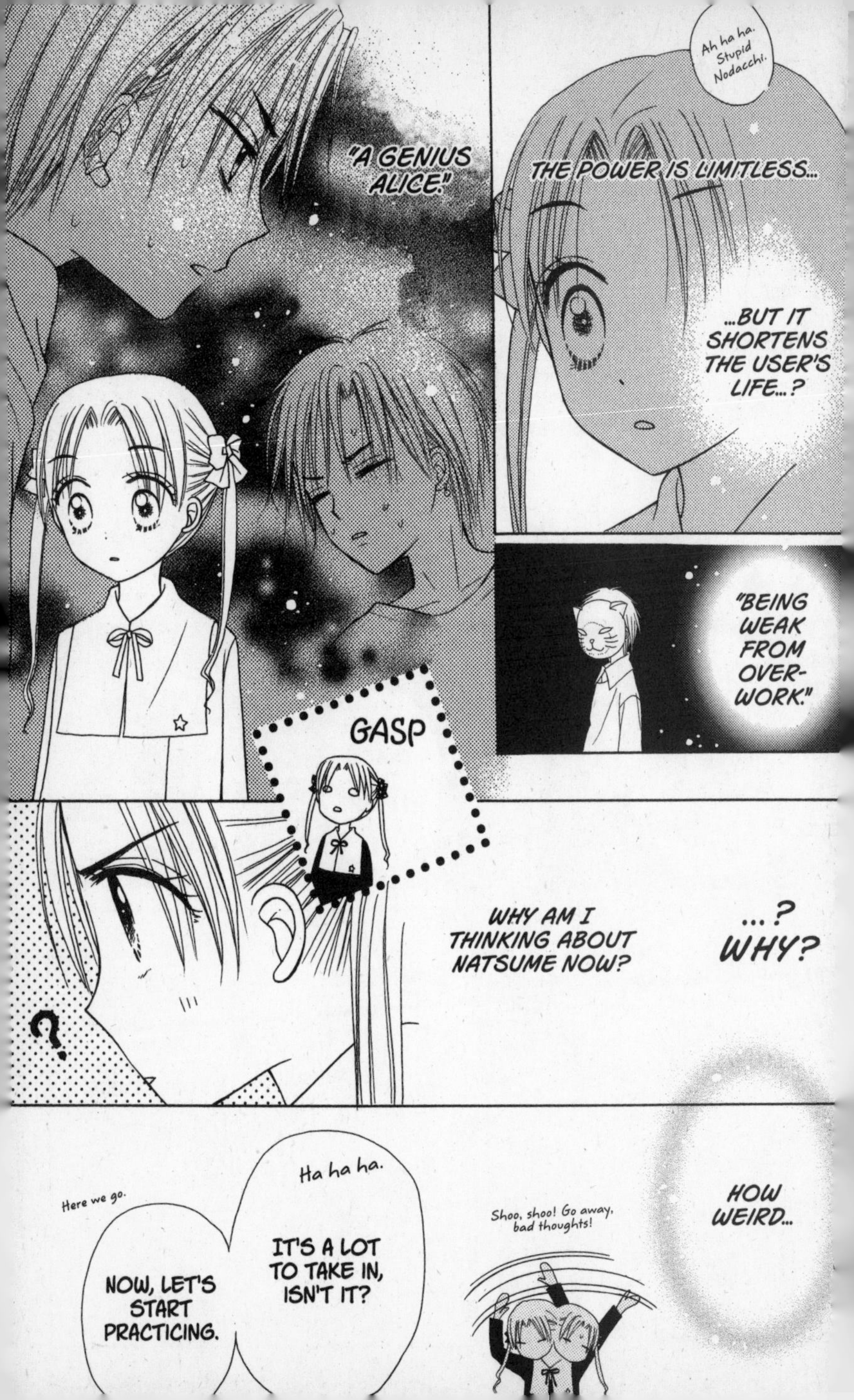
Ah ha ha. Stupid Nodacchi.
THE POWER IS LIMITLESS...
...BUT IT SHORTENS THE USER'S LIFE...?
"BEING WEAK FROM OVER-WORK."
"A GENIUS ALICE."
GASP
...? WHY?
WHY AM I THINKING ABOUT NATSUME NOW?
HOW WEIRD...
Shoo, shoo! Go away, bad thoughts!
Ha ha ha.
IT'S A LOT TO TAKE IN, ISN'T IT?
Here we go.
NOW, LET'S START PRACTICING.

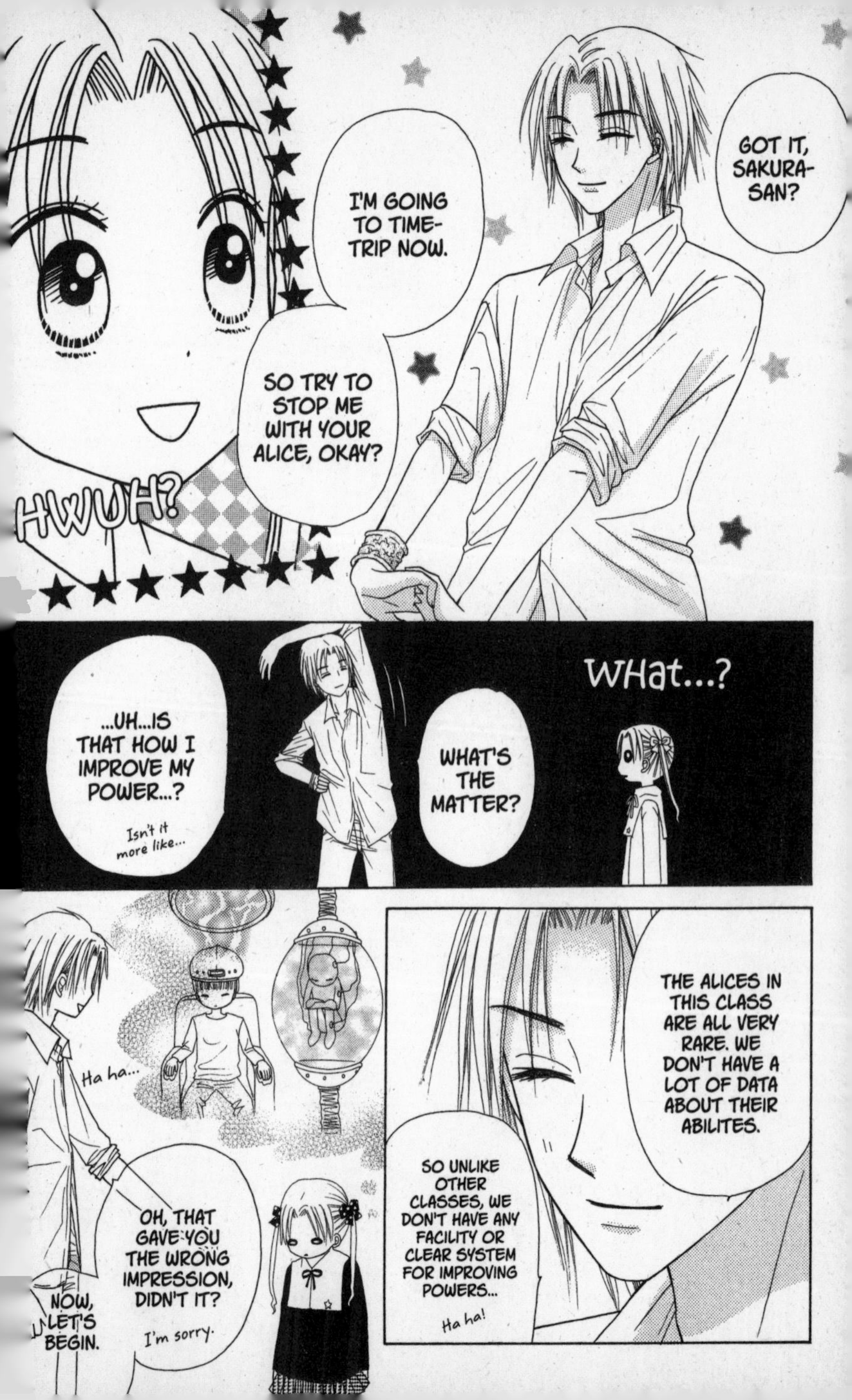
GOT IT, SAKURA-SAN?
I'M GOING TO TIME-TRIP NOW.
SO TRY TO STOP ME WITH YOUR ALICE, OKAY?
HWUH?
WHAt...?
WHAT'S THE MATTER?
...UH...IS THAT HOW I IMPROVE MY POWER...?
Isn't it more like...
THE ALICES IN THIS CLASS ARE ALL VERY RARE. WE DON'T HAVE A LOT OF DATA ABOUT THEIR ABILITES.
SO UNLIKE OTHER CLASSES, WE DON'T HAVE ANY FACILITY OR CLEAR SYSTEM FOR IMPROVING POWERS...
Ha ha!
Ha ha...
OH, THAT GAVE YOU THE WRONG IMPRESSION, DIDN'T IT?
I'm sorry.
NOW, LET'S BEGIN.

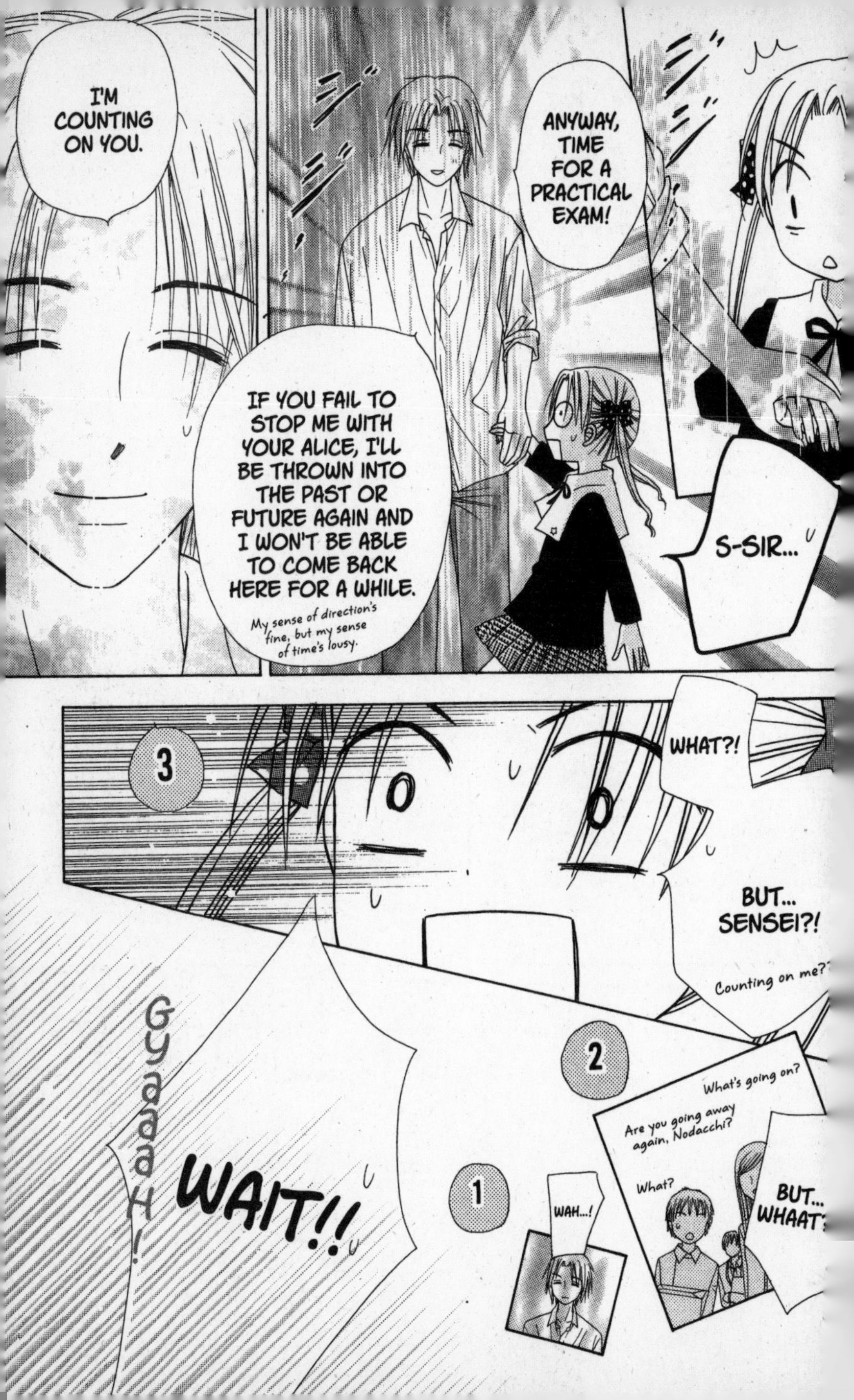
S-SIR...
ANYWAY, TIME FOR A PRACTICAL EXAM!
IF YOU FAIL TO STOP ME WITH YOUR ALICE, I'LL BE THROWN INTO THE PAST OR FUTURE AGAIN AND I WON'T BE ABLE TO COME BACK HERE FOR A WHILE.
My sense of direction's fine, but my sense of time's lousy.
I'M COUNTING ON YOU.
WHAT?!
BUT... SENSEI?!
Counting on me??
3
What's going on?
Are you going away again, Nodacchi?
What?
BUT... WHAAT?
2
WAH...!
1
WAIT!!
Gyaaaah!!

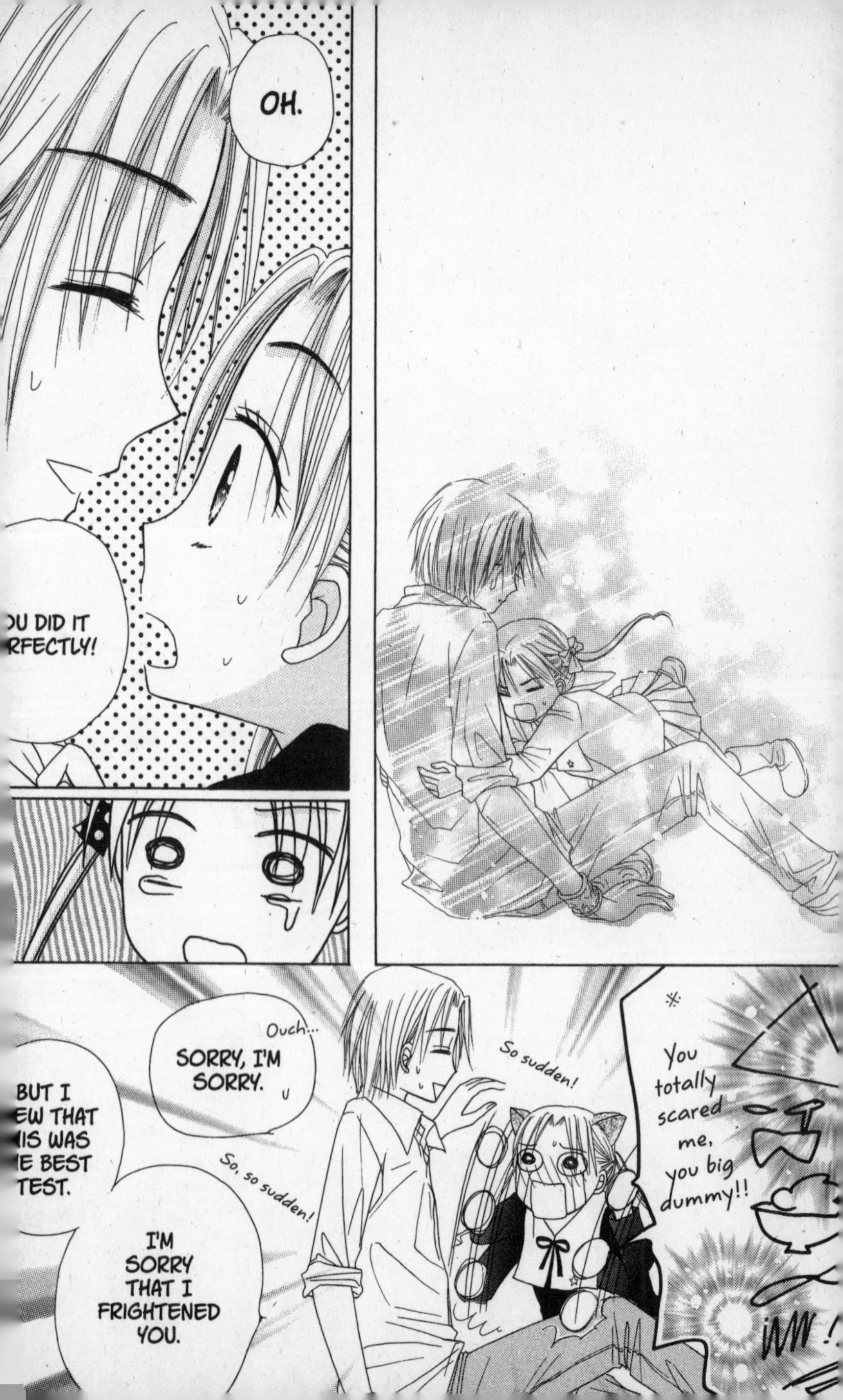
OH.
OU DID IT RFECTLY!
You totally scared me, you big dummy!!
So sudden!
So, so sudden!
Ouch...
SORRY, I'M SORRY.
BUT I EW THAT IS WAS E BEST TEST.
I'M SORRY THAT I FRIGHTENED YOU.

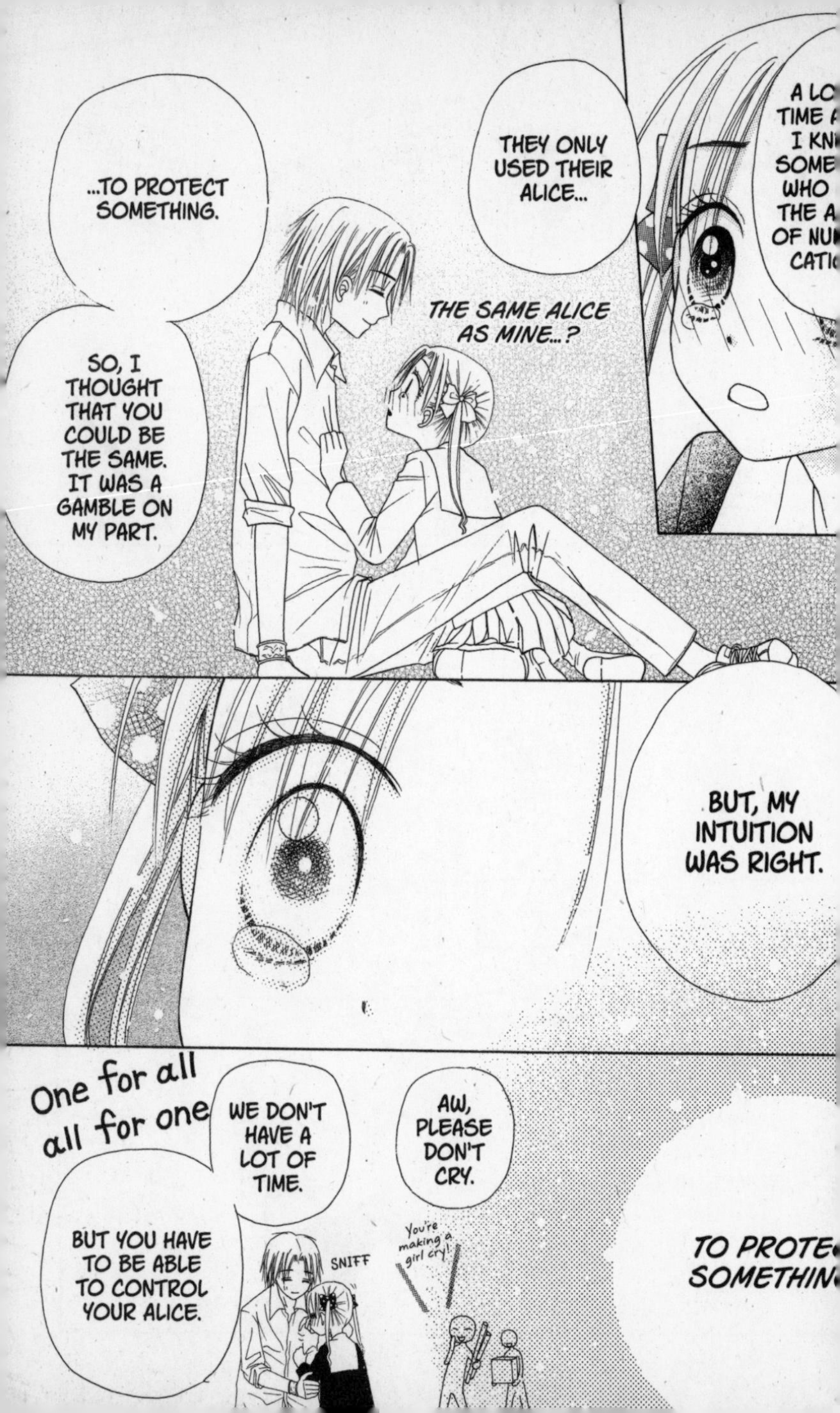
A LO
TIME A
I KN
SOME
WHO
THE A
OF NU
CATI
THEY ONLY USED THEIR ALICE...
...TO PROTECT SOMETHING.
THE SAME ALICE AS MINE...?
SO, I THOUGHT THAT YOU COULD BE THE SAME. IT WAS A GAMBLE ON MY PART.
BUT, MY INTUITION WAS RIGHT.
TO PROTE
SOMETHIN
AW, PLEASE DON'T CRY.
WE DON'T HAVE A LOT OF TIME.
One for all all for one
BUT YOU HAVE TO BE ABLE TO CONTROL YOUR ALICE.
You're making a girl cry!
SNIFF

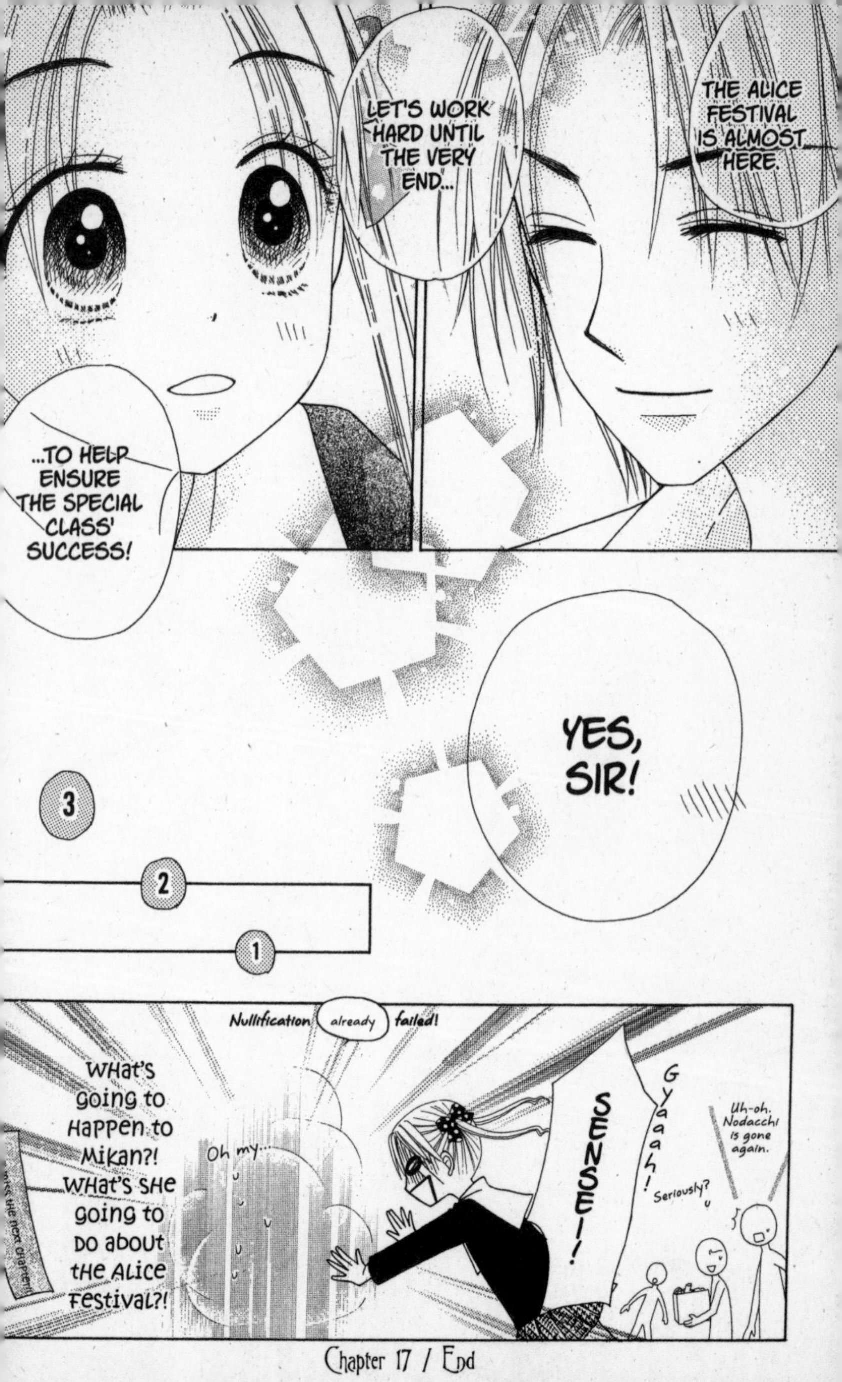
THE ALICE FESTIVAL IS ALMOST HERE.
LET'S WORK HARD UNTIL THE VERY END...
...TO HELP ENSURE THE SPECIAL CLASS' SUCCESS!
YES, SIR!
3
2
1
Nullification already failed!
Uh-oh. Nodacchi is gone again.
Seriously?
Gyaaah!
SENSEI!!
Oh my...
What's going to happen to Mikan?! What's she going to do about the Alice Festival?!

Chapter 17 / End

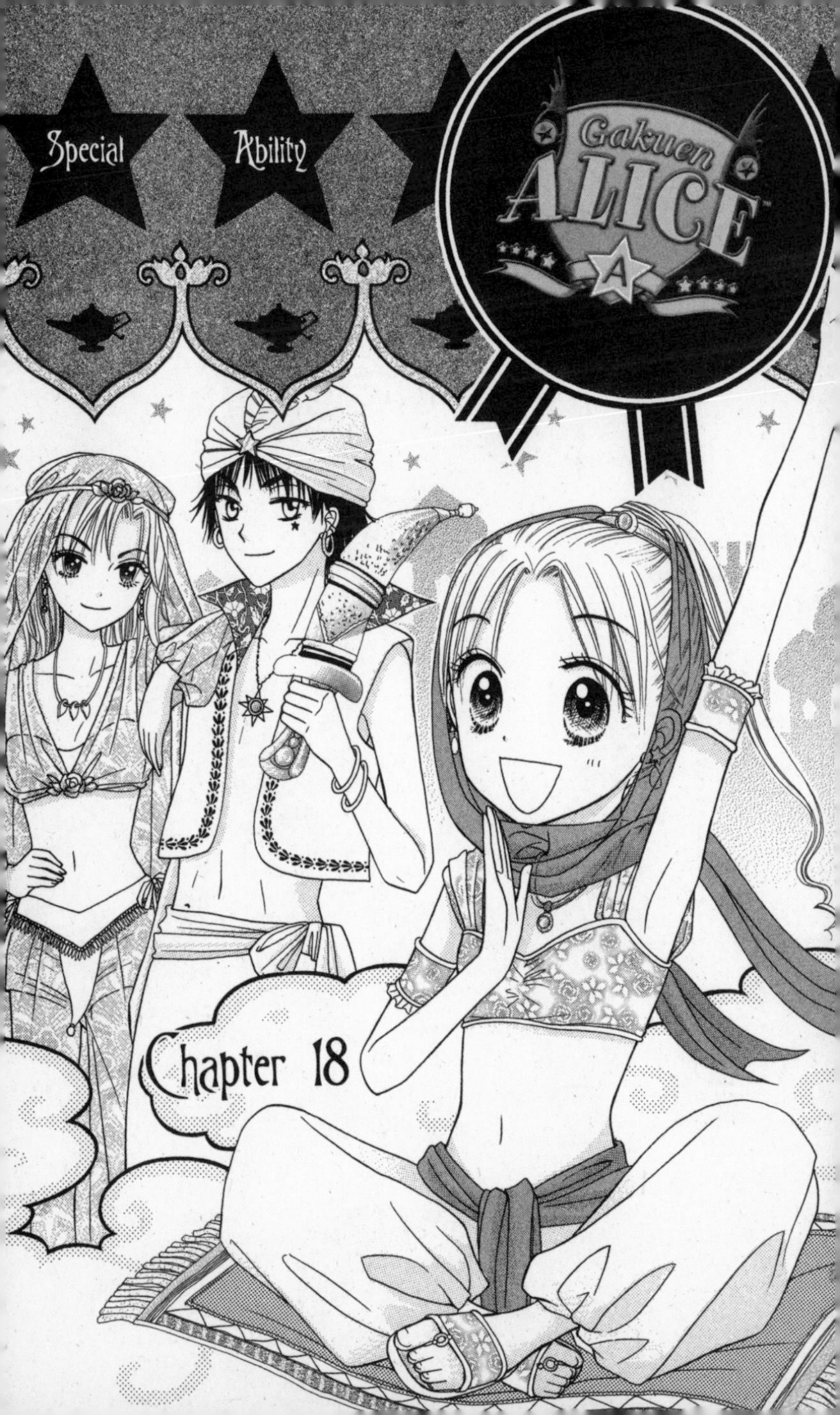
Special Ability
Gakuen ALICE
Chapter 18

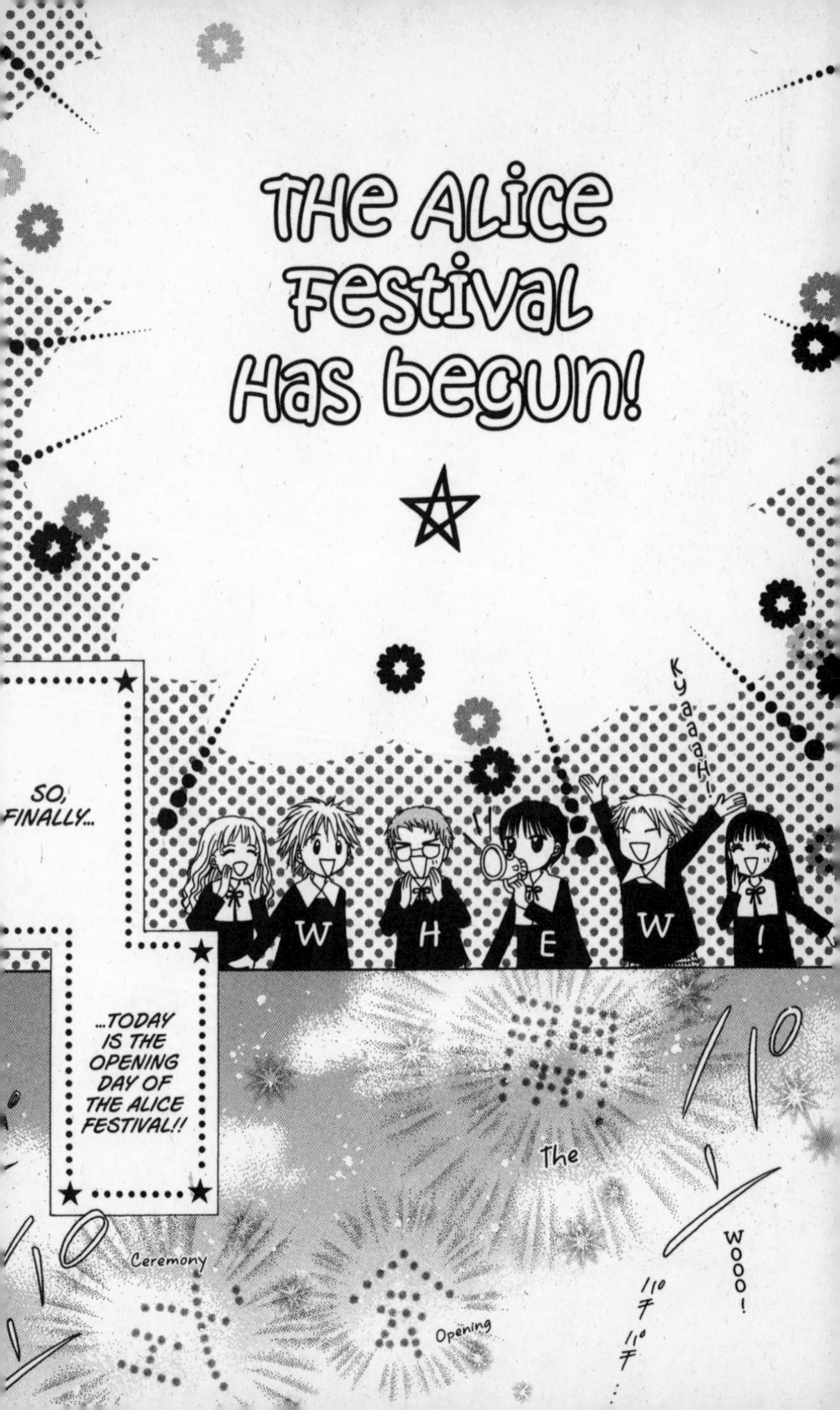
THE ALICE FESTIVAL HAS BEGUN!
KYAAAAH!
WHEW!
SO, FINALLY...
...TODAY IS THE OPENING DAY OF THE ALICE FESTIVAL!!
WOOO!
パチ パチ
The
Opening
Ceremony

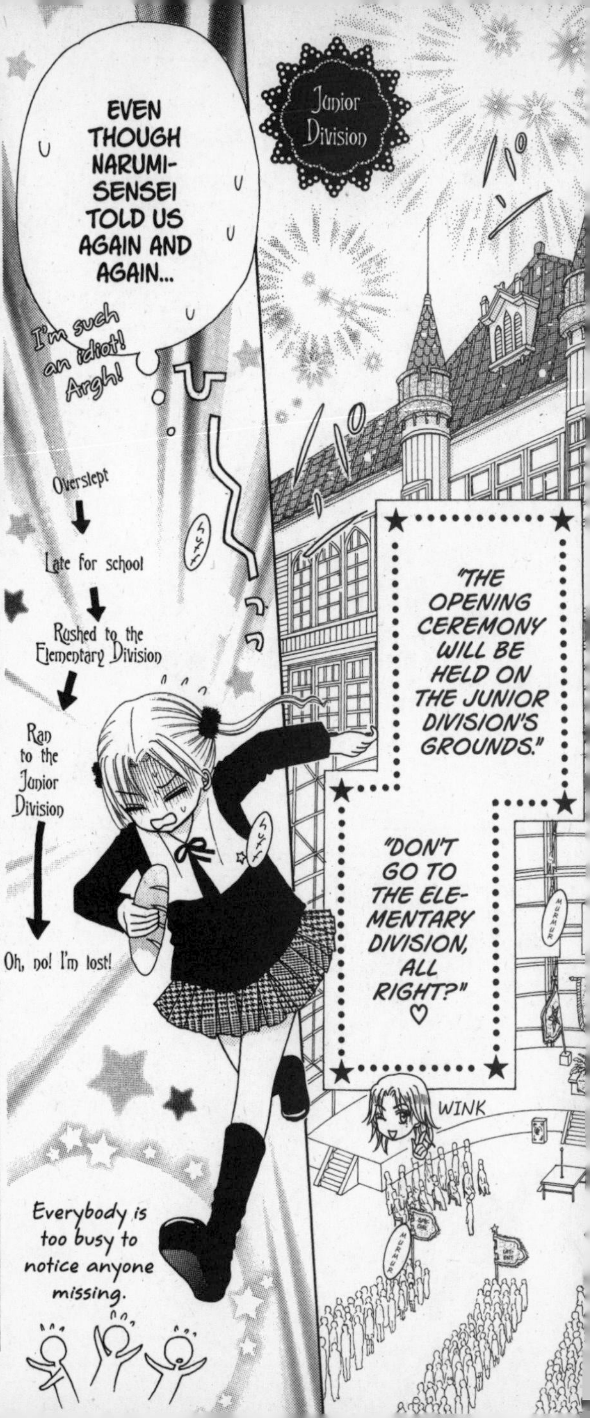
Junior Division
"THE OPENING CEREMONY WILL BE HELD ON THE JUNIOR DIVISION'S GROUNDS."
"DON'T GO TO THE ELE-MENTARY DIVISION, ALL RIGHT?" ♡
WINK
EVEN THOUGH NARUMI-SENSEI TOLD US AGAIN AND AGAIN...
I'm such an idiot! Argh!
Overslept
Late for school
Rushed to the Elementary Division
Ran to the Junior Division
Oh, no! I'm lost!
Everybody is too busy to notice anyone missing.

Read at your own discretion.

Higuchi's Room 2

PROFILE 10

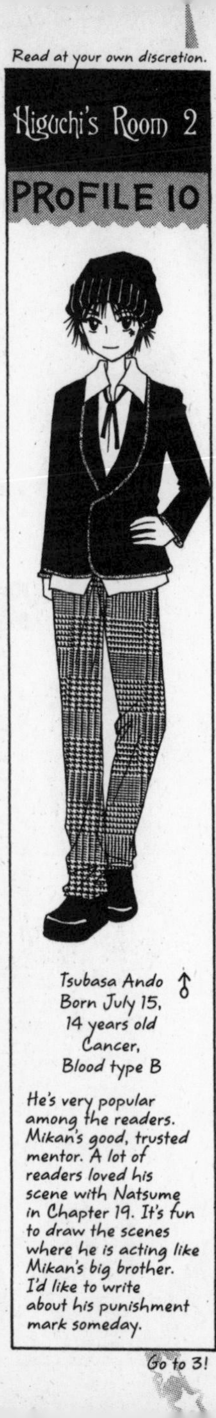

Tsubasa Ando ♂
Born July 15,
14 years old
Cancer,
Blood type B

He's very popular among the readers. Mikan's good, trusted mentor. A lot of readers loved his scene with Natsume in Chapter 19. It's fun to draw the scenes where he is acting like Mikan's big brother. I'd like to write about his punishment mark someday.

Go to 3!

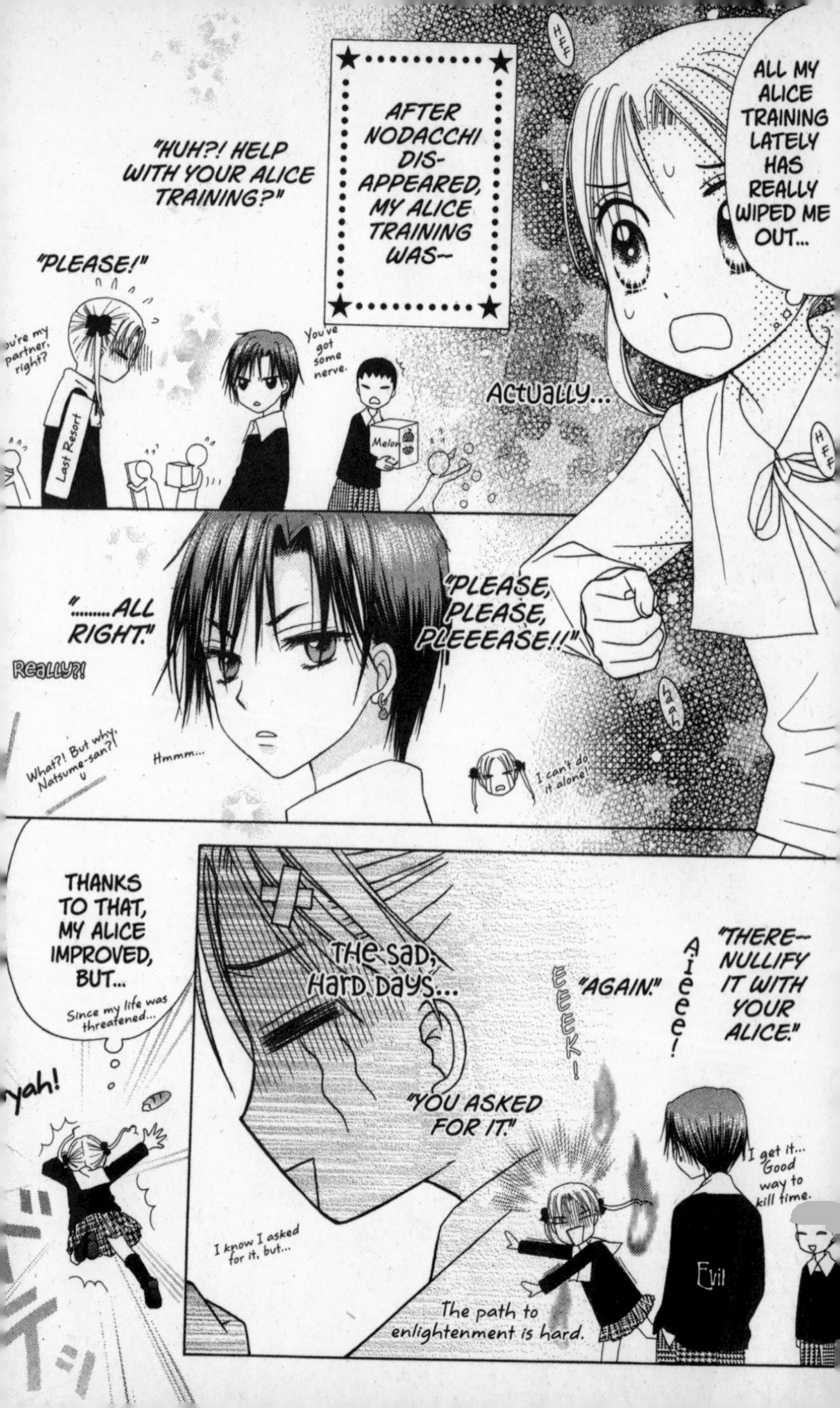
HEFF
ALL MY ALICE TRAINING LATELY HAS REALLY WIPED ME OUT...
HEFF
ACTUALLY...
AFTER NODACCHI DIS- APPEARED, MY ALICE TRAINING WAS~
"HUH?! HELP WITH YOUR ALICE TRAINING?"
You've got some nerve.
Melon
"PLEASE!"
ou're my partner, right?
Last Resort
"PLEASE, PLEASE, PLEEEASE!!"
haah
I can't do it alone!
".........ALL RIGHT."
Really?!
Hmmm...
What?! But why, Natsume-san?!
"THERE— NULLIFY IT WITH YOUR ALICE."
Aieee!
"AGAIN."
EEEEK!
I get it... Good way to kill time.
Evil
The path to enlightenment is hard.
THE SAD, HARD DAYS...
"YOU ASKED FOR IT."
I know I asked for it, but...
THANKS TO THAT, MY ALICE IMPROVED, BUT...
Since my life was threatened...
yah!

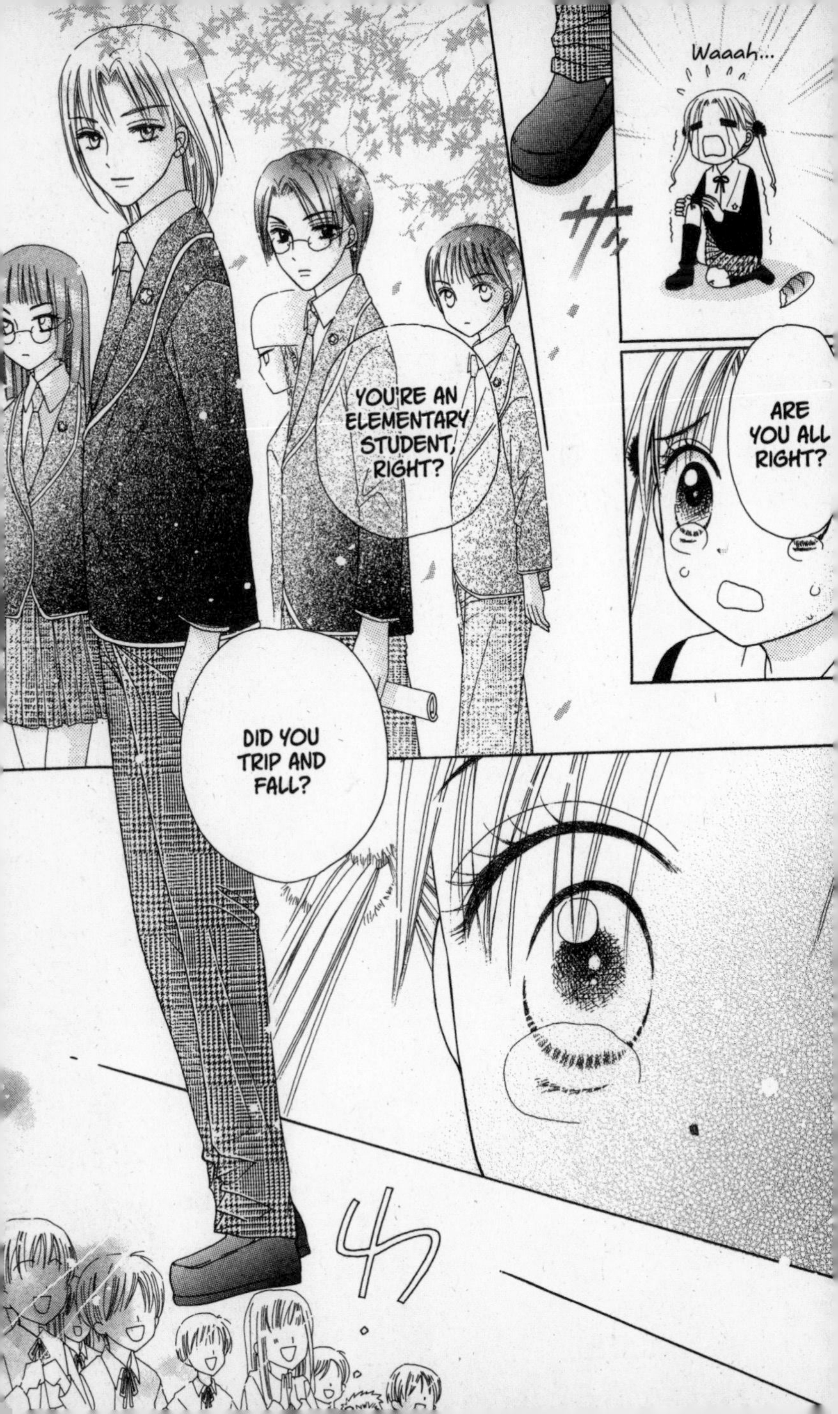
Waaah...
ARE YOU ALL RIGHT?
YOU'RE AN ELEMENTARY STUDENT, RIGHT?
DID YOU TRIP AND FALL?

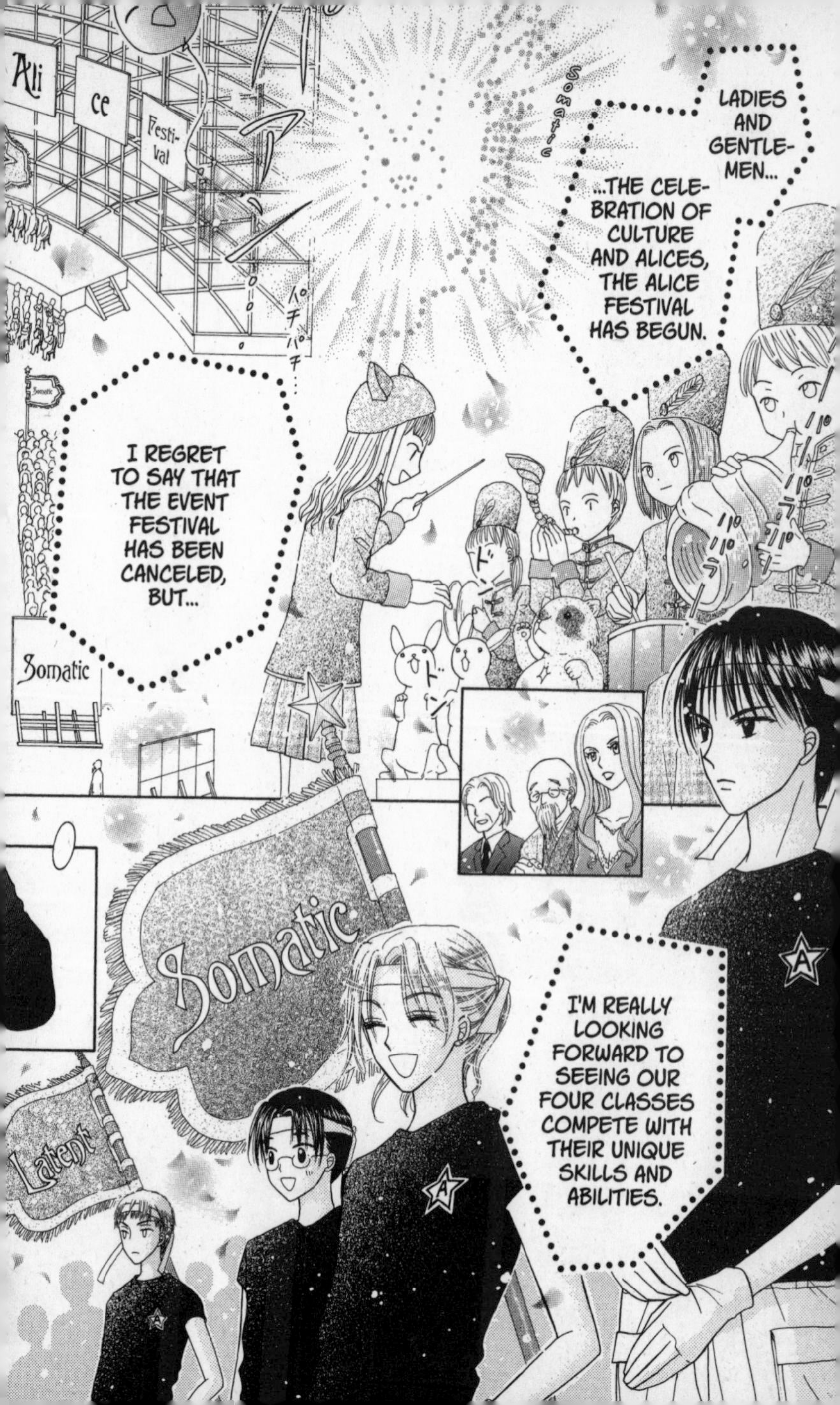
LADIES AND GENTLE-MEN...
...THE CELE-BRATION OF CULTURE AND ALICES, THE ALICE FESTIVAL HAS BEGUN.
Somatic
Ali ce Festi-val
I REGRET TO SAY THAT THE EVENT FESTIVAL HAS BEEN CANCELED, BUT...
Somatic
I'M REALLY LOOKING FORWARD TO SEEING OUR FOUR CLASSES COMPETE WITH THEIR UNIQUE SKILLS AND ABILITIES.
Somatic
Latent

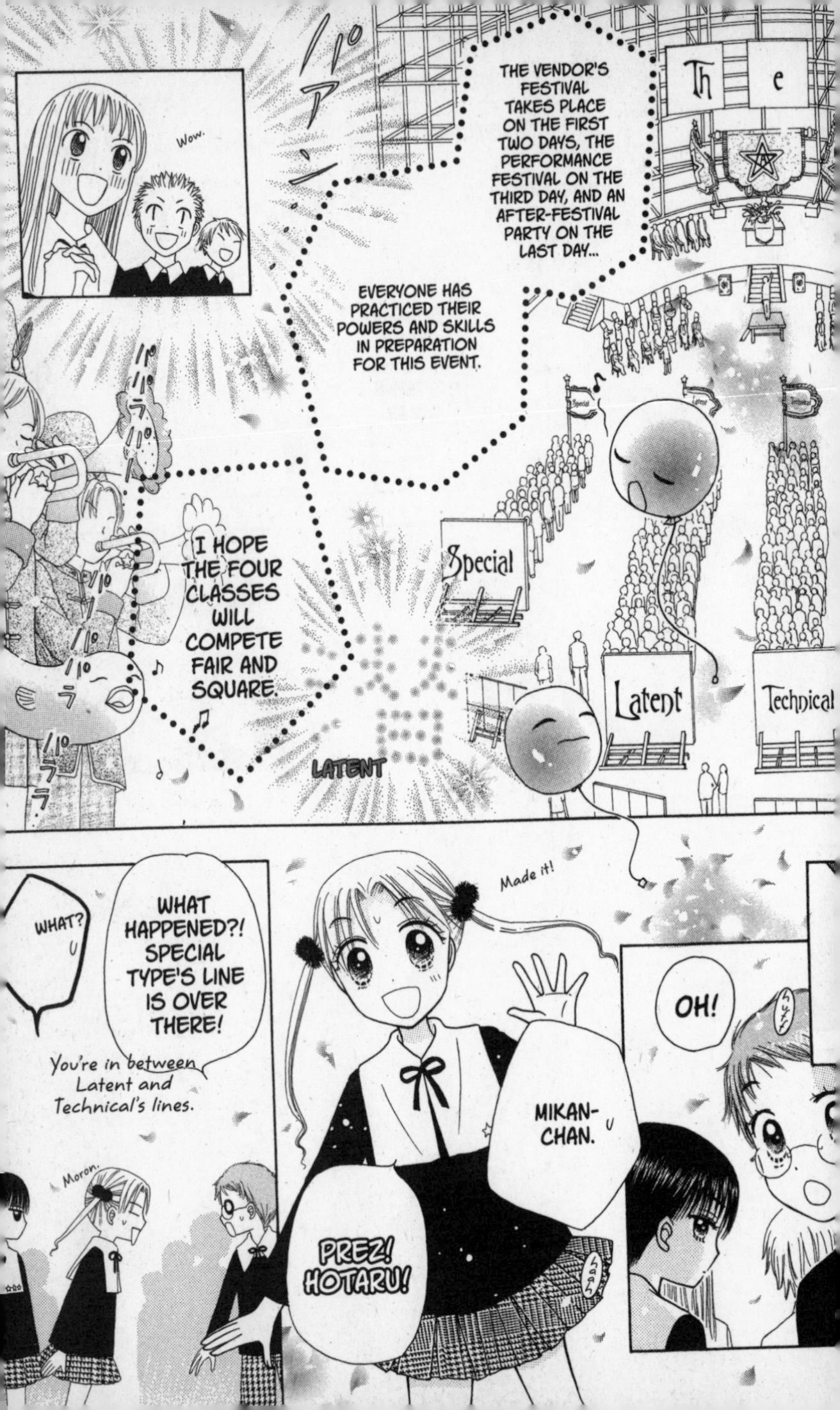

Th e
THE VENDOR'S FESTIVAL TAKES PLACE ON THE FIRST TWO DAYS, THE PERFORMANCE FESTIVAL ON THE THIRD DAY, AND AN AFTER-FESTIVAL PARTY ON THE LAST DAY...
EVERYONE HAS PRACTICED THEIR POWERS AND SKILLS IN PREPARATION FOR THIS EVENT.
Special
Latent
Technical
I HOPE THE FOUR CLASSES WILL COMPETE FAIR AND SQUARE.
LATENT
Wow.
OH!
Made it!
MIKAN-CHAN.
PREZ! HOTARU!
WHAT HAPPENED?! SPECIAL TYPE'S LINE IS OVER THERE!
WHAT?
You're in between Latent and Technical's lines.
Moron.

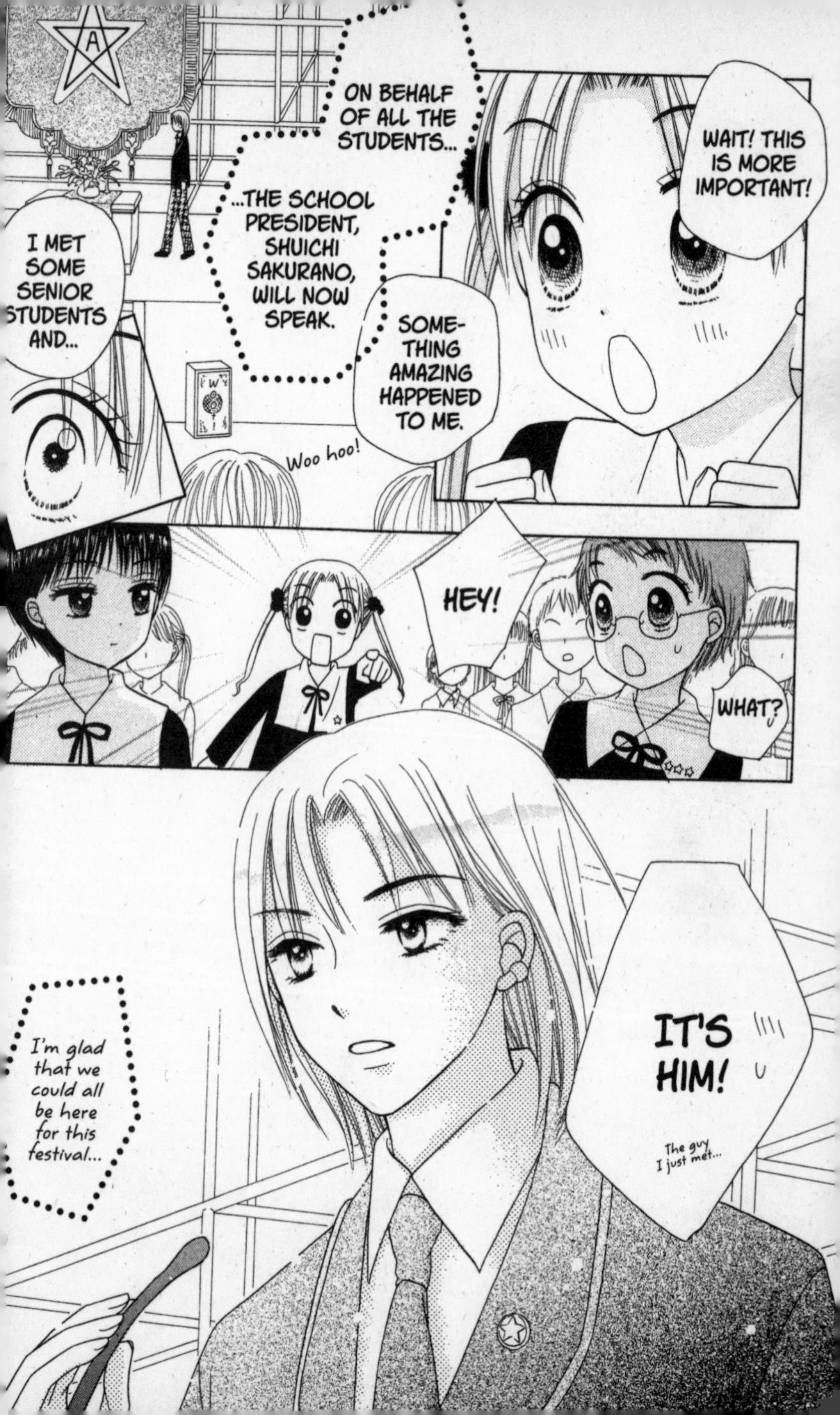
WAIT! THIS IS MORE IMPORTANT!
SOME-THING AMAZING HAPPENED TO ME.
ON BEHALF OF ALL THE STUDENTS...
...THE SCHOOL PRESIDENT, SHUICHI SAKURANO, WILL NOW SPEAK.
I MET SOME SENIOR STUDENTS AND...
Woo hoo!
WHAT?
HEY!
IT'S HIM!
The guy I just met...
I'm glad that we could all be here for this festival...

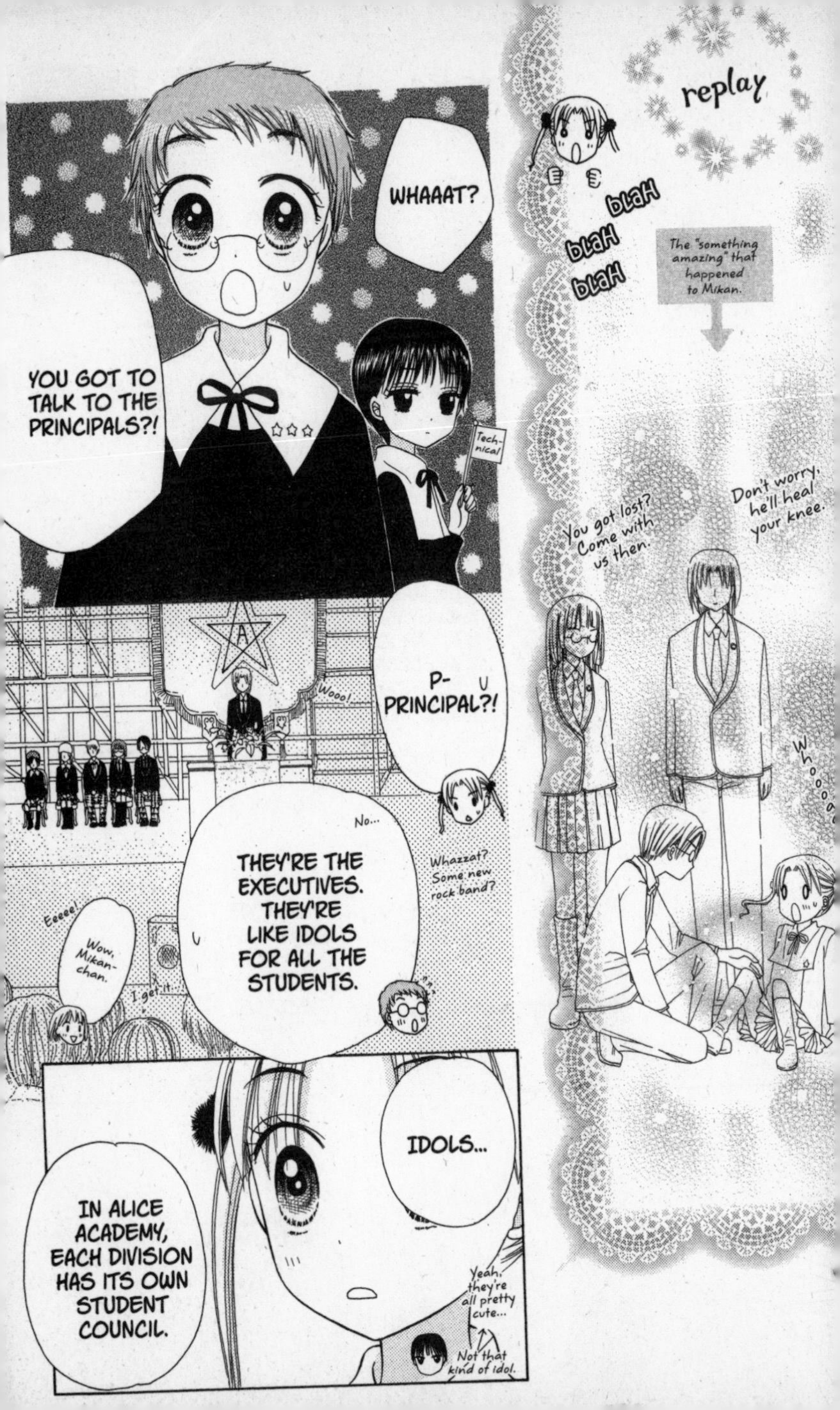
replay
blah
blah
blah
The "something amazing" that happened to Mikan.
Don't worry, he'll heal your knee.
You got lost? Come with us then.
Whoooo
WHAAAT?
YOU GOT TO TALK TO THE PRINCIPALS?!
Tech-nical
P-PRINCIPAL?!
Wooo!
No...
Whazzat? Some new rock band?
THEY'RE THE EXECUTIVES. THEY'RE LIKE IDOLS FOR ALL THE STUDENTS.
Eeeee!
Wow, Mikan-chan.
I get it.
IDOLS...
IN ALICE ACADEMY, EACH DIVISION HAS ITS OWN STUDENT COUNCIL.
Yeah, they're all pretty cute...
Not that kind of idol.

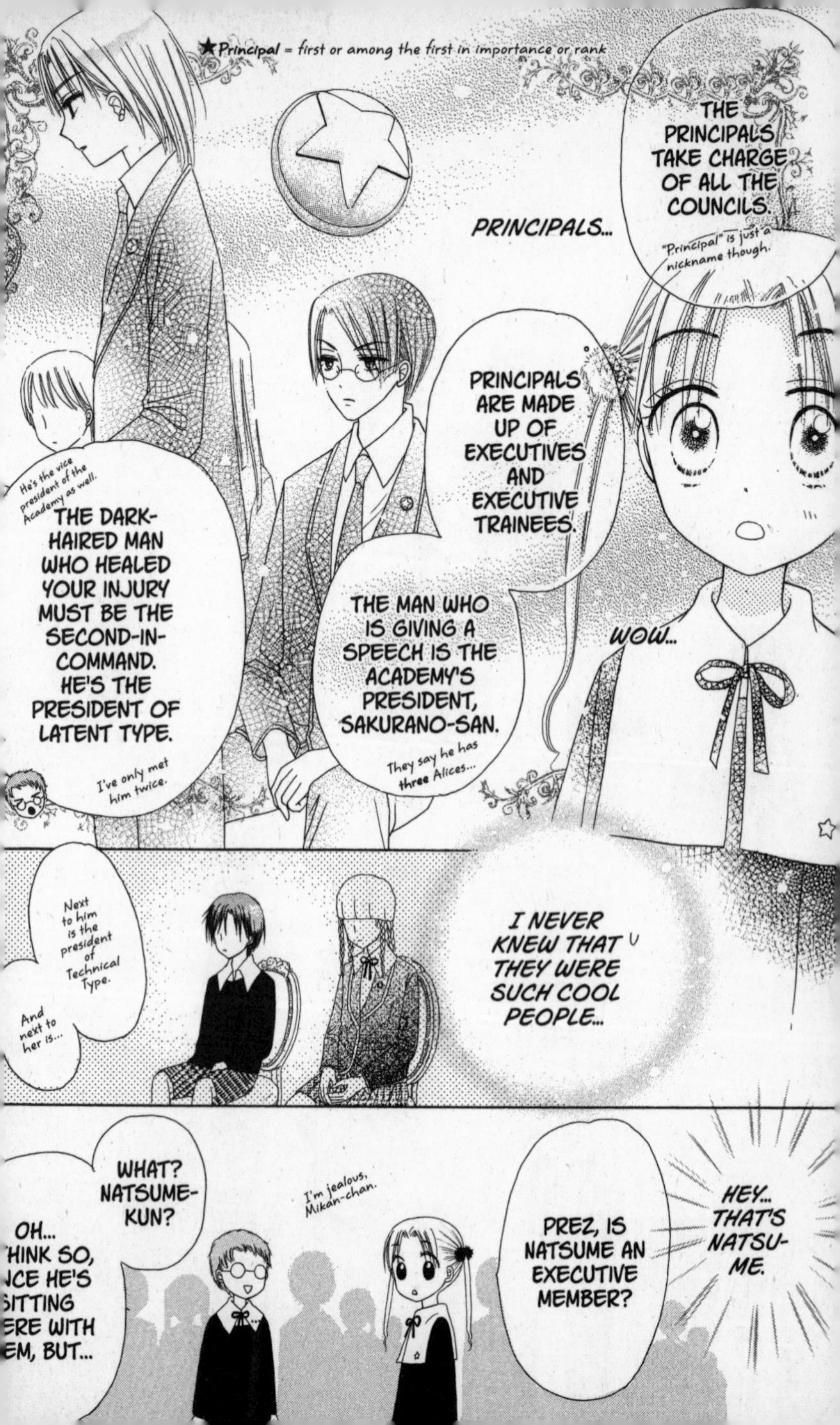
★Principal = first or among the first in importance or rank
THE PRINCIPALS TAKE CHARGE OF ALL THE COUNCILS.
"Principal" is just a nickname though.
PRINCIPALS...
PRINCIPALS ARE MADE UP OF EXECUTIVES AND EXECUTIVE TRAINEES.
WOW...
THE MAN WHO IS GIVING A SPEECH IS THE ACADEMY'S PRESIDENT, SAKURANO-SAN.
They say he has three Alices...
He's the vice president of the Academy as well.
THE DARK-HAIRED MAN WHO HEALED YOUR INJURY MUST BE THE SECOND-IN-COMMAND. HE'S THE PRESIDENT OF LATENT TYPE.
I've only met him twice.
I NEVER KNEW THAT THEY WERE SUCH COOL PEOPLE...
Next to him is the president of Technical Type.
And next to her is...
HEY... THAT'S NATSUME.
PREZ, IS NATSUME AN EXECUTIVE MEMBER?
I'm jealous, Mikan-chan.
WHAT? NATSUME-KUN?
OH... HINK SO, NCE HE'S SITTING ERE WITH EM, BUT...

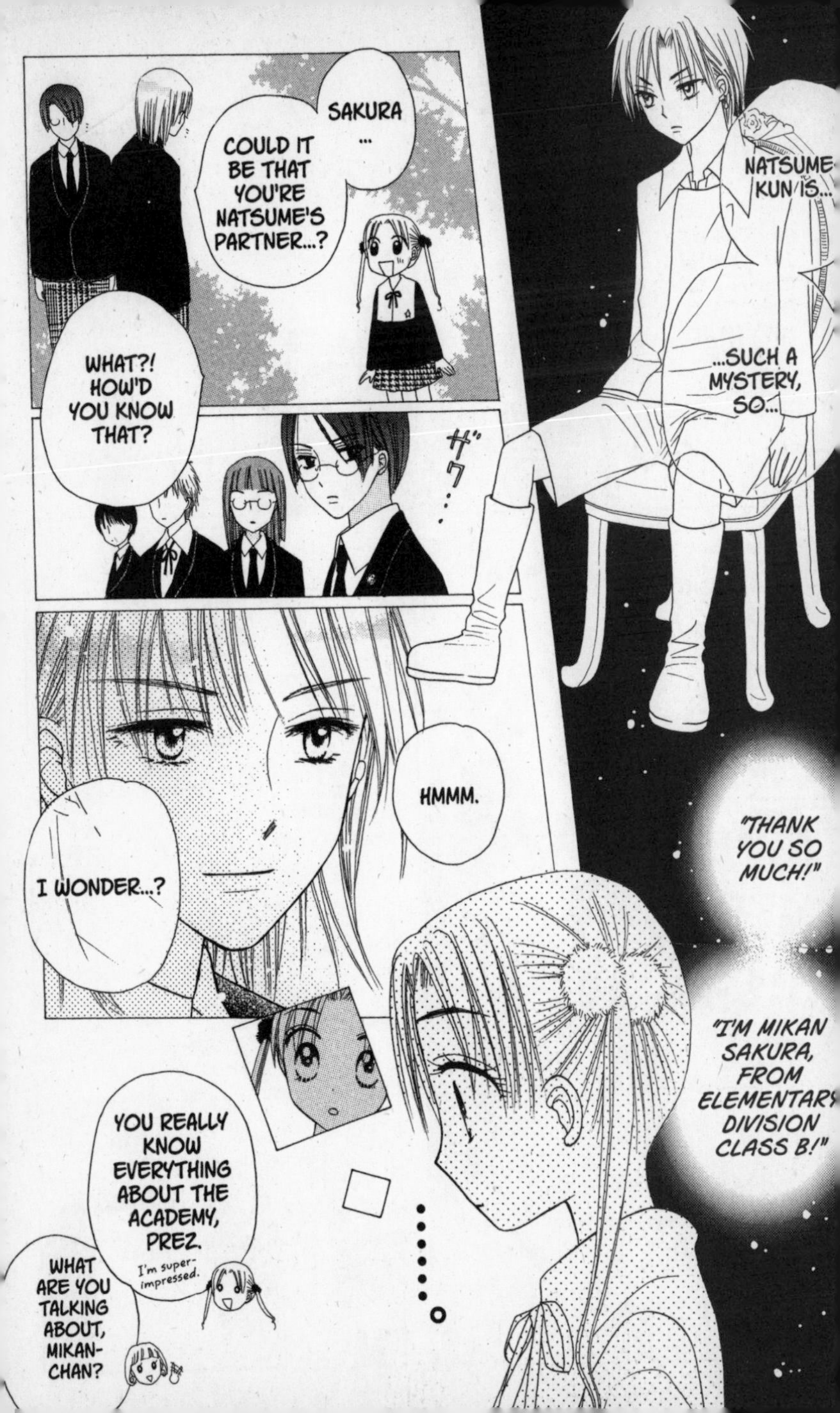

NATSUME KUN IS...
...SUCH A MYSTERY, SO...
"THANK YOU SO MUCH!"
"I'M MIKAN SAKURA, FROM ELEMENTARY DIVISION CLASS B!"
SAKURA ...
COULD IT BE THAT YOU'RE NATSUME'S PARTNER...?
WHAT?! HOW'D YOU KNOW THAT?
ザク...
HMMM.
I WONDER...?
......。
YOU REALLY KNOW EVERYTHING ABOUT THE ACADEMY, PREZ.
I'm super-impressed.
WHAT ARE YOU TALKING ABOUT, MIKAN-CHAN?

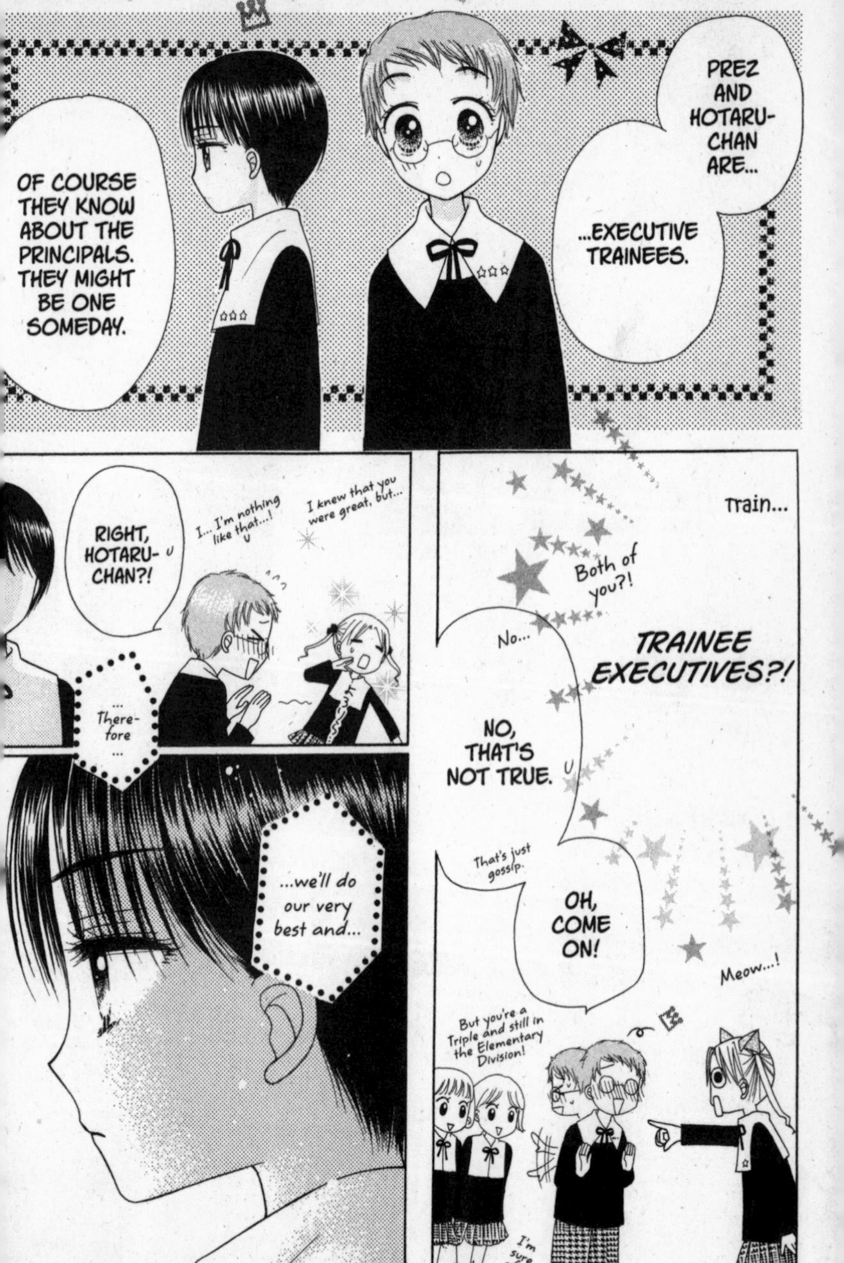

PREZ AND HOTARU-CHAN ARE...
...EXECUTIVE TRAINEES.
OF COURSE THEY KNOW ABOUT THE PRINCIPALS. THEY MIGHT BE ONE SOMEDAY.
Train...
Both of you?!
TRAINEE EXECUTIVES?!
No...
NO, THAT'S NOT TRUE.
That's just gossip.
OH, COME ON!
Meow...!
But you're a Triple and still in the Elementary Division!
I'm sure of it.
Yeah
I knew that you were great, but...
I... I'm nothing like that...!
RIGHT, HOTARU-CHAN?!
...Therefore...
...we'll do our very best and...

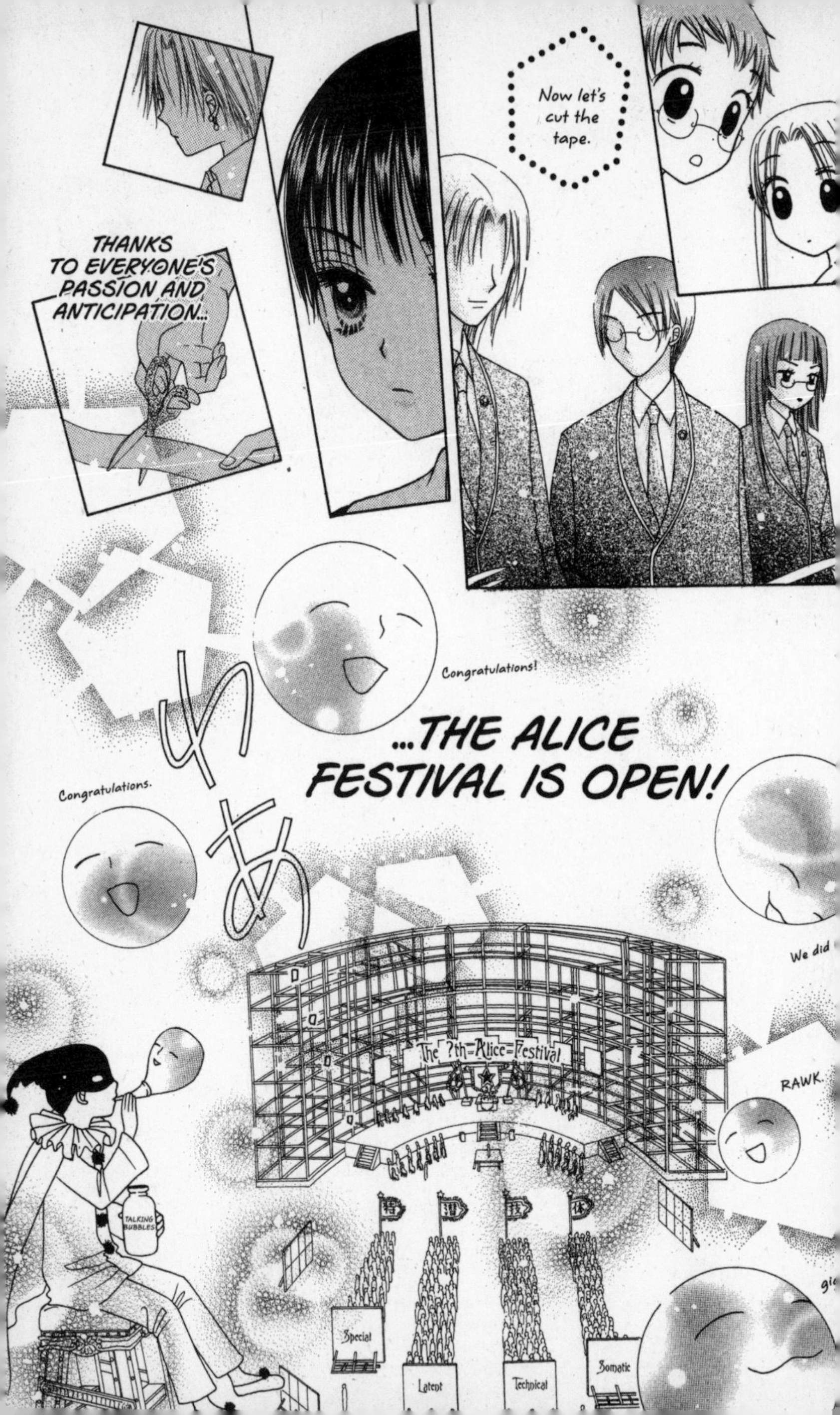
Now let's cut the tape.
THANKS TO EVERYONE'S PASSION AND ANTICIPATION...
Congratulations!
...THE ALICE FESTIVAL IS OPEN!
Congratulations.
We did
RAWK.
The 7th Alice Festival
TALKING BUBBLES
Special
Latent
Technical
Somatic

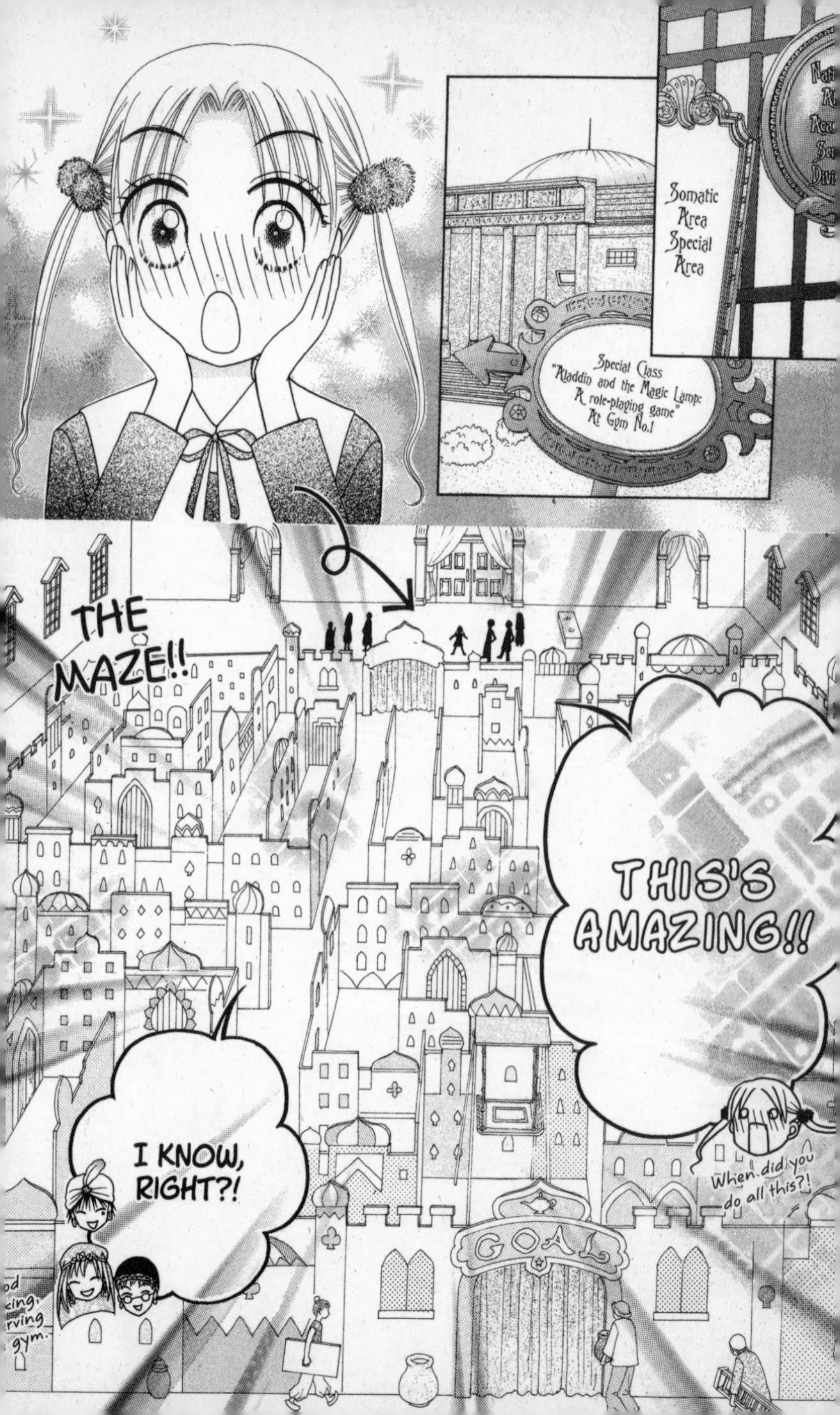
Somatic Area Special Area
Special Class "Aladdin and the Magic Lamp: A role-playing game" At Gym No.1
THIS'S AMAZING!!
When did you do all this?!
THE MAZE!!
I KNOW, RIGHT?!
GOAL

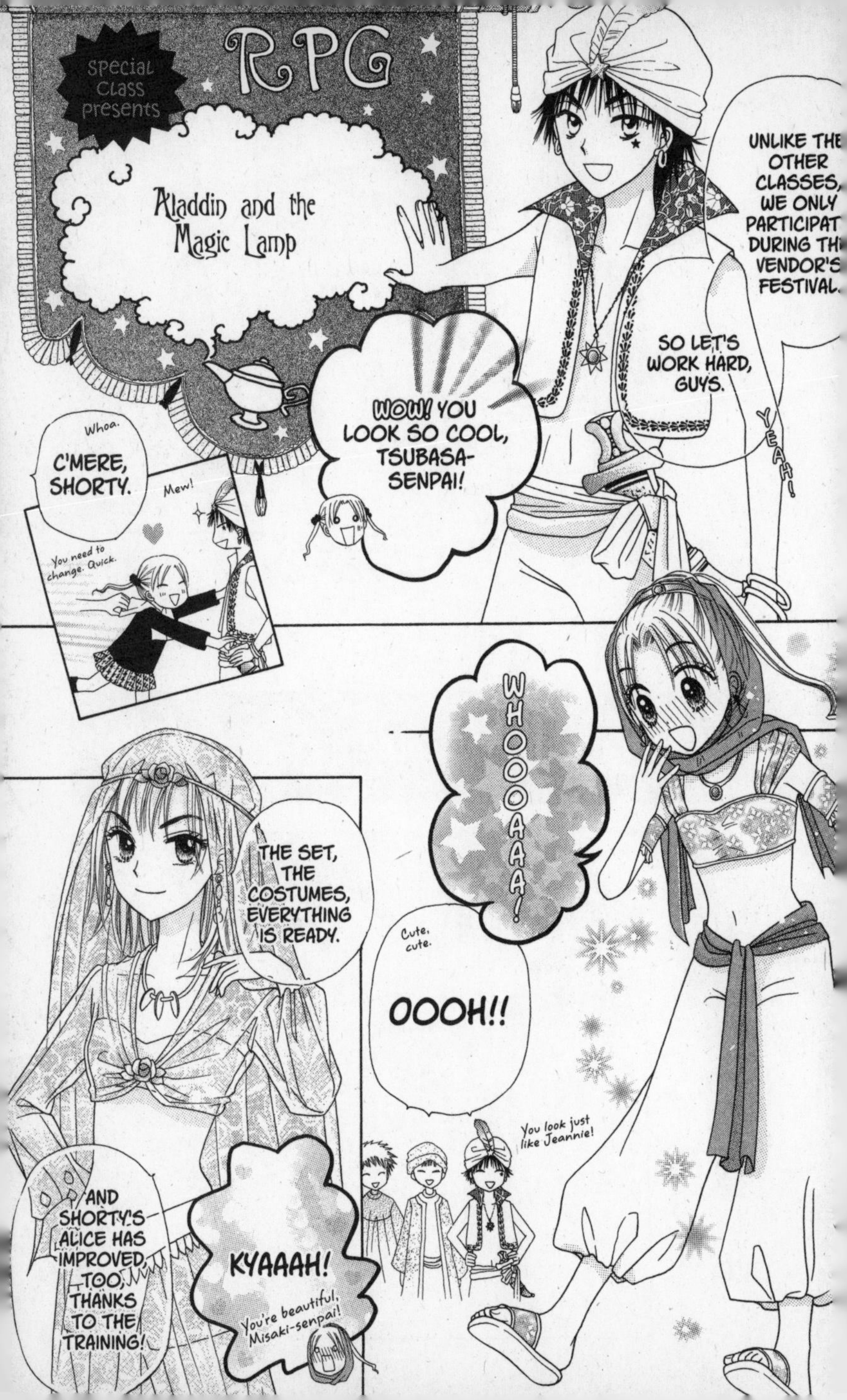
UNLIKE THE OTHER CLASSES, WE ONLY PARTICIPAT DURING TH VENDOR'S FESTIVAL.
SO LET'S WORK HARD, GUYS.
YEAH!
WOW! YOU LOOK SO COOL, TSUBASA-SENPAI!
Special Class presents
RPG
Aladdin and the Magic Lamp
Whoa.
C'MERE, SHORTY.
Mew!
You need to change. Quick.
WHOOOOAAA!
Cute, cute.
OOOH!!
You look just like Jeannie!
THE SET, THE COSTUMES, EVERYTHING IS READY.
AND SHORTY'S ALICE HAS IMPROVED, TOO, THANKS TO THE TRAINING!
KYAAAH!
You're beautiful, Misaki-senpai!

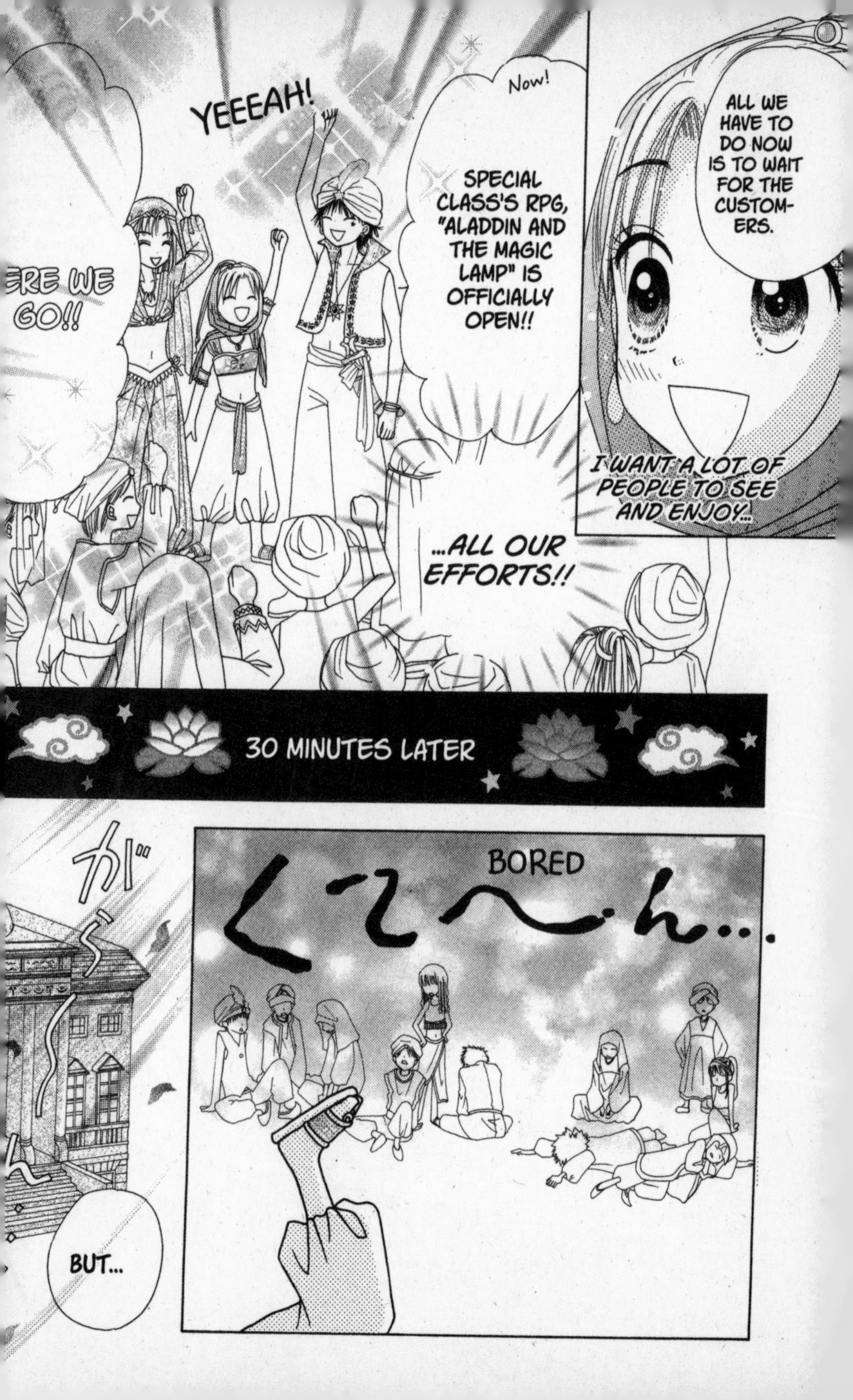
ALL WE HAVE TO DO NOW IS TO WAIT FOR THE CUSTOMERS.
I WANT A LOT OF PEOPLE TO SEE AND ENJOY...
Now!
SPECIAL CLASS'S RPG, "ALADDIN AND THE MAGIC LAMP" IS OFFICIALLY OPEN!!
...ALL OUR EFFORTS!!
YEEEAH!
ERE WE GO!!
30 MINUTES LATER
BORED
くて〜ん...
がら〜ん
BUT...

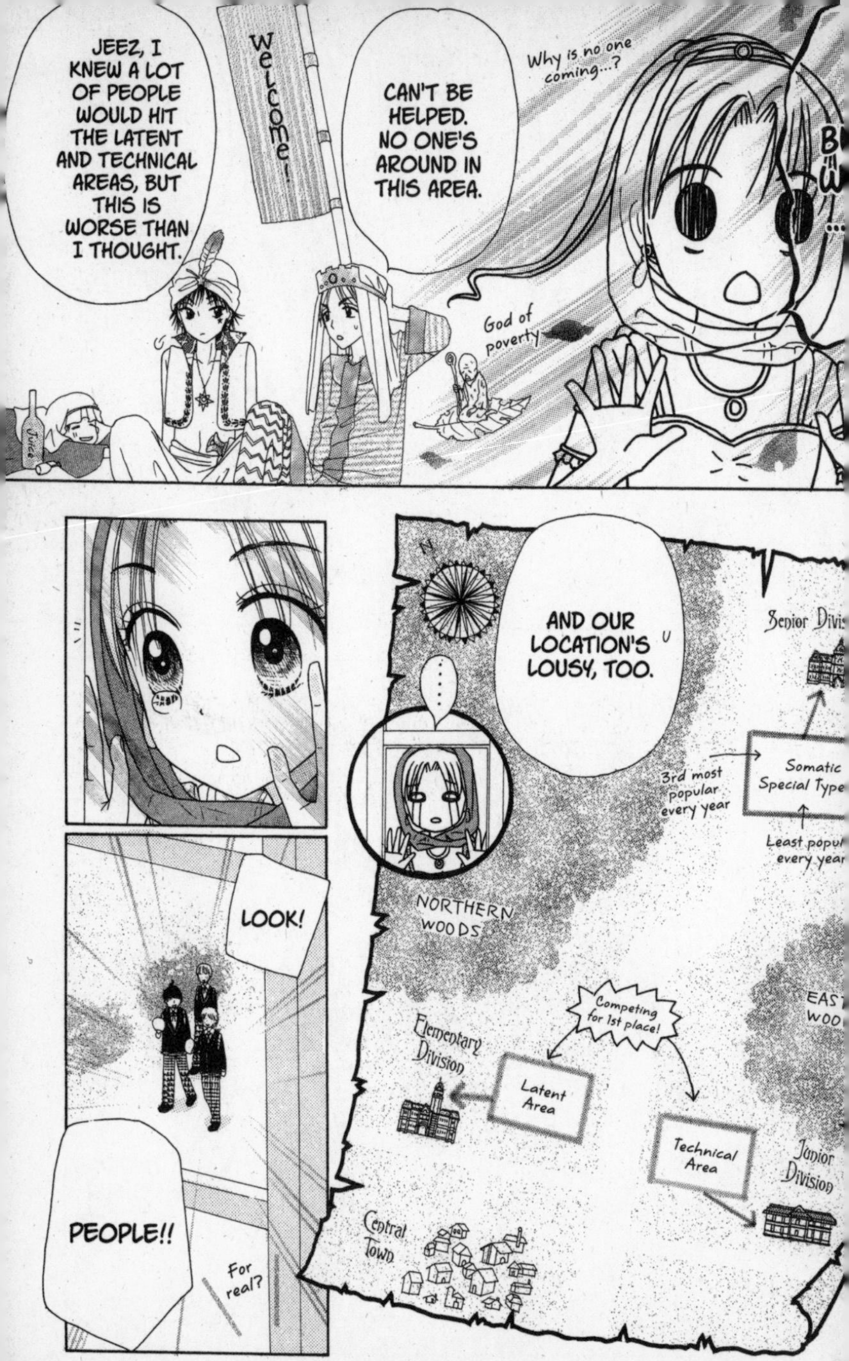
Why is no one coming...?
CAN'T BE HELPED. NO ONE'S AROUND IN THIS AREA.
Welcome!
JEEZ, I KNEW A LOT OF PEOPLE WOULD HIT THE LATENT AND TECHNICAL AREAS, BUT THIS IS WORSE THAN I THOUGHT.
God of poverty
Juice
AND OUR LOCATION'S LOUSY, TOO.
......
Senior Divis
Somatic Special Type
3rd most popular every year
Least popul every year
NORTHERN WOODS
EAS WOO
Competing for 1st place!
Elementary Division
Latent Area
Technical Area
Junior Division
Central Town
LOOK!
PEOPLE!!
For real?

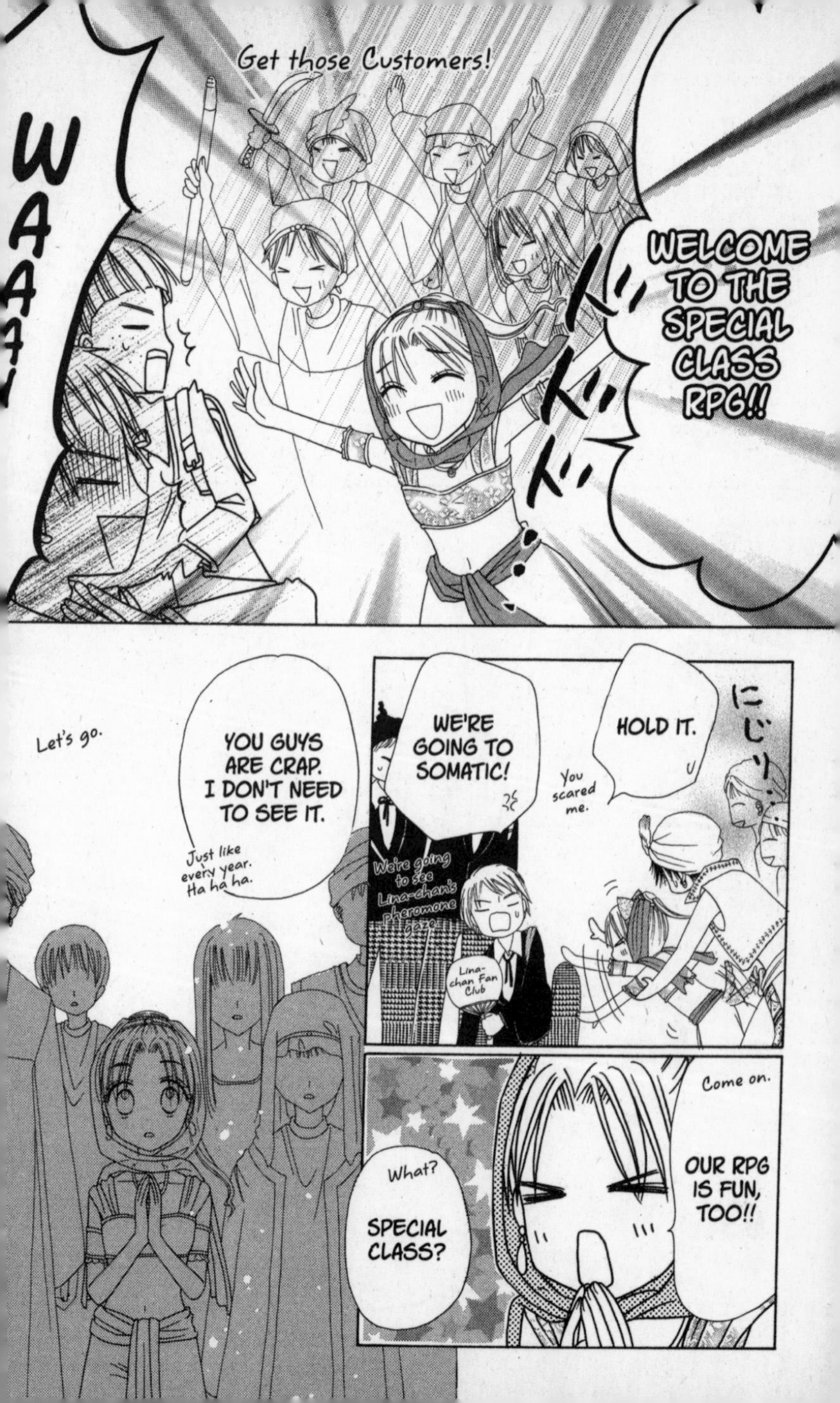
WELCOME TO THE SPECIAL CLASS RPG!!
Get those Customers!
WAAAA
にじり…
HOLD IT.
You scared me.
WE'RE GOING TO SOMATIC!
We're going to see Lina-chan's pheromone gaze
Lina-chan Fan Club
Come on.
OUR RPG IS FUN, TOO!!
What?
SPECIAL CLASS?
YOU GUYS ARE CRAP. I DON'T NEED TO SEE IT.
Let's go.
Just like every year. Ha ha ha.

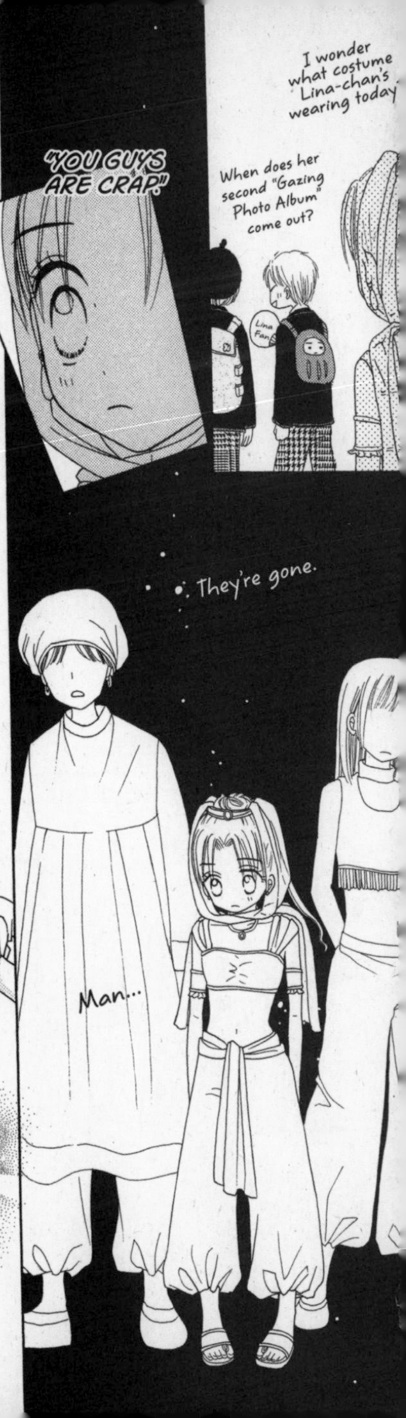
I wonder what costume Lina-chan's wearing today
When does her second "Gazing Photo Album" come out?
Lina Fan
"YOU GUYS ARE CRAP."
They're gone.
Man...
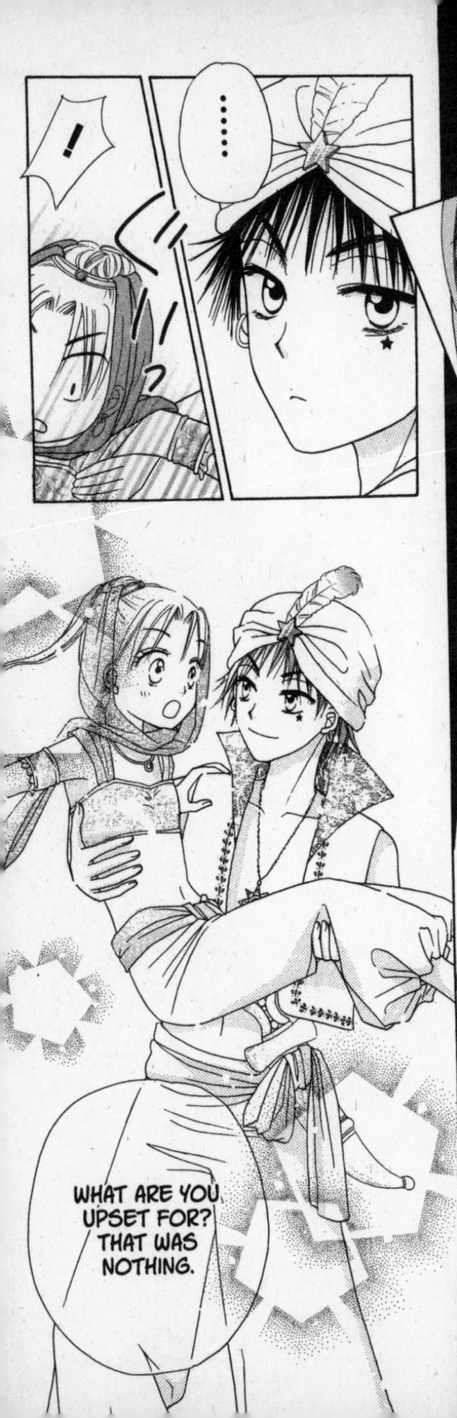
......
!
WHAT ARE YOU UPSET FOR? THAT WAS NOTHING.

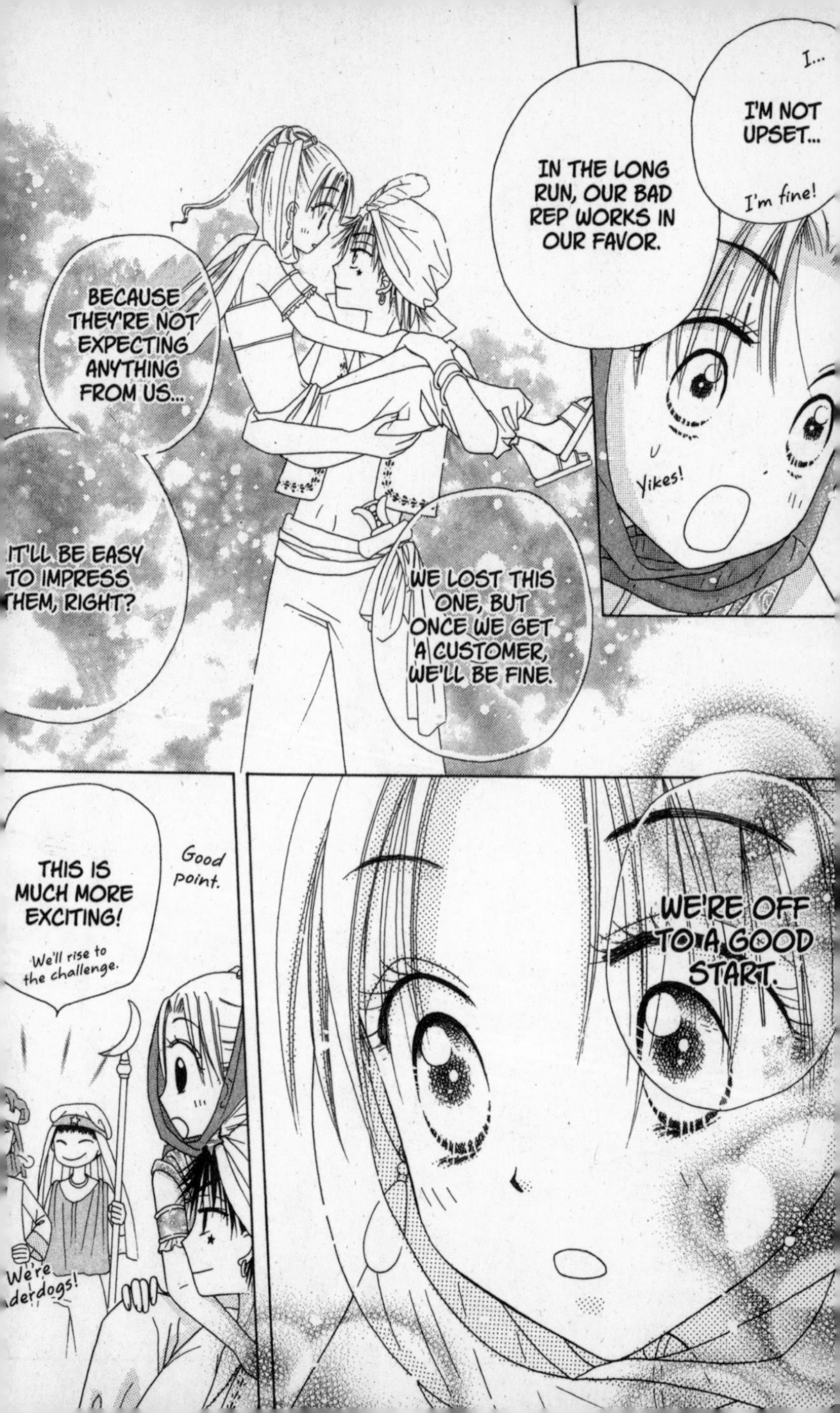
I...
I'M NOT UPSET...
I'm fine!
IN THE LONG RUN, OUR BAD REP WORKS IN OUR FAVOR.
Yikes!
BECAUSE THEY'RE NOT EXPECTING ANYTHING FROM US...
WE LOST THIS ONE, BUT ONCE WE GET A CUSTOMER, WE'LL BE FINE.
IT'LL BE EASY TO IMPRESS THEM, RIGHT?
WE'RE OFF TO A GOOD START.
Good point.
THIS IS MUCH MORE EXCITING!
We'll rise to the challenge.
We're
derdogs!

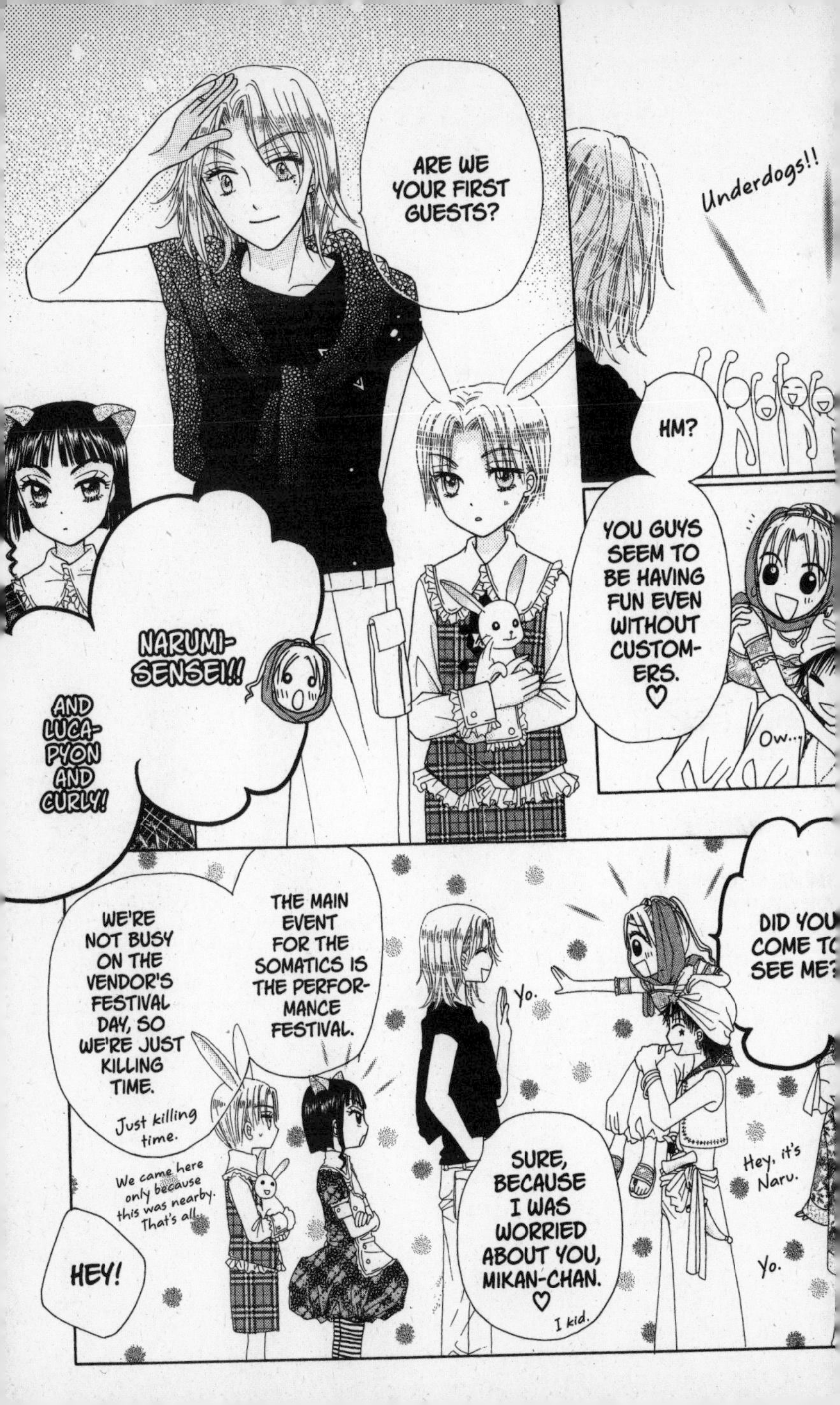
Underdogs!!
HM?
YOU GUYS SEEM TO BE HAVING FUN EVEN WITHOUT CUSTOMERS. ♡
Ow...
ARE WE YOUR FIRST GUESTS?
NARUMI-SENSEI!!
AND LUCA-PYON AND CURLY!
DID YOU COME TO SEE ME?
Hey, it's Naru.
Yo.
Yo.
SURE, BECAUSE I WAS WORRIED ABOUT YOU, MIKAN-CHAN. ♡
I kid.
THE MAIN EVENT FOR THE SOMATICS IS THE PERFORMANCE FESTIVAL.
WE'RE NOT BUSY ON THE VENDOR'S FESTIVAL DAY, SO WE'RE JUST KILLING TIME.
Just killing time.
We came here only because this was nearby. That's all.
HEY!

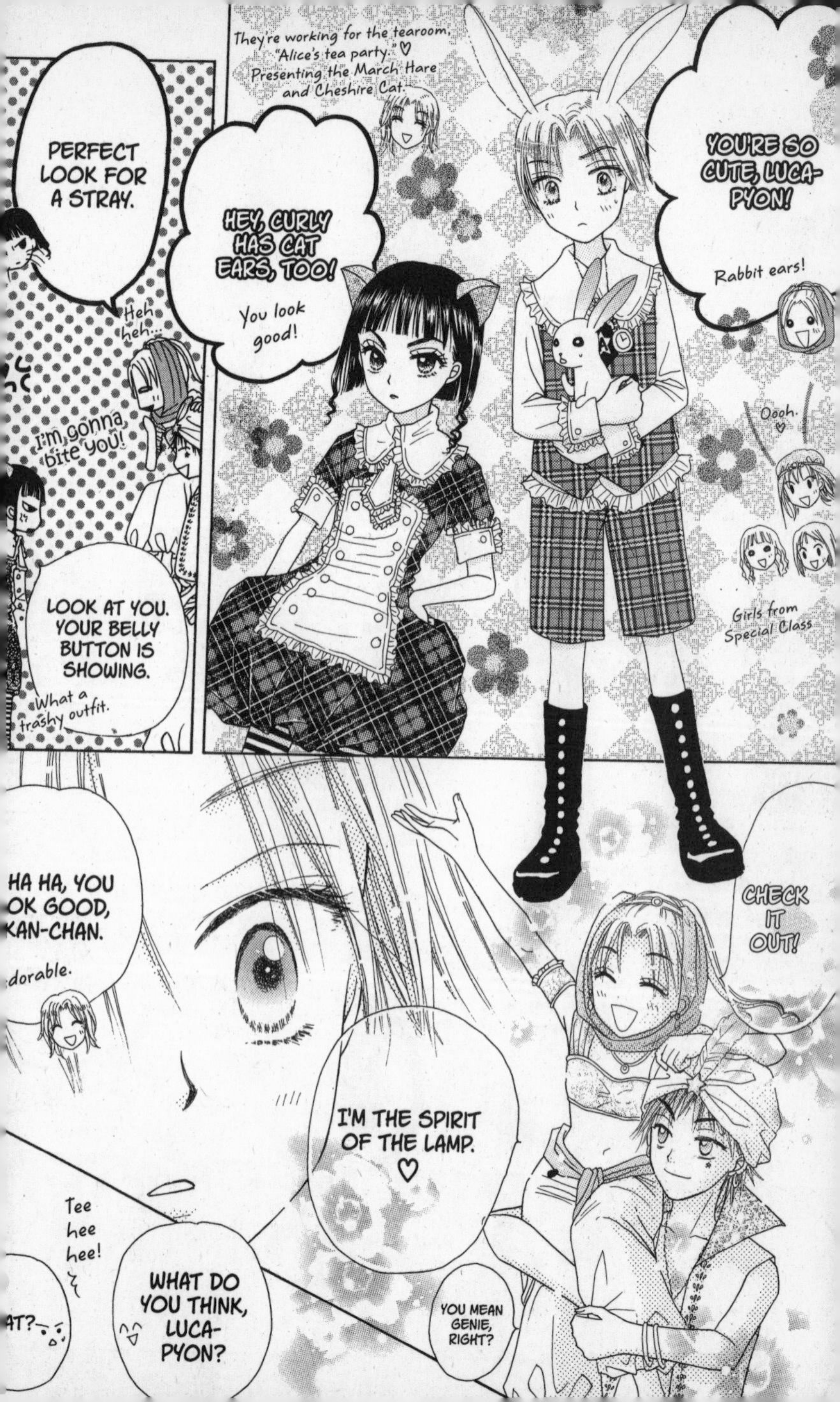
They're working for the tearoom, "Alice's tea party." ♡ Presenting the March Hare and Cheshire Cat.
YOU'RE SO CUTE, LUCA-PYON!
Rabbit ears!
HEY, CURLY HAS CAT EARS, TOO!
You look good!
Oooh. ♡
Girls from Special Class
PERFECT LOOK FOR A STRAY.
Heh heh...
I'm gonna bite you!
LOOK AT YOU. YOUR BELLY BUTTON IS SHOWING.
What a trashy outfit.
CHECK IT OUT!
I'M THE SPIRIT OF THE LAMP. ♡
YOU MEAN GENIE, RIGHT?
WHAT DO YOU THINK, LUCA-PYON?
Tee hee hee!
HA HA, YOU
OK GOOD,
KAN-CHAN.
dorable.
AT?

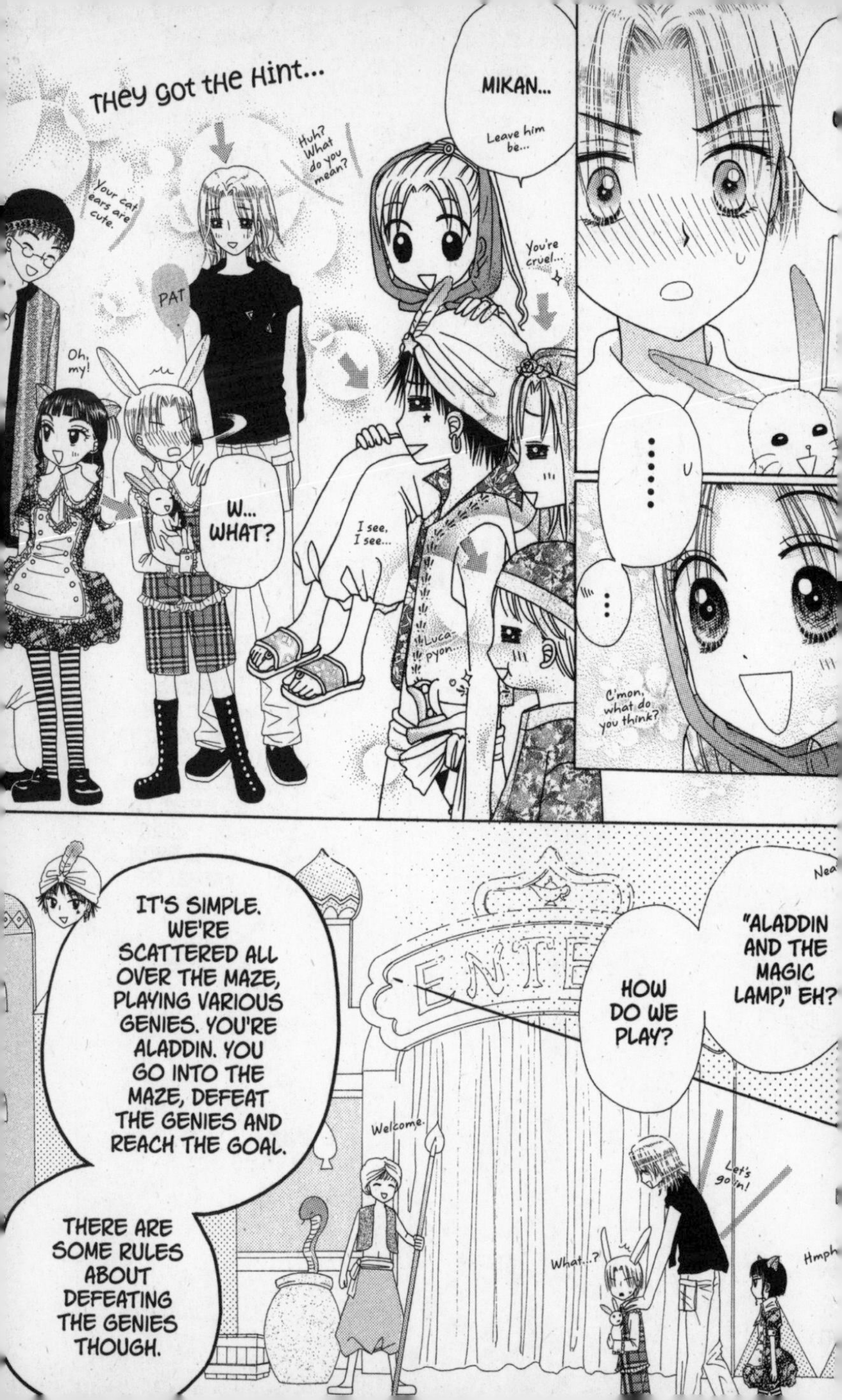

......
...
C'mon, what do you think?
MIKAN...
Leave him be...
You're cruel...
Huh? What do you mean?
They got the Hint...
Your cat ears are cute.
PAT
W... WHAT?
Oh, my!
I see, I see...
Luca-pyon...
"ALADDIN AND THE MAGIC LAMP," EH?
HOW DO WE PLAY?
Let's go in!
Hmph
What...?
Welcome.
IT'S SIMPLE. WE'RE SCATTERED ALL OVER THE MAZE, PLAYING VARIOUS GENIES. YOU'RE ALADDIN. YOU GO INTO THE MAZE, DEFEAT THE GENIES AND REACH THE GOAL.
THERE ARE SOME RULES ABOUT DEFEATING THE GENIES THOUGH.

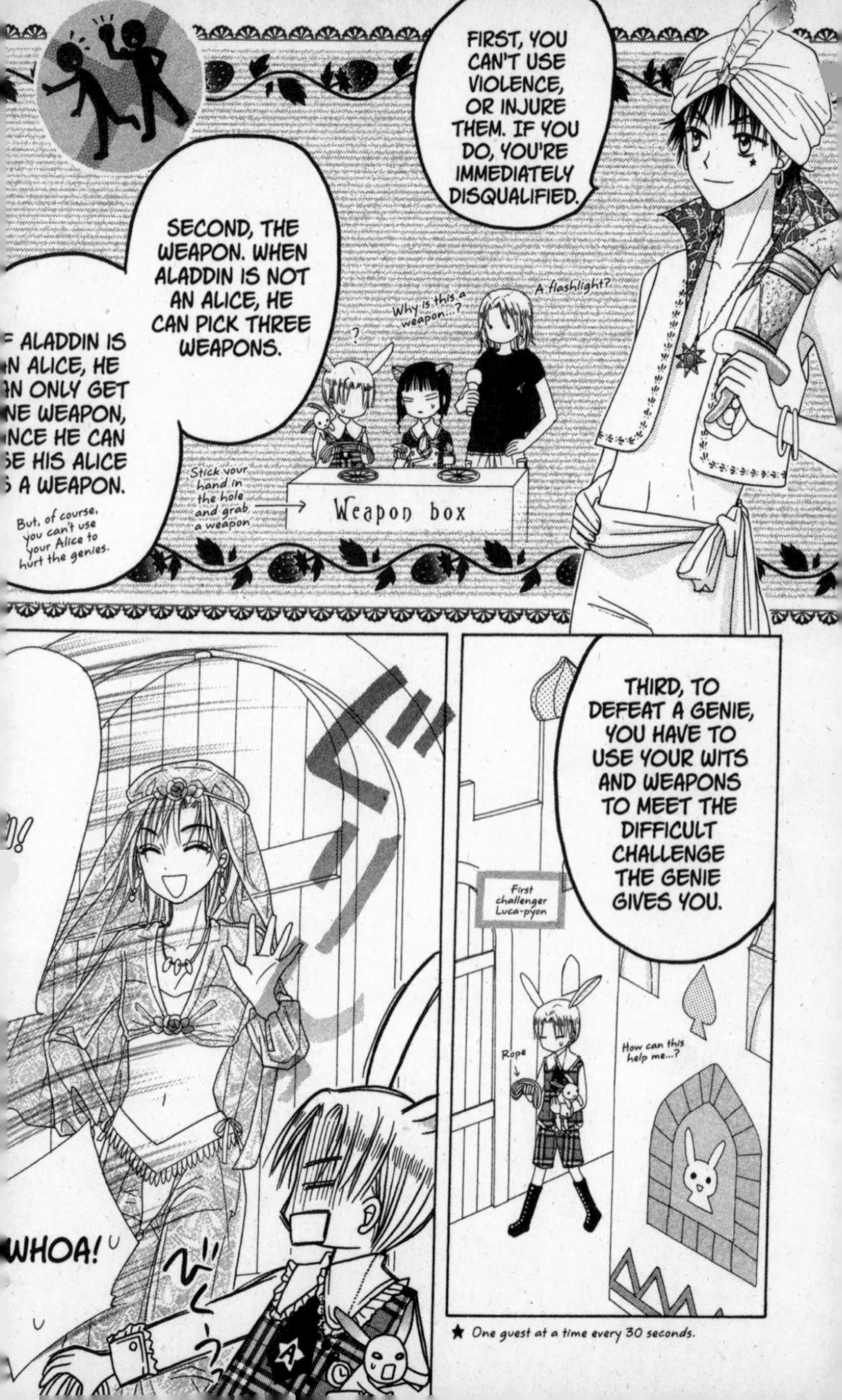
FIRST, YOU CAN'T USE VIOLENCE, OR INJURE THEM. IF YOU DO, YOU'RE IMMEDIATELY DISQUALIFIED.
A flashlight?
Why is this a weapon...?
?
SECOND, THE WEAPON. WHEN ALADDIN IS NOT AN ALICE, HE CAN PICK THREE WEAPONS.
Stick your hand in the hole and grab a weapon
Weapon box
F ALADDIN IS N ALICE, HE AN ONLY GET NE WEAPON, NCE HE CAN SE HIS ALICE S A WEAPON.
But, of course, you can't use your Alice to hurt the genies.
THIRD, TO DEFEAT A GENIE, YOU HAVE TO USE YOUR WITS AND WEAPONS TO MEET THE DIFFICULT CHALLENGE THE GENIE GIVES YOU.
First challenger Luca-pyon
How can this help me...?
Rope
WHOA!
★ One guest at a time every 30 seconds.

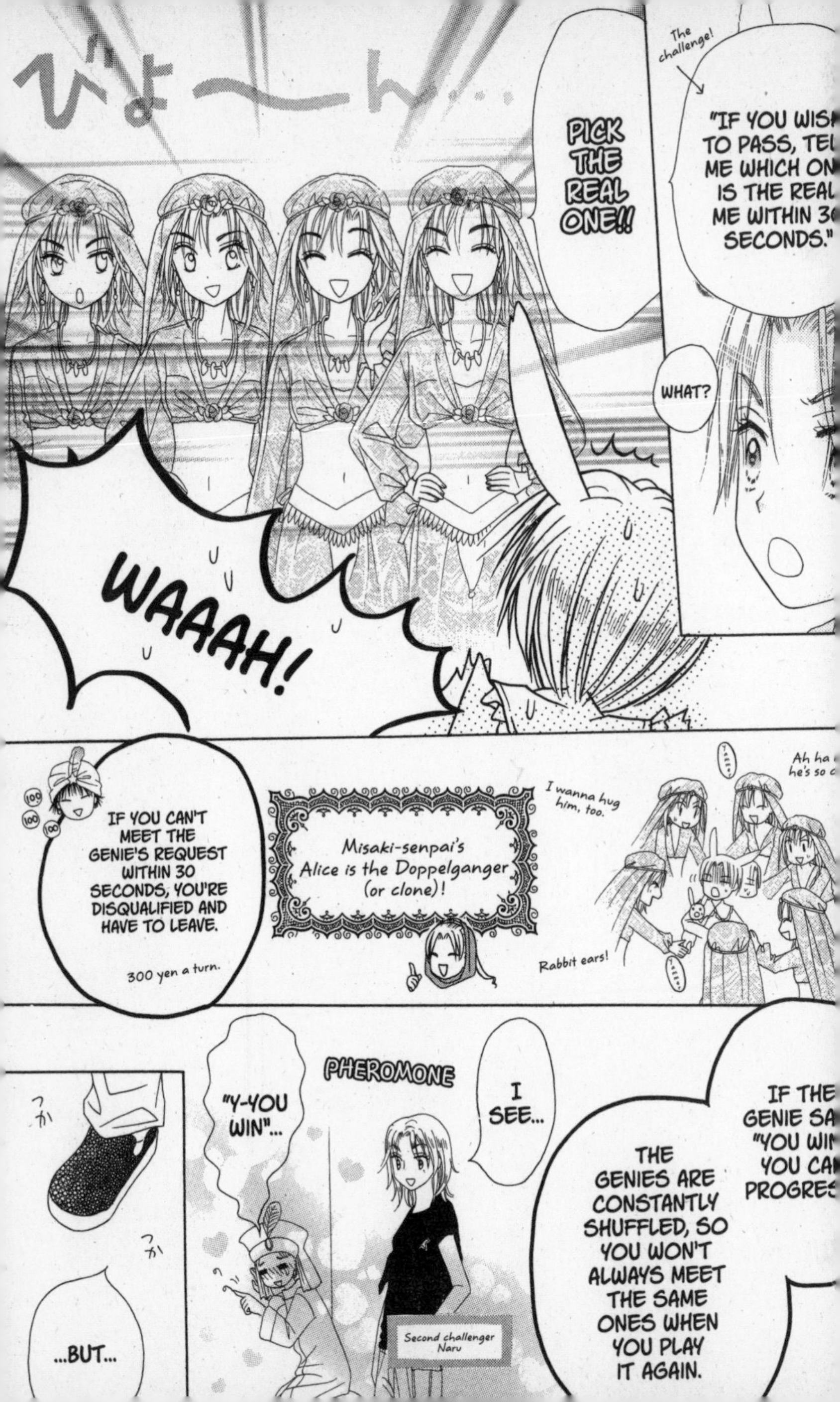
The challenge!
"IF YOU WIS TO PASS, TEL ME WHICH ON IS THE REAL ME WITHIN 3 SECONDS."
WHAT?
ぴよ〜ん…
PICK THE REAL ONE!!
WAAAH!
Ah ha he's so
I wanna hug him, too.
Rabbit ears!
Misaki-senpai's Alice is the Doppelganger (or clone)!
IF YOU CAN'T MEET THE GENIE'S REQUEST WITHIN 30 SECONDS, YOU'RE DISQUALIFIED AND HAVE TO LEAVE.
300 yen a turn.
IF THE GENIE SA "YOU WI YOU CA PROGRES
THE GENIES ARE CONSTANTLY SHUFFLED, SO YOU WON'T ALWAYS MEET THE SAME ONES WHEN YOU PLAY IT AGAIN.
I SEE...
PHEROMONE
"Y-YOU WIN"...
Second challenger Naru
つか
つか
...BUT...

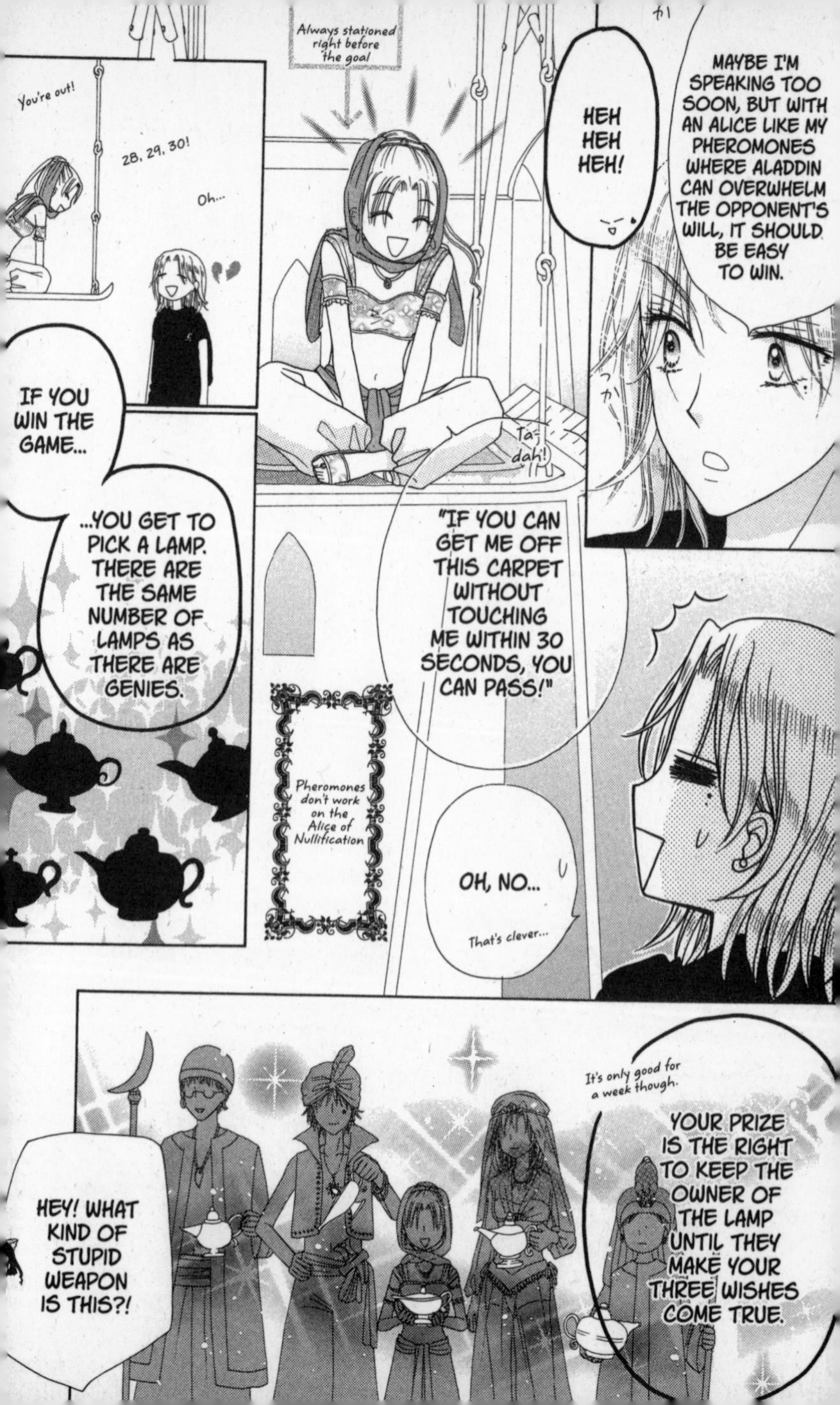
HEH HEH HEH!
MAYBE I'M SPEAKING TOO SOON, BUT WITH AN ALICE LIKE MY PHEROMONES WHERE ALADDIN CAN OVERWHELM THE OPPONENT'S WILL, IT SHOULD BE EASY TO WIN.
Always stationed right before the goal
"IF YOU CAN GET ME OFF THIS CARPET WITHOUT TOUCHING ME WITHIN 30 SECONDS, YOU CAN PASS!"
Ta-dah!
You're out!
28, 29, 30!
Oh...
OH, NO...
That's clever...
Pheromones don't work on the Alice of Nullification
IF YOU WIN THE GAME...
...YOU GET TO PICK A LAMP. THERE ARE THE SAME NUMBER OF LAMPS AS THERE ARE GENIES.
YOUR PRIZE IS THE RIGHT TO KEEP THE OWNER OF THE LAMP UNTIL THEY MAKE YOUR THREE WISHES COME TRUE.
It's only good for a week though.
HEY! WHAT KIND OF STUPID WEAPON IS THIS?!

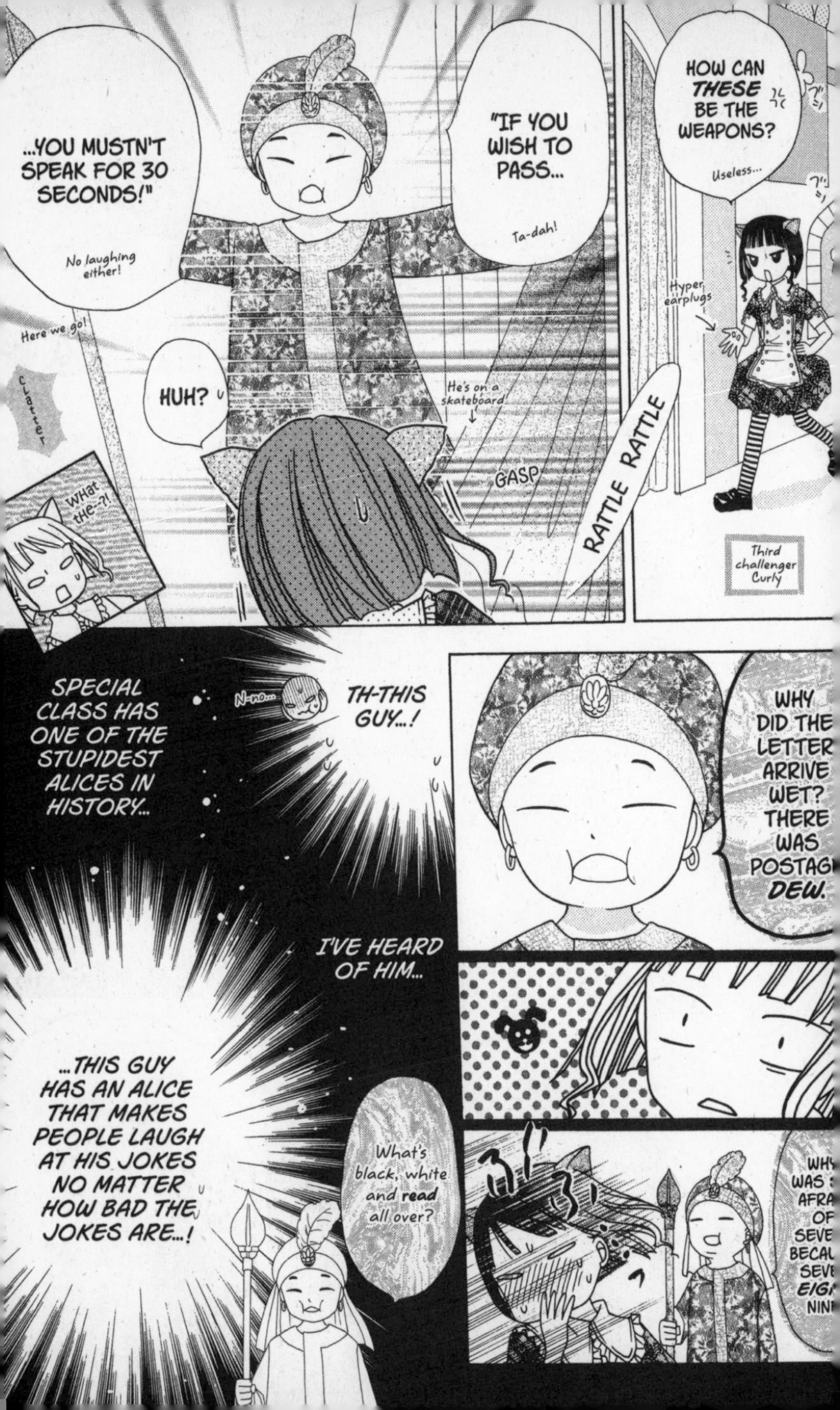

HOW CAN THESE BE THE WEAPONS?
Useless...
Hyper earplugs
Third challenger Curly
"IF YOU WISH TO PASS...
Ta-dah!
...YOU MUSTN'T SPEAK FOR 30 SECONDS!"
No laughing either!
Here we go!
He's on a skateboard
RATTLE RATTLE
GASP
HUH?
Clatter
WHAT THE-?!
WHY DID THE LETTER ARRIVE WET? THERE WAS POSTAG DEW.
WHY WAS AFRA OF SEVE BECAU SEVE EIGH NINE
TH-THIS GUY...!
N-no...
SPECIAL CLASS HAS ONE OF THE STUPIDEST ALICES IN HISTORY...
I'VE HEARD OF HIM...
What's black, white and read all over?
...THIS GUY HAS AN ALICE THAT MAKES PEOPLE LAUGH AT HIS JOKES NO MATTER HOW BAD THE JOKES ARE...!

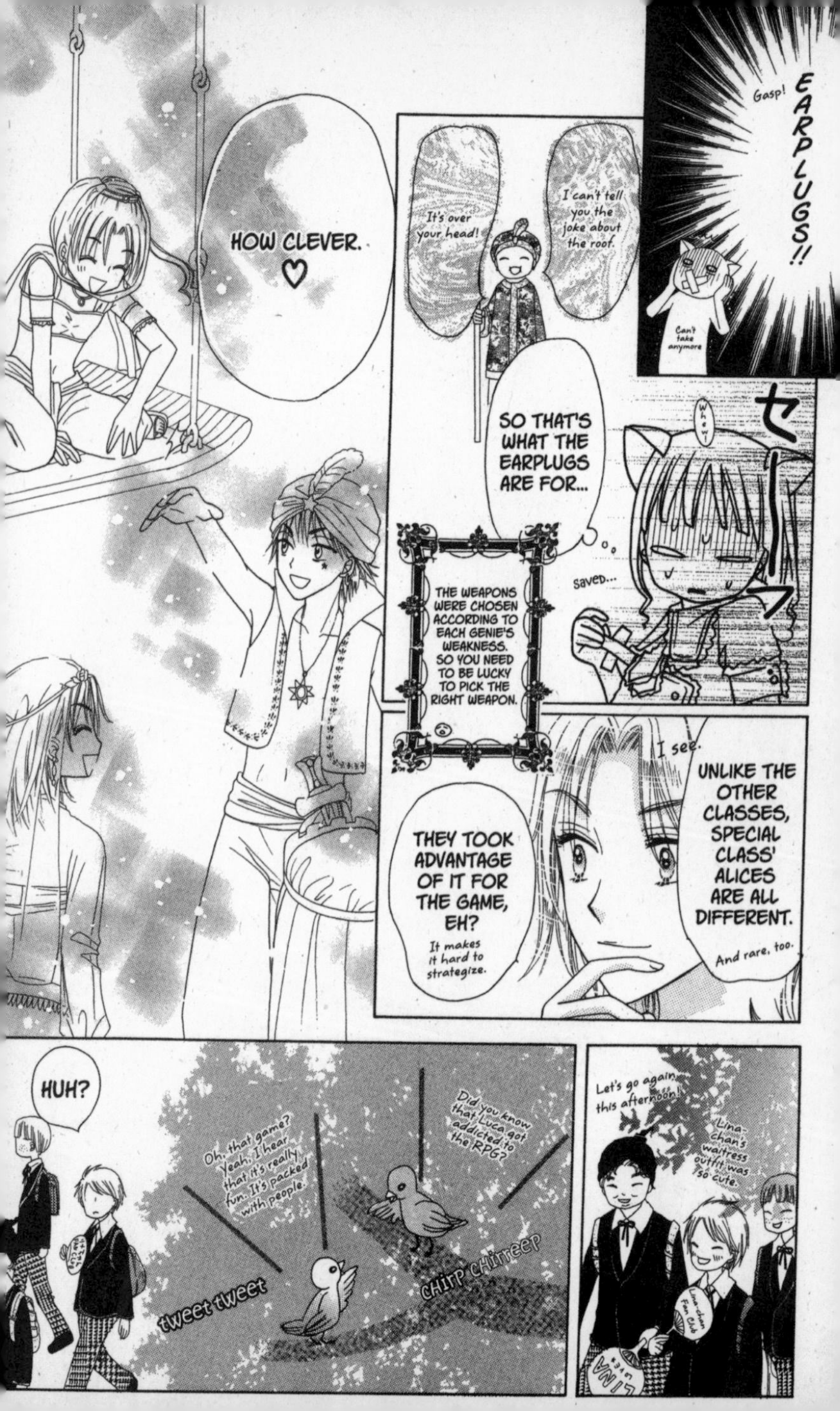

Gasp!
EARPLUGS!!
Can't take anymore
I can't tell you the joke about the roof.
It's over your head!
Whew
SO THAT'S WHAT THE EARPLUGS ARE FOR...
saved...
THE WEAPONS WERE CHOSEN ACCORDING TO EACH GENIE'S WEAKNESS. SO YOU NEED TO BE LUCKY TO PICK THE RIGHT WEAPON.
I see.
UNLIKE THE OTHER CLASSES, SPECIAL CLASS' ALICES ARE ALL DIFFERENT.
And rare, too.
THEY TOOK ADVANTAGE OF IT FOR THE GAME, EH?
It makes it hard to strategize.
HOW CLEVER. ♡
Let's go again this afternoon!
Lina-chan's waitress outfit was so cute.
Lina-chan Fan Club
Did you know that Luca got addicted to the RPG?
Oh, that game? Yeah, I hear that it's really fun. It's packed with people.
CHIRP CHIRREEP
tweet tweet
HUH?

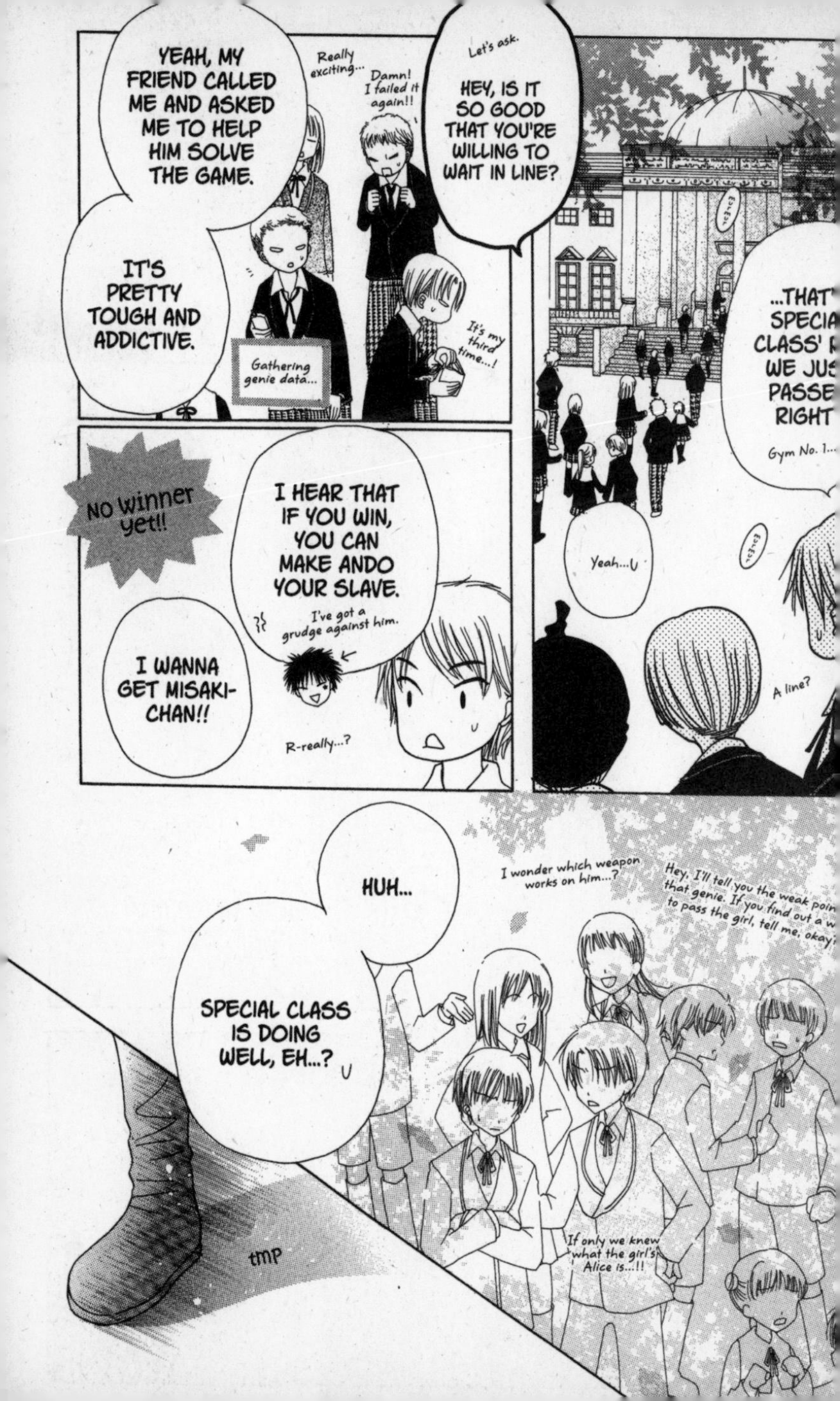
...THAT'
SPECIA
CLASS'
WE JUS
PASSE
RIGHT
Gym No. 1...
Yeah...
A line?
Let's ask.
HEY, IS IT SO GOOD THAT YOU'RE WILLING TO WAIT IN LINE?
Damn! I failed it again!!
Really exciting...
It's my third time...!
YEAH, MY FRIEND CALLED ME AND ASKED ME TO HELP HIM SOLVE THE GAME.
IT'S PRETTY TOUGH AND ADDICTIVE.
Gathering genie data...
I HEAR THAT IF YOU WIN, YOU CAN MAKE ANDO YOUR SLAVE.
I've got a grudge against him.
No winner yet!!
I WANNA GET MISAKI-CHAN!!
R-really...?
Hey, I'll tell you the weak poin
that genie. If you find out a w
to pass the girl, tell me, okay
I wonder which weapon works on him...?
HUH...
SPECIAL CLASS IS DOING WELL, EH...?
If only we knew what the girl's Alice is...!!
tmp

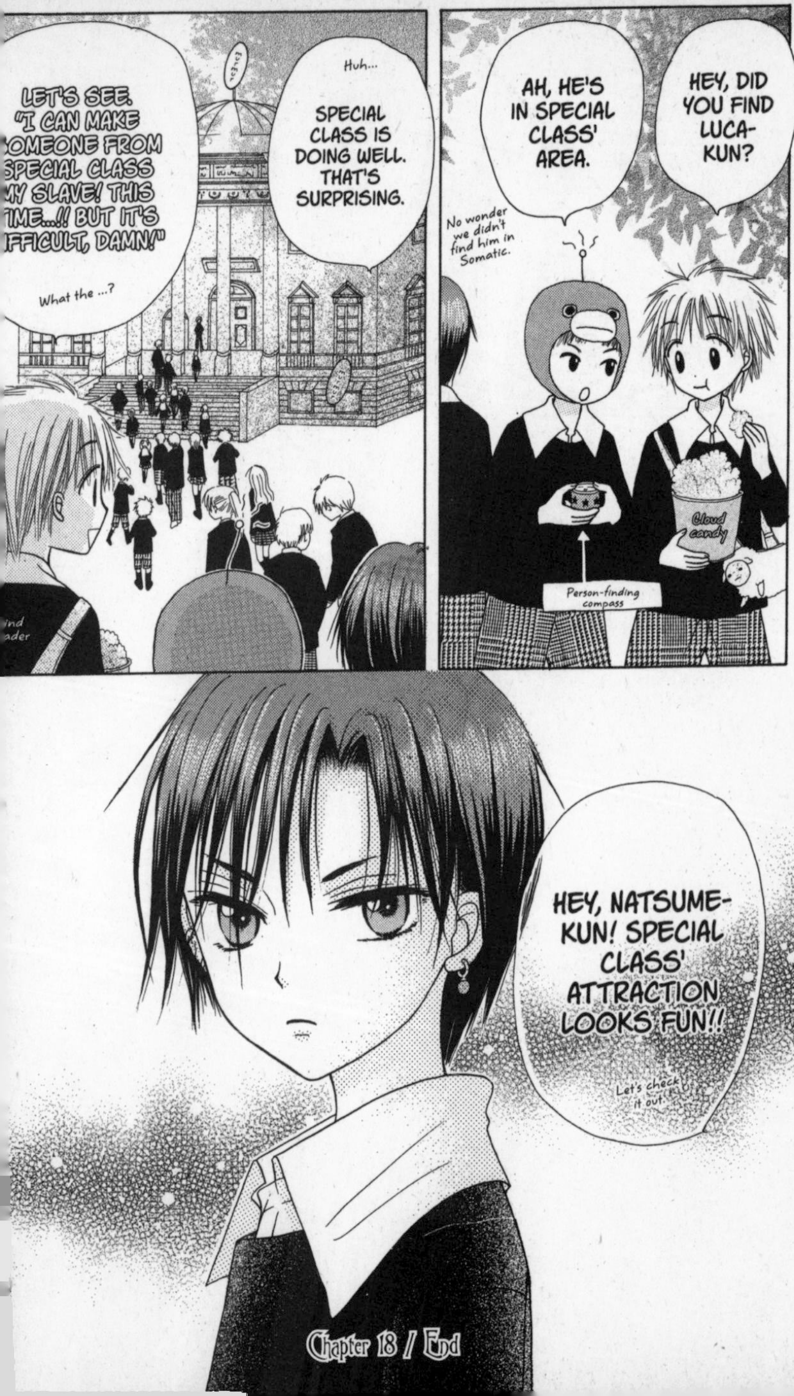
HEY, DID YOU FIND LUCA-KUN?
AH, HE'S IN SPECIAL CLASS' AREA.
No wonder we didn't find him in Somatic.
Person-finding compass
Cloud candy
Huh...
SPECIAL CLASS IS DOING WELL. THAT'S SURPRISING.
LET'S SEE. "I CAN MAKE SOMEONE FROM SPECIAL CLASS MY SLAVE! THIS TIME...!! BUT IT'S DIFFICULT, DAMN!"
What the ...?
HEY, NATSUME-KUN! SPECIAL CLASS' ATTRACTION LOOKS FUN!!
Let's check it out.
Chapter 18 / End

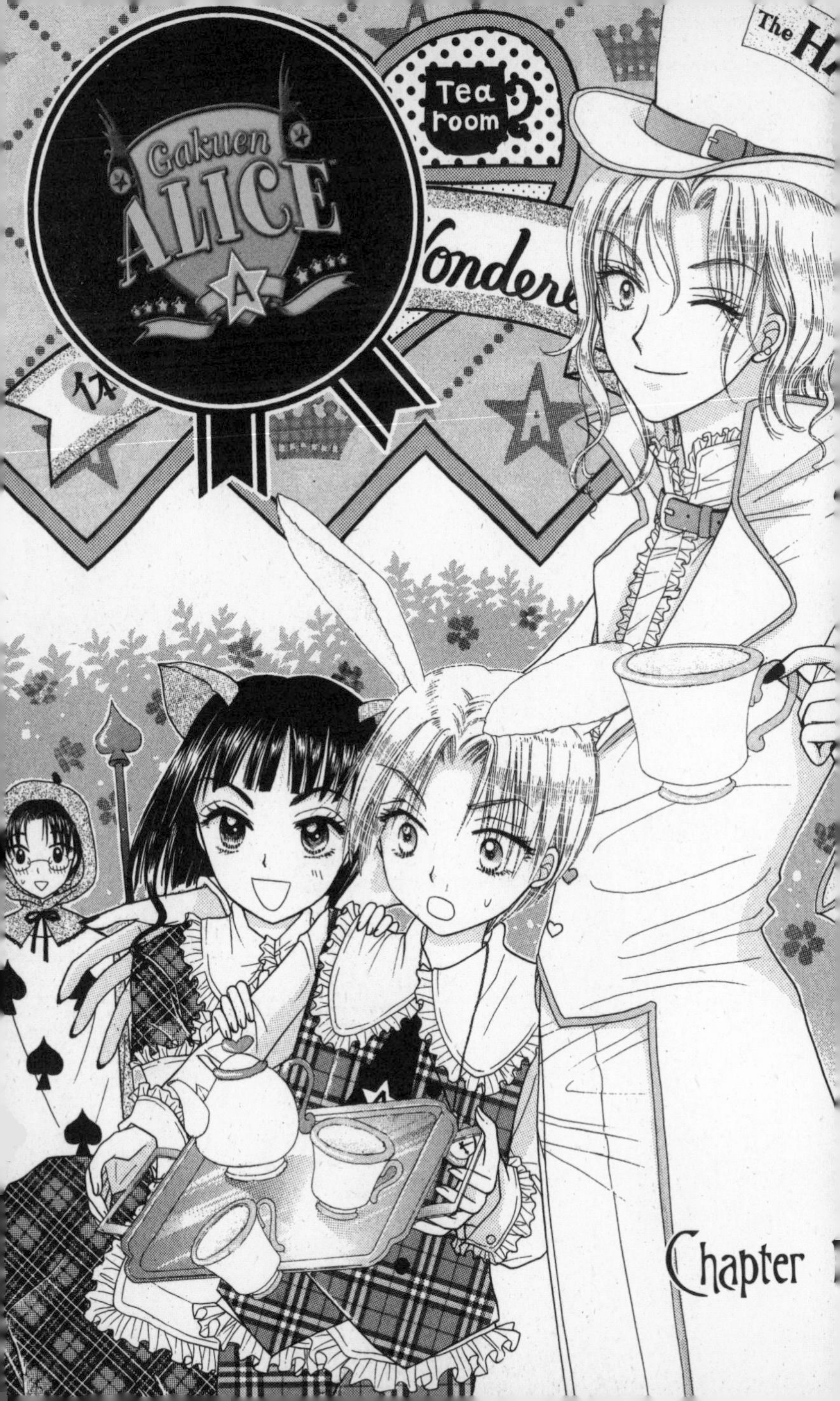
Gakuen ALICE
Tea room
The HA
onderl
Chapter

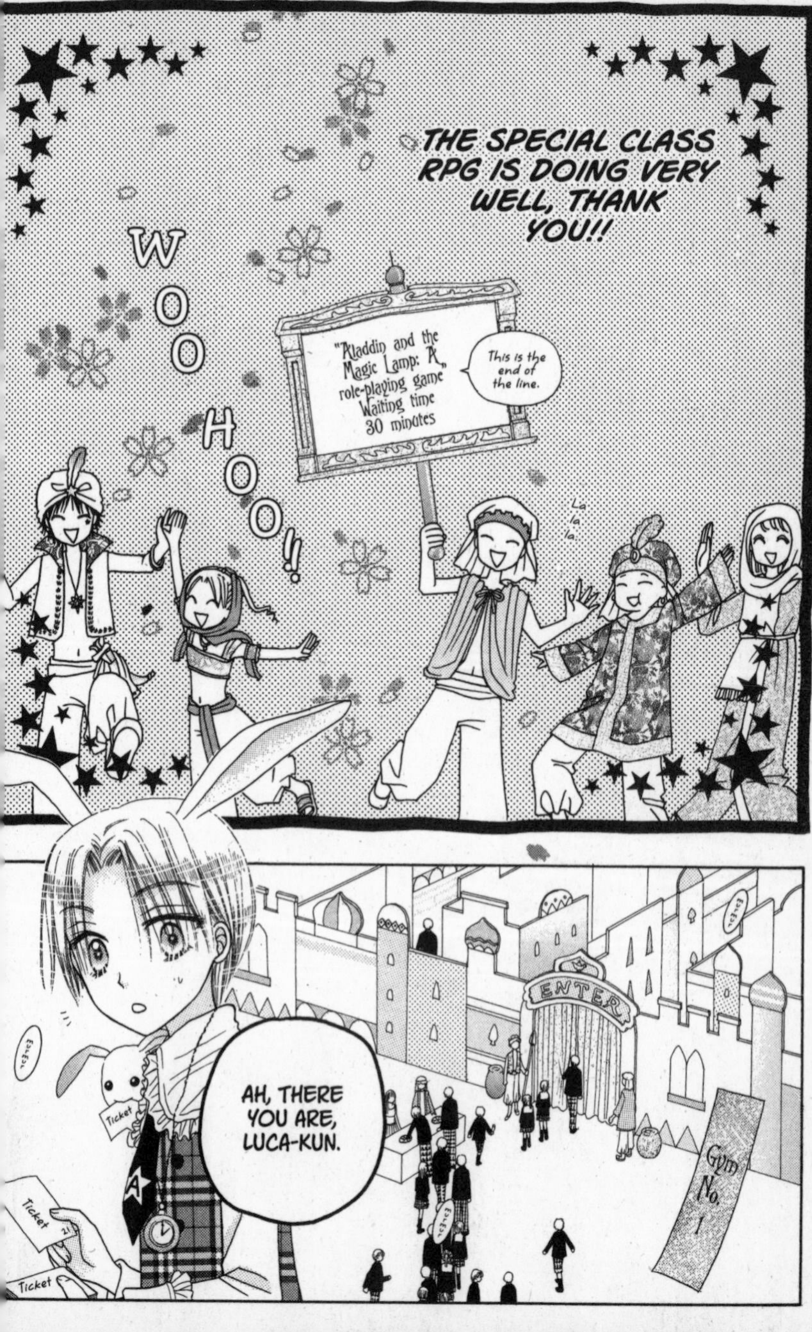
THE SPECIAL CLASS RPG IS DOING VERY WELL, THANK YOU!!
"Aladdin and the Magic Lamp: A role-playing game" Waiting time 30 minutes
This is the end of the line.
La la la
WOO HOO HOO!!
ENTER
Gym No. 1
AH, THERE YOU ARE, LUCA-KUN.
Ticket
Ticket 21
Ticket

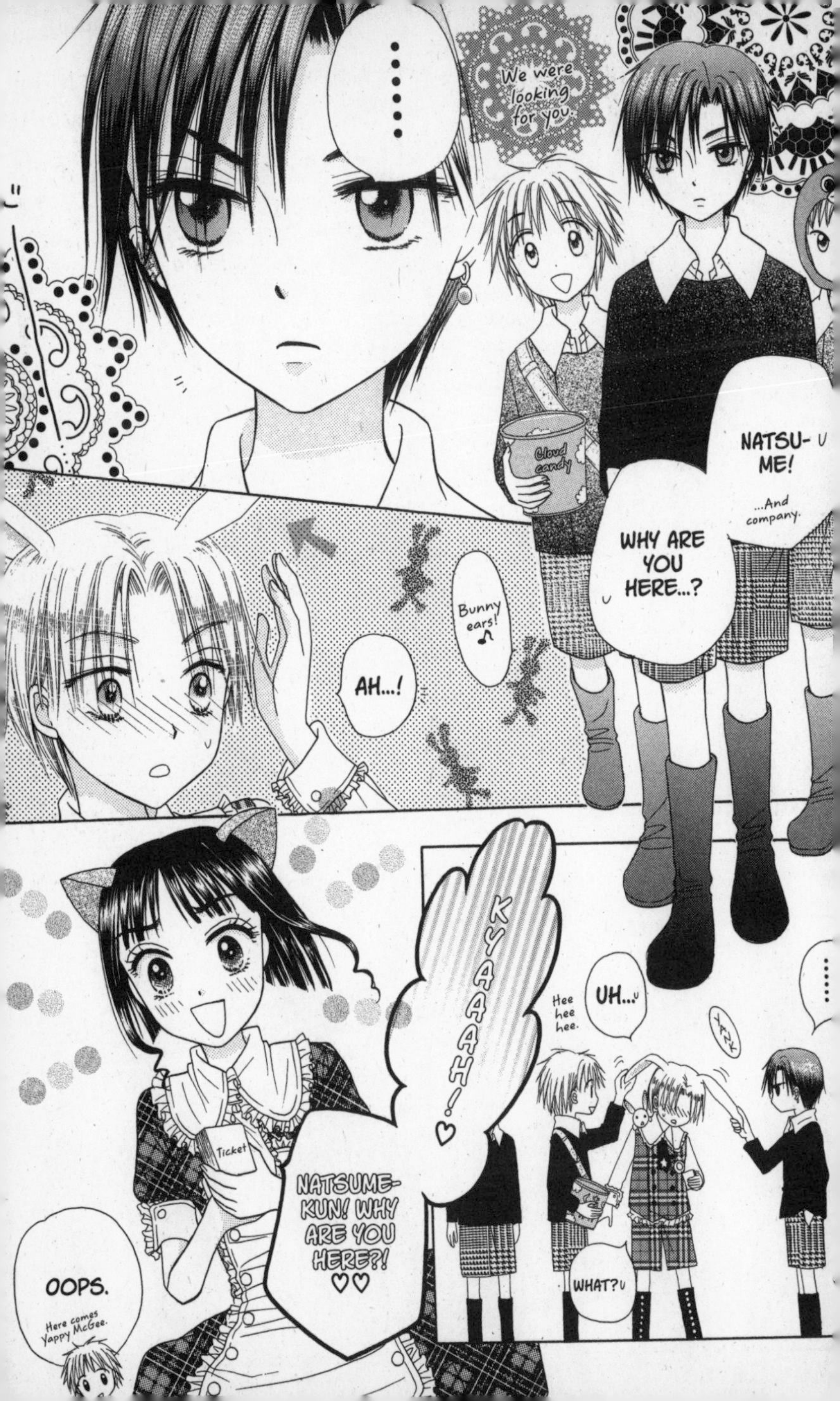
We were looking for you.
NATSU-ME!
...And company.
WHY ARE YOU HERE...?
......
AH...!
Bunny ears! ♪
......
UH...
Hee hee hee.
YANK
WHAT?
KYAAAAAH!♥
NATSUME-KUN! WHY ARE YOU HERE?! ♡♡
Ticket
OOPS.
Here comes Yappy McGee.

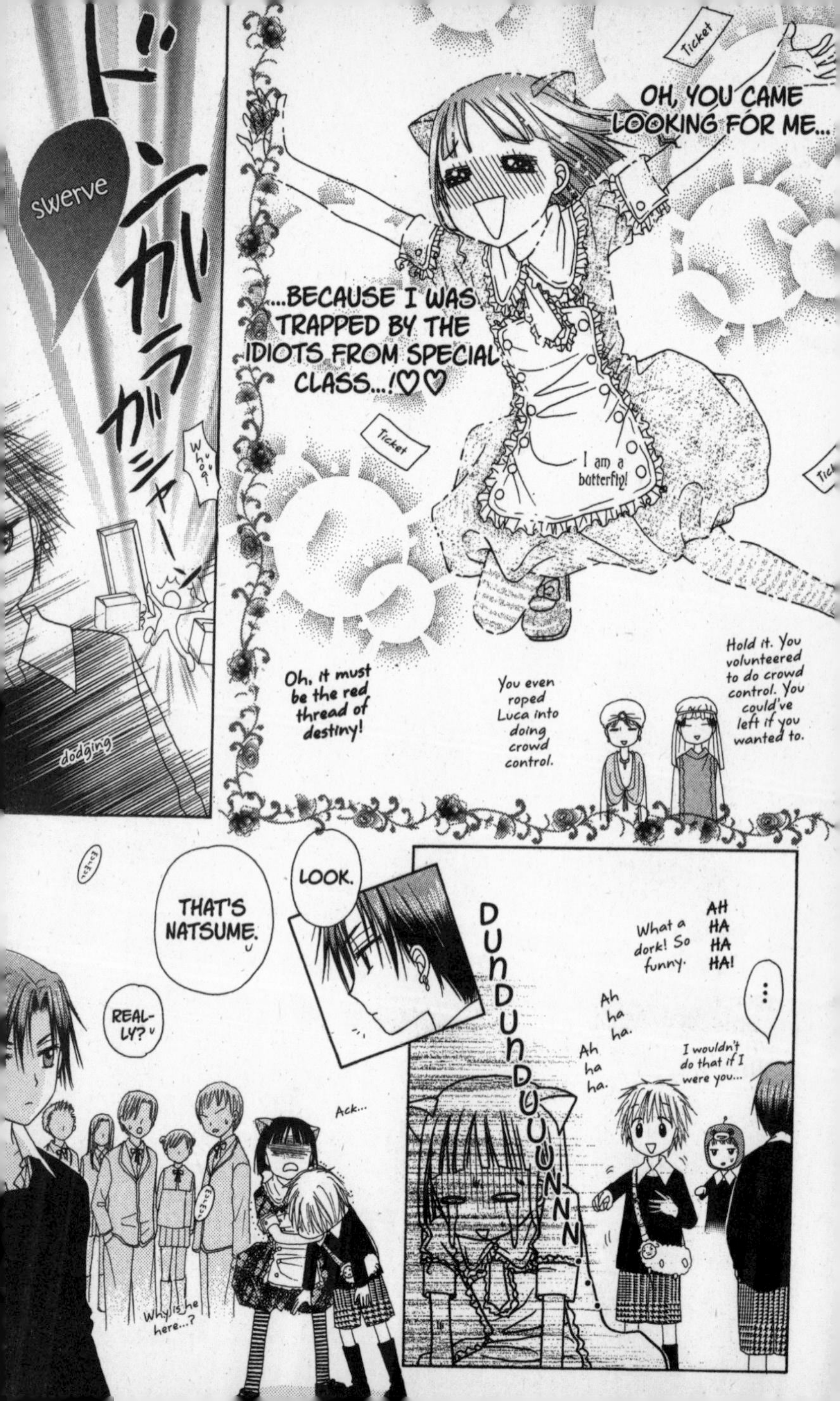

Ticket
OH, YOU CAME LOOKING FOR ME...
...BECAUSE I WAS TRAPPED BY THE IDIOTS FROM SPECIAL CLASS...!♡♡
Ticket
I am a butterfly!
Hold it. You volunteered to do crowd control. You could've left if you wanted to.
You even roped Luca into doing crowd control.
Oh, it must be the red thread of destiny!
ドンガラガラガシャーン
Swerve
Whoa!
dodging
AH HA HA HA!
What a dork! So funny.
...
Ah ha ha.
Ah ha ha.
I wouldn't do that if I were you...
DUNDUNDUUUNNN...
LOOK.
THAT'S NATSUME.
REAL-LY?
Ack...
Why is he here...?

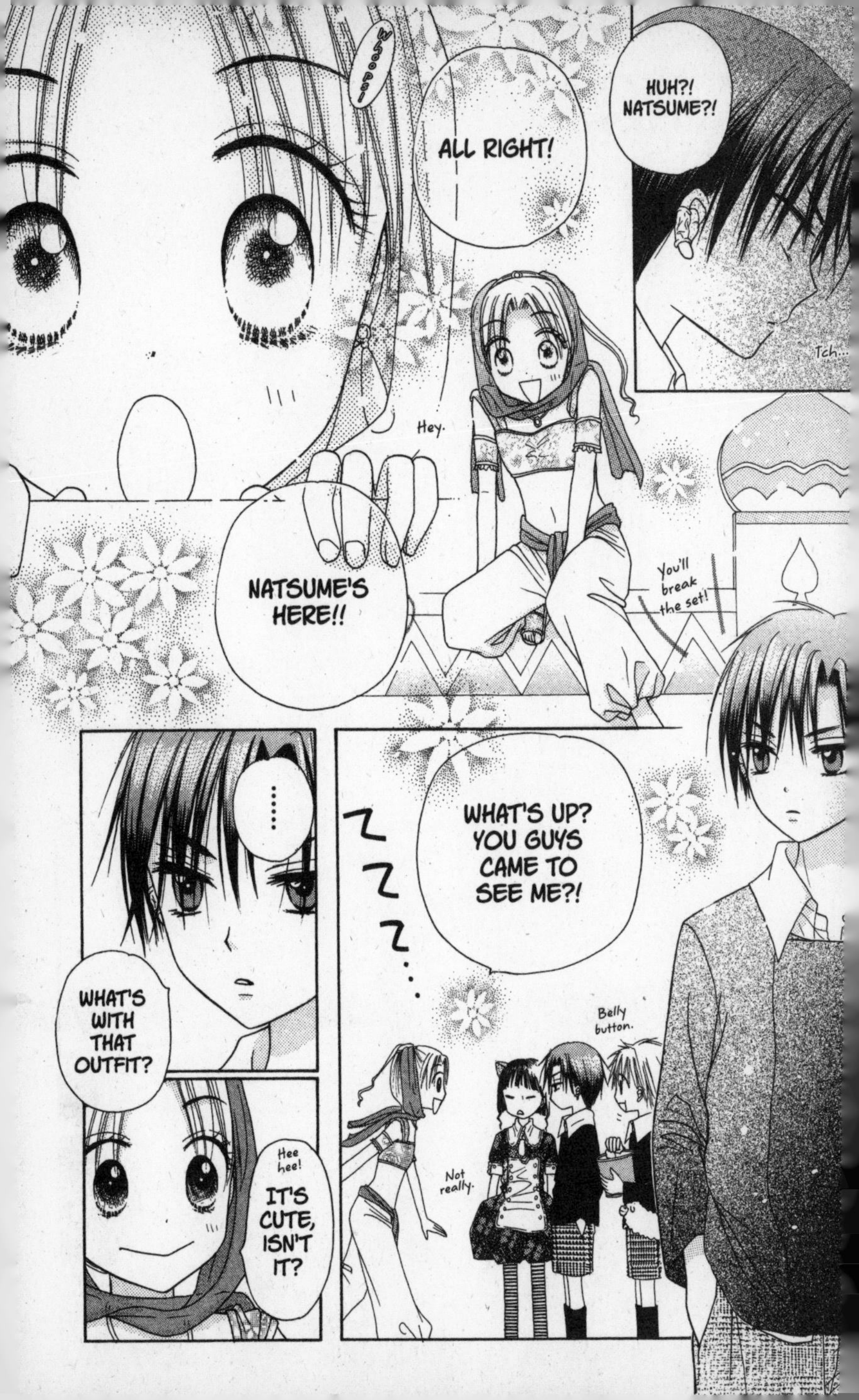
HUH?! NATSUME?!
Tch...
Whoops!
ALL RIGHT!
Hey.
NATSUME'S HERE!!
You'll break the set!
WHAT'S UP? YOU GUYS CAME TO SEE ME?!
ZZZ...
Belly button.
Not really.
......
WHAT'S WITH THAT OUTFIT?
Hee hee!
IT'S CUTE, ISN'T IT?

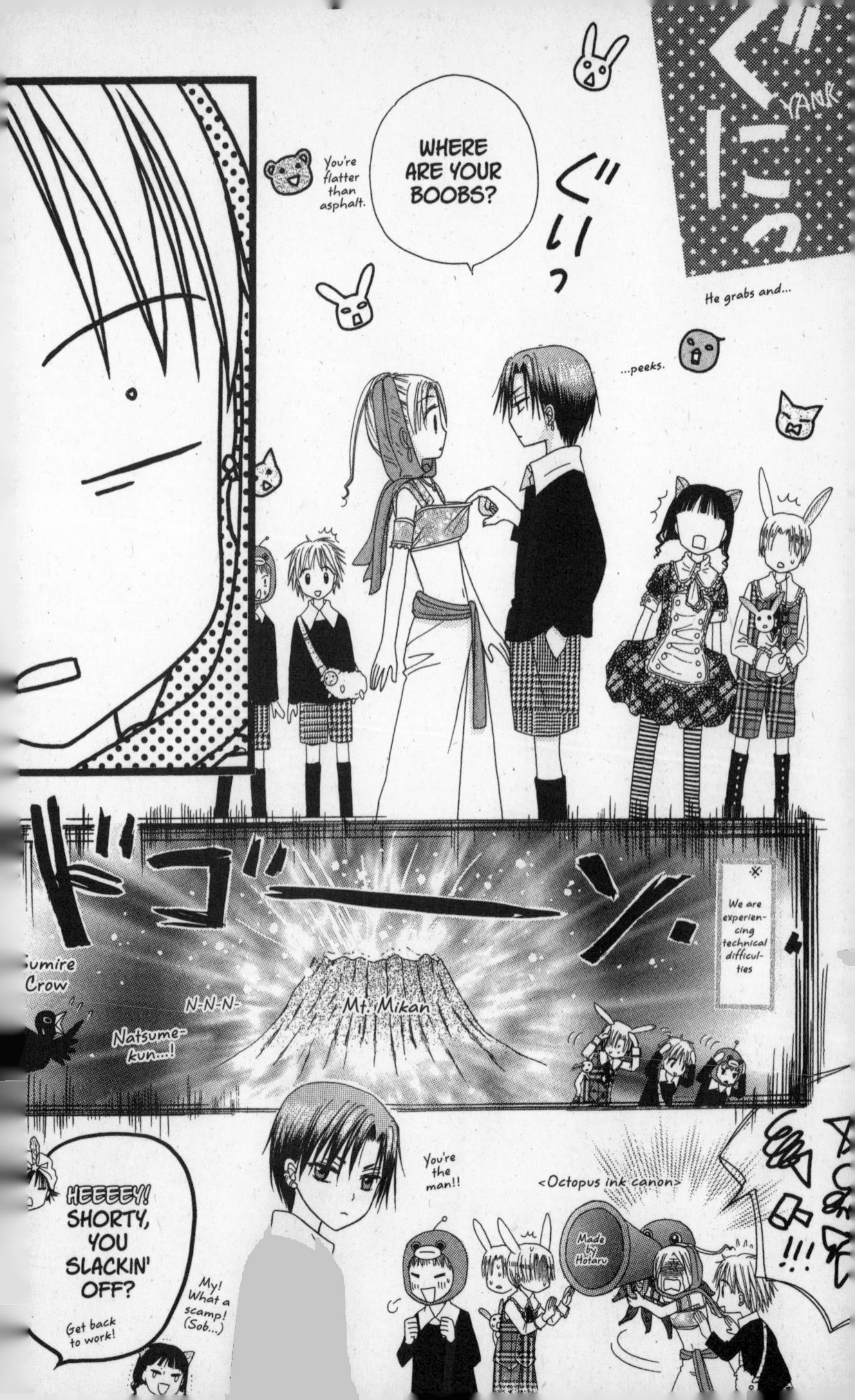
YANK
ぐいっ
WHERE ARE YOUR BOOBS?
You're flatter than asphalt.
He grabs and...
...peeks.
※ We are experiencing technical difficulties
Mt. Mikan
N-N-N-
Natsume-kun...!
umire Crow
<Octopus ink canon>
Made by Hotaru
You're the man!!
My! What a scamp! (Sob...)
HEEEEEY! SHORTY, YOU SLACKIN' OFF?
Get back to work!

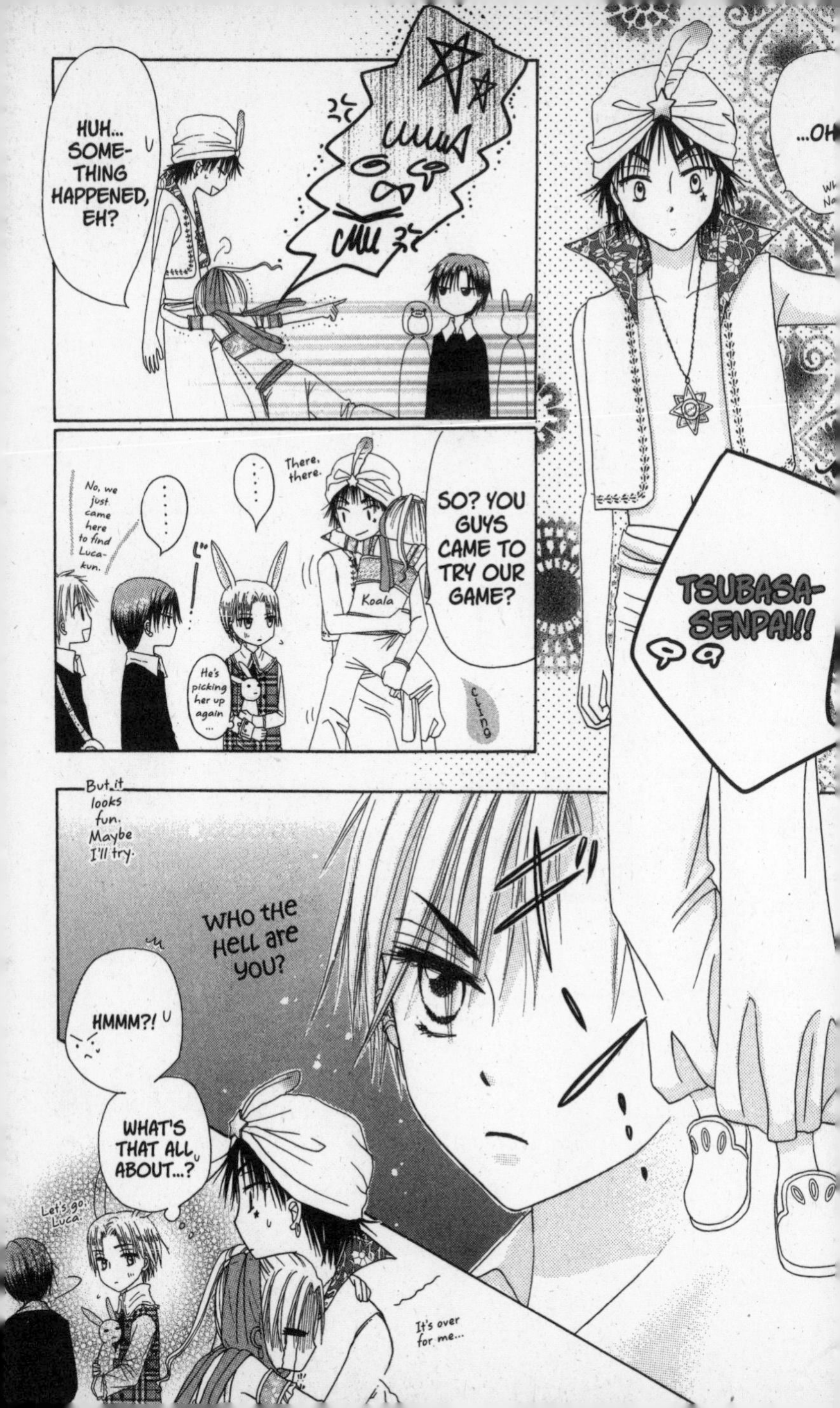
...OH
TSUBASA-SENPAI!!
HUH... SOME-THING HAPPENED, EH?
SO? YOU GUYS CAME TO TRY OUR GAME?
There, there.
Koala
cling
......
......
No, we just came here to find Luca-kun.
He's picking her up again...
But it looks fun. Maybe I'll try.
WHO THE HELL ARE YOU?
HMMM?!
WHAT'S THAT ALL ABOUT...?
Let's go, Luca.
It's over for me...

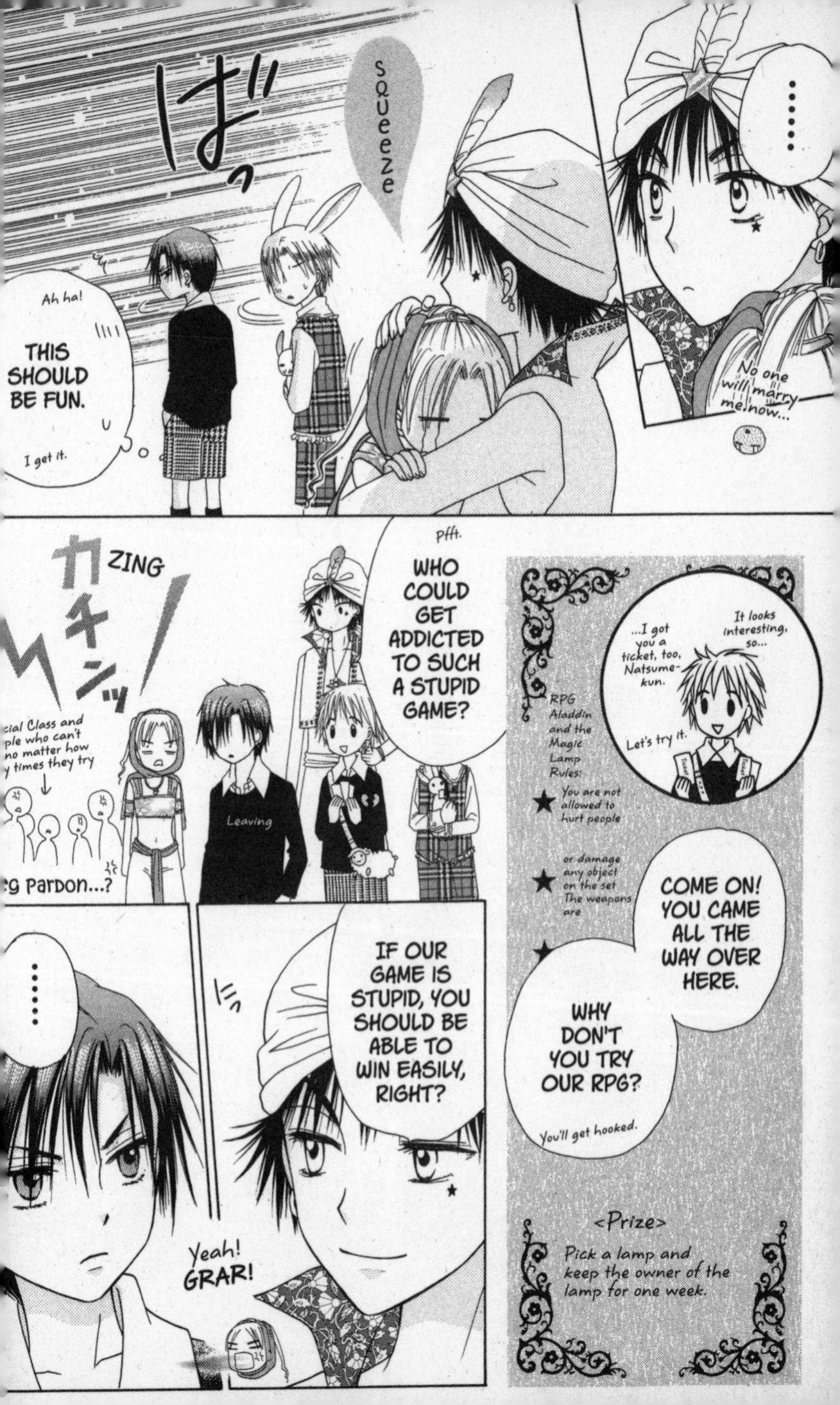

......
No one will marry me now...
SQUEEZE
ばっ
Ah ha!
THIS SHOULD BE FUN.
I get it.
RPG Aladdin and the Magic Lamp Rules:
★ You are not allowed to hurt people
★ or damage any object on the set The weapons are
★
It looks interesting, so...
...I got you a ticket, too, Natsume-kun.
Let's try it.
COME ON! YOU CAME ALL THE WAY OVER HERE.
WHY DON'T YOU TRY OUR RPG?
You'll get hooked.
<Prize>
Pick a lamp and keep the owner of the lamp for one week.
Pfft.
WHO COULD GET ADDICTED TO SUCH A STUPID GAME?
カチンッ
ZING
Leaving
cial Class and
ple who can't
no matter how
y times they try
g Pardon...?
IF OUR GAME IS STUPID, YOU SHOULD BE ABLE TO WIN EASILY, RIGHT?
Yeah! GRAR!
......

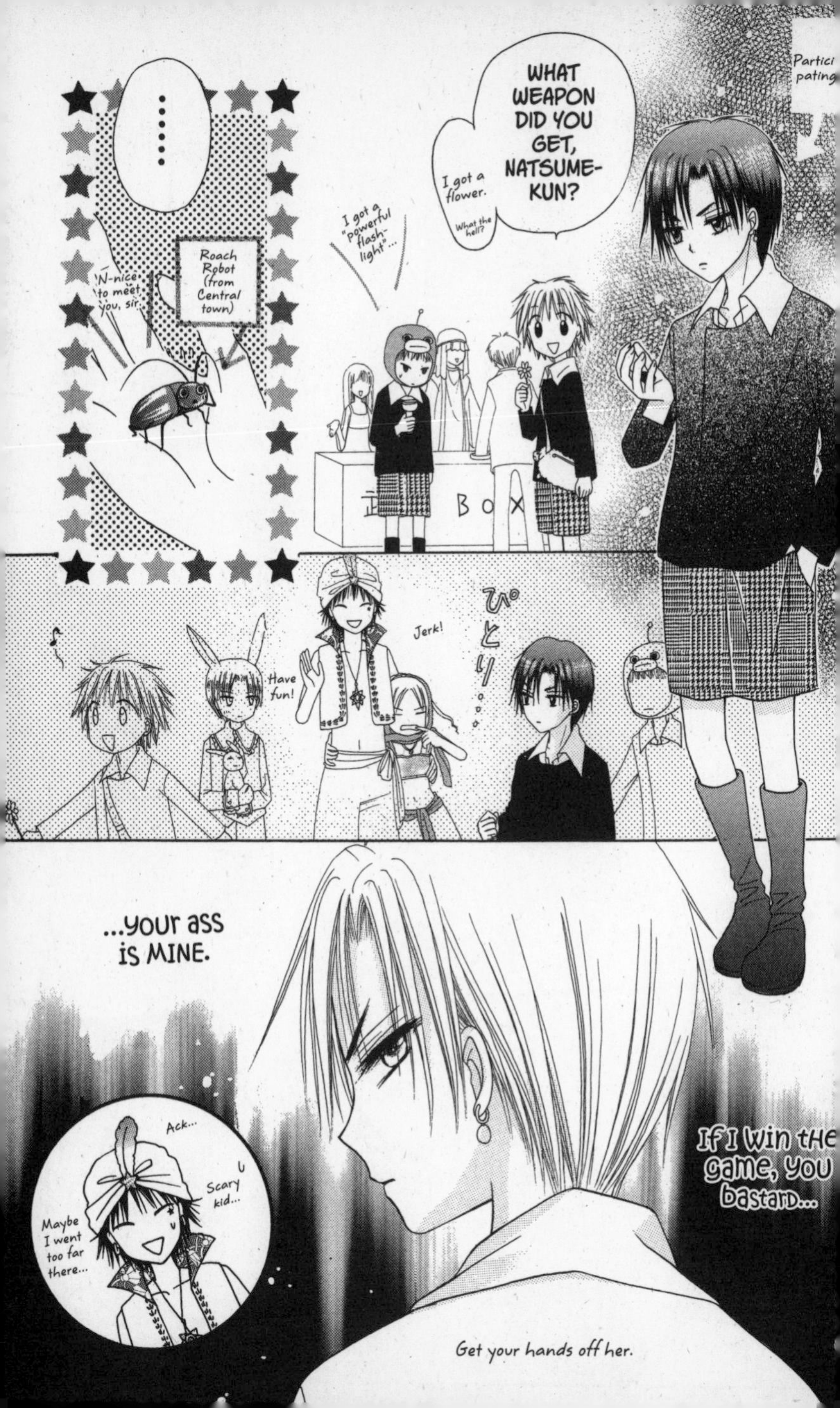
Partici pating
WHAT WEAPON DID YOU GET, NATSUME-KUN?
I got a flower.
What the hell?
I got a "powerful flash-light"...
......
Roach Robot (from Central town)
N-nice to meet you, sir.
ぴとりっ
Jerk!
Have fun!
If I win the game, you bastard...
...your ass is MINE.
Get your hands off her.
Ack...
Scary kid...
Maybe I went too far there...

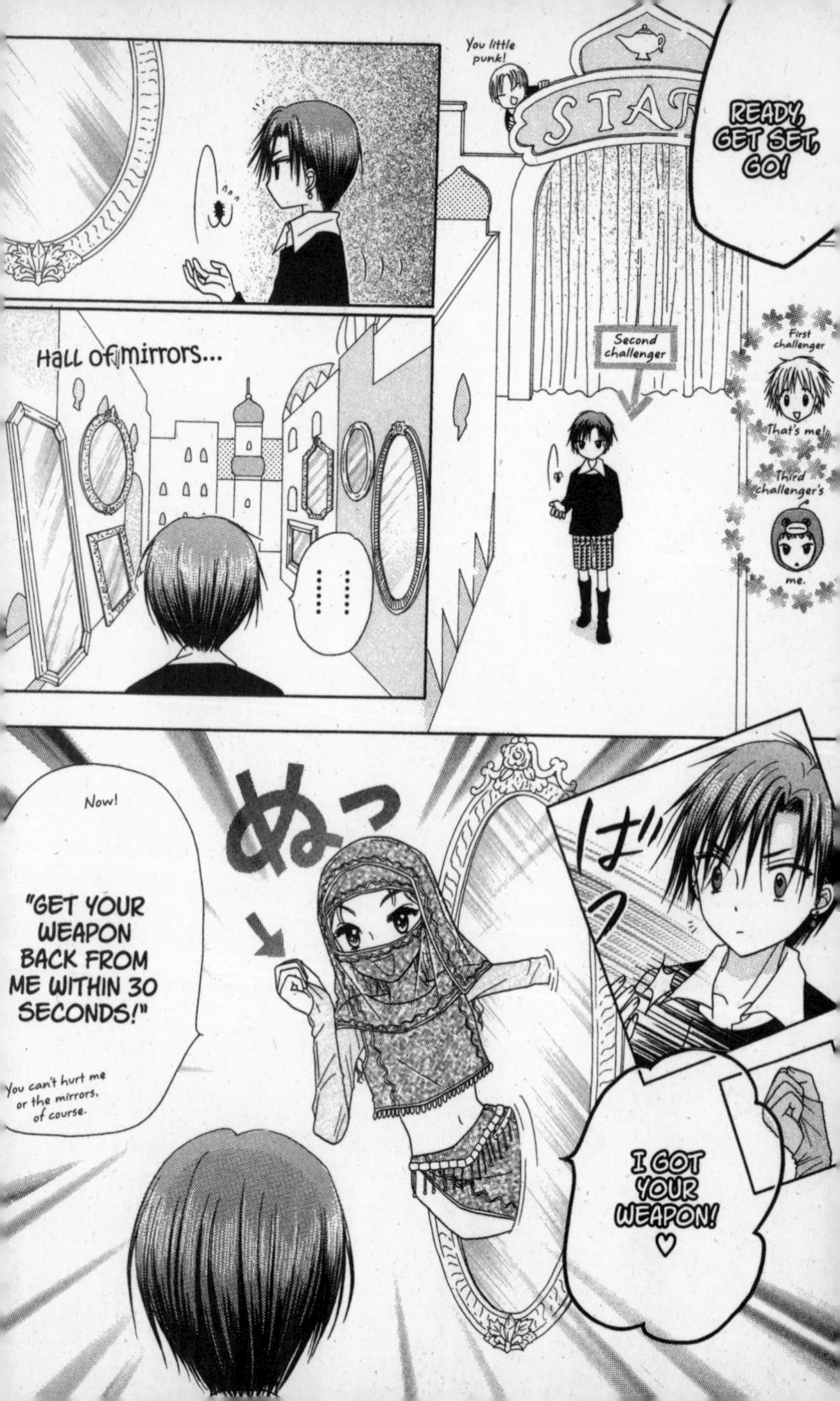
READY, GET SET, GO!
You little punk!
First challenger
That's me!
Third challenger's
me.
Second challenger
Hall of mirrors...
......
ばっ
I GOT YOUR WEAPON! ♥
ぬっ
Now!
"GET YOUR WEAPON BACK FROM ME WITHIN 30 SECONDS!"
You can't hurt me or the mirrors, of course.

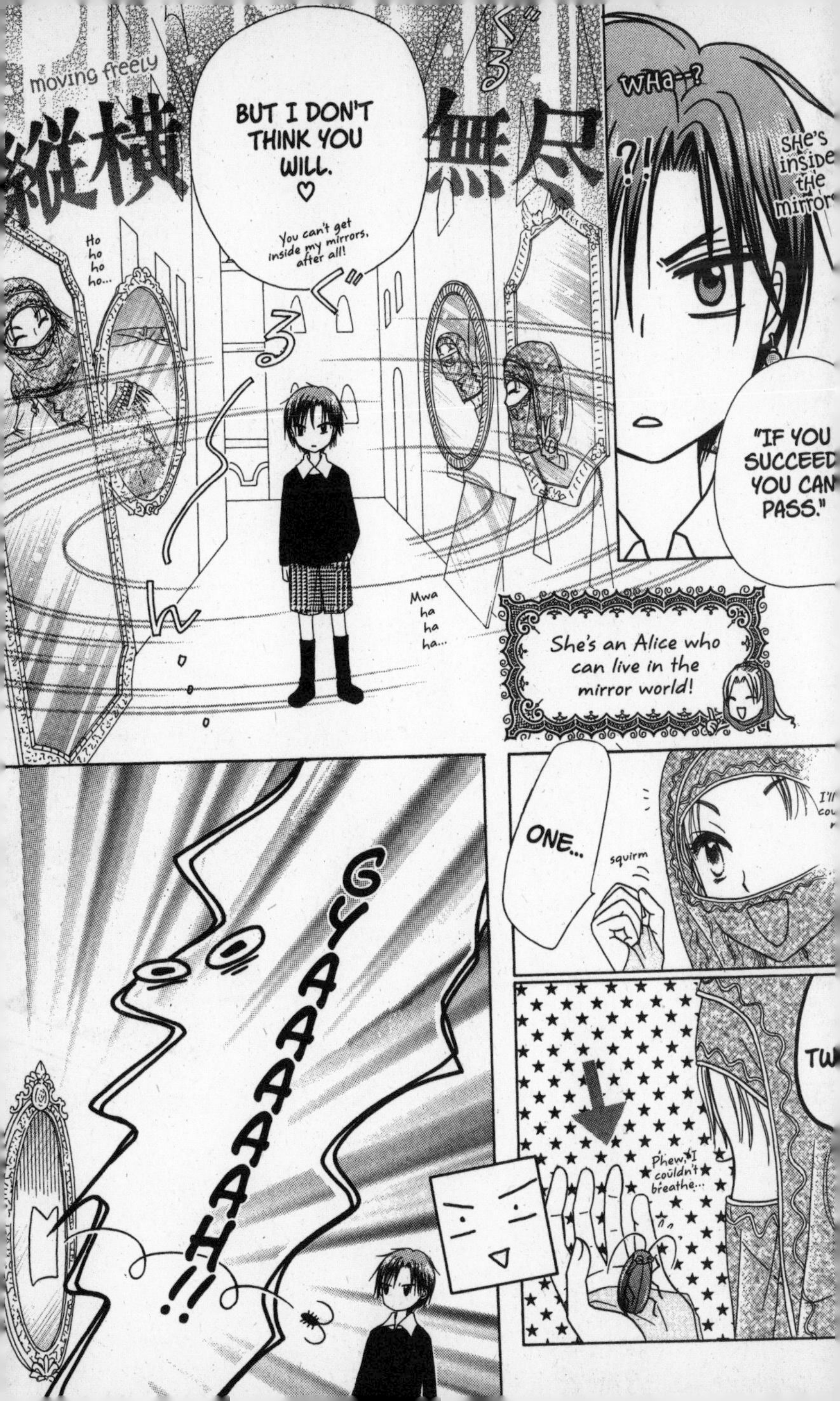

WHA--?
?!
SHE'S INSIDE THE MIRROR
"IF YOU SUCCEED YOU CAN PASS."
She's an Alice who can live in the mirror world!
moving freely
縦横
無尽
BUT I DON'T THINK YOU WILL. ♡
You can't get inside my mirrors, after all!
ぐるぐるぐるん
Ho ho ho ho...
Mwa ha ha ha...
ONE...
squirm
Phew, I couldn't breathe...
GYAAAAAAAAH!!

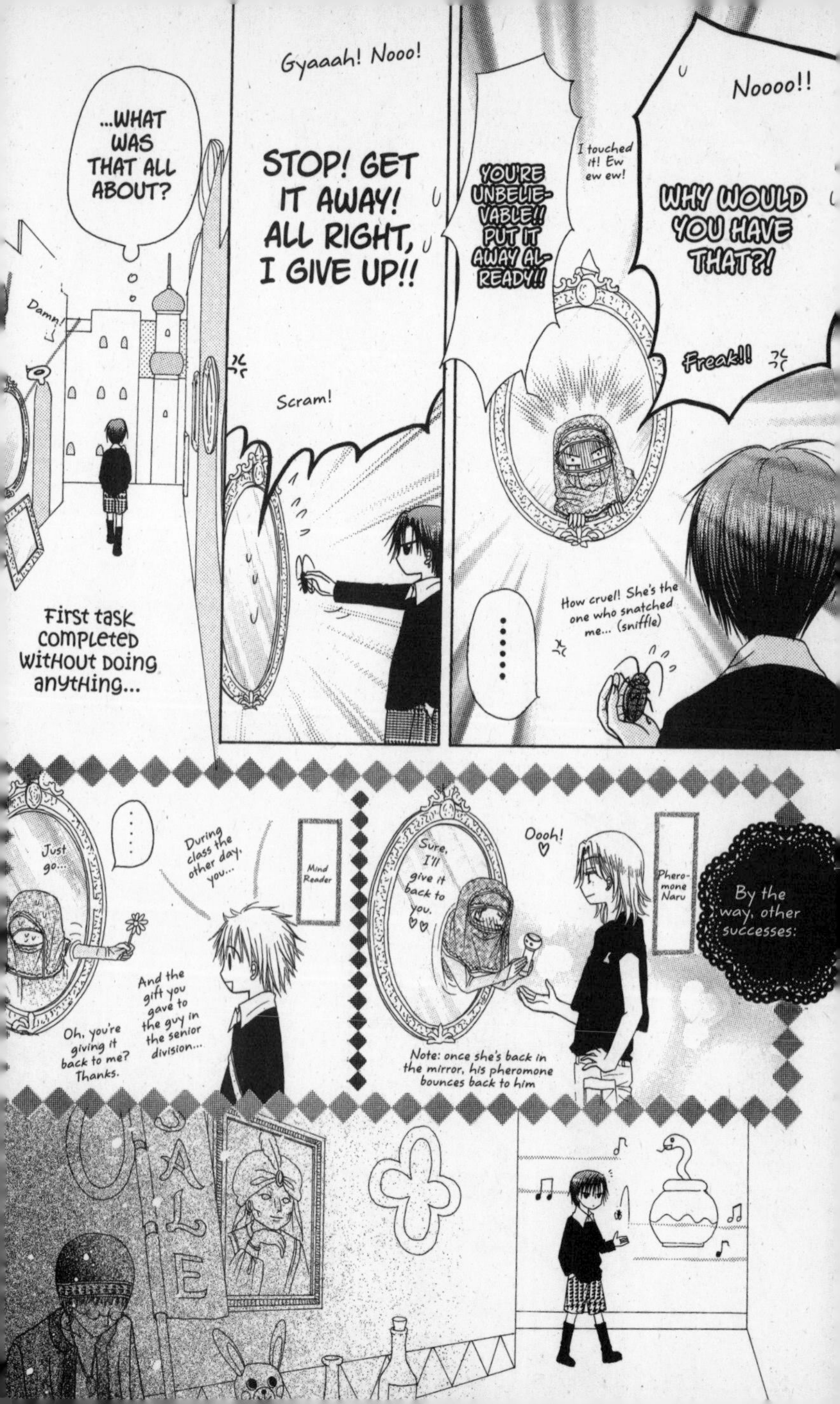
Noooo!!
WHY WOULD YOU HAVE THAT?!
I touched it! Ew ew ew!
YOU'RE UNBELIEVABLE!! PUT IT AWAY ALREADY!!
Freak!!
How cruel! She's the one who snatched me... (sniffle)
......
Gyaaah! Nooo!
STOP! GET IT AWAY! ALL RIGHT, I GIVE UP!!
Scram!
...WHAT WAS THAT ALL ABOUT?
Damn!
First task completed without doing anything...
By the way, other successes:
Oooh! ♡
Phero-mone Naru
Sure, I'll give it back to you. ♡♡
Note: once she's back in the mirror, his pheromone bounces back to him
Mind Reader
During class the other day, you...
And the gift you gave to the guy in the senior division...
......
Just go...
Oh, you're giving it back to me? Thanks.

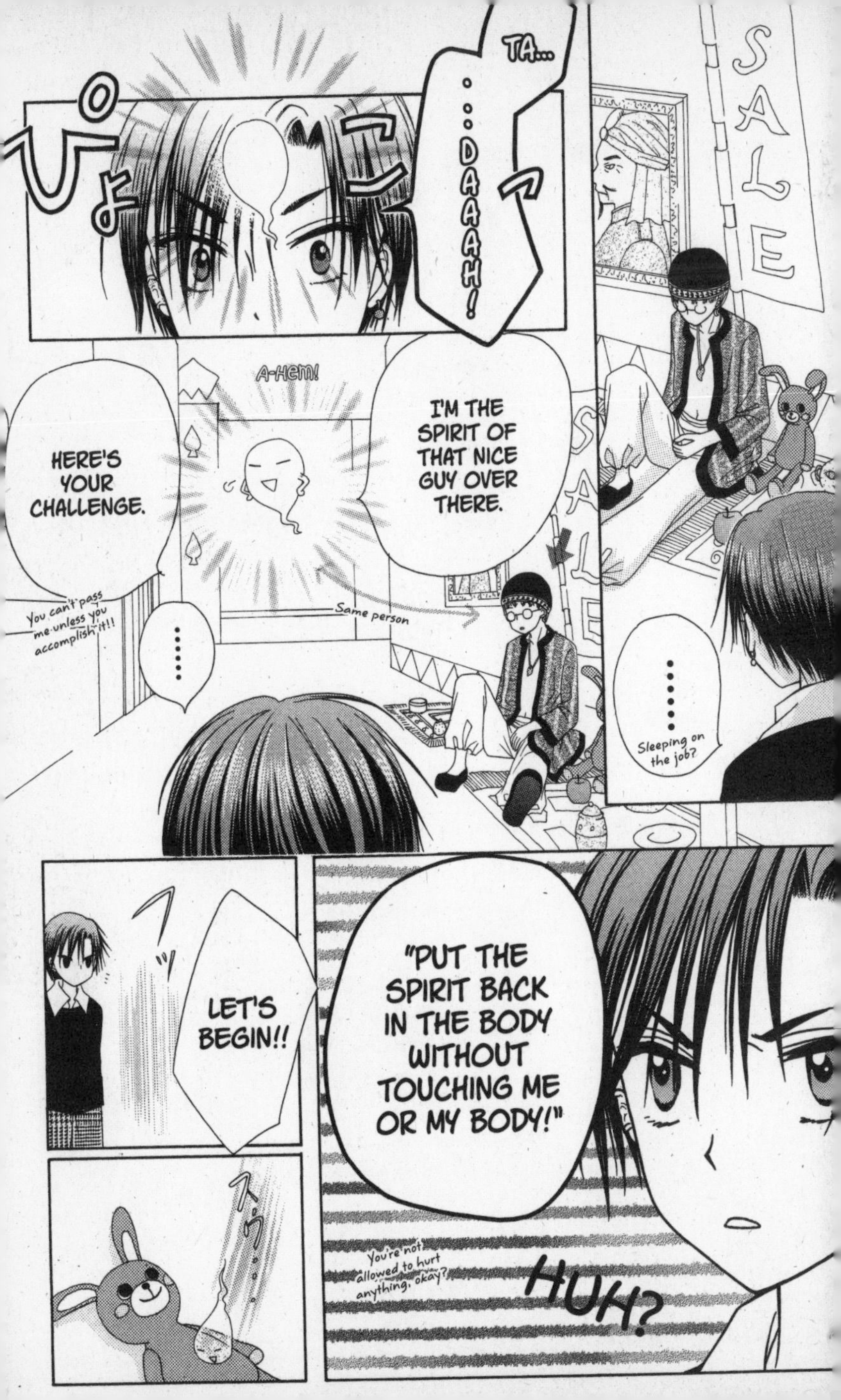

SALE
......
Sleeping on the job?
ぴょこ
TA... ...DAAAAH!
A-HEM!
I'M THE SPIRIT OF THAT NICE GUY OVER THERE.
Same person
HERE'S YOUR CHALLENGE.
You can't pass me unless you accomplish it!!
......
"PUT THE SPIRIT BACK IN THE BODY WITHOUT TOUCHING ME OR MY BODY!"
You're not allowed to hurt anything, okay?
HUH?
LET'S BEGIN!!

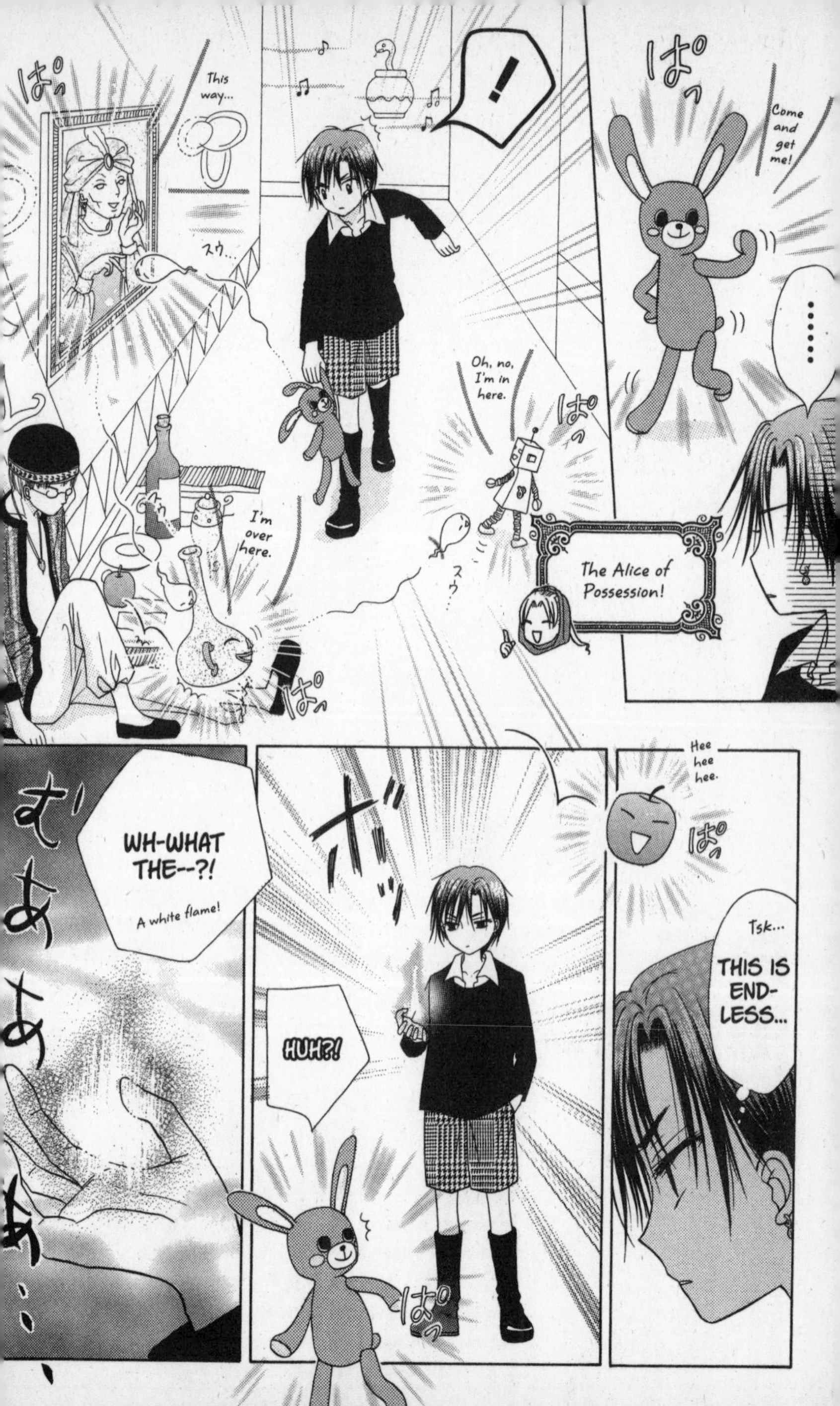
ぱっ
Come and get me!
......
The Alice of Possession!
!
ぱっ
Oh, no, I'm in here.
スウ...
ぱっ
This way...
スウ...
I'm over here.
ぱっ
Hee hee hee.
ぱっ
Tsk...
THIS IS END-LESS...
HUH?!
ぱっ
WH-WHAT THE--?!
A white flame!

Read at your own discretion.

Higuchi's room 3

PROFILE 11

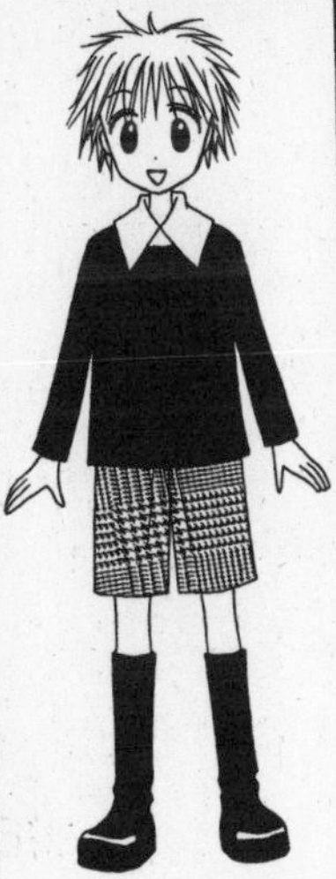

♂

Mind Reader-kun!
Born March 18,
9 years old
Pisces,
Blood type AB

He was supposed to be just one of Mikan's classmates, but because of his power, he's unexpectedly popular amongst readers. A lot of people say, "Please give him a name!" Well, he does have a name, but I'm waiting for a good time to reveal it. Heh heh. By the way, he's a year younger than Mikan and the others. He has very little facial expression (or none at all) and it's both easy and tough to draw him. He's that kind of mysterious character.

Go to 4!

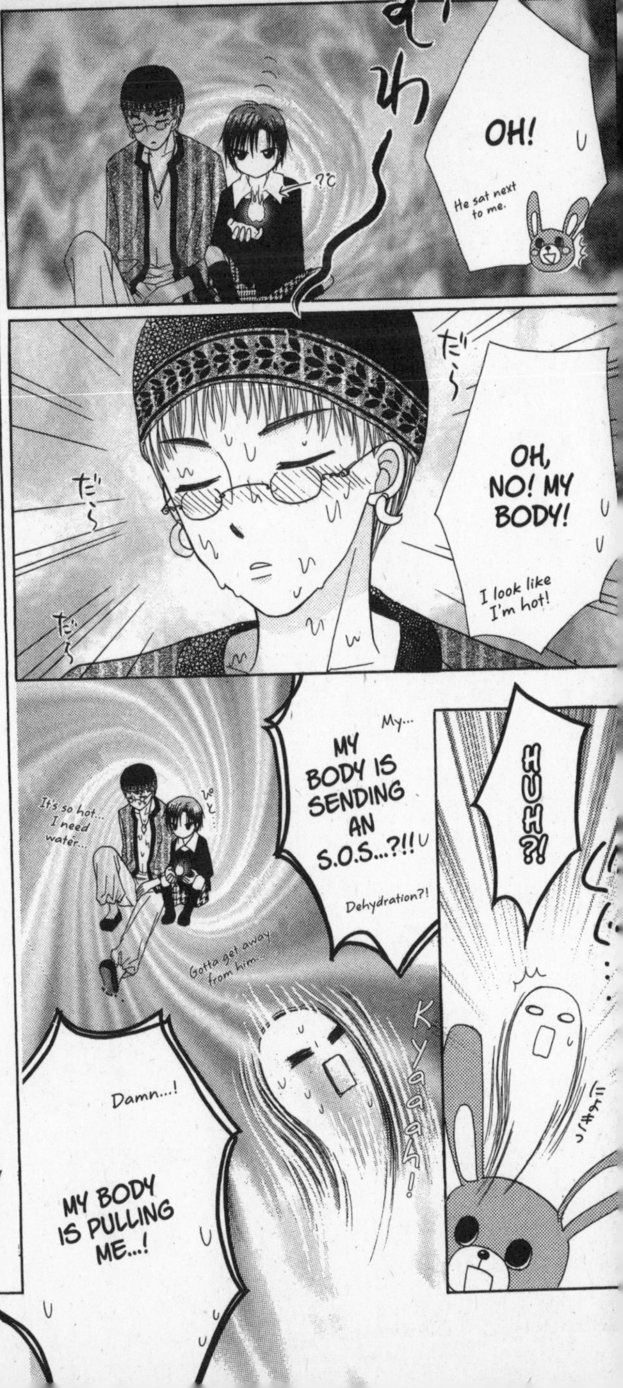
OH!
He sat next to me.
OH, NO! MY BODY!
I look like I'm hot!
HUH?!
My...
MY BODY IS SENDING AN S.O.S...?!!
Dehydration?!
It's so hot... I need water...
Gotta get away from him...
Kyaaaaa!
Damn...!
MY BODY IS PULLING ME...!

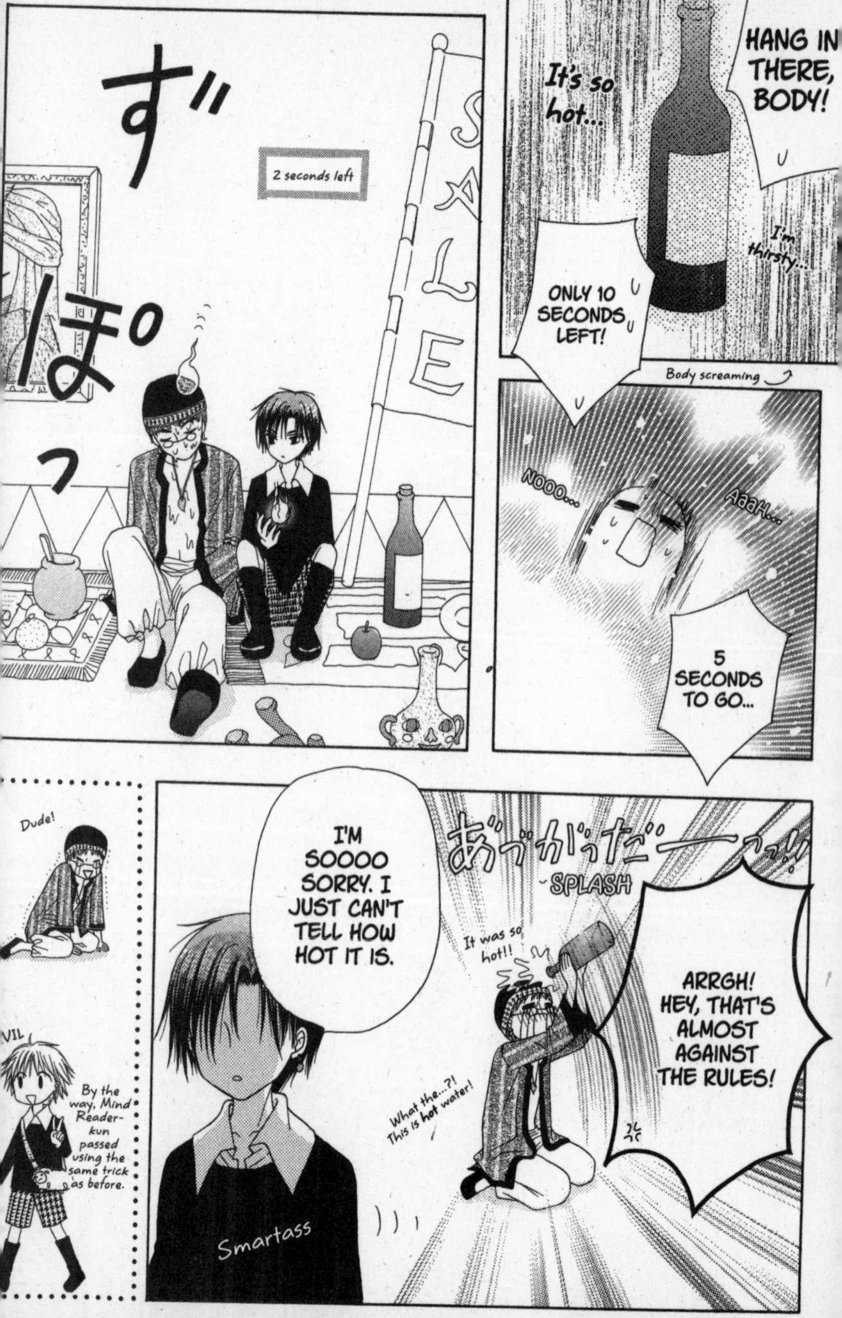

HANG IN THERE, BODY!
It's so hot...
I'm thirsty...
ONLY 10 SECONDS LEFT!
Body screaming
NOOO...
AAAH...
5 SECONDS TO GO...
ずぽっ
2 seconds left
SALE
SPLASH
ARRGH! HEY, THAT'S ALMOST AGAINST THE RULES!
It was so hot!!
What the...?! This is hot water!
I'M SOOOO SORRY. I JUST CAN'T TELL HOW HOT IT IS.
Smartass
Dude!
By the way, Mind Reader-kun passed using the same trick as before.

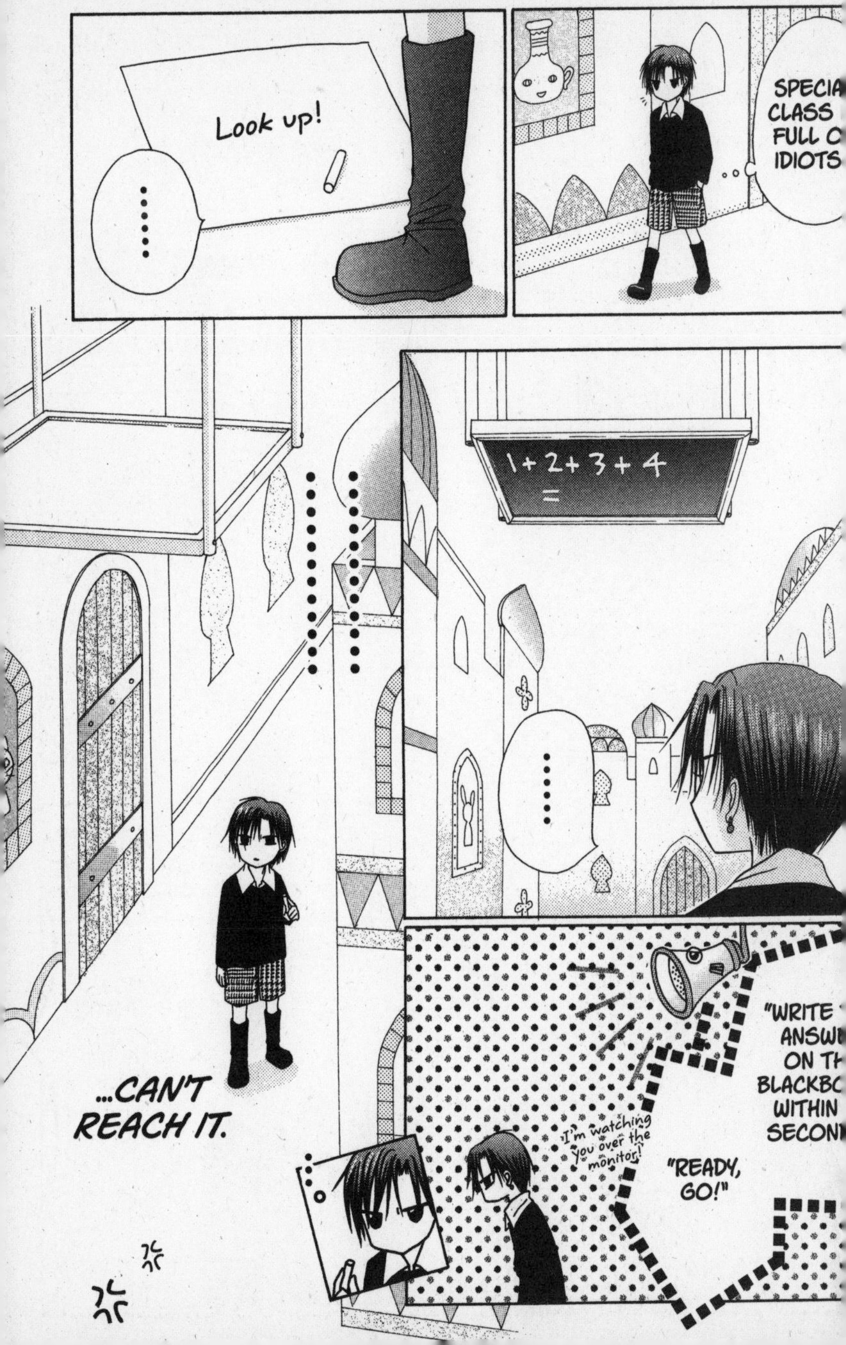
SPECIA CLASS FULL C IDIOTS
Look up!
......
1+2+3+4 =
......
"WRITE ANSW ON TH BLACKBO WITHIN SECON
"READY, GO!"
I'm watching you over the monitor!
......
......
...CAN'T REACH IT.

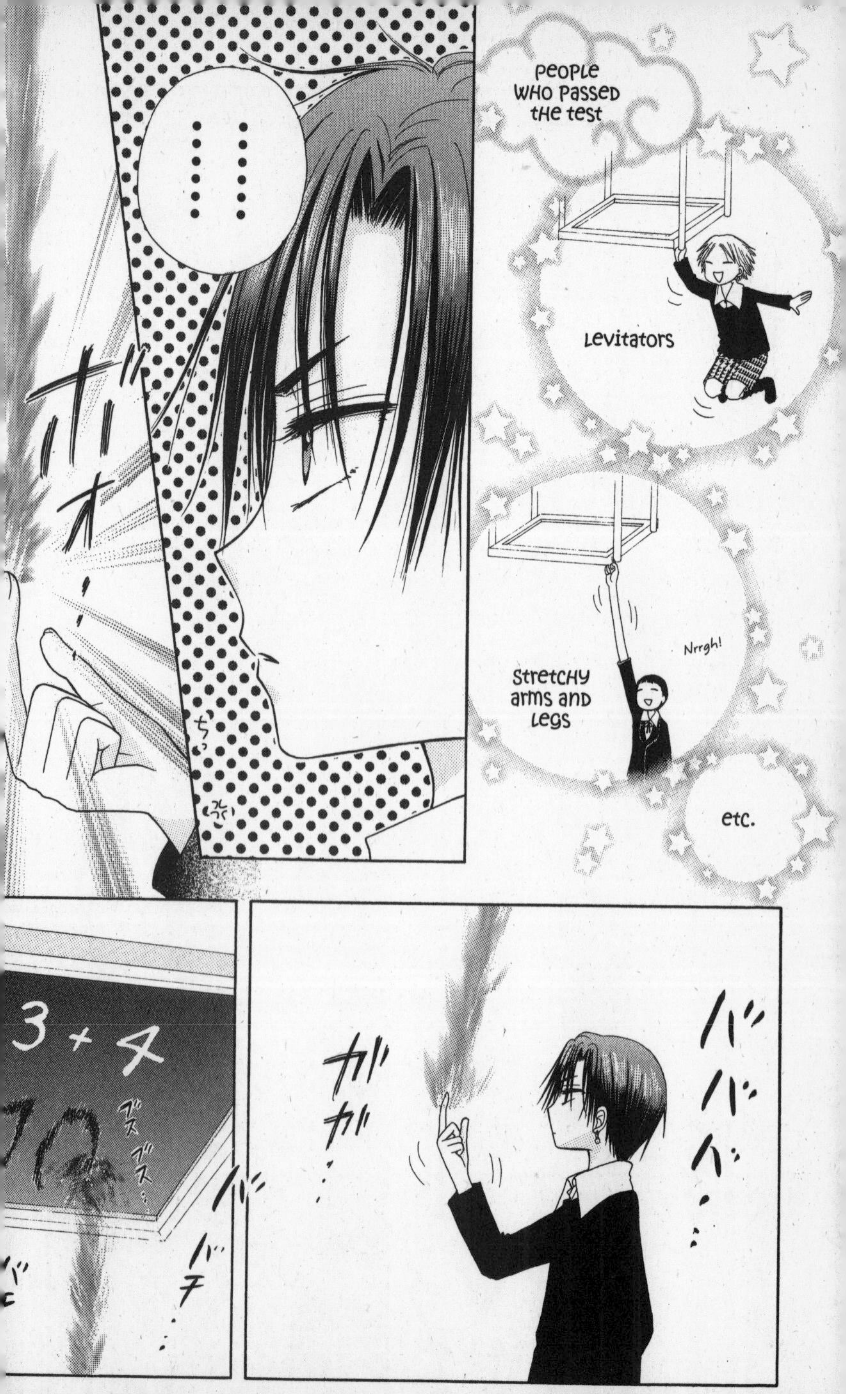
People who passed the test
Levitators
Stretchy arms and legs
Nrrgh!
etc.
......
ちっ
バババ...
ガガ...
バ
バチ...
ブスブス...

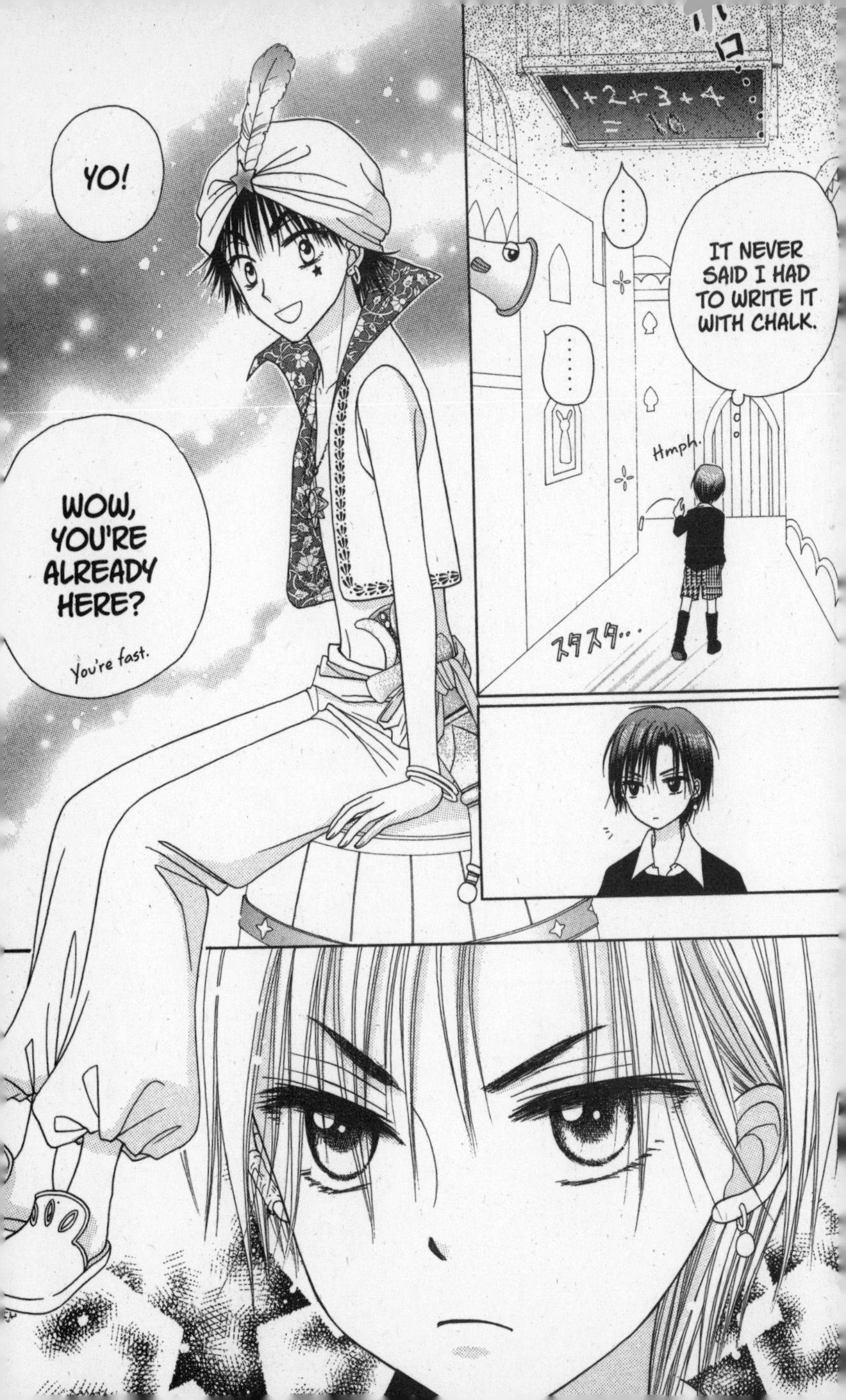
1+2+3+4
= 10
IT NEVER SAID I HAD TO WRITE IT WITH CHALK.
......
......
Hmph.
スタスタ...
YO!
WOW, YOU'RE ALREADY HERE?
You're fast.

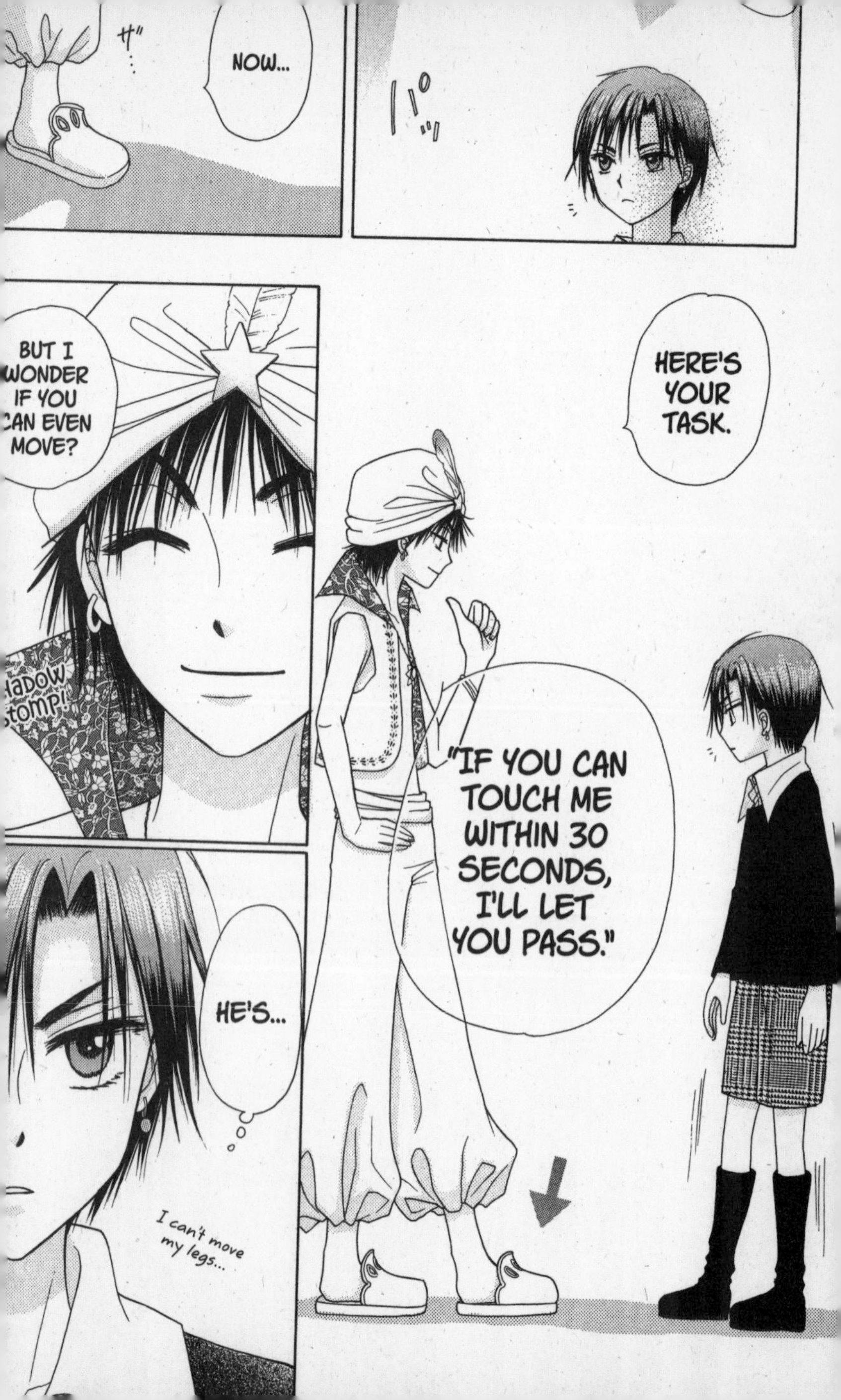

ザ"
NOW...
HERE'S YOUR TASK.
"IF YOU CAN TOUCH ME WITHIN 30 SECONDS, I'LL LET YOU PASS."
BUT I WONDER IF YOU CAN EVEN MOVE?
HADOW STOMP!
HE'S...
I can't move my legs...

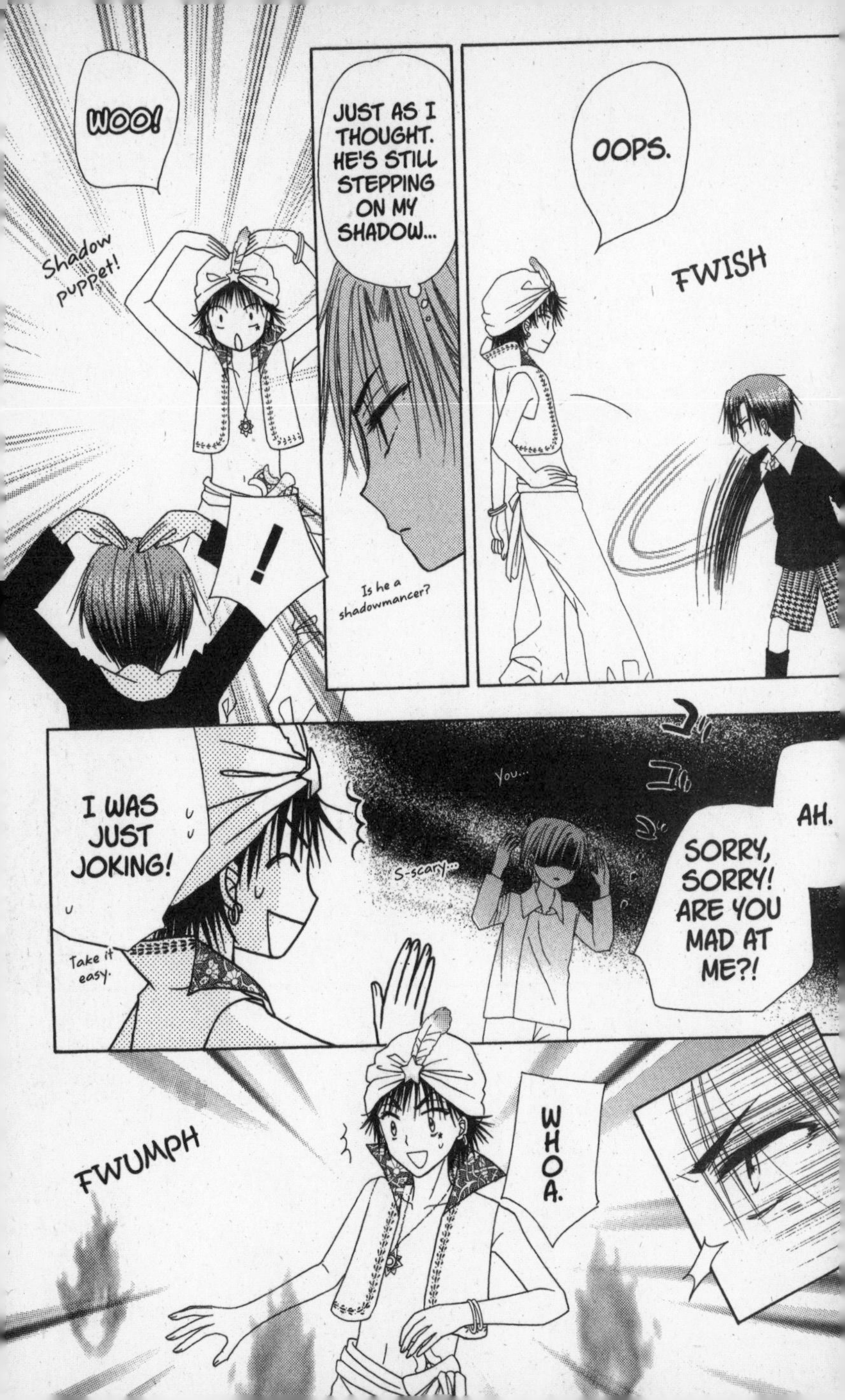
OOPS.
FWISH
JUST AS I THOUGHT. HE'S STILL STEPPING ON MY SHADOW...
Is he a shadowmancer?
WOO!
Shadow puppet!
!
AH.
SORRY, SORRY! ARE YOU MAD AT ME?!
You...
S-scary...
I WAS JUST JOKING!
Take it easy.
WHOA.
FWUMPH

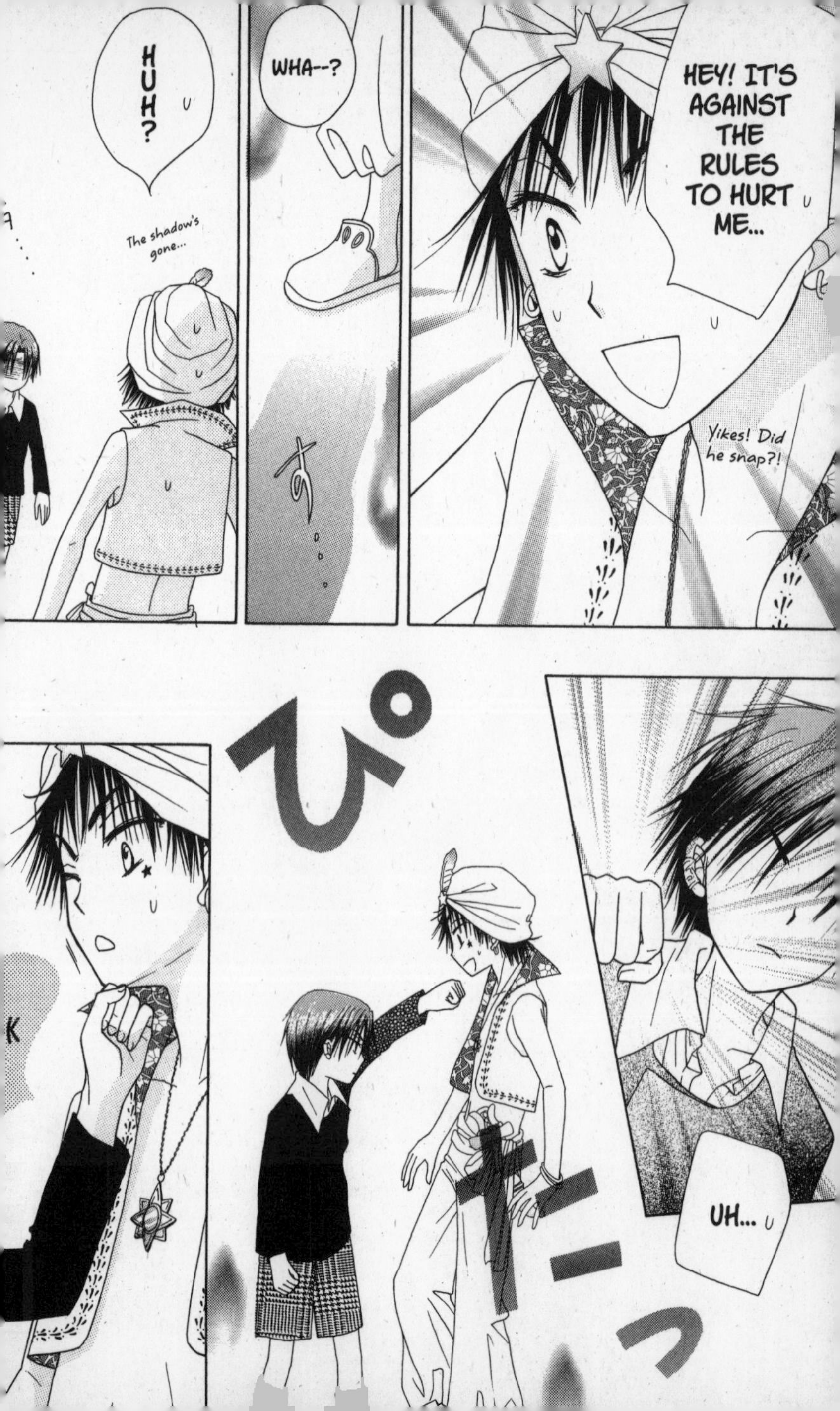
HEY! IT'S AGAINST THE RULES TO HURT ME...
Yikes! Did he snap?!
WHA--?
HUH?
The shadow's gone...
UH...
ぴ

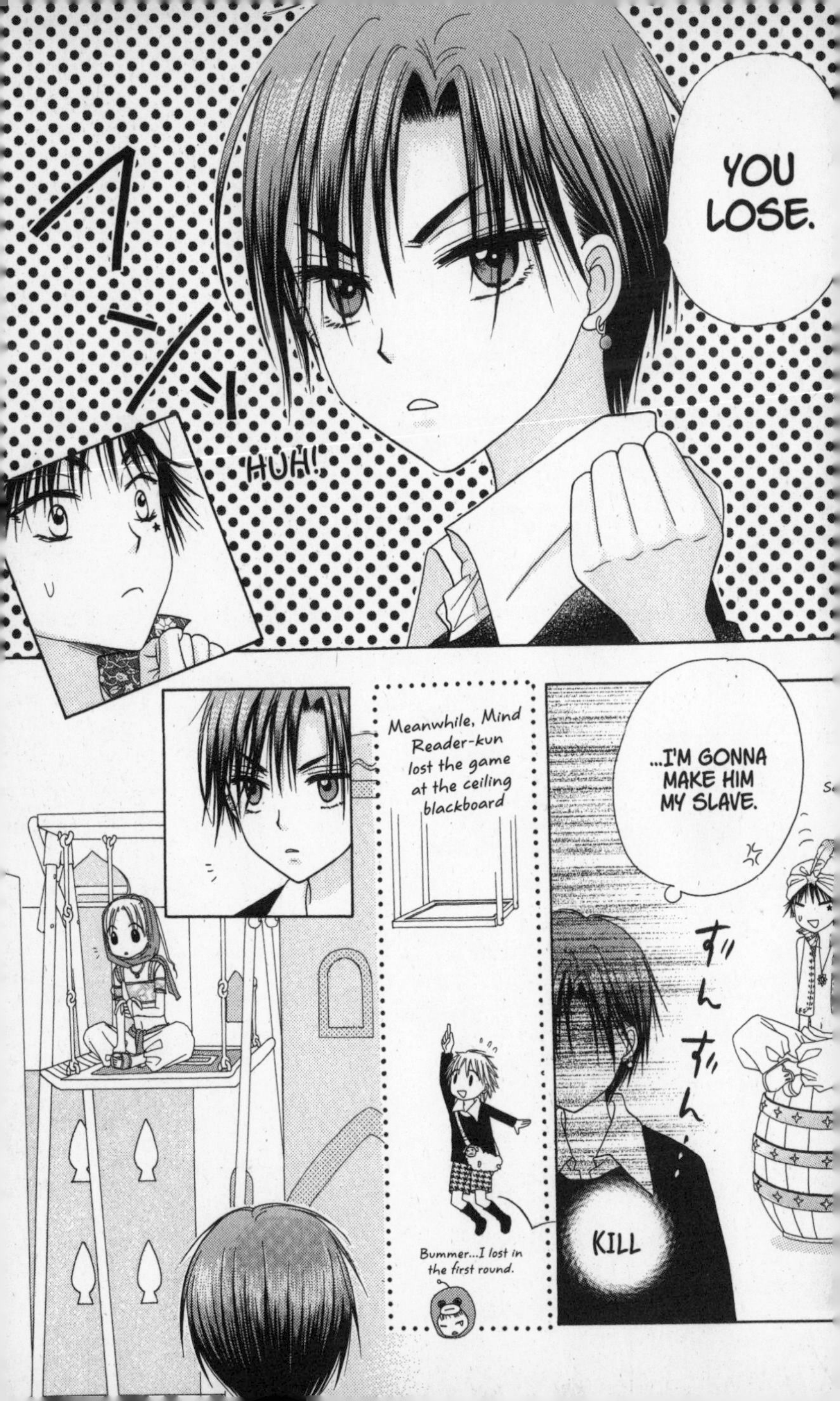
YOU LOSE.
HUH!
...I'M GONNA MAKE HIM MY SLAVE.
ずん ずん ずん
KILL
Meanwhile, Mind Reader-kun lost the game at the ceiling blackboard
Bummer...I lost in the first round.

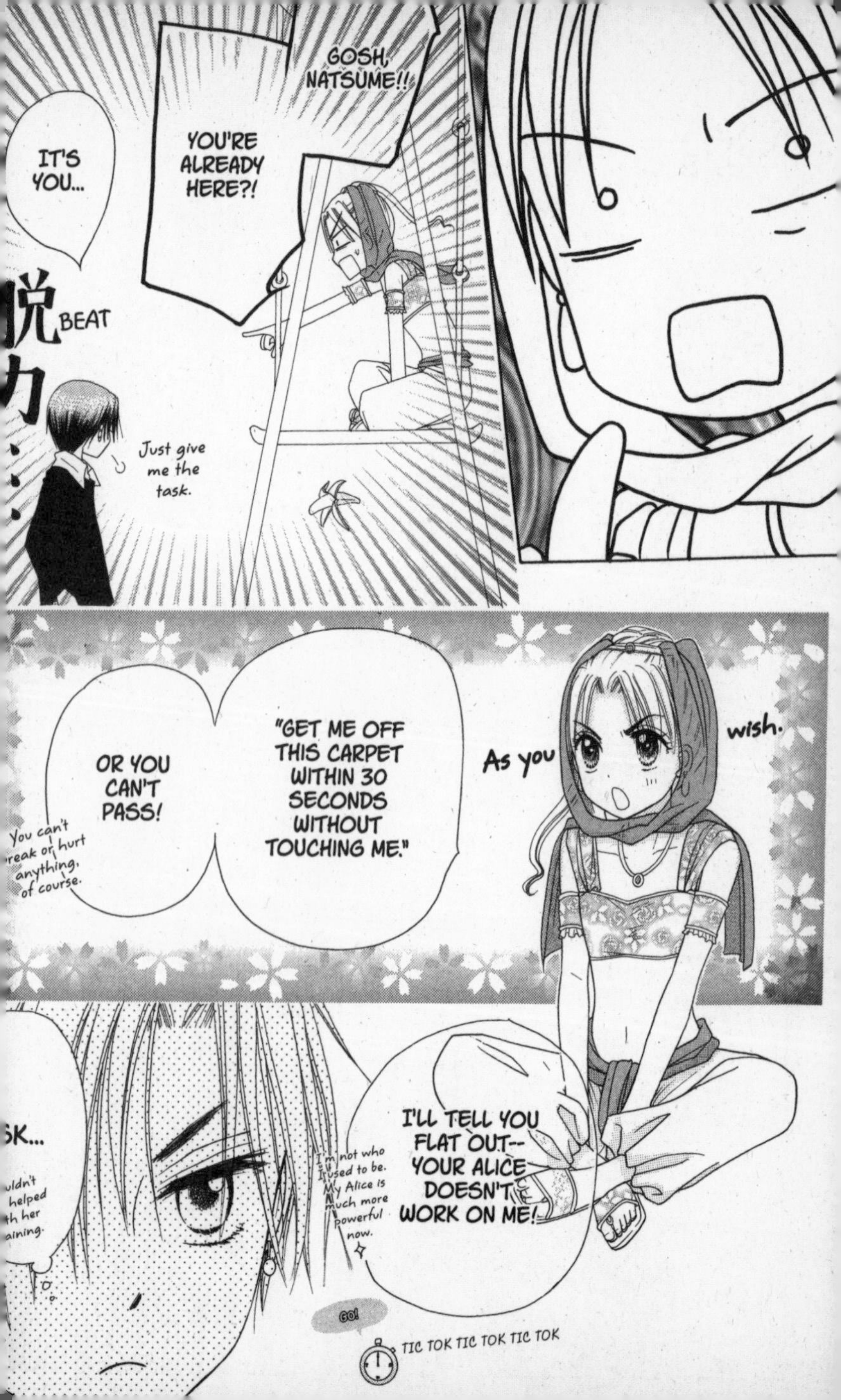

GOSH, NATSUME!!
YOU'RE ALREADY HERE?!
IT'S YOU...
脱力 BEAT
Just give me the task.
As you wish.
"GET ME OFF THIS CARPET WITHIN 30 SECONDS WITHOUT TOUCHING ME."
OR YOU CAN'T PASS!
You can't reak or hurt anything, of course.
I'LL TELL YOU FLAT OUT-- YOUR ALICE DOESN'T WORK ON ME!
I'm not who I used to be. My Alice is much more powerful now.
SK...
uldn't helped th her aining.
Go!
TIC TOK TIC TOK TIC TOK

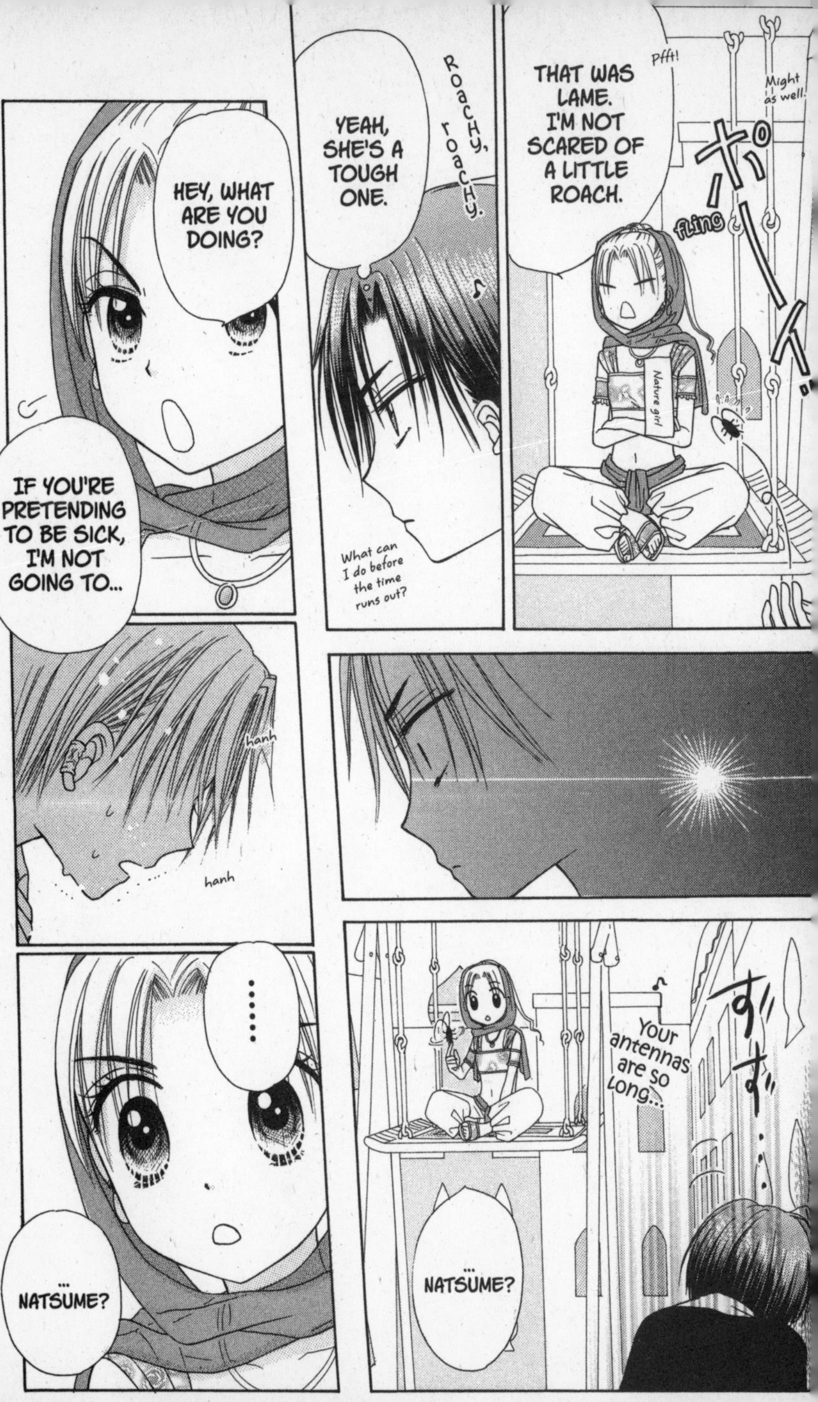
Might as well!
Pfft!
THAT WAS LAME. I'M NOT SCARED OF A LITTLE ROACH.
fling
Nature girl
YEAH, SHE'S A TOUGH ONE.
Roachy, roachy, roachy.
What can I do before the time runs out?
HEY, WHAT ARE YOU DOING?
IF YOU'RE PRETENDING TO BE SICK, I'M NOT GOING TO...
hanh
hanh
Your antennas are so long...
...NATSUME?
......
...NATSUME?

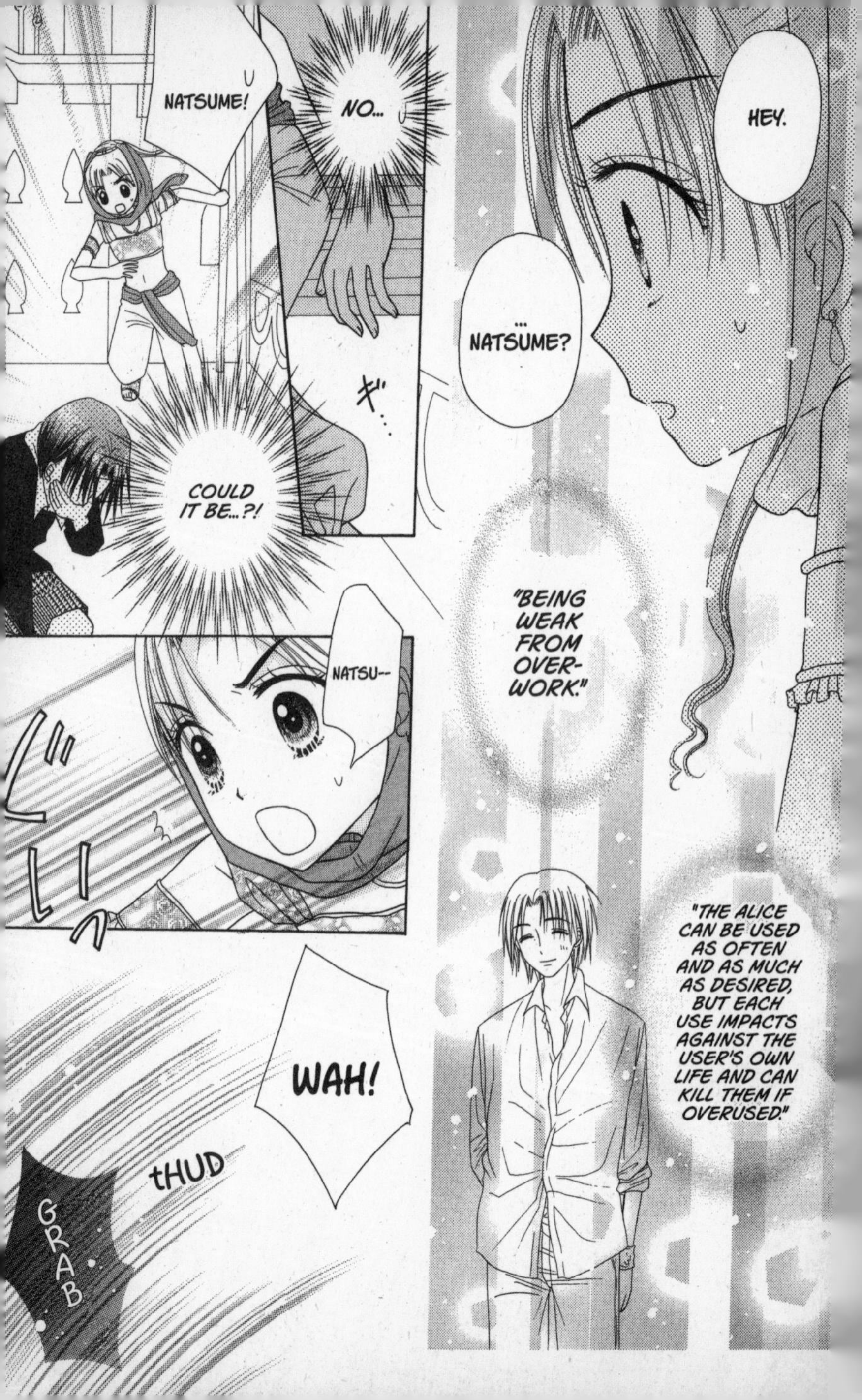
HEY.
...NATSUME?
"BEING WEAK FROM OVER-WORK."
"THE ALICE CAN BE USED AS OFTEN AND AS MUCH AS DESIRED, BUT EACH USE IMPACTS AGAINST THE USER'S OWN LIFE AND CAN KILL THEM IF OVERUSED."
NO...
NATSUME!
ギ…
COULD IT BE...?!
NATSU--
WAH!
tHUD
GRAB

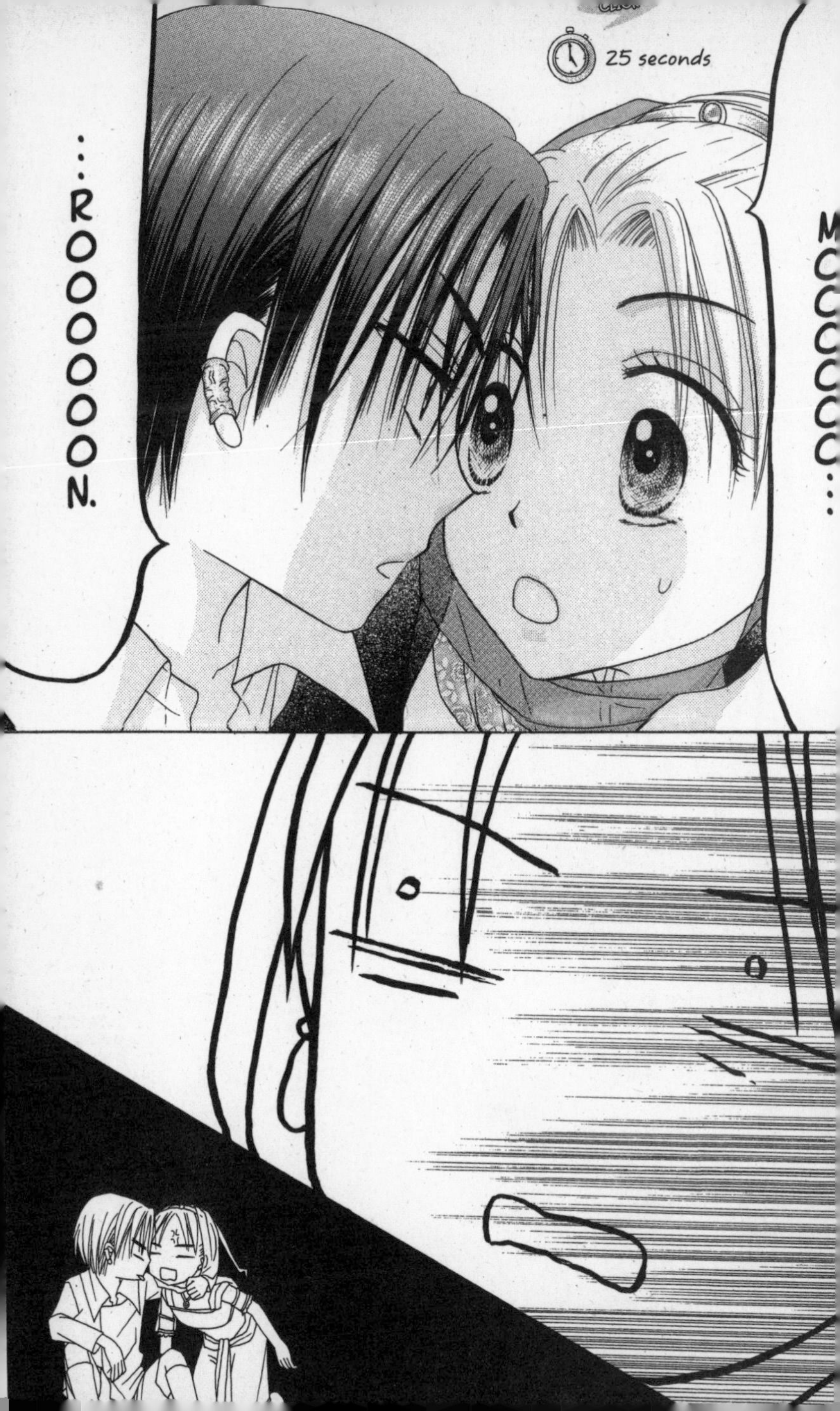
25 seconds
MOOOOOO...
...ROOOOOON.

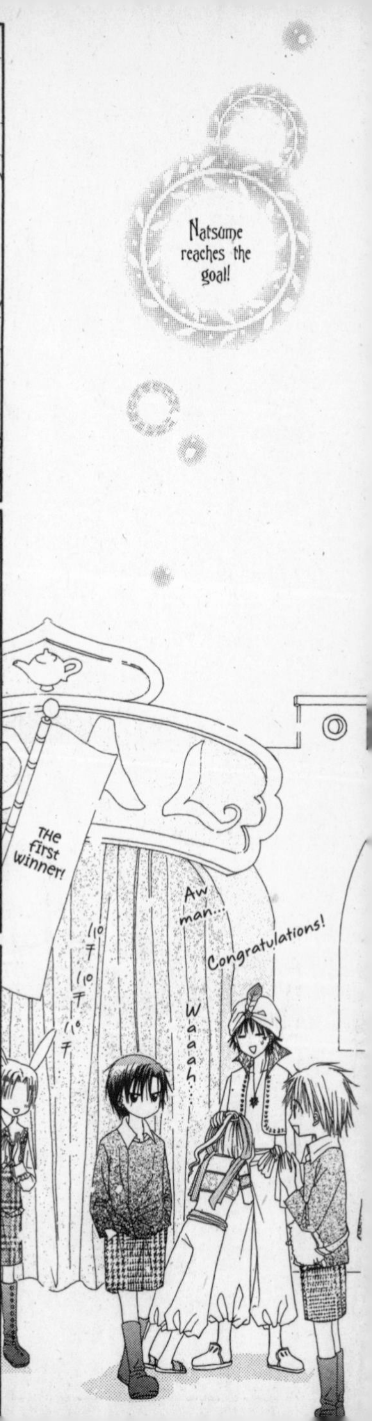
Natsume reaches the goal!
The first winner!
Aw man...
Congratulations!
Waaah...
パチパチパチ
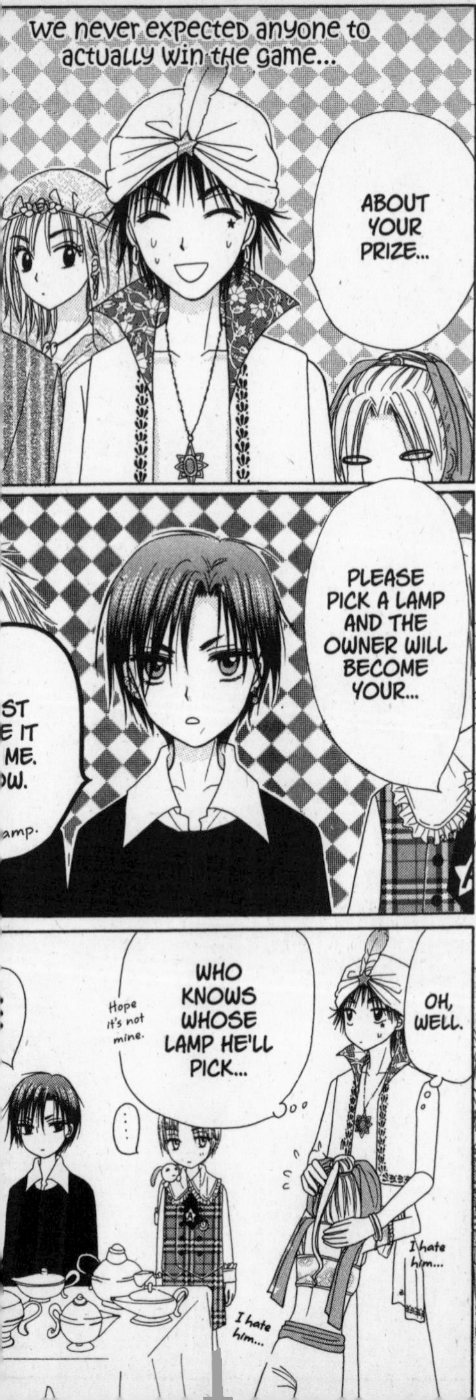
we never expected anyone to actually win the game...
ABOUT YOUR PRIZE...
PLEASE PICK A LAMP AND THE OWNER WILL BECOME YOUR...
OH, WELL.
WHO KNOWS WHOSE LAMP HE'LL PICK...
Hope it's not mine.
....
I hate him...
I hate him...

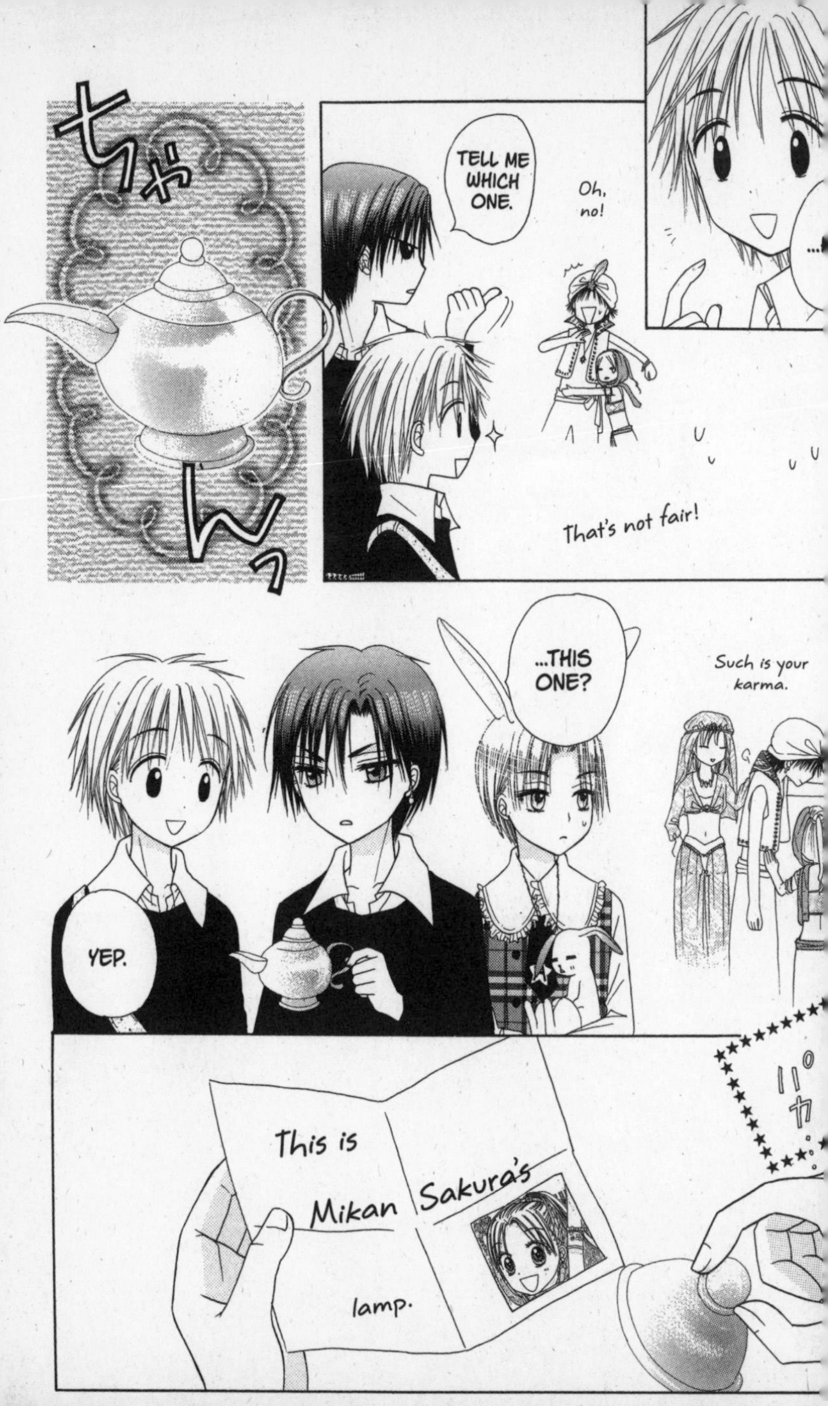
...
TELL ME WHICH ONE.
Oh, no!
That's not fair!
ちゃん
Such is your karma.
...THIS ONE?
YEP.
パカ
This is Mikan Sakura's lamp.

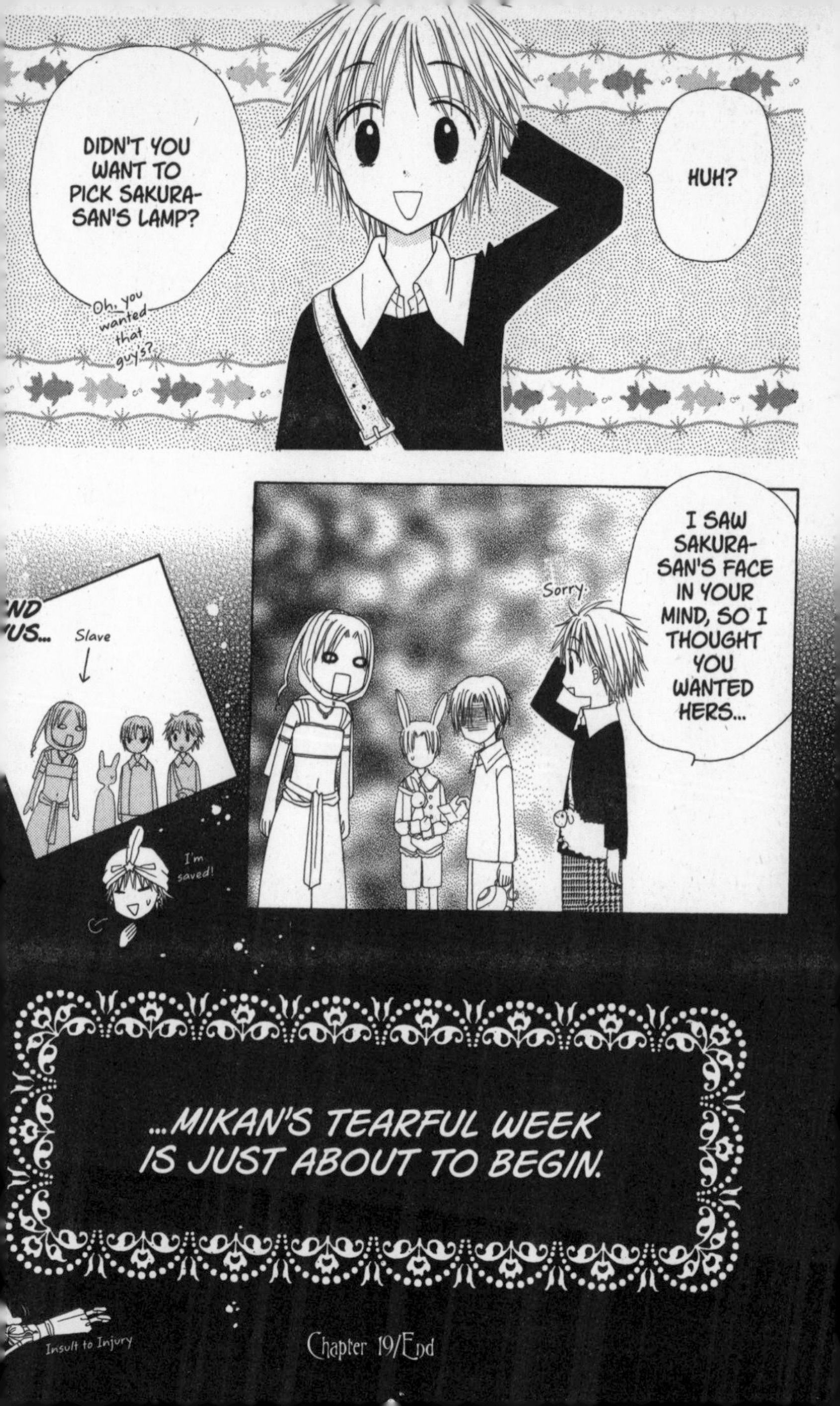
HUH?
DIDN'T YOU WANT TO PICK SAKURA-SAN'S LAMP?
Oh, you wanted that guy's?
I SAW SAKURA-SAN'S FACE IN YOUR MIND, SO I THOUGHT YOU WANTED HERS...
Sorry.
Slave
I'm saved!
...MIKAN'S TEARFUL WEEK IS JUST ABOUT TO BEGIN.
Insult to Injury
Chapter 19/End

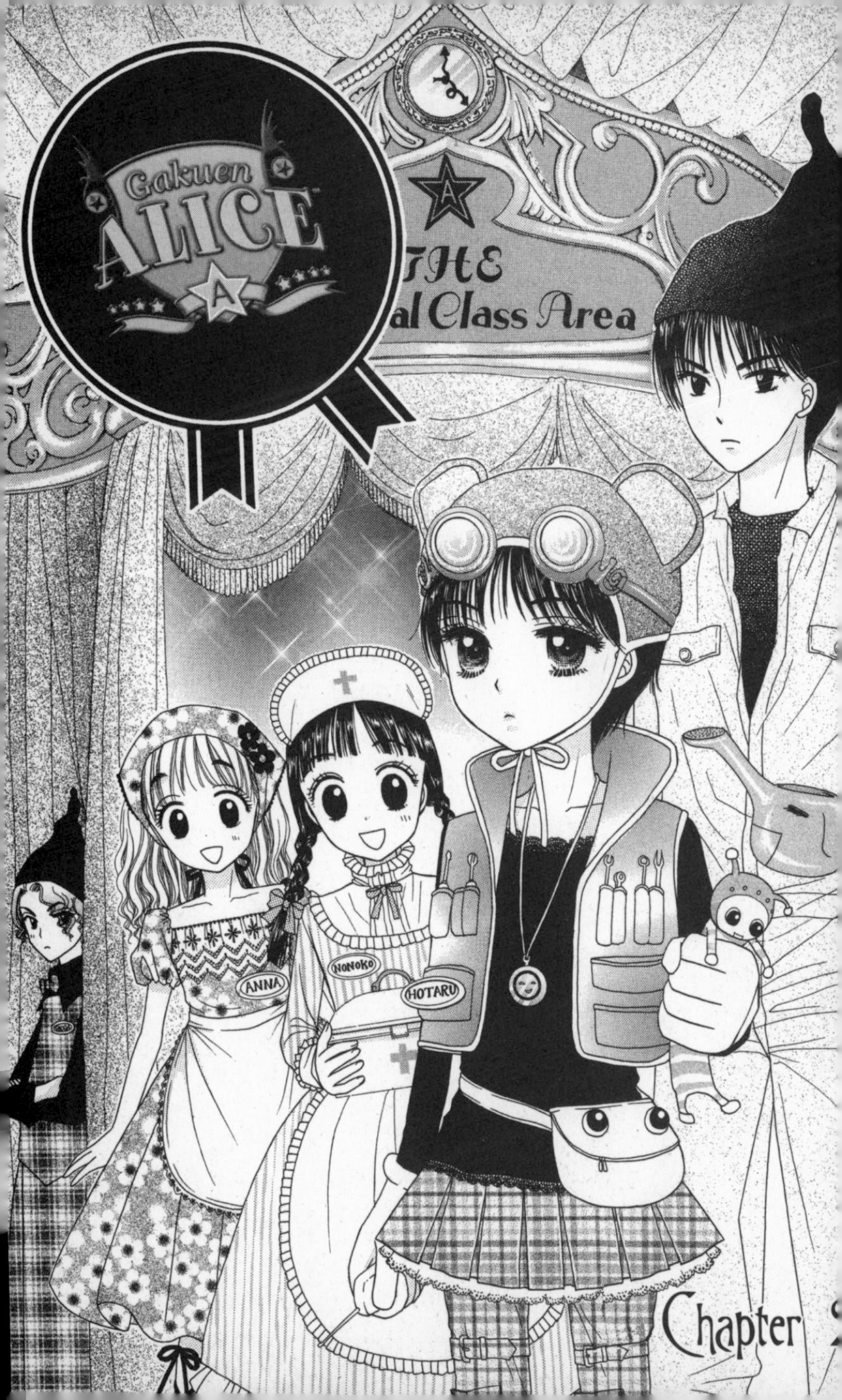

Gakuen ALICE
THE
al Class Area
ANNA
NONOKO
HOTARU
Chapter

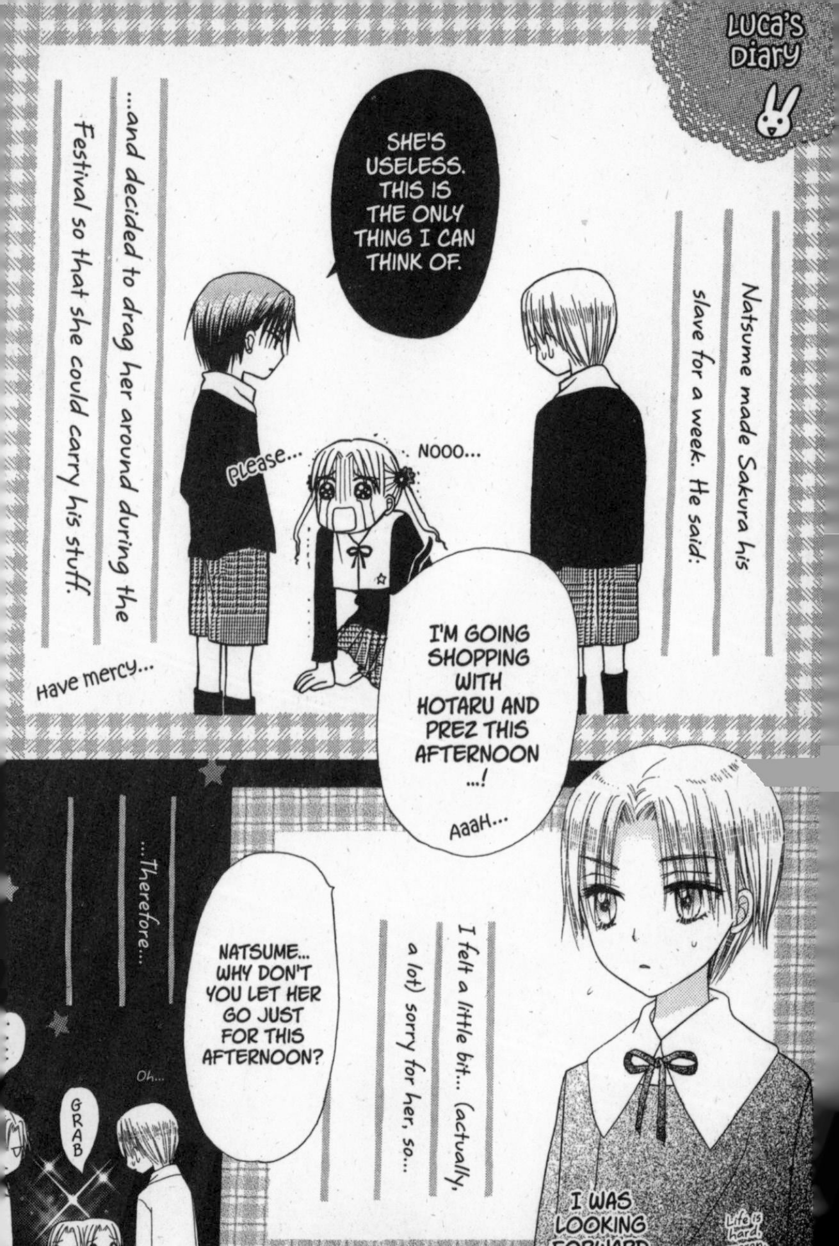
LUCA'S DIARY
Natsume made Sakura his slave for a week. He said:
SHE'S USELESS. THIS IS THE ONLY THING I CAN THINK OF.
NOOO...
PLEASE...
...and decided to drag her around during the Festival so that she could carry his stuff.
Have mercy...
I'M GOING SHOPPING WITH HOTARU AND PREZ THIS AFTERNOON ...!
AaaH...
I felt a little bit... (actually, a lot) sorry for her, so...
I WAS LOOKING FORWARD TO IT...!
Life is hard, moron.
NATSUME... WHY DON'T YOU LET HER GO JUST FOR THIS AFTERNOON?
...Therefore...
Oh...
GRAB

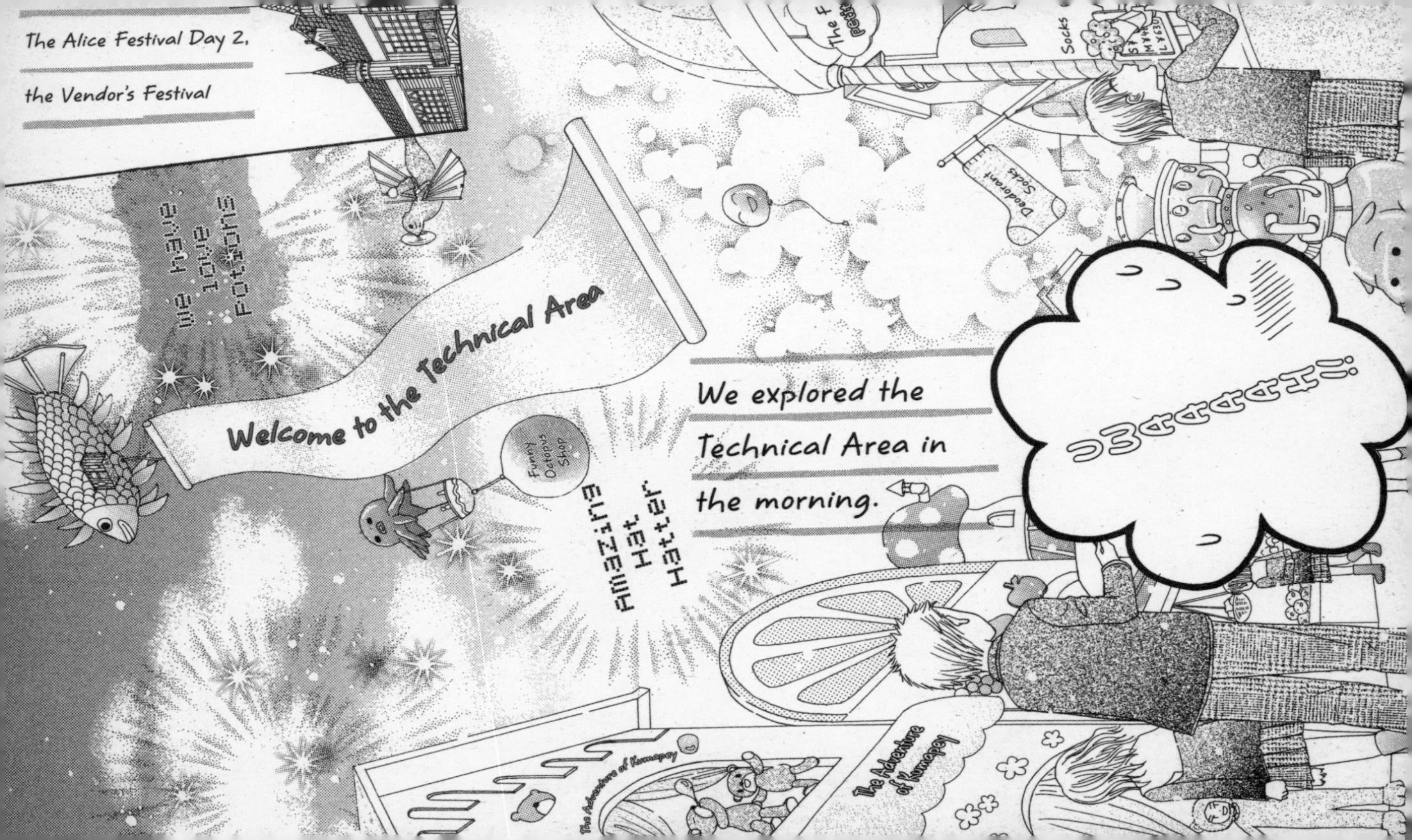
The Alice Festival Day 2,
the Vendor's Festival
We have love potions
Welcome to the Technical Area
Funny Octopus Shop
Amazing Hat Hatter
We explored the Technical Area in the morning.
Deodorant Socks
Socks
The Adventure of Kumapey
The Adventure of Kumapey
UWAAAAAH!!

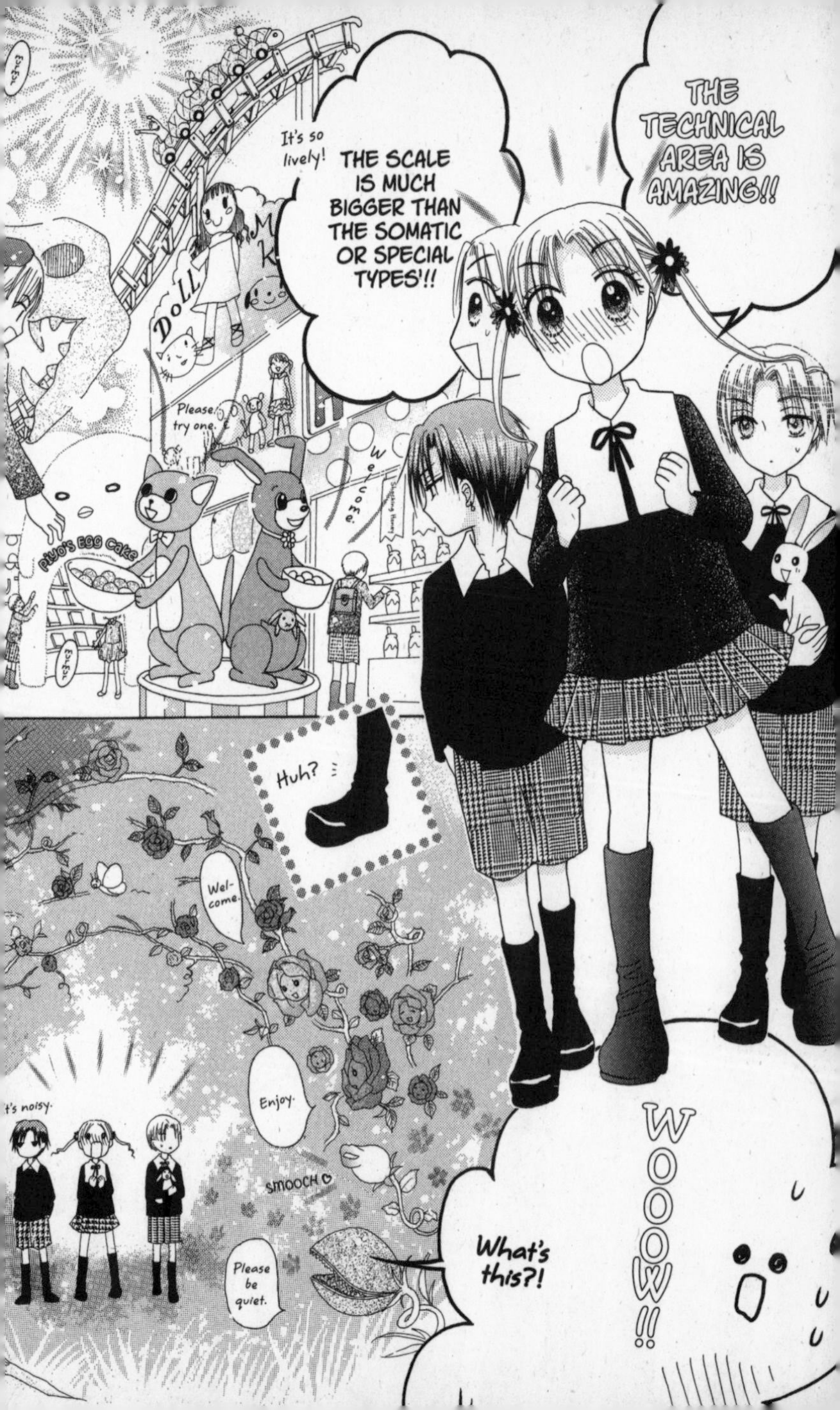
THE TECHNICAL AREA IS AMAZING!!
THE SCALE IS MUCH BIGGER THAN THE SOMATIC OR SPECIAL TYPES'!!
It's so lively!
Please try one.
Welcome.
Piyo's Egg Cake
Huh?
WOOOOW!!
What's this?!
Welcome.
Enjoy.
SMOOCH
Please be quiet.
t's noisy.

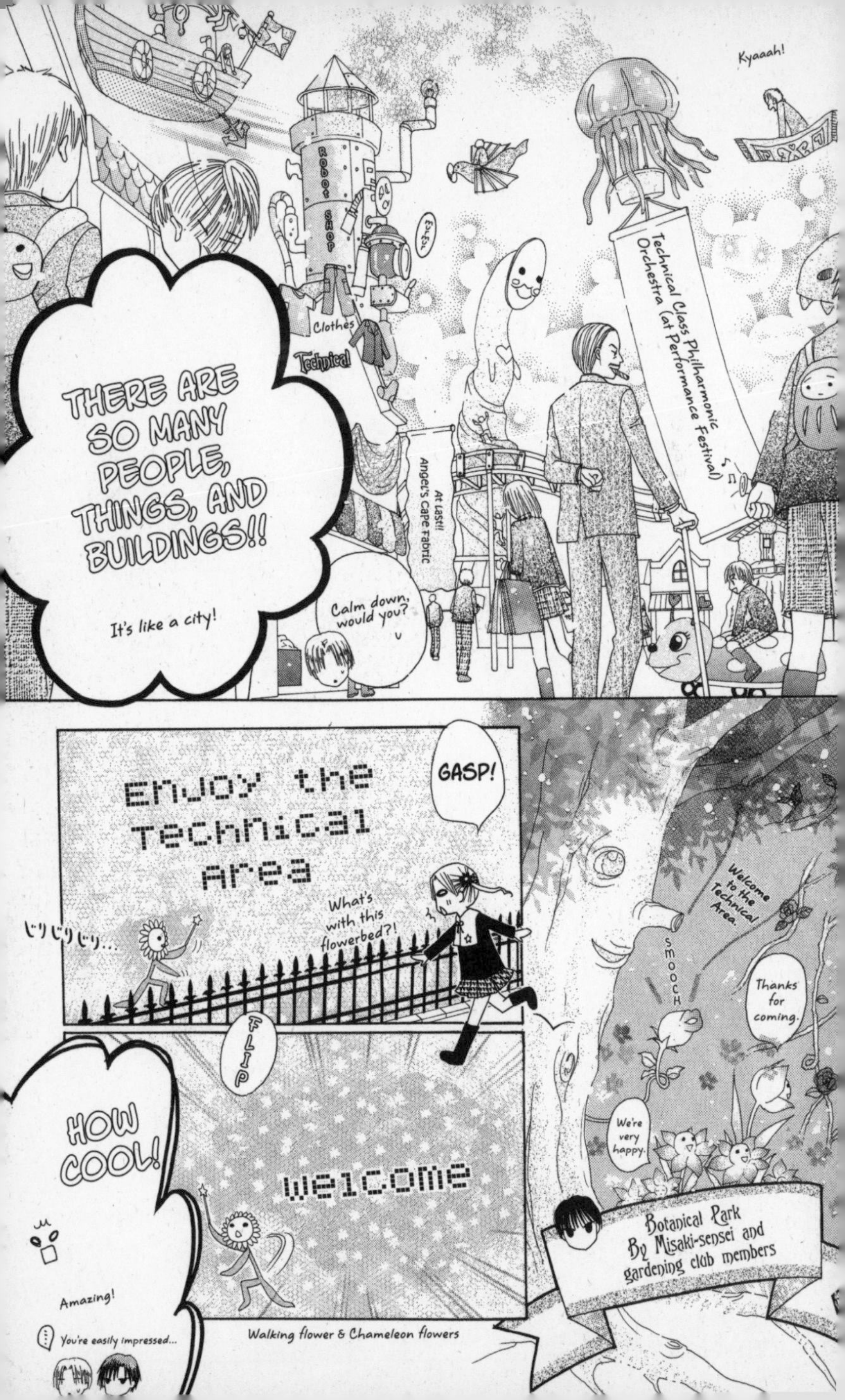
Kyaaah!
Technical Class Philharmonic Orchestra (at Performance Festival)
Robot SHOP
Clothes
Technical
At last!! Angel's Cape fabric
Calm down, would you?
THERE ARE SO MANY PEOPLE, THINGS, AND BUILDINGS!!
It's like a city!
Welcome to the Technical Area.
SMOOCH
Thanks for coming.
We're very happy.
Botanical Park By Misaki-sensei and gardening club members
GASP!
Enjoy the Technical Area
What's with this flowerbed?!
ジリジリジリ…
FLIP
HOW COOL!
Welcome
Amazing!
You're easily impressed...
Walking flower & Chameleon flowers

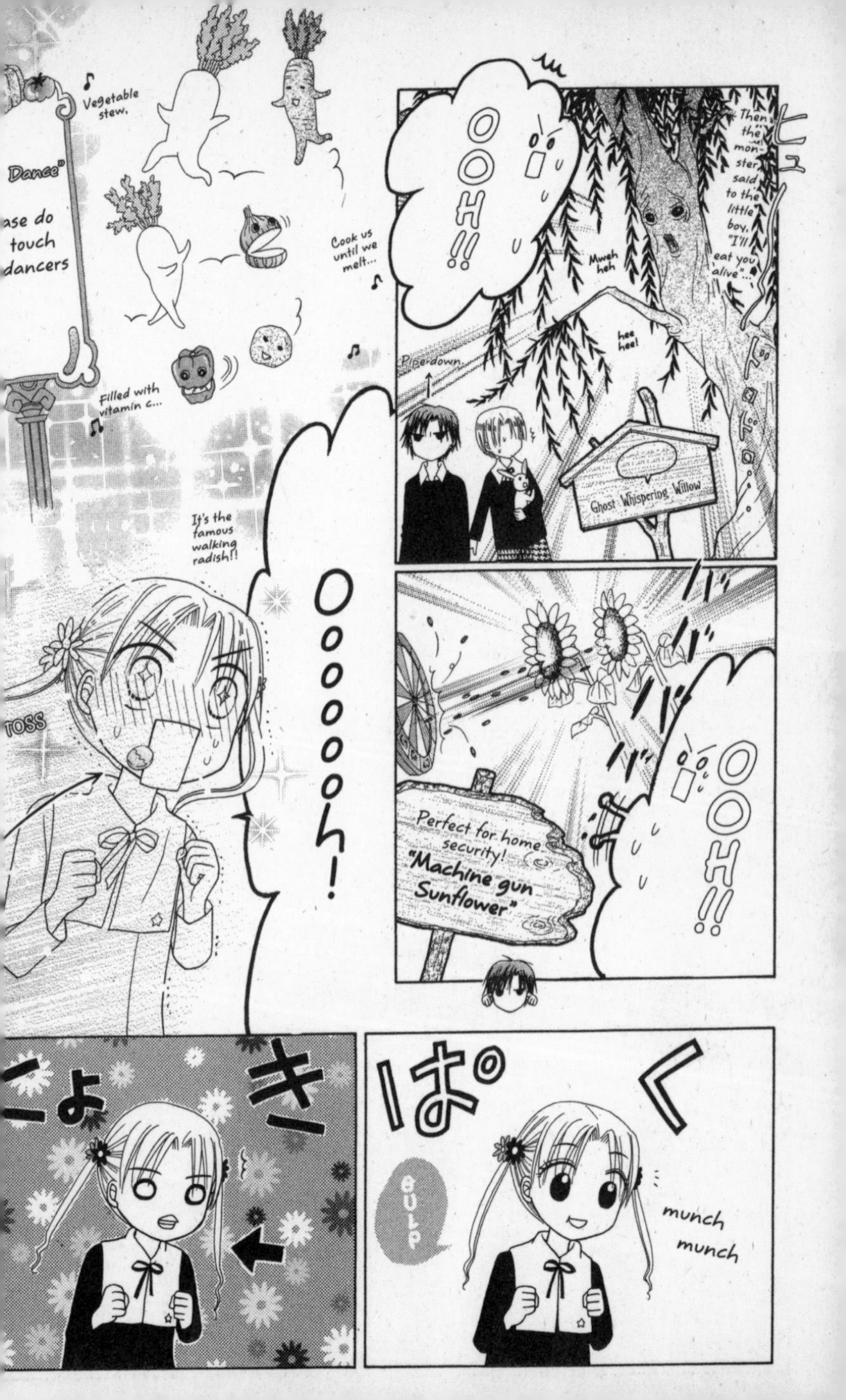
OOOH!!
Then the monster said to the little boy, "I'll eat you alive"...
ヒュ
ドロドロ
Mweh heh
hee hee!
Pipe down.
Ghost Whispering Willow
バババババ
OOOH!!
Perfect for home security! "Machine gun Sunflower"
Dance"
ase do touch dancers
Vegetable stew,
Cook us until we melt...
Filled with vitamin c...
It's the famous walking radish!!
TOSS
Oooooooh!
ぱく
GULP
munch munch
にょき

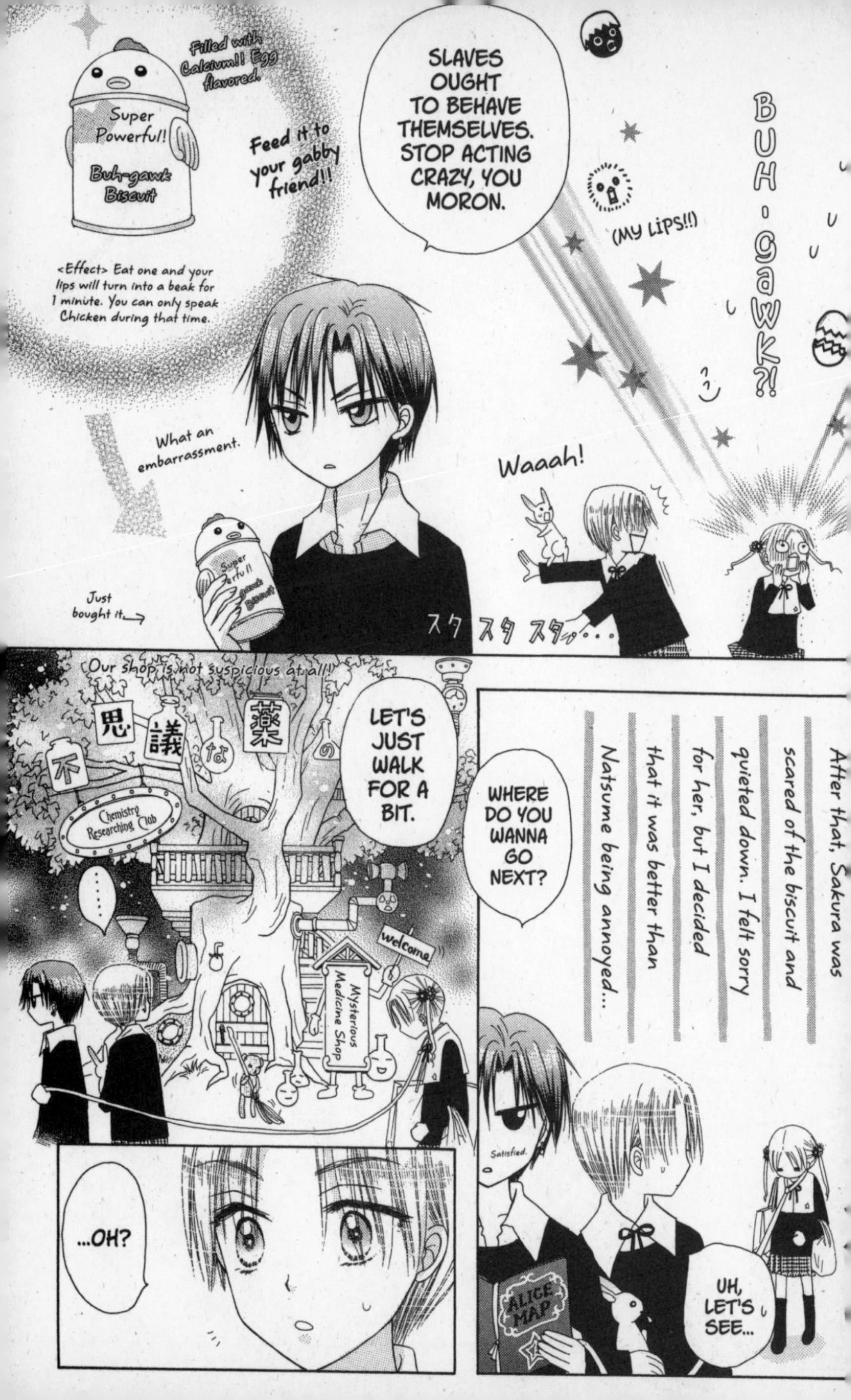
BUH-GAWK?!
(MY LIPS!!)
Waaah!
SLAVES OUGHT TO BEHAVE THEMSELVES. STOP ACTING CRAZY, YOU MORON.
Feed it to your gabby friend!!
Filled with Calcium!! Egg flavored.
Super Powerful!!
Buh-gawk Biscuit
<Effect> Eat one and your lips will turn into a beak for 1 minute. You can only speak Chicken during that time.
What an embarrassment.
Just bought it
スタ スタ スタ
After that, Sakura was scared of the biscuit and quieted down. I felt sorry for her, but I decided that it was better than Natsume being annoyed...
WHERE DO YOU WANNA GO NEXT?
Satisfied.
UH, LET'S SEE...
ALICE MAP
Our shop is not suspicious at all!
LET'S JUST WALK FOR A BIT.
不思議な薬の
Chemistry Researching Club
welcome
Mysterious Medicine Shop
......
...OH?

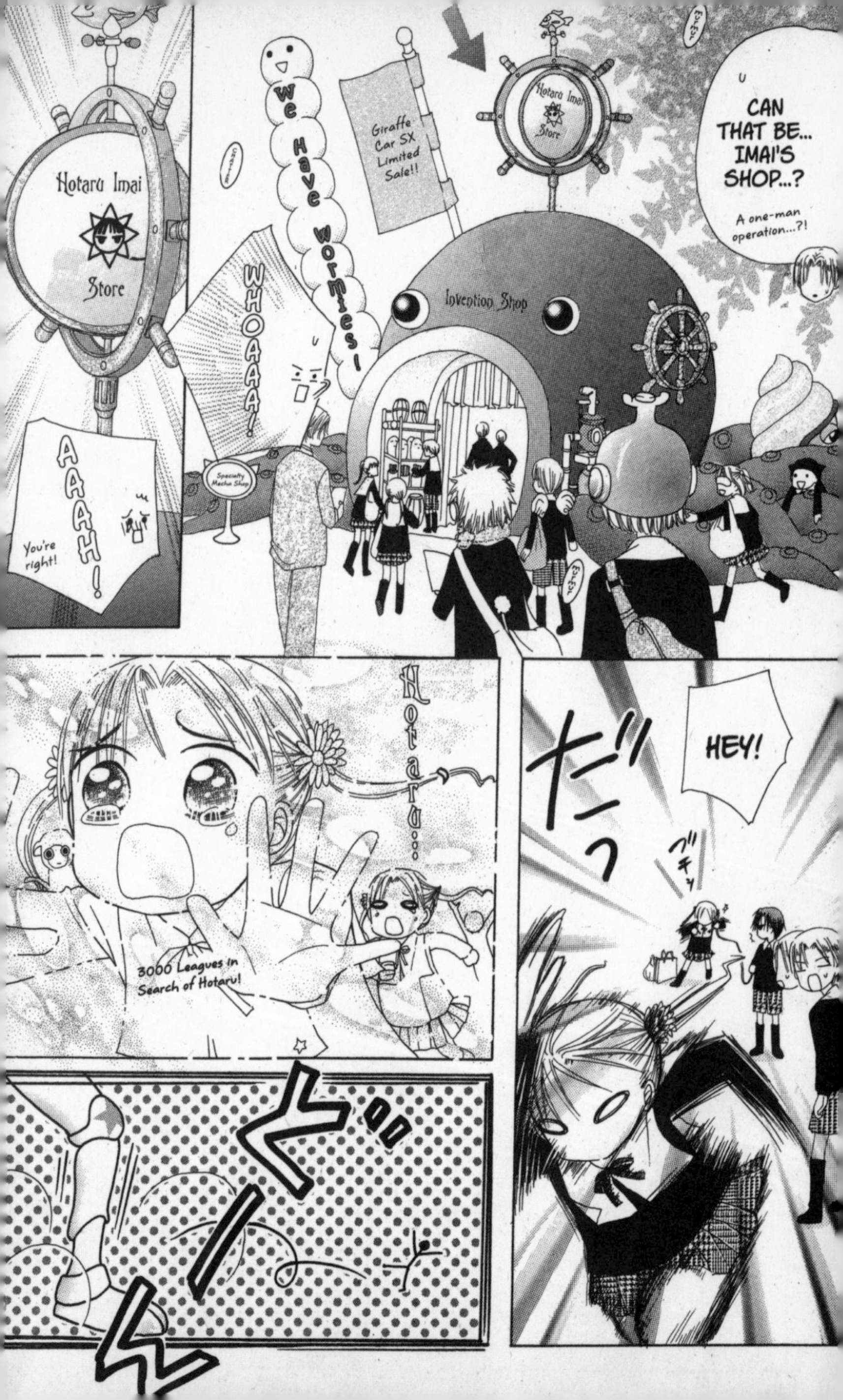
CAN THAT BE... IMAI'S SHOP...?
A one-man operation...?!
Hotaru Imai Store
Giraffe Car SX Limited Sale!!
We have wormies!
WHOAAAA!
Invention Shop
Specialty Mecha Shop
Hotaru Imai Store
AAAAH!
You're right!
HEY!
Hotaru...
3000 Leagues in Search of Hotaru!

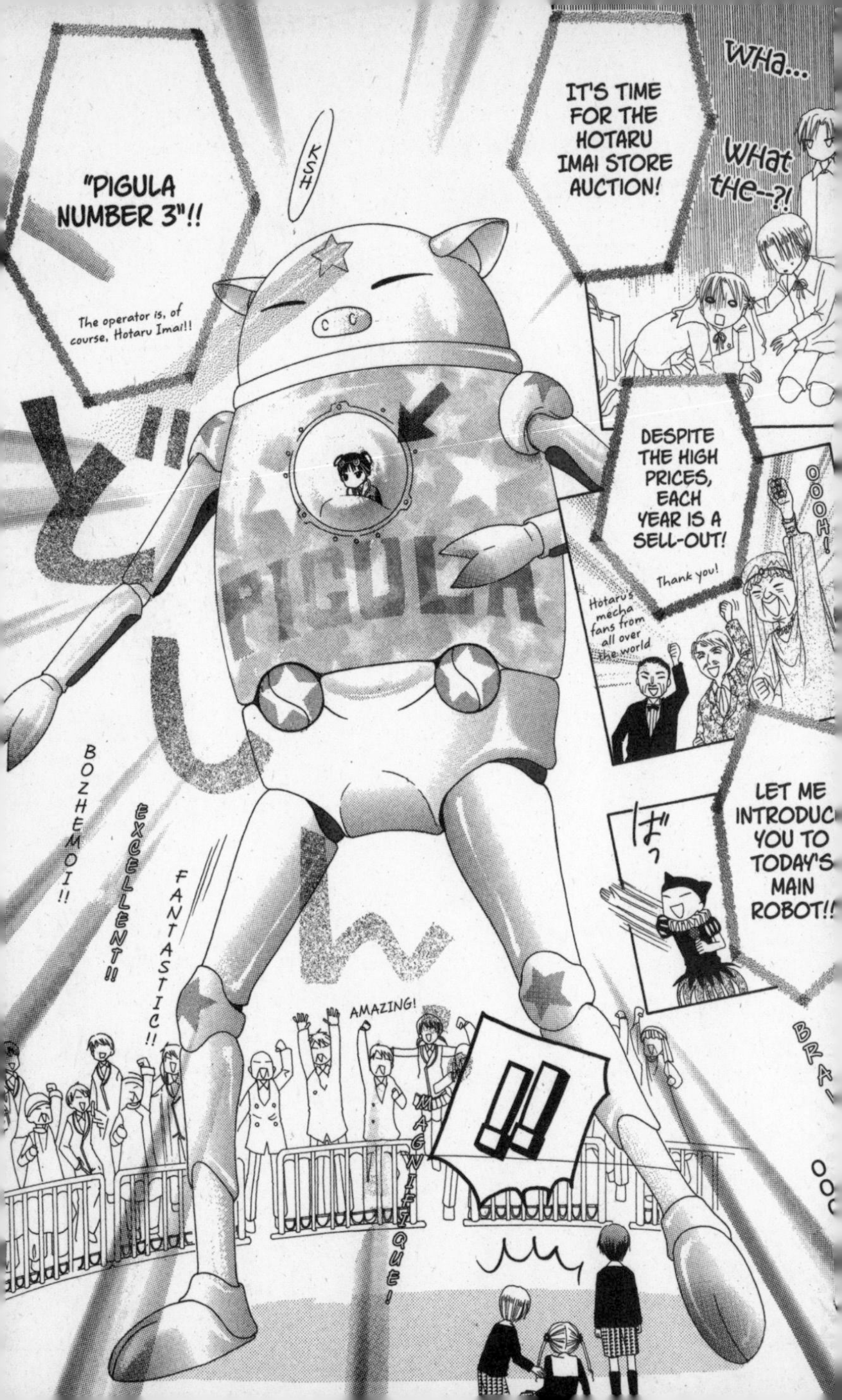
IT'S TIME FOR THE HOTARU IMAI STORE AUCTION!
WHA...
WHAT THE--?!
DESPITE THE HIGH PRICES, EACH YEAR IS A SELL-OUT!
Thank you!
OOOH!
Hotaru's mecha fans from all over the world
LET ME INTRODUC YOU TO TODAY'S MAIN ROBOT!!
KSH
"PIGULA NUMBER 3"!!
The operator is, of course, Hotaru Imai!!
PIGULA
BRA- OOO
AMAZING!
MAGNIFIQUE!
FANTASTIC!!
EXCELLENT!!
BOZHEMOI!!
!!

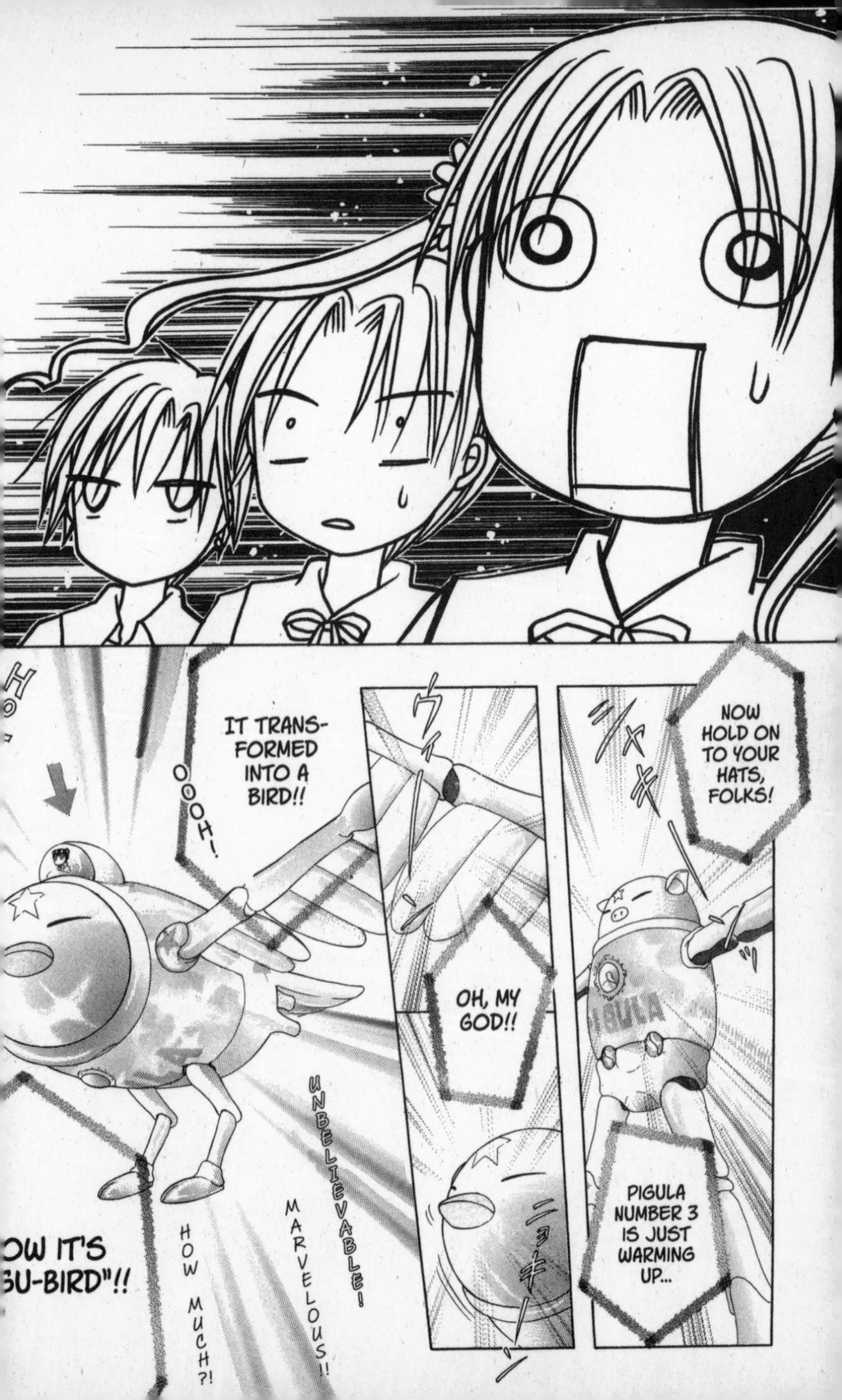

NOW HOLD ON TO YOUR HATS, FOLKS!
PIGULA NUMBER 3 IS JUST WARMING UP...
OH, MY GOD!!
IT TRANS-FORMED INTO A BIRD!!
OOOH!
UNBELIEVABLE!
MARVELOUS!!
HOW MUCH?!
OW IT'S
SU-BIRD"!!

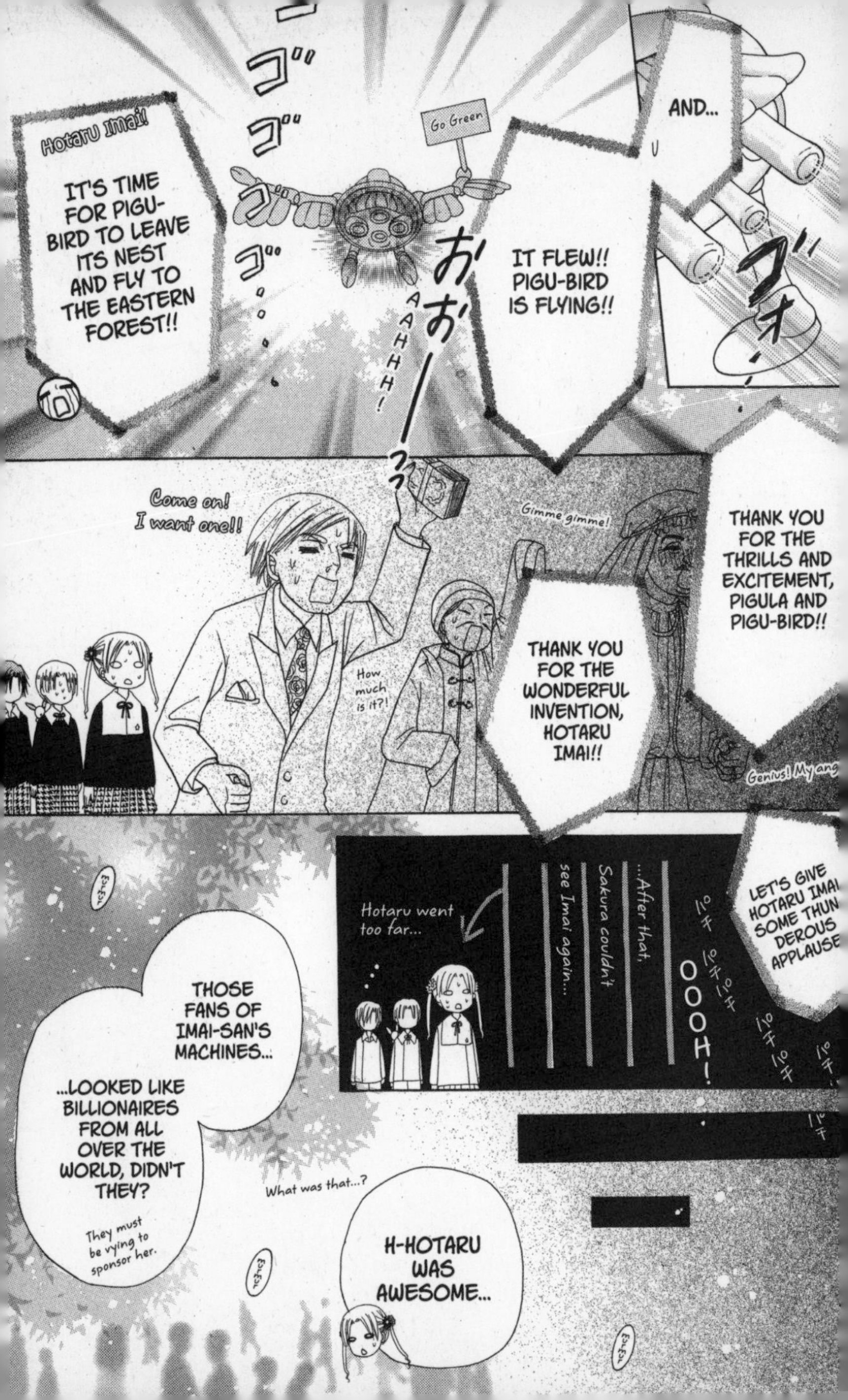

AND...
IT FLEW!! PIGU-BIRD IS FLYING!!
AAHHHH!
Go Green
Hotaru Imai!
IT'S TIME FOR PIGU-BIRD TO LEAVE ITS NEST AND FLY TO THE EASTERN FOREST!!
THANK YOU FOR THE THRILLS AND EXCITEMENT, PIGULA AND PIGU-BIRD!!
Genius! My ang
THANK YOU FOR THE WONDERFUL INVENTION, HOTARU IMAI!!
Gimme gimme!
How much is it?!
Come on! I want one!!
LET'S GIVE HOTARU IMAI SOME THUNDEROUS APPLAUSE
OOOOH!
...After that, Sakura couldn't see Imai again...
Hotaru went too far...
THOSE FANS OF IMAI-SAN'S MACHINES...
...LOOKED LIKE BILLIONAIRES FROM ALL OVER THE WORLD, DIDN'T THEY?
They must be vying to sponsor her.
What was that...?
H-HOTARU WAS AWESOME...

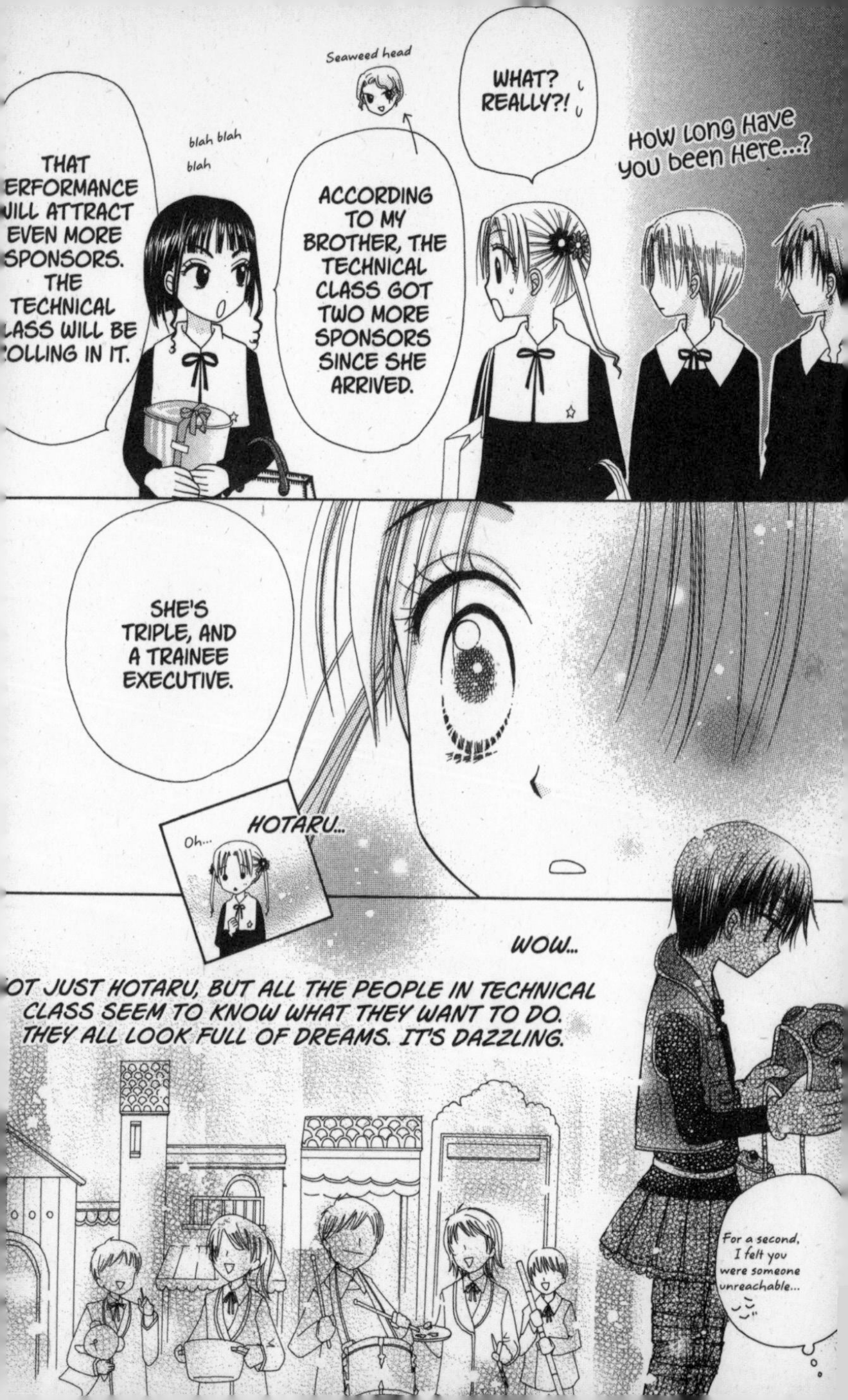
How long have you been here...?
WHAT? REALLY?!
Seaweed head
ACCORDING TO MY BROTHER, THE TECHNICAL CLASS GOT TWO MORE SPONSORS SINCE SHE ARRIVED.
blah blah blah
THAT ERFORMANCE VILL ATTRACT EVEN MORE SPONSORS. THE TECHNICAL LASS WILL BE OLLING IN IT.
SHE'S TRIPLE, AND A TRAINEE EXECUTIVE.
HOTARU...
Oh...
WOW...
OT JUST HOTARU, BUT ALL THE PEOPLE IN TECHNICAL CLASS SEEM TO KNOW WHAT THEY WANT TO DO. THEY ALL LOOK FULL OF DREAMS. IT'S DAZZLING.
For a second, I felt you were someone unreachable...

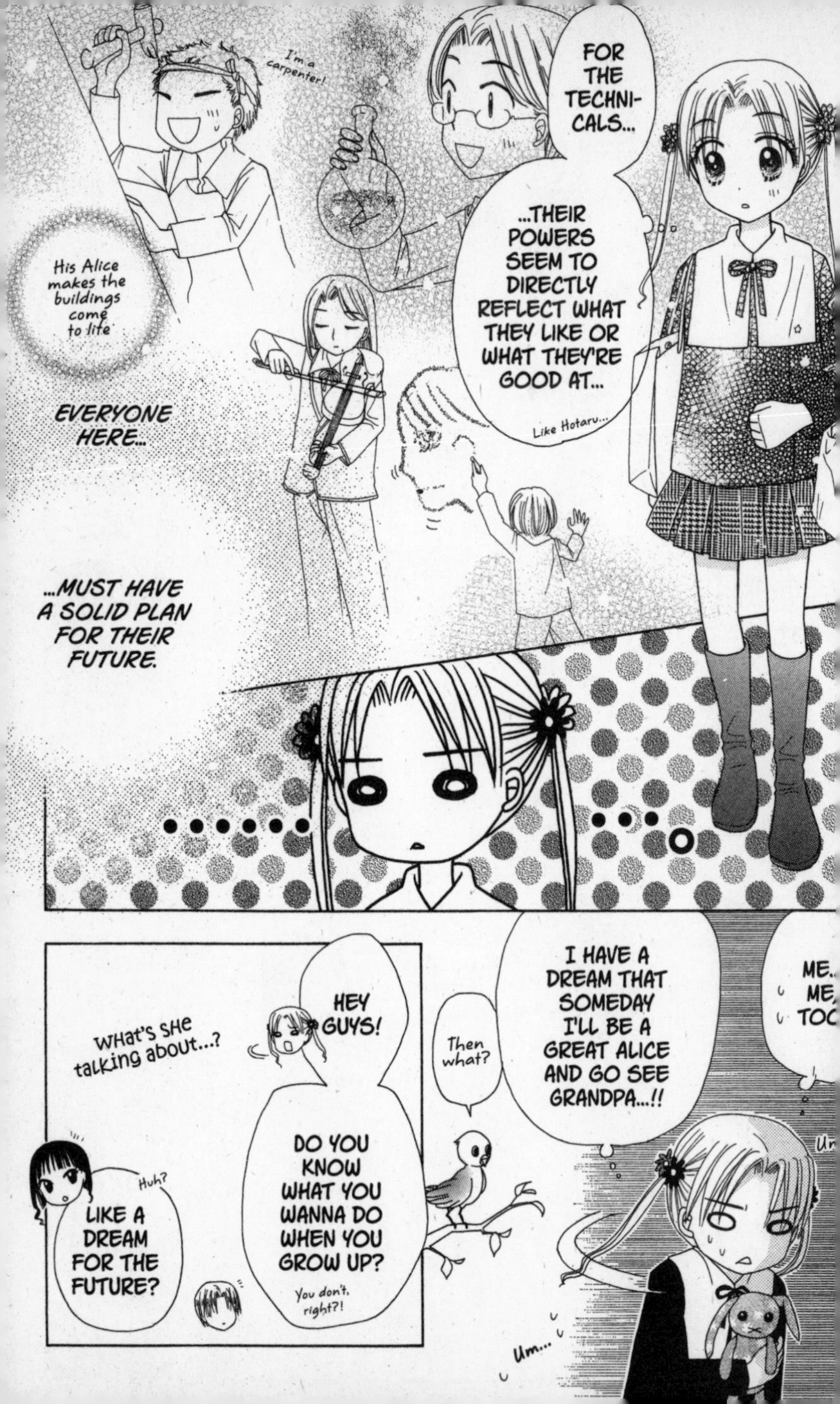
FOR THE TECHNICALS...
...THEIR POWERS SEEM TO DIRECTLY REFLECT WHAT THEY LIKE OR WHAT THEY'RE GOOD AT...
Like Hotaru...
I'm a carpenter!
His Alice makes the buildings come to life
EVERYONE HERE...
...MUST HAVE A SOLID PLAN FOR THEIR FUTURE.
ME...
ME,
I HAVE A DREAM THAT SOMEDAY I'LL BE A GREAT ALICE AND GO SEE GRANDPA...!!
Then what?
Um...
HEY GUYS!
What's she talking about...?
DO YOU KNOW WHAT YOU WANNA DO WHEN YOU GROW UP?
You don't, right?!
Huh?
LIKE A DREAM FOR THE FUTURE?

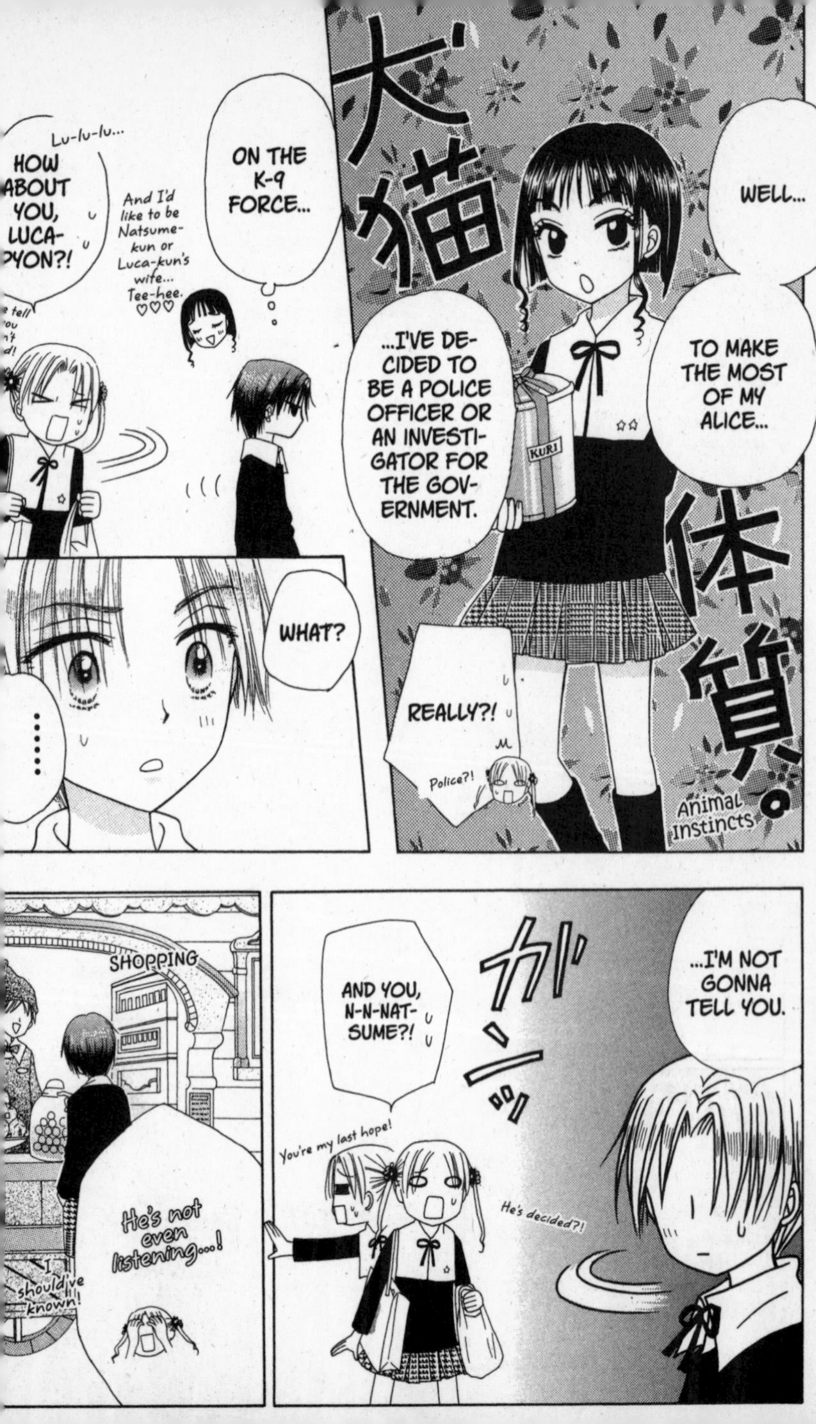
犬猫
WELL...
TO MAKE THE MOST OF MY ALICE...
...I'VE DECIDED TO BE A POLICE OFFICER OR AN INVESTIGATOR FOR THE GOVERNMENT.
体質
Animal Instincts
REALLY?!
Police?!
ON THE K-9 FORCE...
And I'd like to be Natsume-kun or Luca-kun's wife... Tee-hee. ♡♡♡
Lu-lu-lu...
HOW ABOUT YOU, LUCA-PYON?!
WHAT?
......
...I'M NOT GONNA TELL YOU.
ガーン
AND YOU, N-N-NAT-SUME?!
You're my last hope!
He's decided?!
SHOPPING
He's not even listening...!
I should've known!

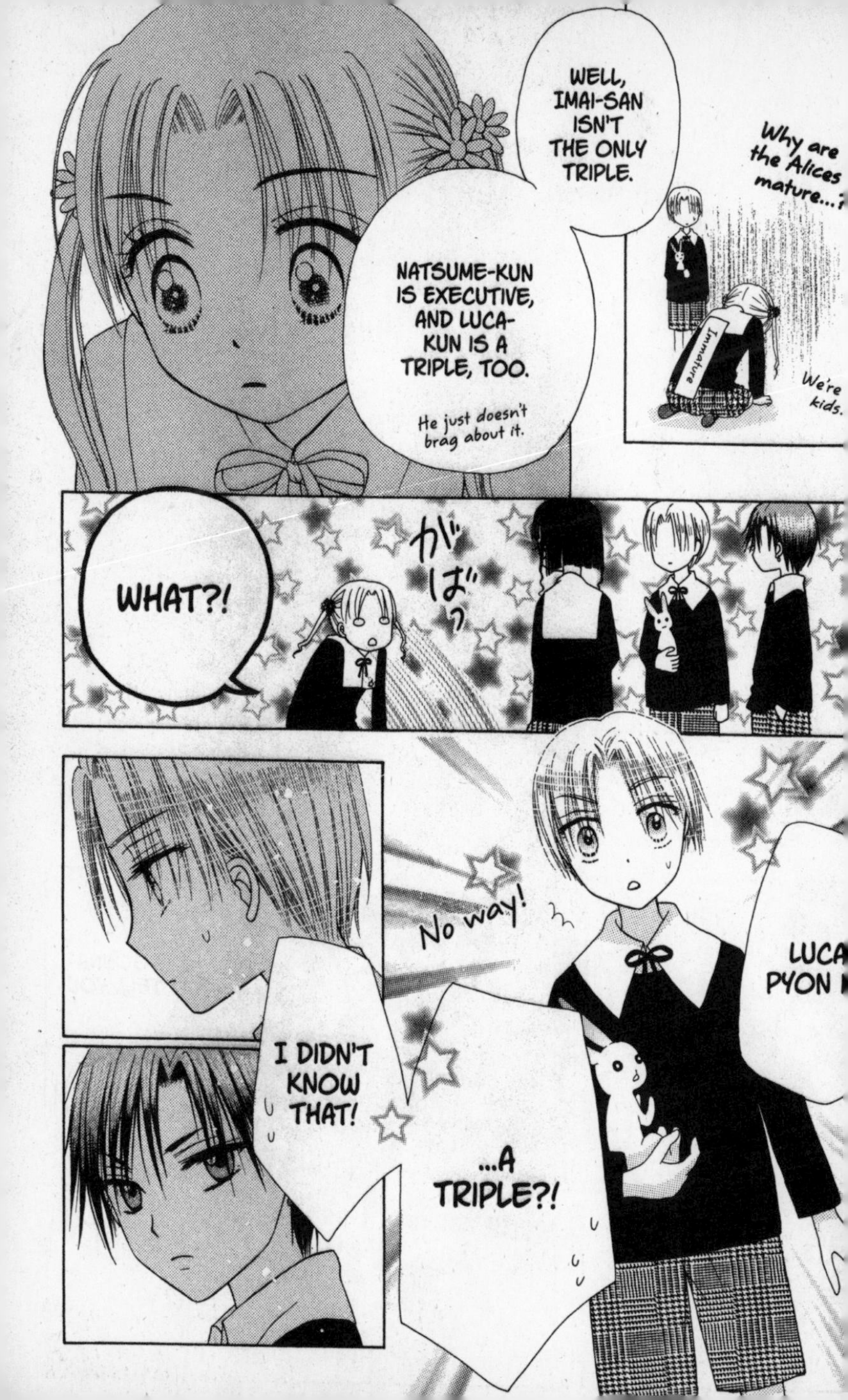
Why are the Alices mature...?
Immature
We're kids.
WELL, IMAI-SAN ISN'T THE ONLY TRIPLE.
NATSUME-KUN IS EXECUTIVE, AND LUCA-KUN IS A TRIPLE, TOO.
He just doesn't brag about it.
がばっ
WHAT?!
LUCA PYON
No way!
...A TRIPLE?!
I DIDN'T KNOW THAT!

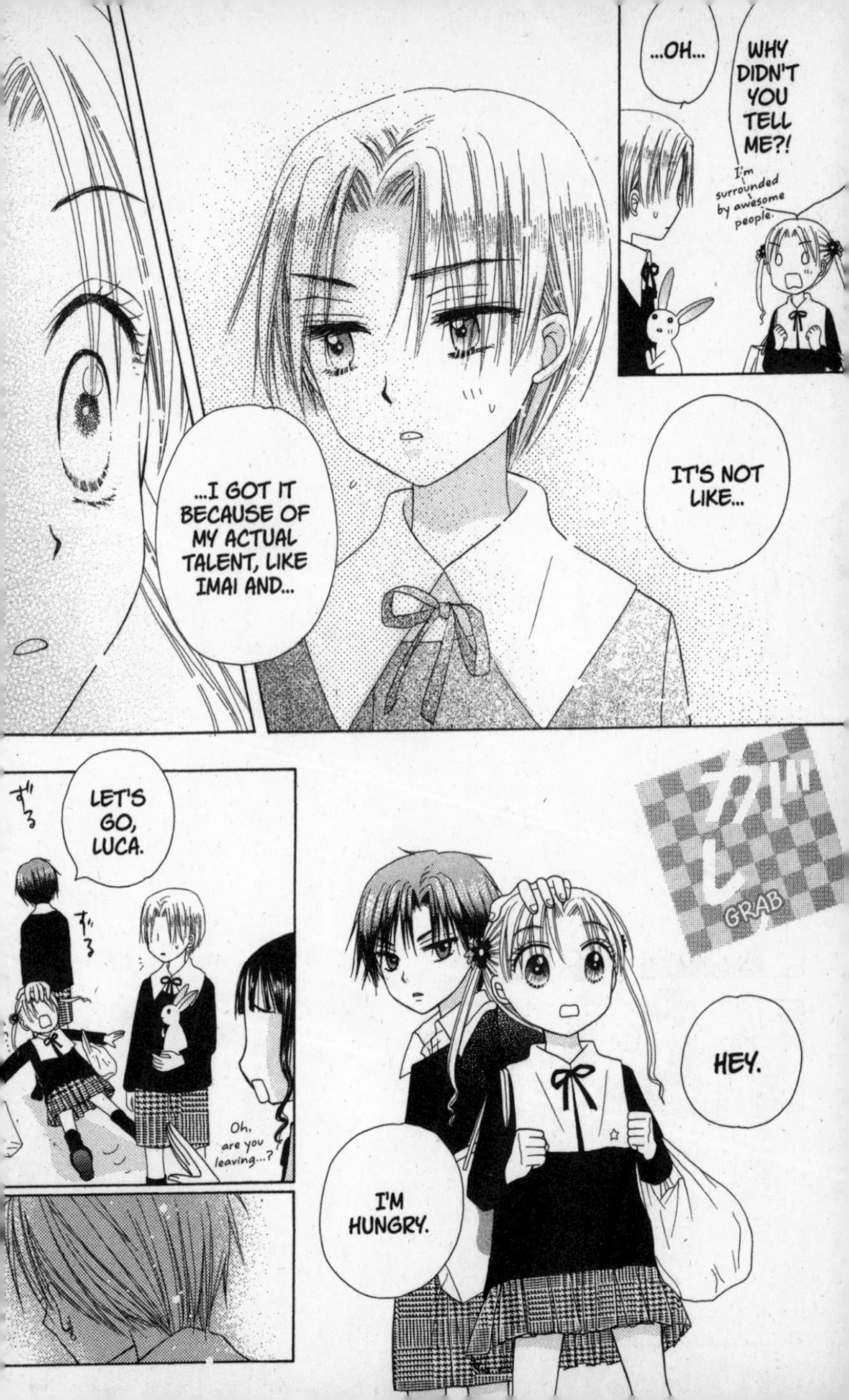

WHY DIDN'T YOU TELL ME?!
...OH...
I'm surrounded by awesome people.
IT'S NOT LIKE...
...I GOT IT BECAUSE OF MY ACTUAL TALENT, LIKE IMAI AND...
GRAB
HEY.
I'M HUNGRY.
LET'S GO, LUCA.
Oh, are you leaving...?

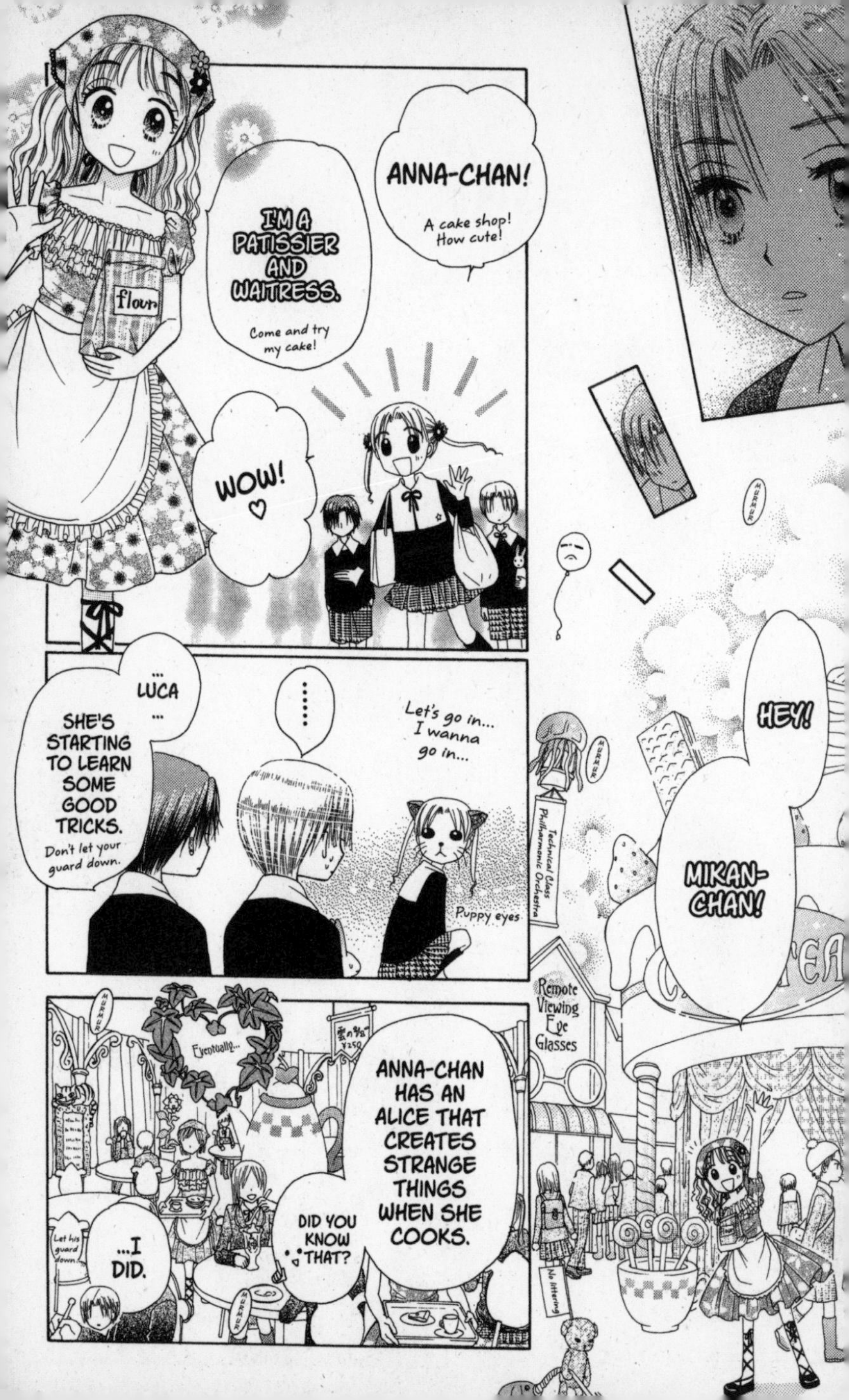

MURMUR
HEY!
MIKAN-CHAN!
Technical Class Philharmonic Orchestra
MURMUR
Remote Viewing Eye Glasses
No littering
ANNA-CHAN!
A cake shop! How cute!
I'M A PATISSIER AND WAITRESS.
Come and try my cake!
flour
WOW! ♡
Let's go in... I wanna go in...
Puppy eyes
......
...LUCA...
SHE'S STARTING TO LEARN SOME GOOD TRICKS.
Don't let your guard down.
MURMUR
Eventually...
¥250
ANNA-CHAN HAS AN ALICE THAT CREATES STRANGE THINGS WHEN SHE COOKS.
DID YOU KNOW THAT?
...I DID.
Let his guard down.
MURMUR

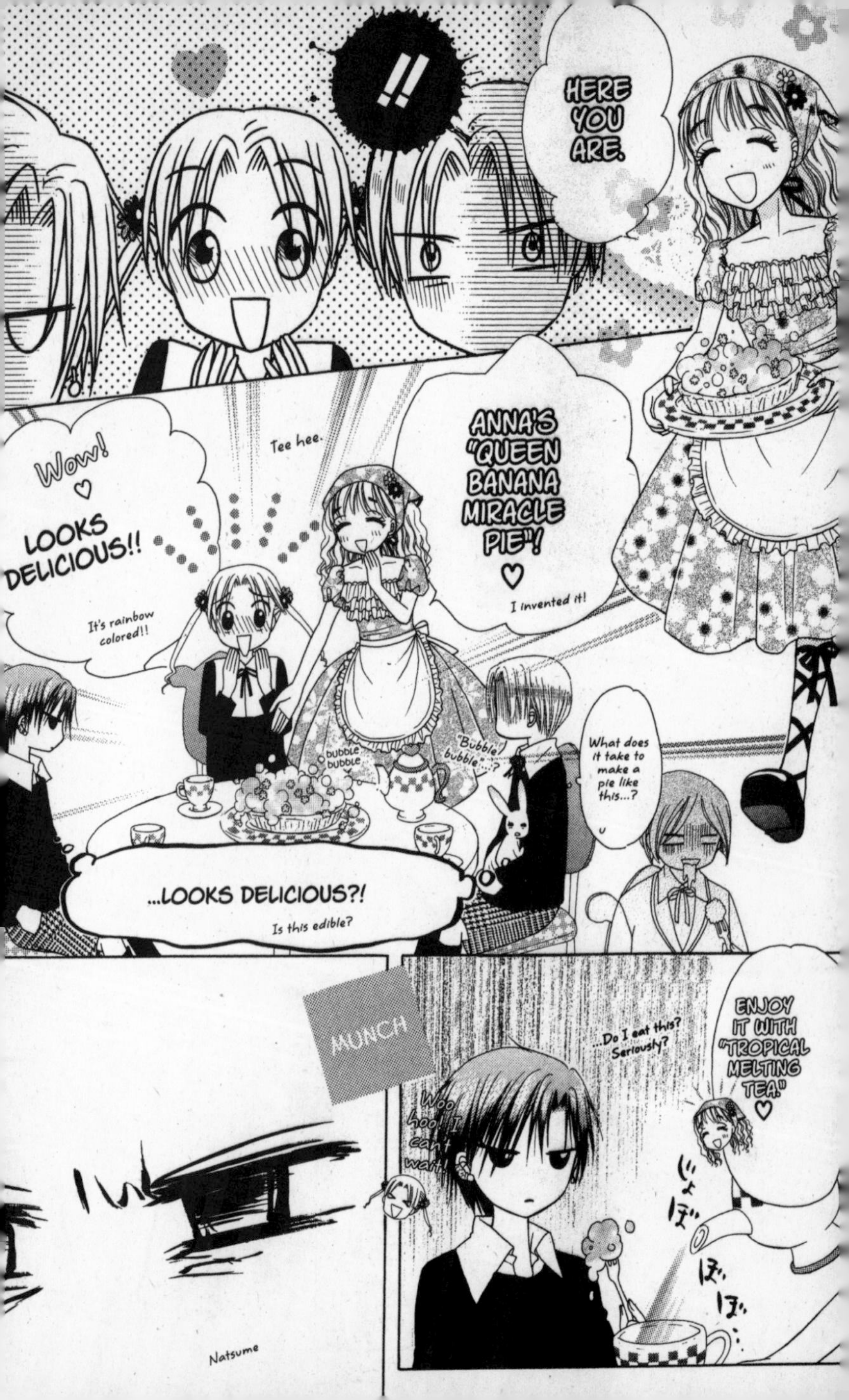
HERE YOU ARE.
!!
ANNA'S "QUEEN BANANA MIRACLE PIE"! ♡
I invented it!
Tee hee.
Wow! ♡ LOOKS DELICIOUS!!
It's rainbow colored!!
What does it take to make a pie like this...?
"Bubble bubble"...?
bubble bubble
...LOOKS DELICIOUS?!
Is this edible?
ENJOY IT WITH "TROPICAL MELTING TEA." ♡
じょぼぼぼ
...Do I eat this? Seriously?
Woo hoo!! I can't wait.
MUNCH
Natsume

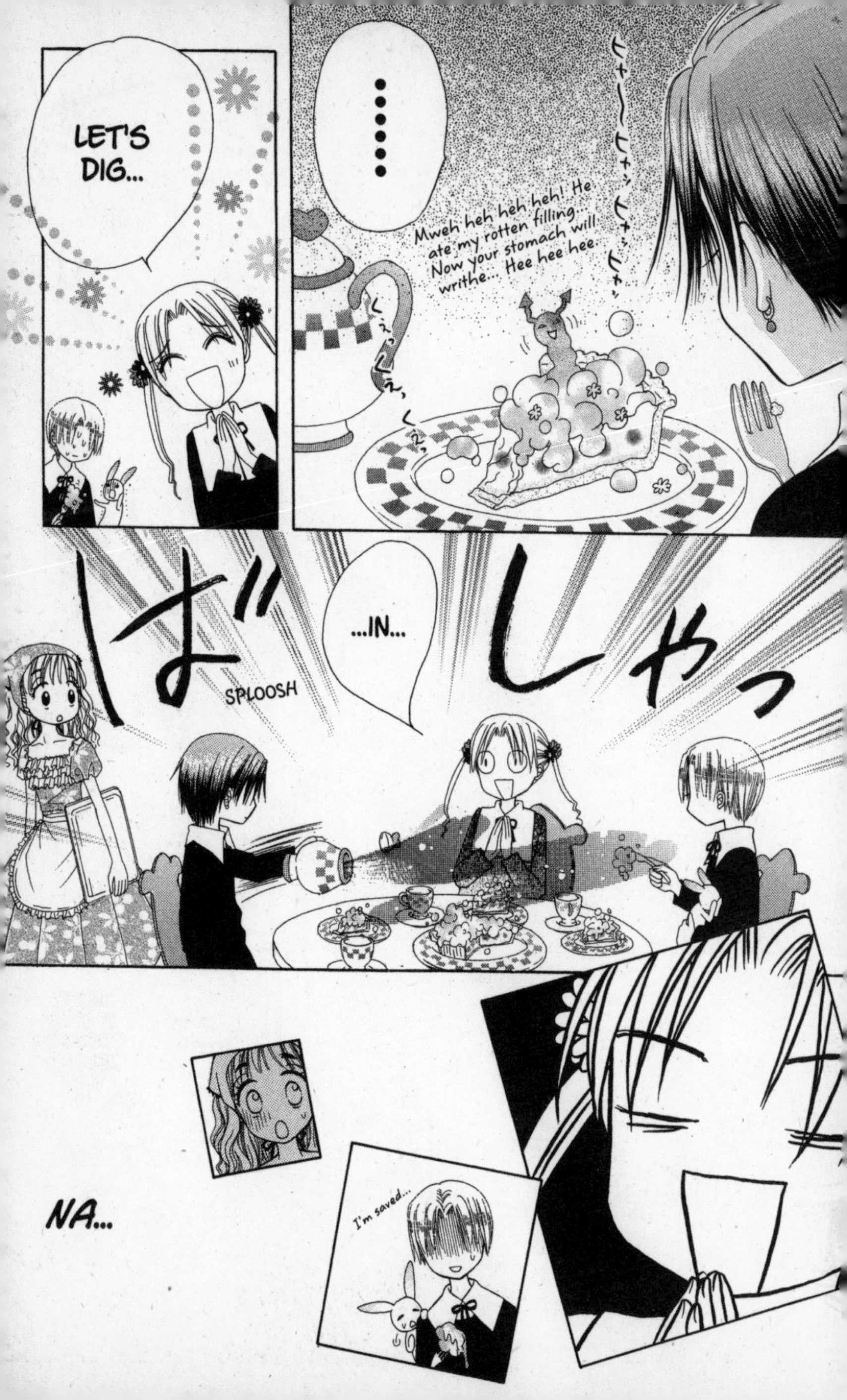
•••••
Mweh heh heh heh! He ate my rotten filling... Now your stomach will writhe... Hee hee hee.
LET'S DIG...
...IN...
SPLOOSH
I'm saved...
NA...

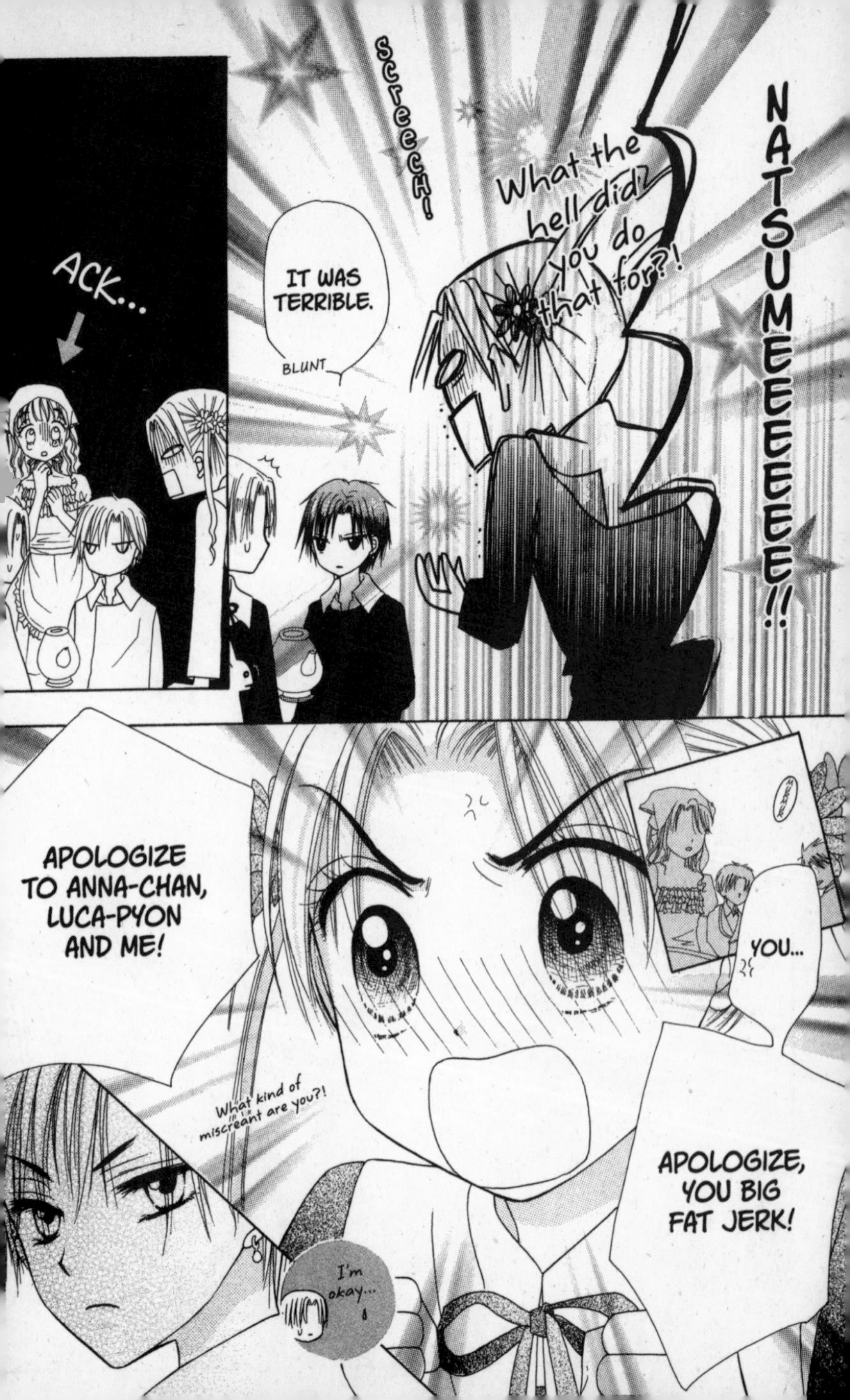
NATSUMEEEEEEE!!
What the hell did you do that for?!
SCREECH!
IT WAS TERRIBLE.
BLUNT
ACK...
YOU...
APOLOGIZE, YOU BIG FAT JERK!
APOLOGIZE TO ANNA-CHAN, LUCA-PYON AND ME!
What kind of miscreant are you?!
I'm okay...

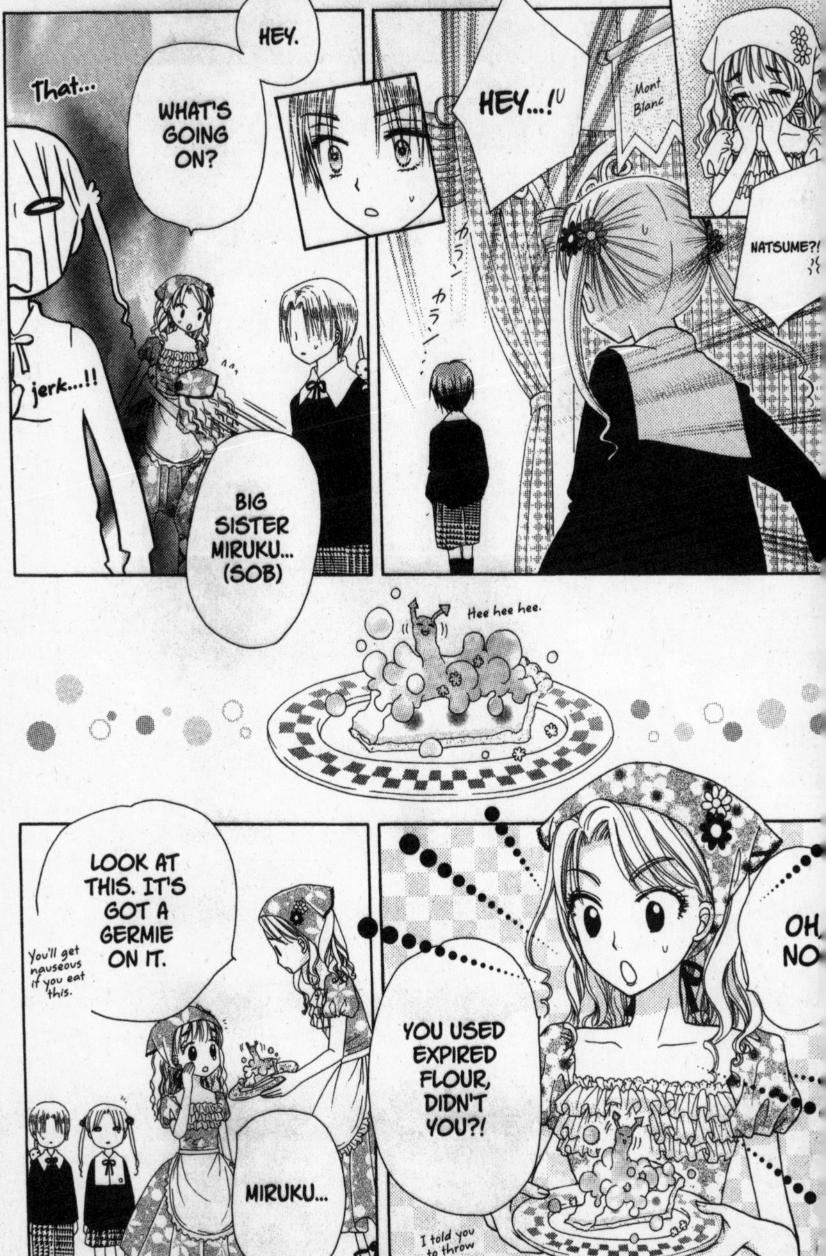

NATSUME?!
HEY...!
Mont Blanc
HEY.
WHAT'S GOING ON?
That...
jerk...!!
BIG SISTER MIRUKU... (SOB)
Hee hee hee.
OH, NO
YOU USED EXPIRED FLOUR, DIDN'T YOU?!
I told you to throw it away.
LOOK AT THIS. IT'S GOT A GERMIE ON IT.
You'll get nauseous if you eat this.
MIRUKU...

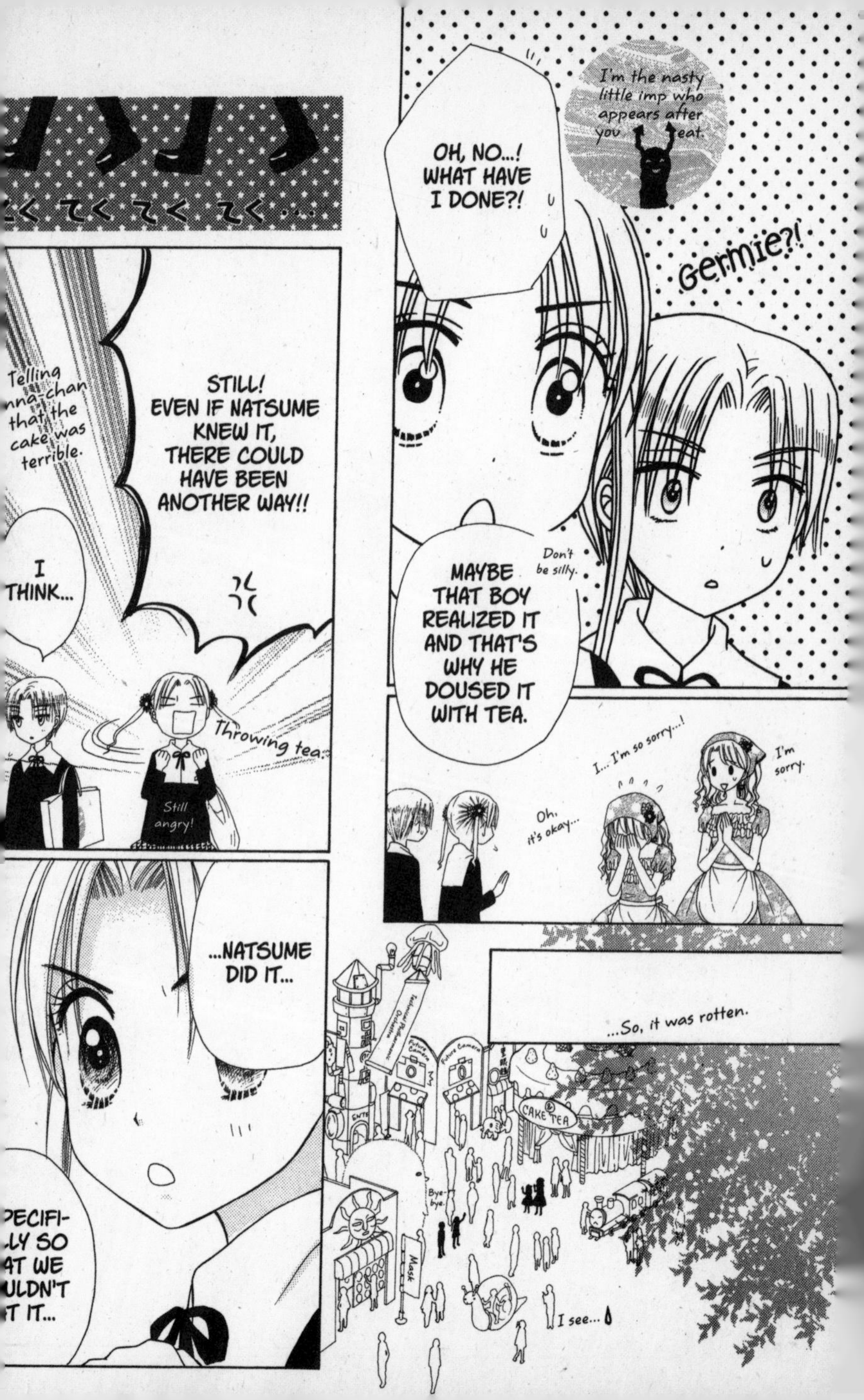

OH, NO...! WHAT HAVE I DONE?!
I'm the nasty little imp who appears after you eat.
Germie?!
Don't be silly.
MAYBE THAT BOY REALIZED IT AND THAT'S WHY HE DOUSED IT WITH TEA.
I'm sorry.
I... I'm so sorry...!
Oh, it's okay...
...So, it was rotten.
CAKE TEA
Future Camera
Future Camera
Bye-bye.
Mask
I see...
く てく てく てく...
STILL! EVEN IF NATSUME KNEW IT, THERE COULD HAVE BEEN ANOTHER WAY!!
Telling nna-chan that the cake was terrible.
I THINK...
Throwing tea.
Still angry!
...NATSUME DID IT...
PECIFI- LLY SO AT WE ULDN'T T IT...

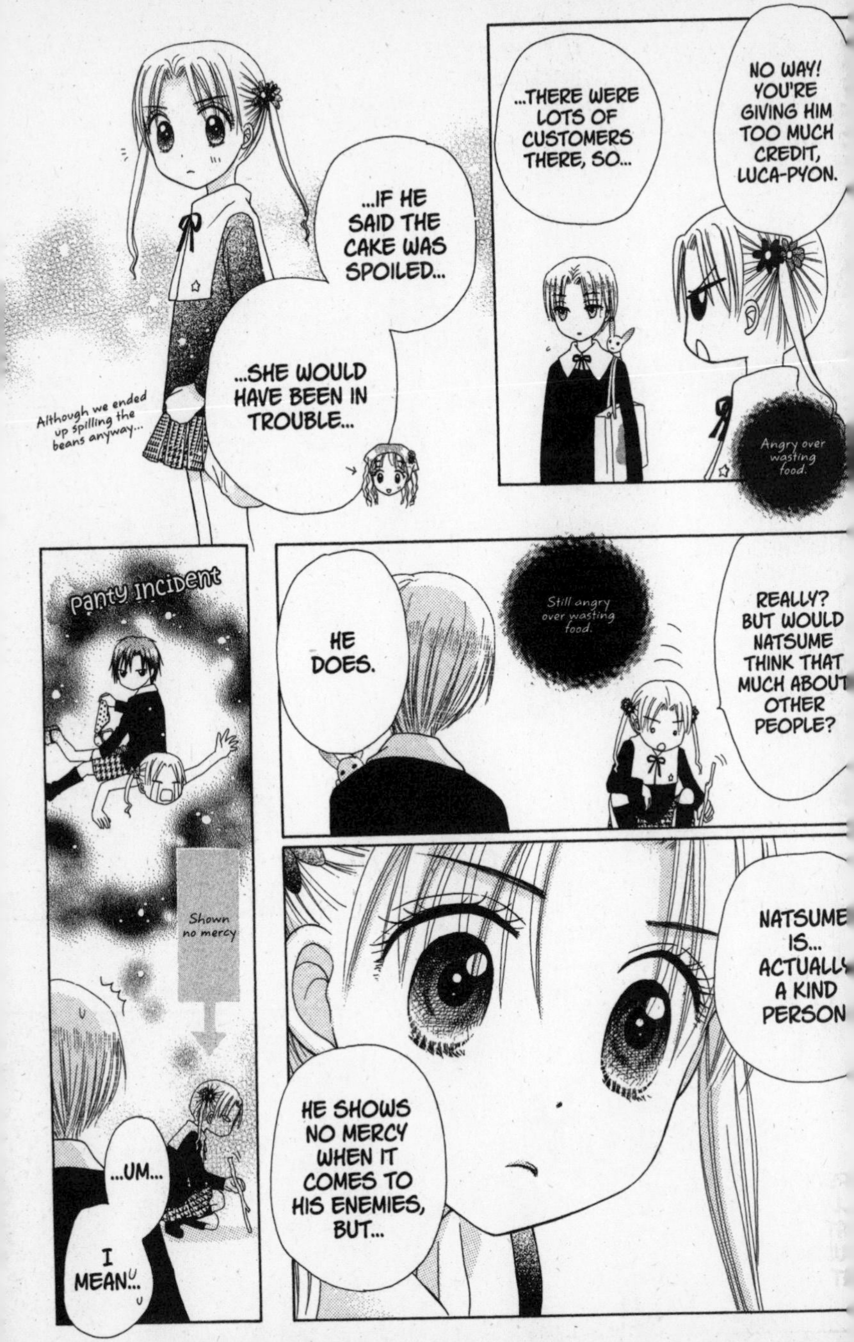
NO WAY! YOU'RE GIVING HIM TOO MUCH CREDIT, LUCA-PYON.
...THERE WERE LOTS OF CUSTOMERS THERE, SO...
Angry over wasting food.
...IF HE SAID THE CAKE WAS SPOILED...
...SHE WOULD HAVE BEEN IN TROUBLE...
Although we ended up spilling the beans anyway...
REALLY? BUT WOULD NATSUME THINK THAT MUCH ABOUT OTHER PEOPLE?
Still angry over wasting food.
HE DOES.
NATSUME IS... ACTUALLY A KIND PERSON
HE SHOWS NO MERCY WHEN IT COMES TO HIS ENEMIES, BUT...
Panty Incident
Shown no mercy
...UM...
I MEAN...

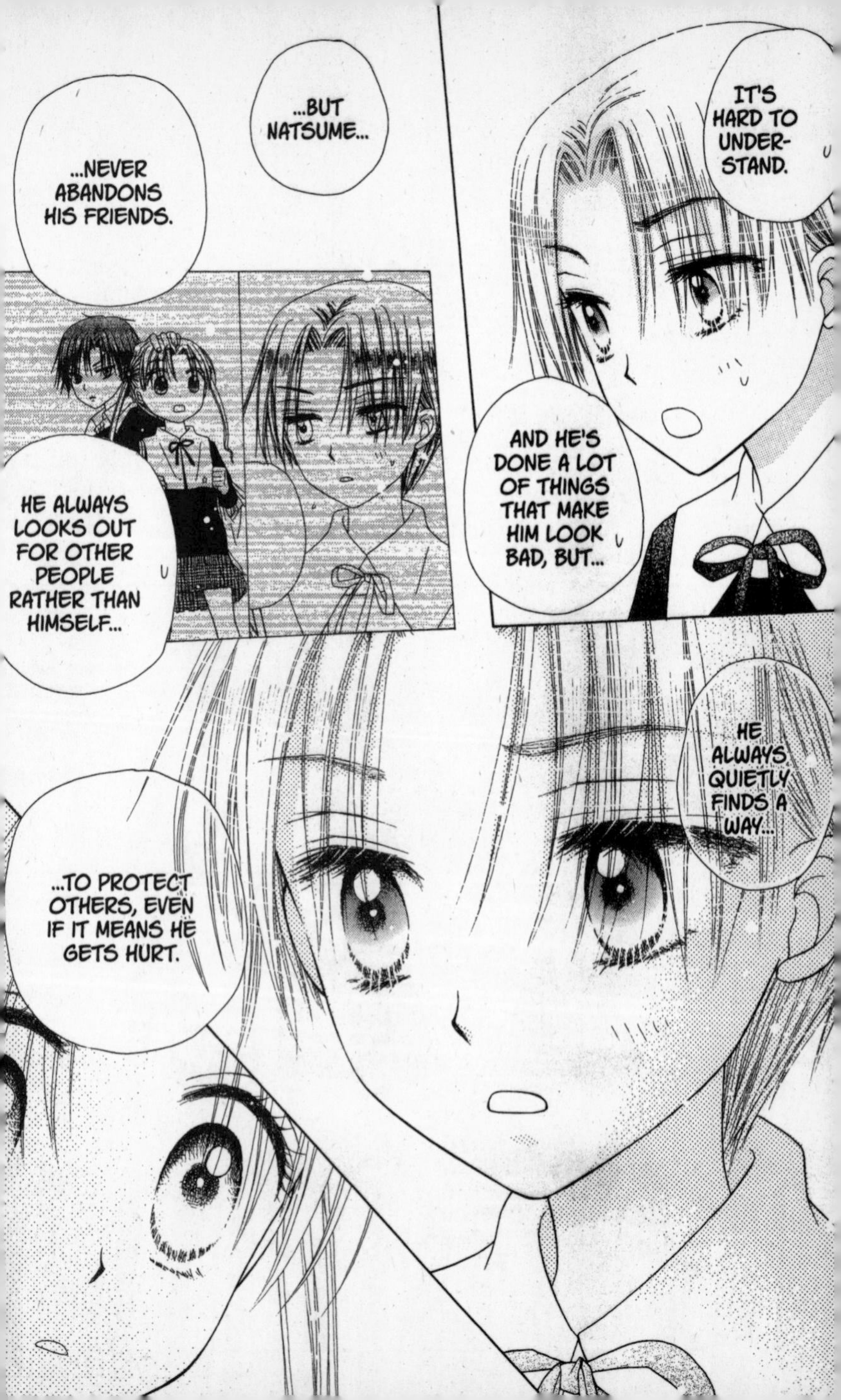
IT'S HARD TO UNDER-STAND.
AND HE'S DONE A LOT OF THINGS THAT MAKE HIM LOOK BAD, BUT...
...BUT NATSUME...
...NEVER ABANDONS HIS FRIENDS.
HE ALWAYS LOOKS OUT FOR OTHER PEOPLE RATHER THAN HIMSELF...
HE ALWAYS QUIETLY FINDS A WAY...
...TO PROTECT OTHERS, EVEN IF IT MEANS HE GETS HURT.

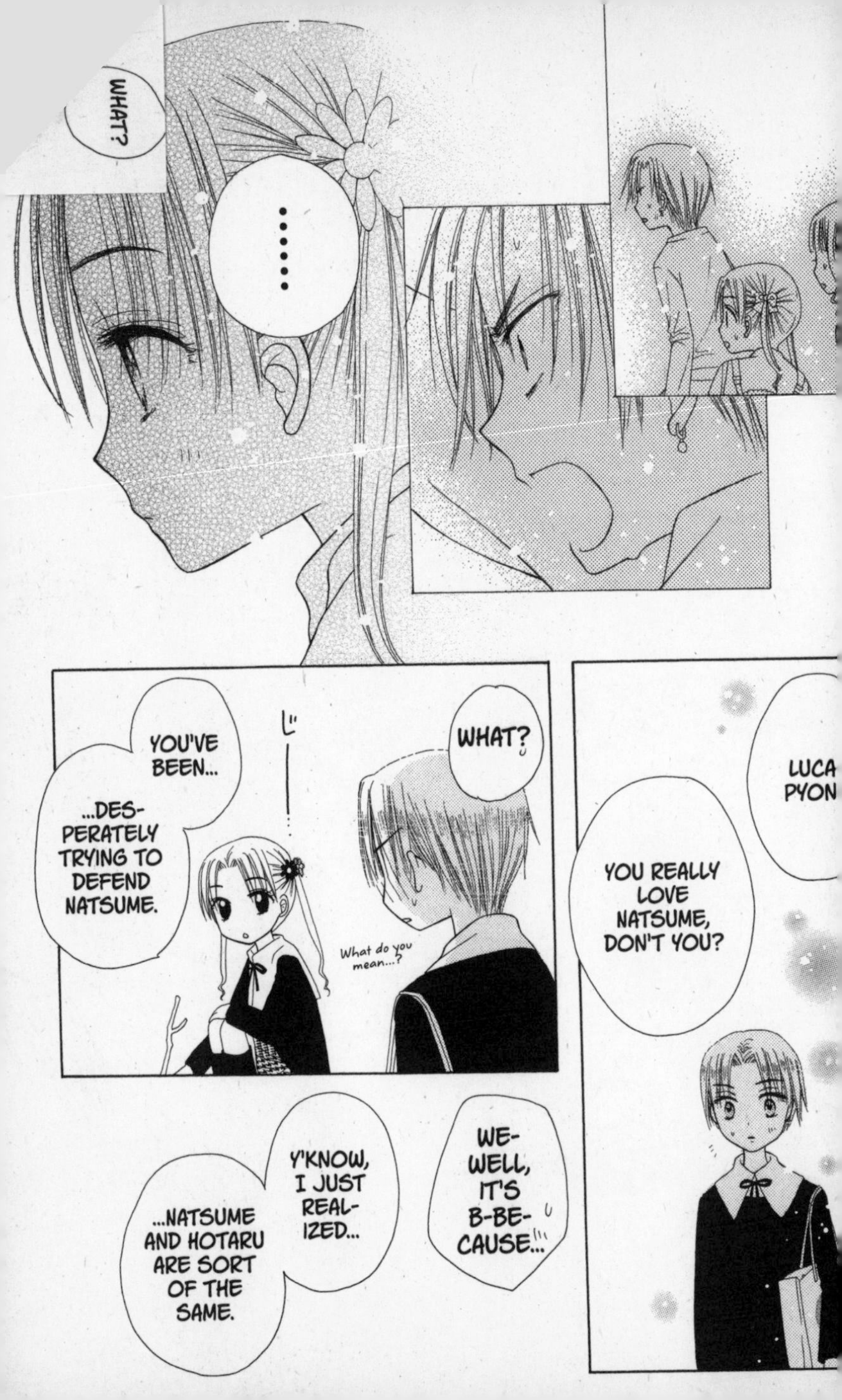
......
WHAT?
LUCA PYON
YOU REALLY LOVE NATSUME, DON'T YOU?
WHAT?
What do you mean...?
YOU'VE BEEN...
...DES-PERATELY TRYING TO DEFEND NATSUME.
WE-WELL, IT'S B-BE-CAUSE...
Y'KNOW, I JUST REAL-IZED...
...NATSUME AND HOTARU ARE SORT OF THE SAME.

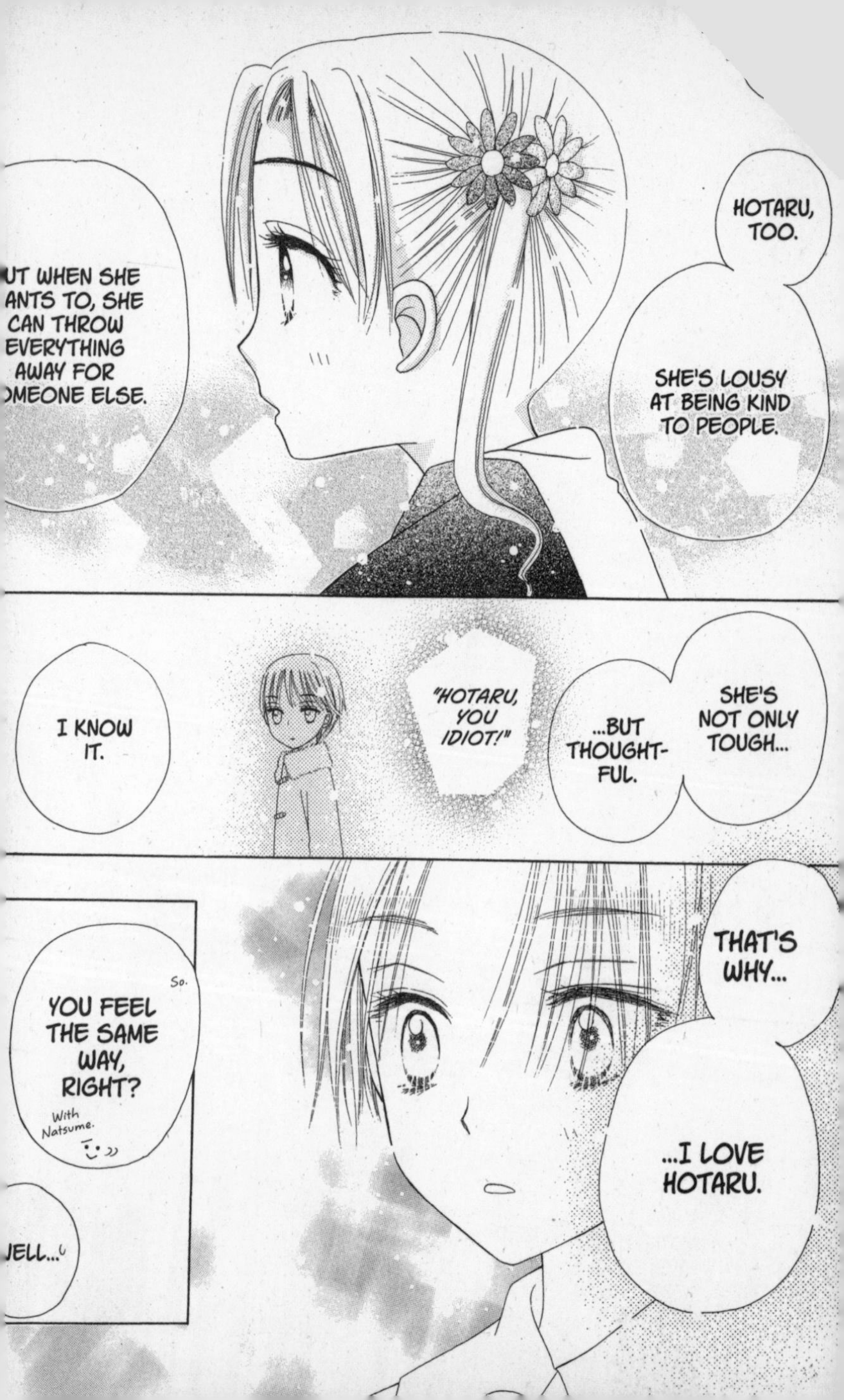
HOTARU, TOO.
SHE'S LOUSY AT BEING KIND TO PEOPLE.
UT WHEN SHE ANTS TO, SHE CAN THROW EVERYTHING AWAY FOR OMEONE ELSE.
SHE'S NOT ONLY TOUGH...
...BUT THOUGHT-FUL.
"HOTARU, YOU IDIOT!"
I KNOW IT.
THAT'S WHY...
...I LOVE HOTARU.
So.
YOU FEEL THE SAME WAY, RIGHT?
With Natsume.
ELL...

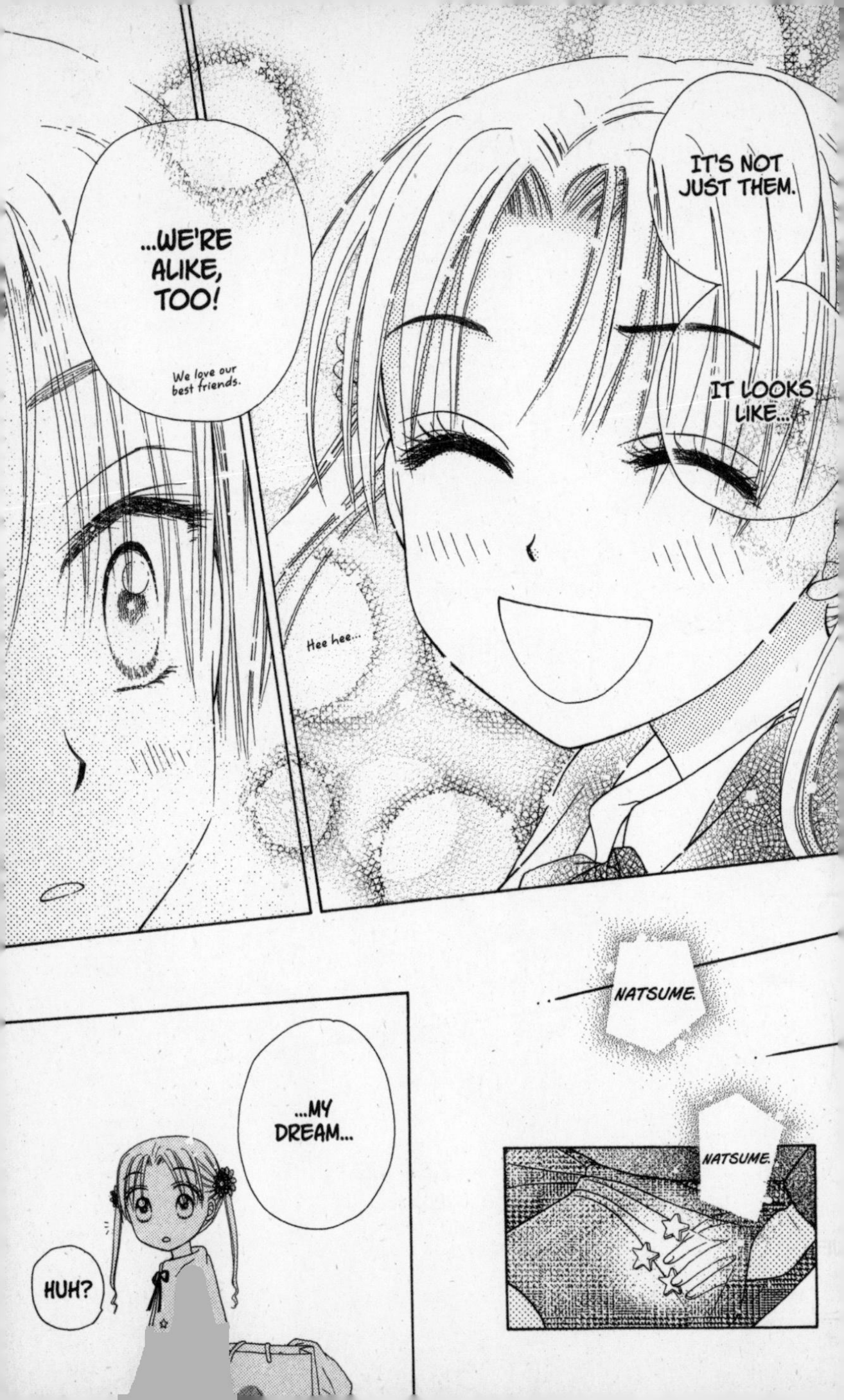
IT'S NOT JUST THEM.
IT LOOKS LIKE...
Hee hee...
...WE'RE ALIKE, TOO!
We love our best friends.
NATSUME.
NATSUME.
...MY DREAM...
HUH?

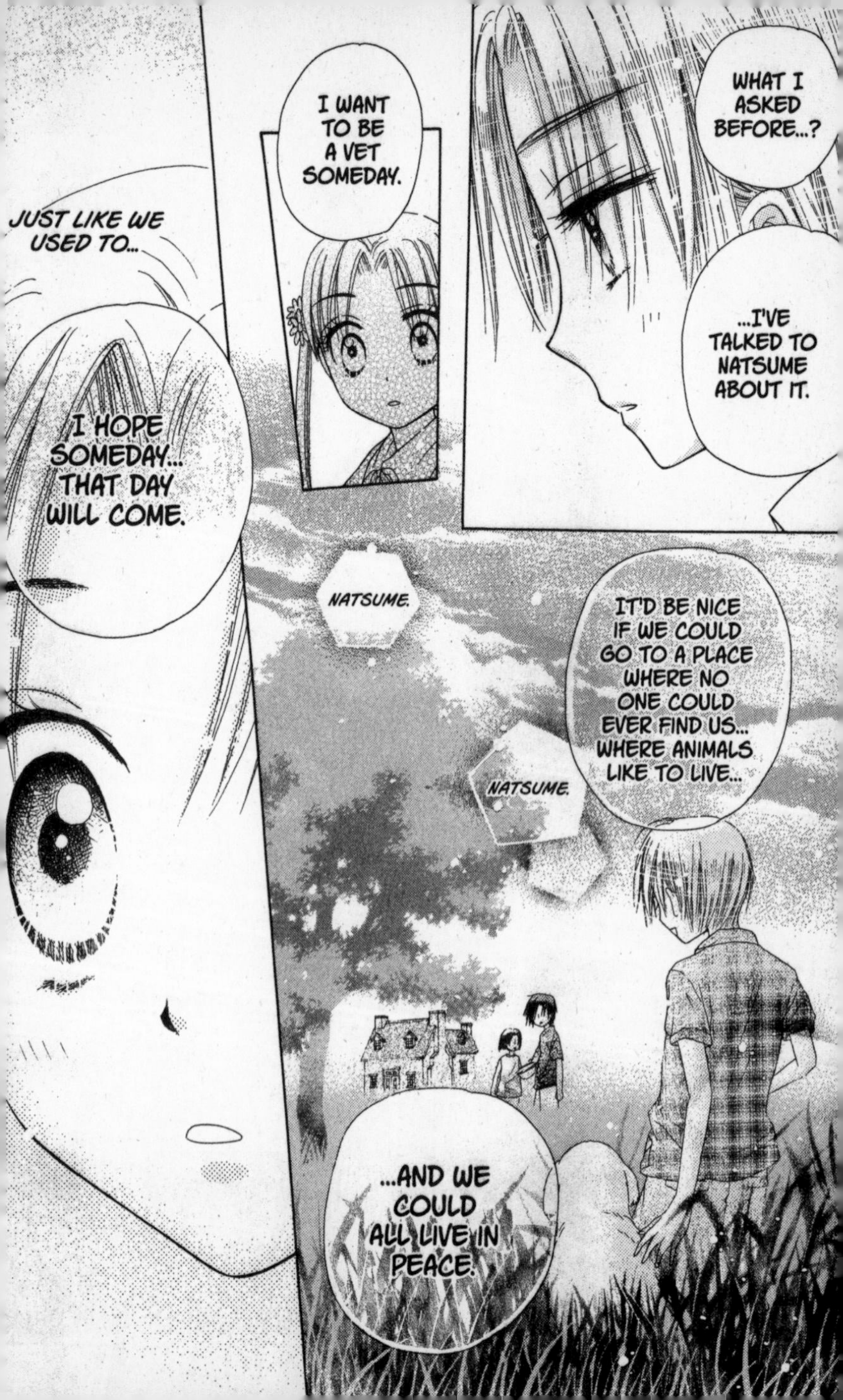
WHAT I ASKED BEFORE...?
...I'VE TALKED TO NATSUME ABOUT IT.
I WANT TO BE A VET SOMEDAY.
NATSUME.
NATSUME.
IT'D BE NICE IF WE COULD GO TO A PLACE WHERE NO ONE COULD EVER FIND US... WHERE ANIMALS LIKE TO LIVE...
...AND WE COULD ALL LIVE IN PEACE.
JUST LIKE WE USED TO...
I HOPE SOMEDAY... THAT DAY WILL COME.

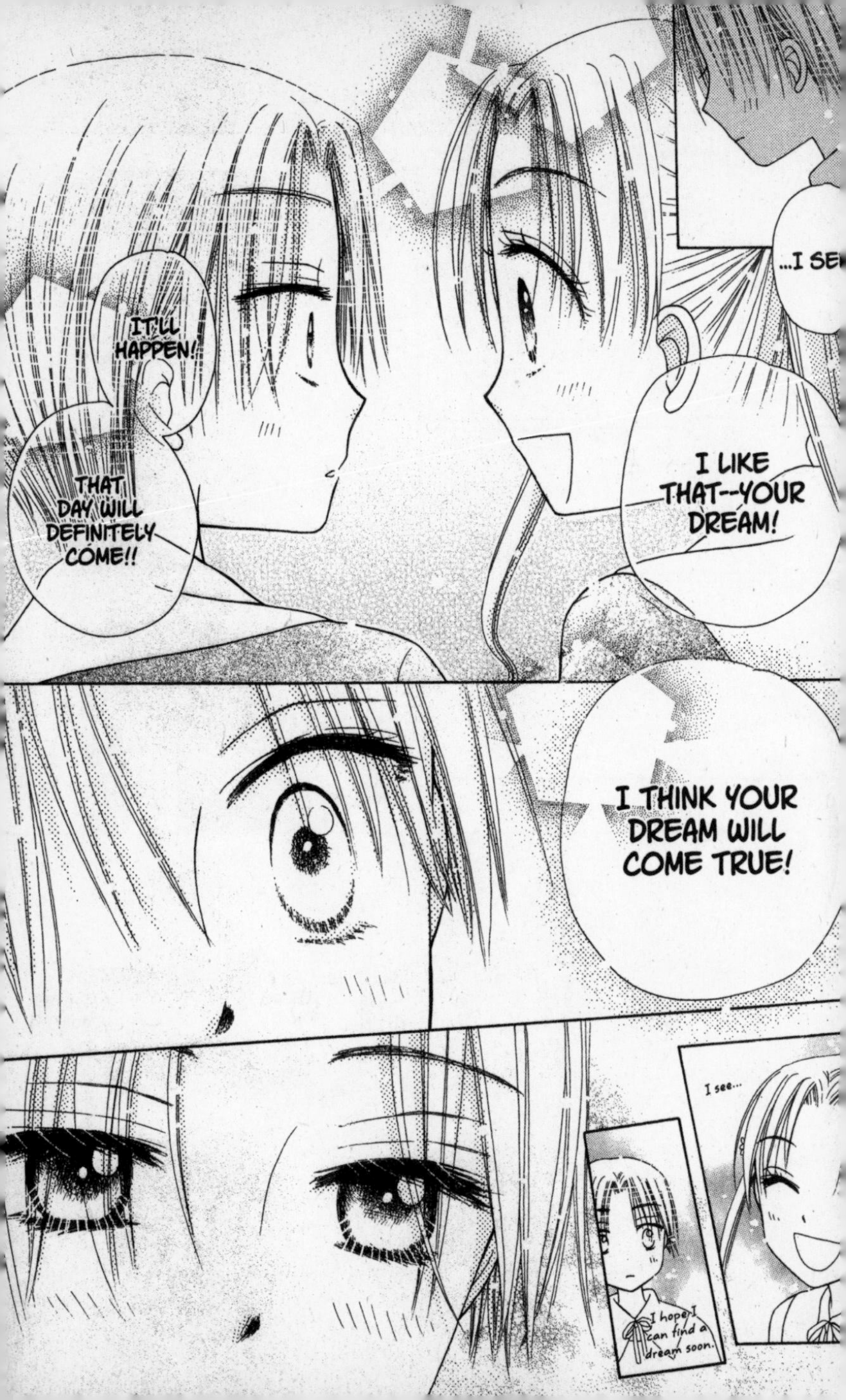
...I SE
I LIKE THAT--YOUR DREAM!
IT'LL HAPPEN!
THAT DAY WILL DEFINITELY COME!!
I THINK YOUR DREAM WILL COME TRUE!
I see...
I hope I can find a dream soon.

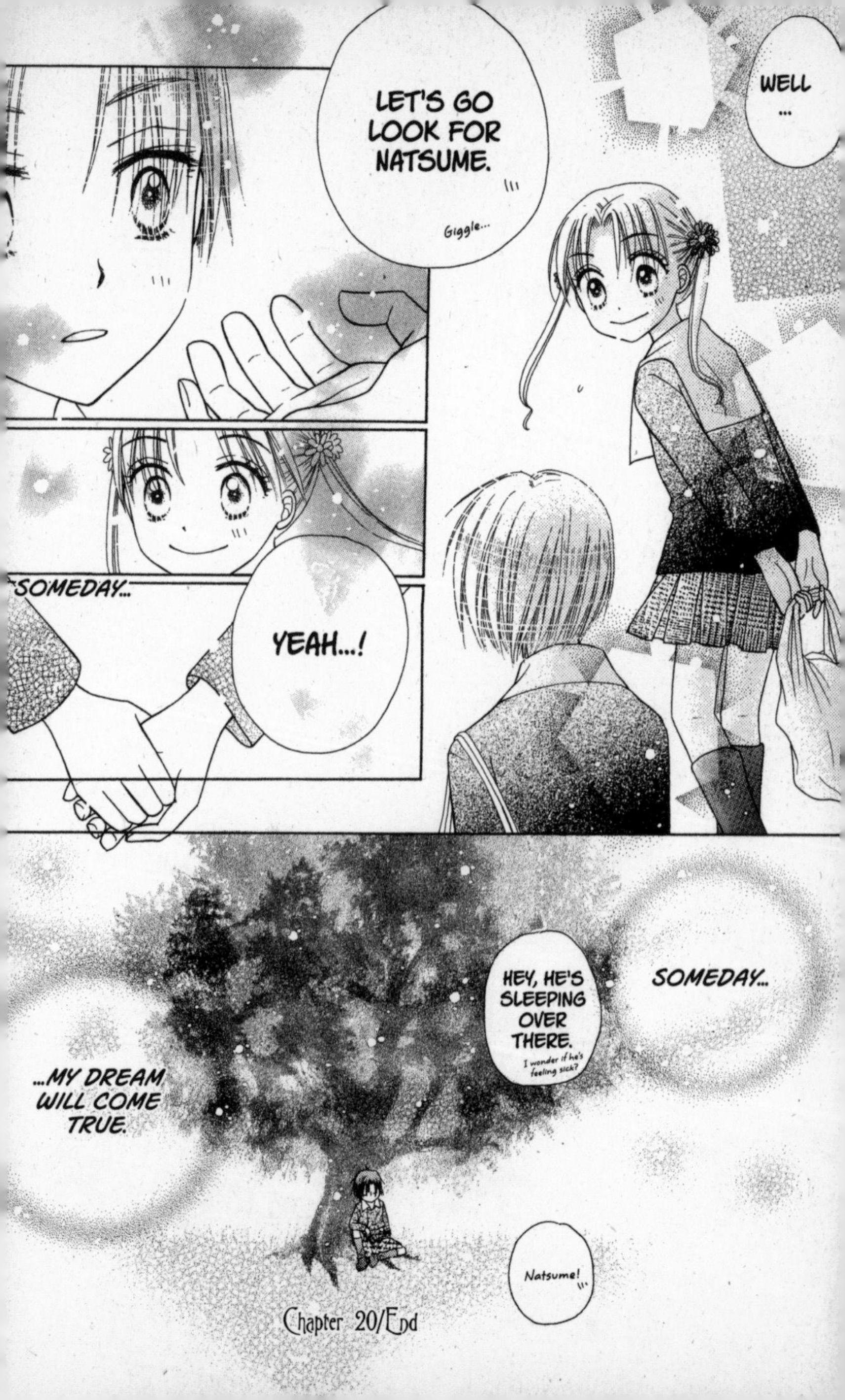
WELL ...
LET'S GO LOOK FOR NATSUME.
Giggle...
SOMEDAY...
YEAH...!
SOMEDAY...
HEY, HE'S SLEEPING OVER THERE.
I wonder if he's feeling sick?
...MY DREAM WILL COME TRUE.
Natsume!
Chapter 20/End

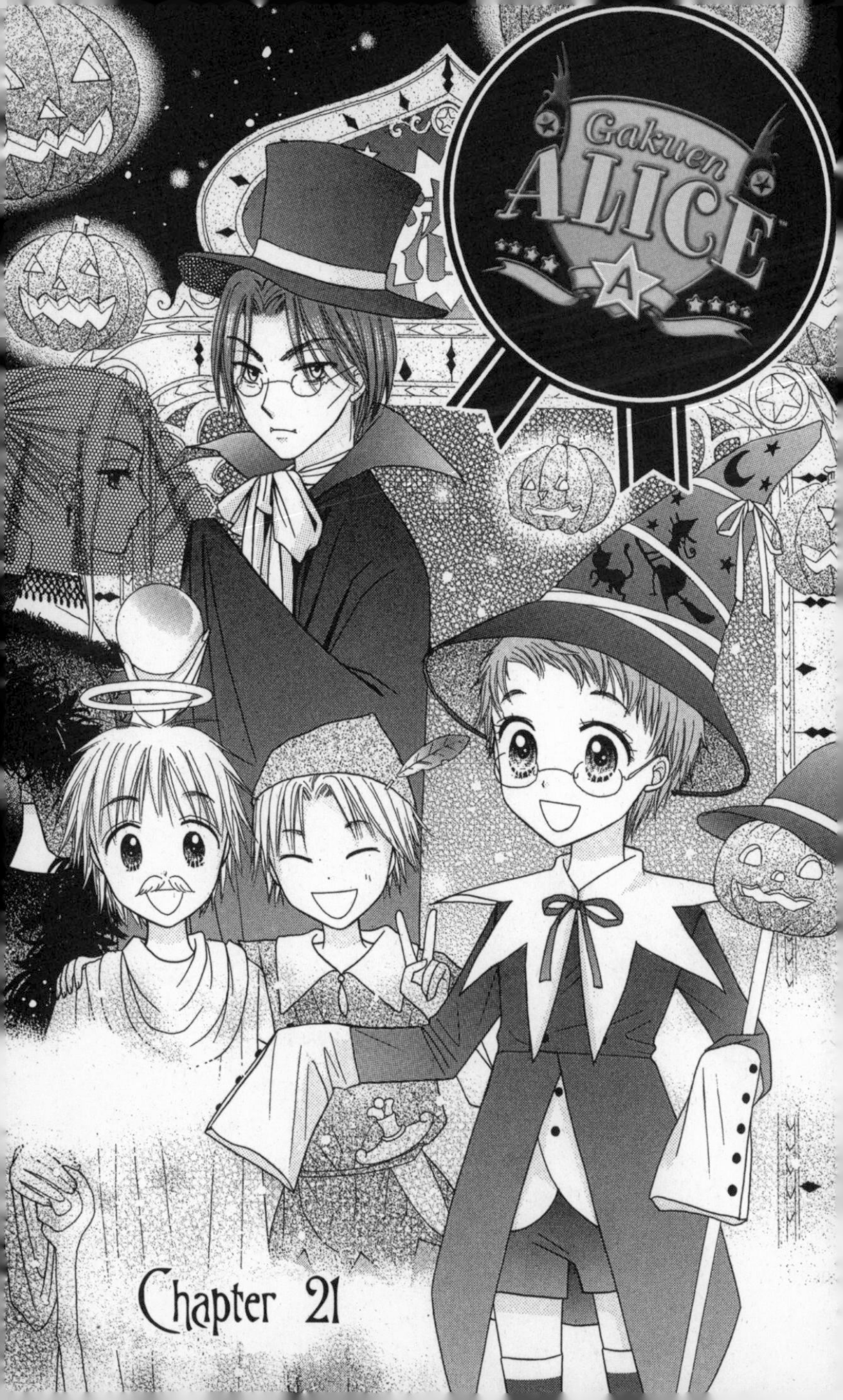
Gakuen ALICE
Chapter 21

THANKS

THANK YOU FOR READING THIS FAR.

SPECIAL THANKS

TOMOE-SAN, TAKANO-SAN, OKABE-SAN, MY FAMILY, FRIENDS, EDITOR
AND
YOU!

SEE YOU AGAIN

I hope to continue making manga that you enjoy.

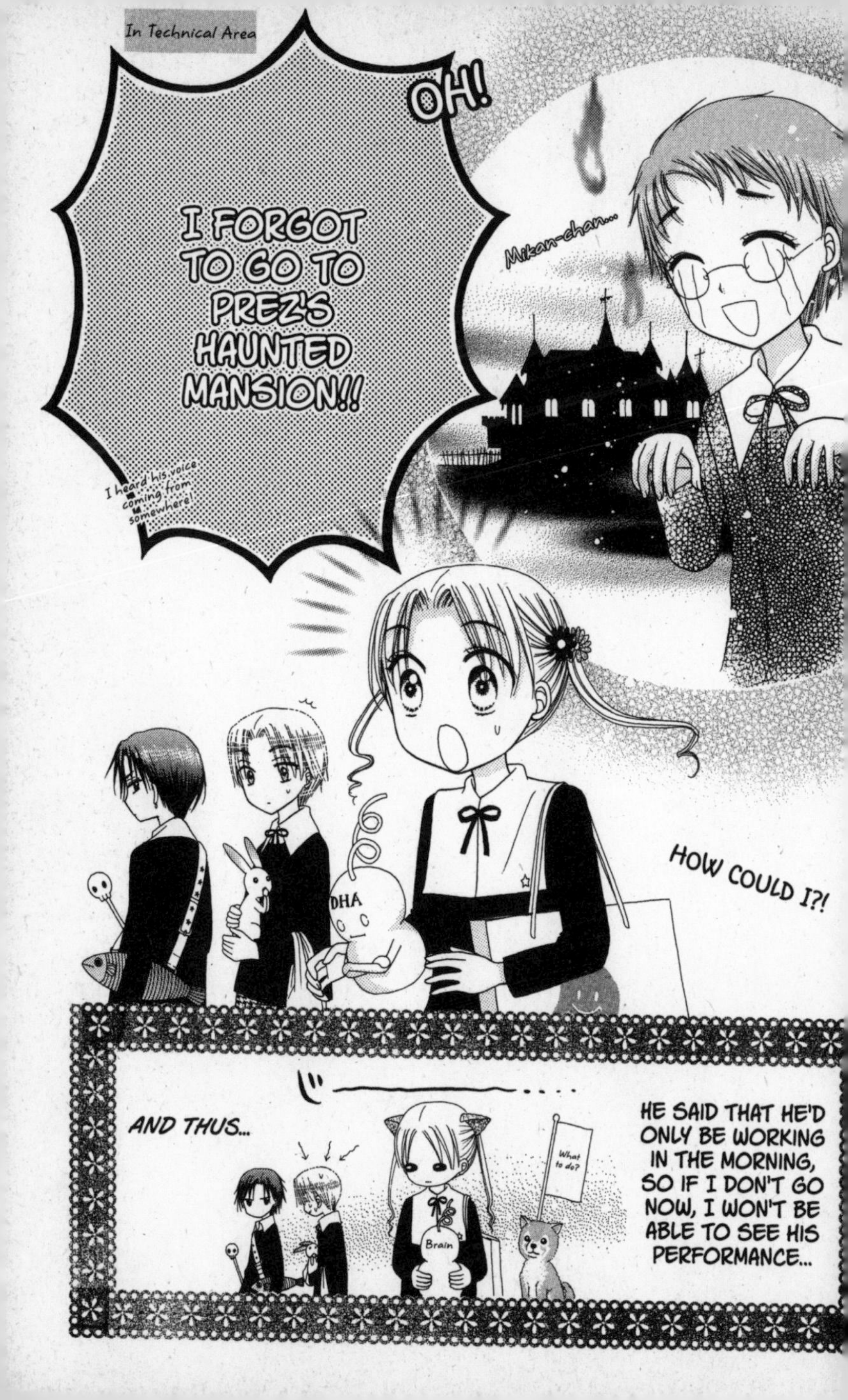
In Technical Area
OH!
Mikan-chan...
I FORGOT TO GO TO PREZ'S HAUNTED MANSION!!
I heard his voice coming from somewhere!
HOW COULD I?!
DHA
HE SAID THAT HE'D ONLY BE WORKING IN THE MORNING, SO IF I DON'T GO NOW, I WON'T BE ABLE TO SEE HIS PERFORMANCE...
じ―――....
What to do?
Brain
AND THUS...

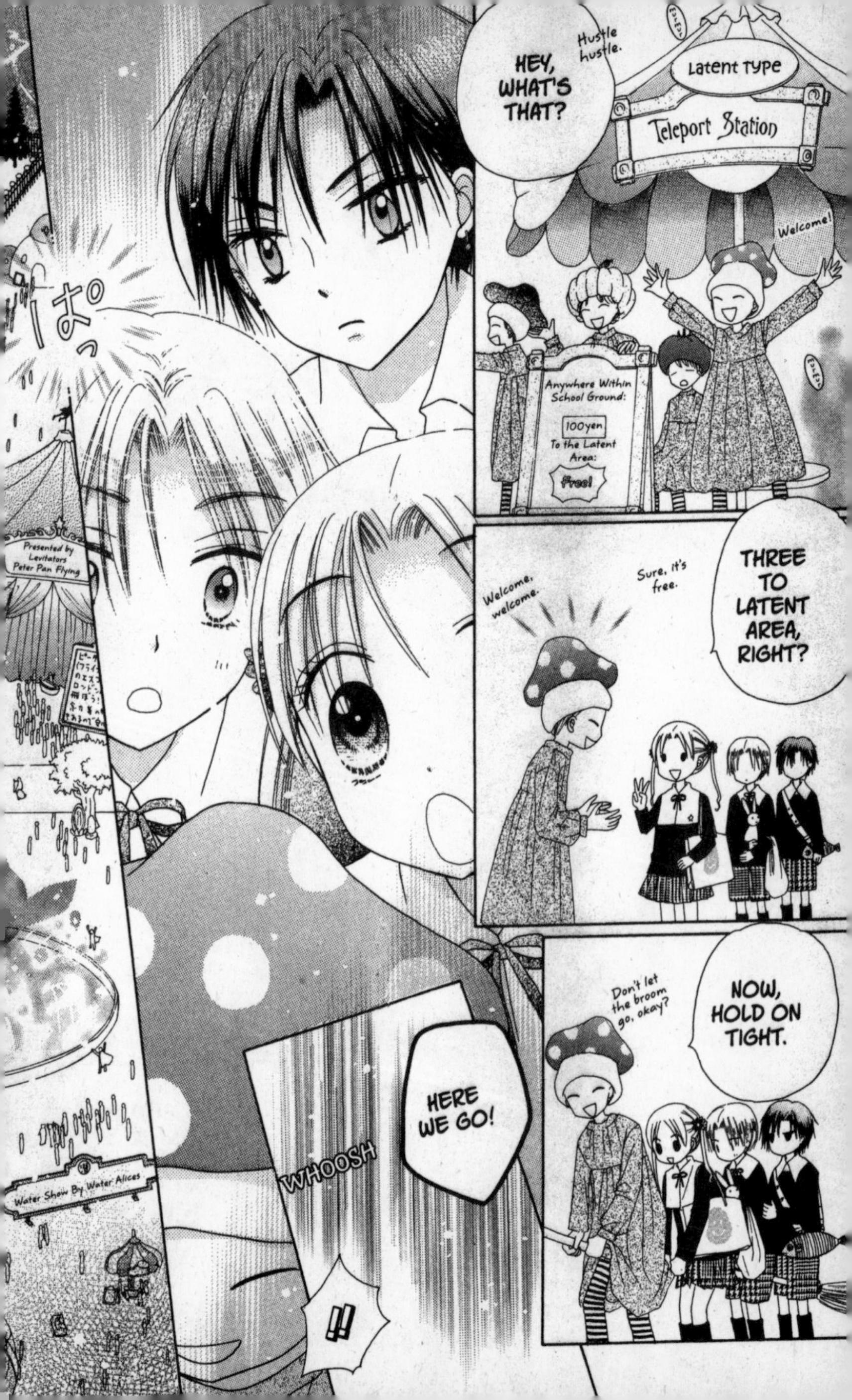
HEY, WHAT'S THAT?
Hustle hustle.
Latent Type
Teleport Station
Welcome!
Anywhere Within School Ground: 100yen To the Latent Area: Free!
THREE TO LATENT AREA, RIGHT?
Sure, it's free.
Welcome, welcome.
NOW, HOLD ON TIGHT.
Don't let the broom go, okay?
ぱっ
Presented by Levitators Peter Pan Flying
HERE WE GO!
WHOOSH
Water Show By Water Alices
!!

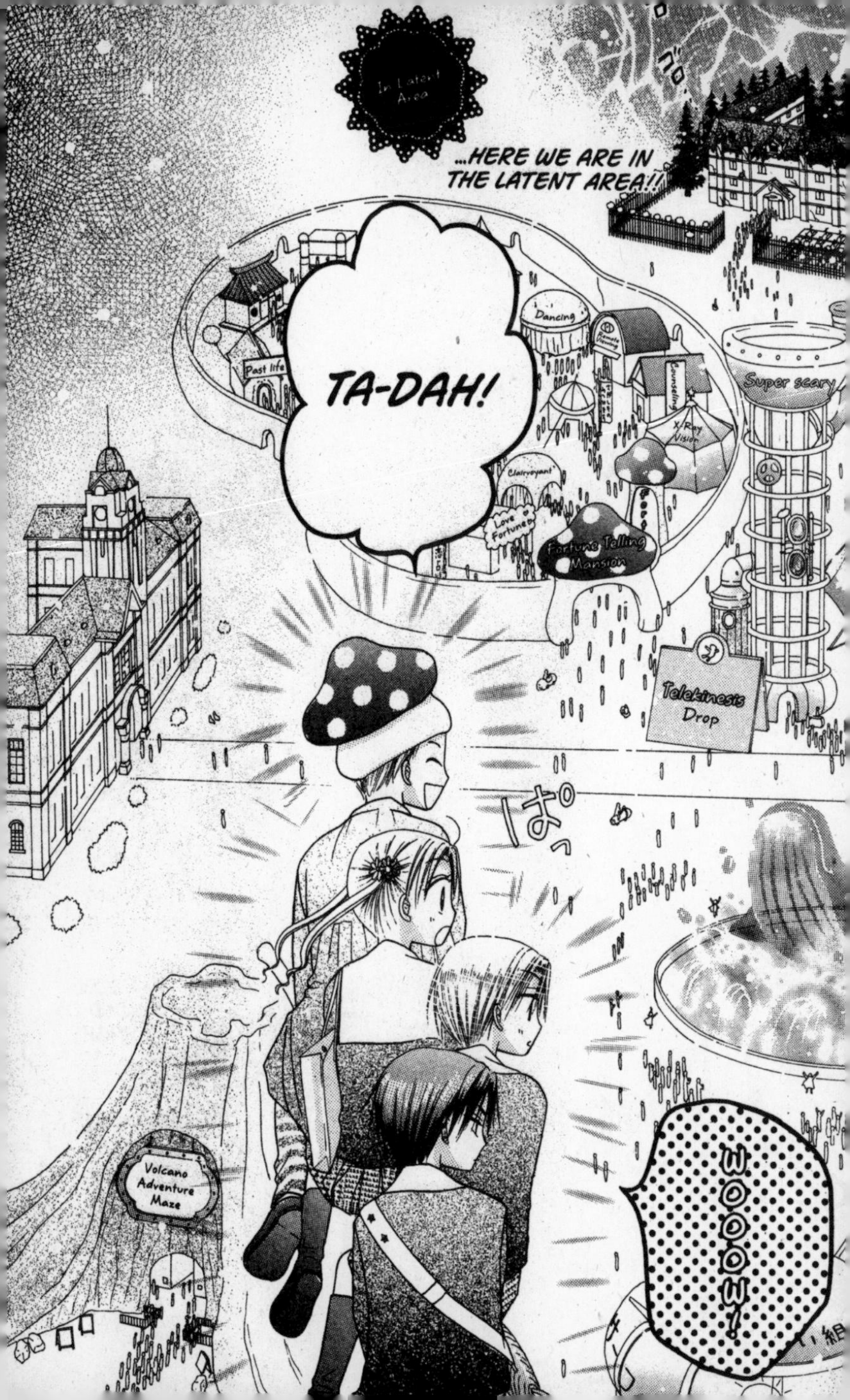ゴロ…
In Latent Area
...HERE WE ARE IN THE LATENT AREA!!
Super scary
Counseling
X-Ray Vision
Dancing
Past life
TA-DAH!
Clairvoyant
Love Fortunes
Fortune Telling Mansion
Telekinesis Drop
ぱっ
WOOOOW!
Volcano Adventure Maze

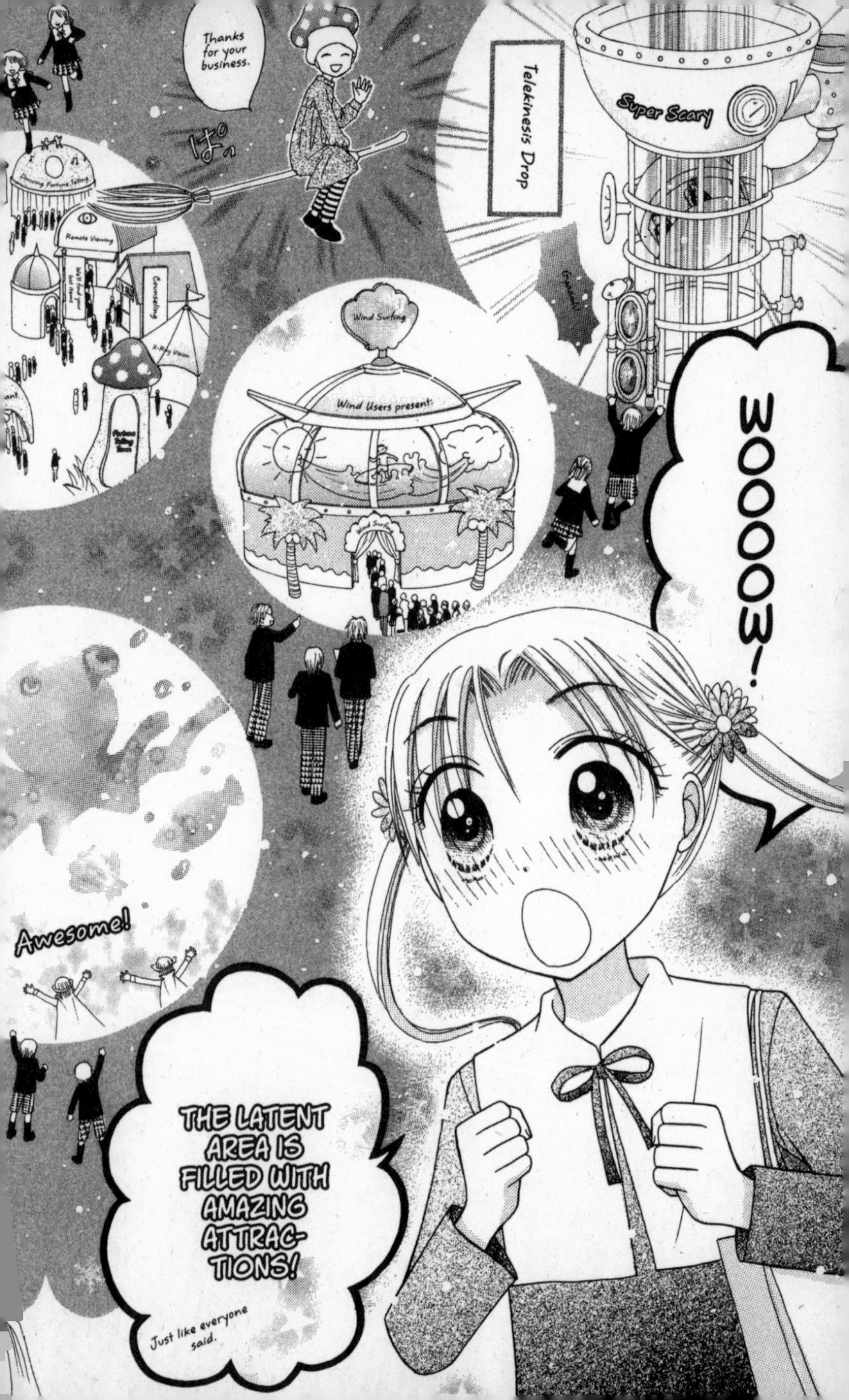
Telekinesis Drop
Super Scary
WOOOOW!
Thanks for your business.
はっ
Dowsing Fortune Telling
Remote Viewing
We'll find your lost items
Counseling
X-Ray Vision
Wind Surfing
Wind Users present:
Awesome!
THE LATENT AREA IS FILLED WITH AMAZING ATTRAC-TIONS!
Just like everyone said.

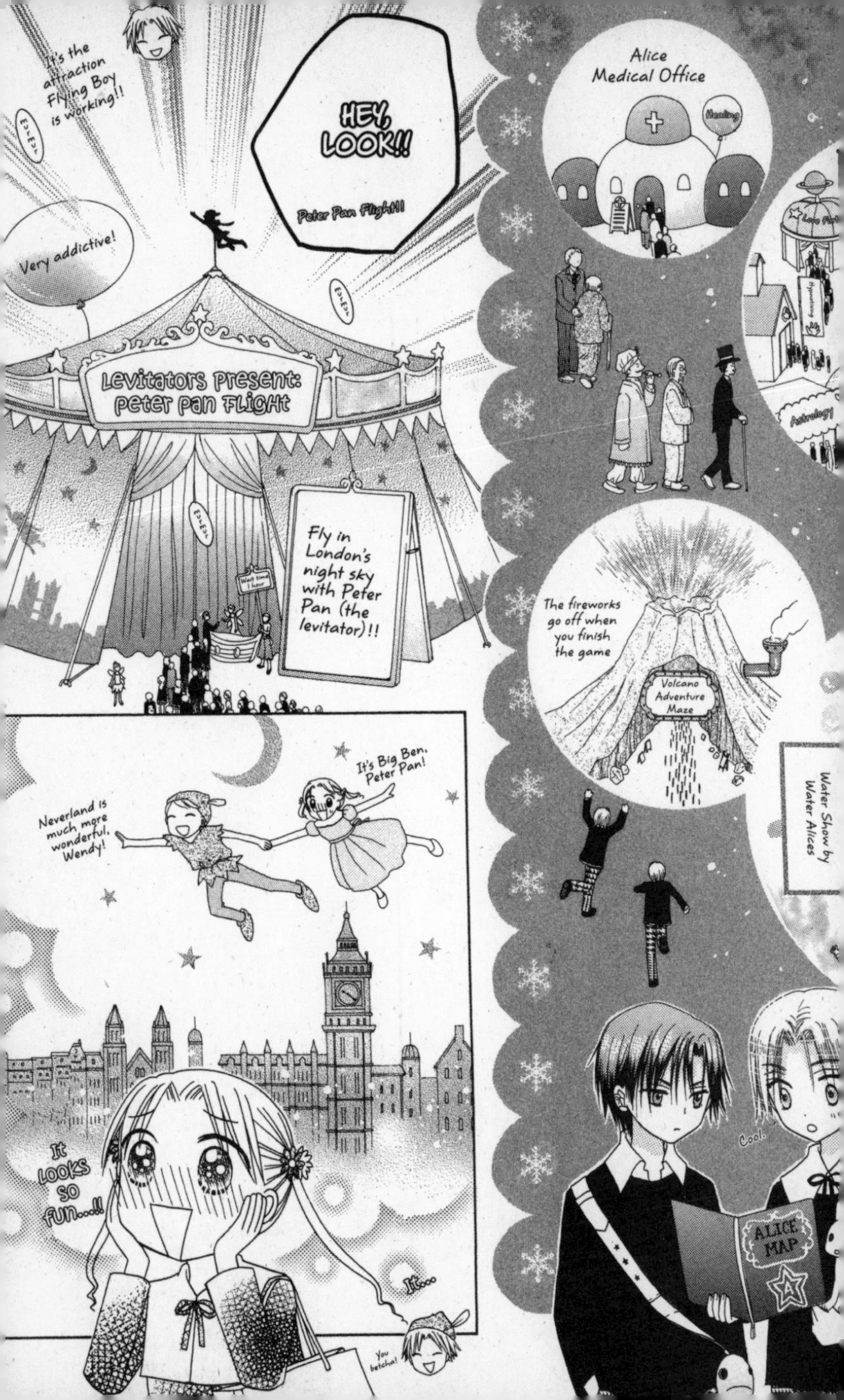
Alice Medical Office
Healing
Hypnotism
Astrology
The fireworks go off when you finish the game
Volcano Adventure Maze
Water Show by Water Alices
Cool.
ALICE MAP
HEY, LOOK!!
Peter Pan Flight!!
It's the attraction Flying Boy is working!!
Very addictive!
Levitators Present: Peter Pan Flight
Fly in London's night sky with Peter Pan (the levitator)!!
Wait time 1 hour
It's Big Ben, Peter Pan!
Neverland is much more wonderful, Wendy!
It looks so fun...!!
It...
You betcha!

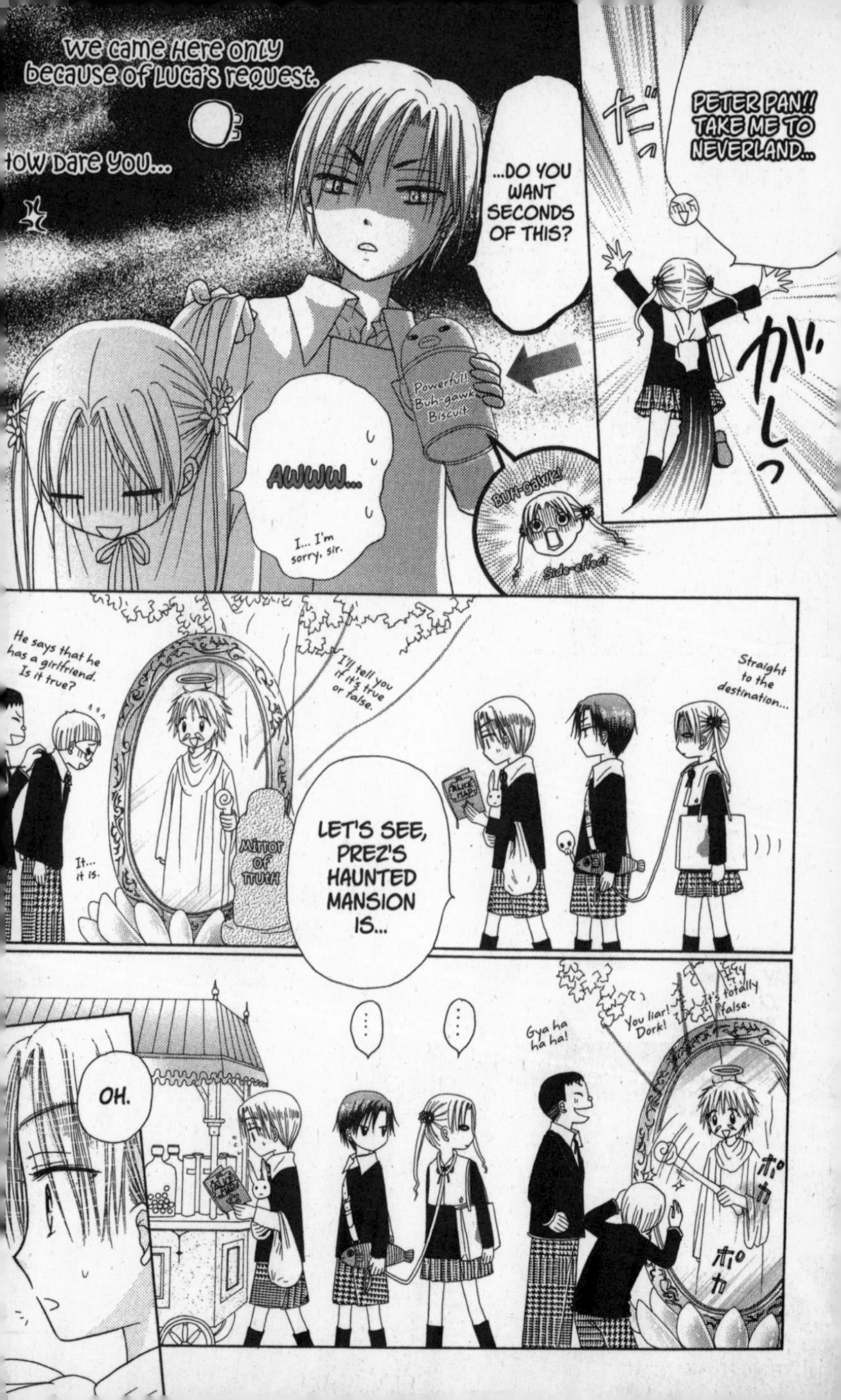
だっ
PETER PAN!! TAKE ME TO NEVERLAND...
がしっ
We came here only because of Luca's request.
How dare you...
...DO YOU WANT SECONDS OF THIS?
Powerful!! Buh-gawk Biscuit
AWWW...
I... I'm sorry, sir.
BUH-GAWK!
Side-effect
Straight to the destination...
LET'S SEE, PREZ'S HAUNTED MANSION IS...
I'll tell you if it's true or false.
He says that he has a girlfriend. Is it true?
It... it is.
Mirror of Truth
It's totally false.
You liar! Dork!
Gya ha ha ha!
ポカ
ポカ
....
....
OH.

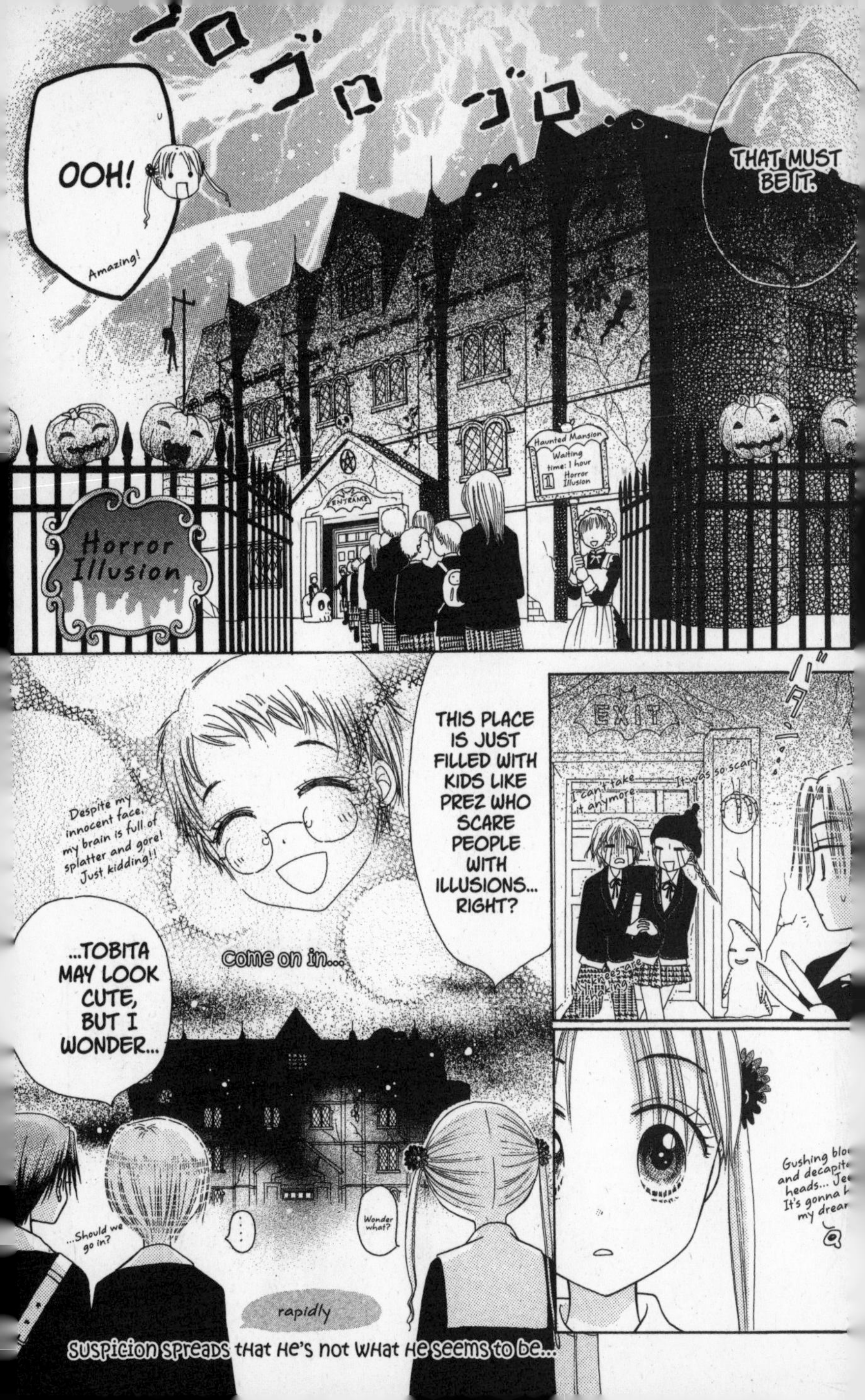
THAT MUST BE IT.
OOH!
Amazing!
Haunted Mansion
Waiting time: 1 hour
1 Horror Illusion
ENTRANCE
Horror Illusion
EXIT
It was so scary
I can't take it anymore
My knees are shaking
Gushing bloo and decapite heads... Jee It's gonna h my drear
THIS PLACE IS JUST FILLED WITH KIDS LIKE PREZ WHO SCARE PEOPLE WITH ILLUSIONS... RIGHT?
Despite my innocent face, my brain is full of splatter and gore! Just kidding!!
...TOBITA MAY LOOK CUTE, BUT I WONDER...
come on in...
Wonder what?
...
...Should we go in?
rapidly
suspicion spreads that he's not what he seems to be...

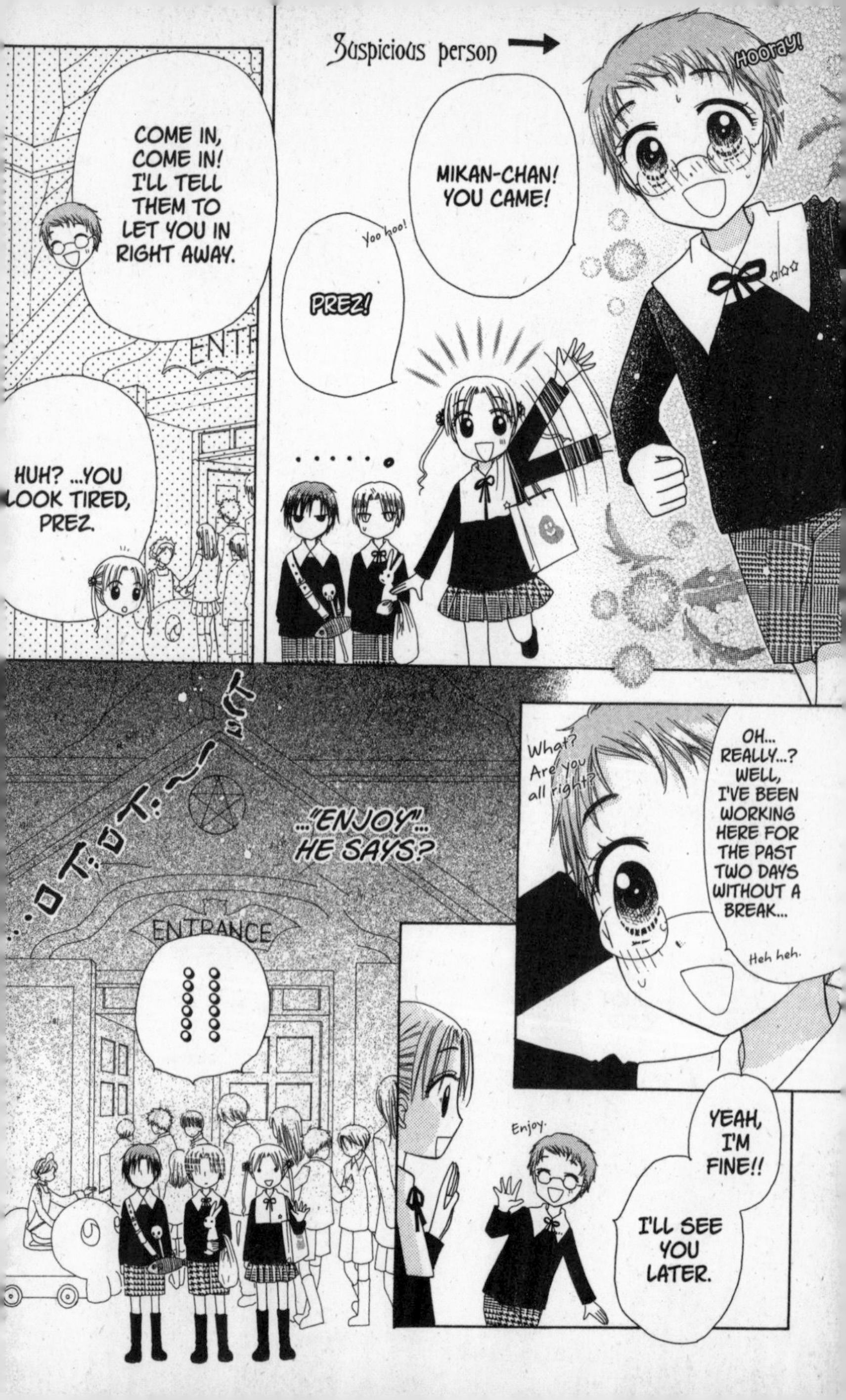

Suspicious person →
HOORAY!
MIKAN-CHAN! YOU CAME!
Yoo hoo!
PREZ!
......
COME IN, COME IN! I'LL TELL THEM TO LET YOU IN RIGHT AWAY.
HUH? ...YOU LOOK TIRED, PREZ.
What? Are you all right?
OH... REALLY...? WELL, I'VE BEEN WORKING HERE FOR THE PAST TWO DAYS WITHOUT A BREAK...
Heh heh.
YEAH, I'M FINE!!
I'LL SEE YOU LATER.
Enjoy.
..."ENJOY"... HE SAYS?
ENTRANCE
....

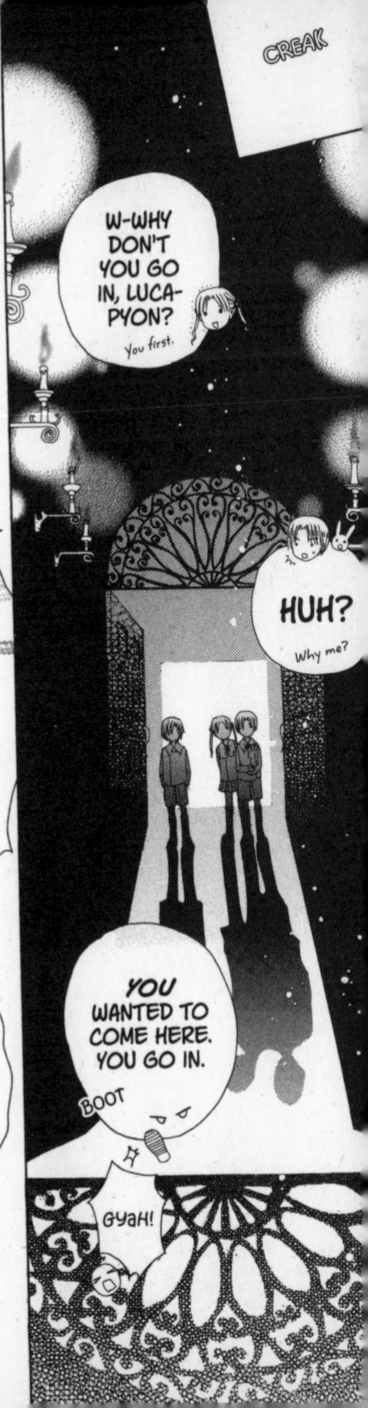
CREAK
W-WHY DON'T YOU GO IN, LUCA-PYON?
You first.
HUH?
Why me?
YOU WANTED TO COME HERE. YOU GO IN.
BOOT
GYaH!

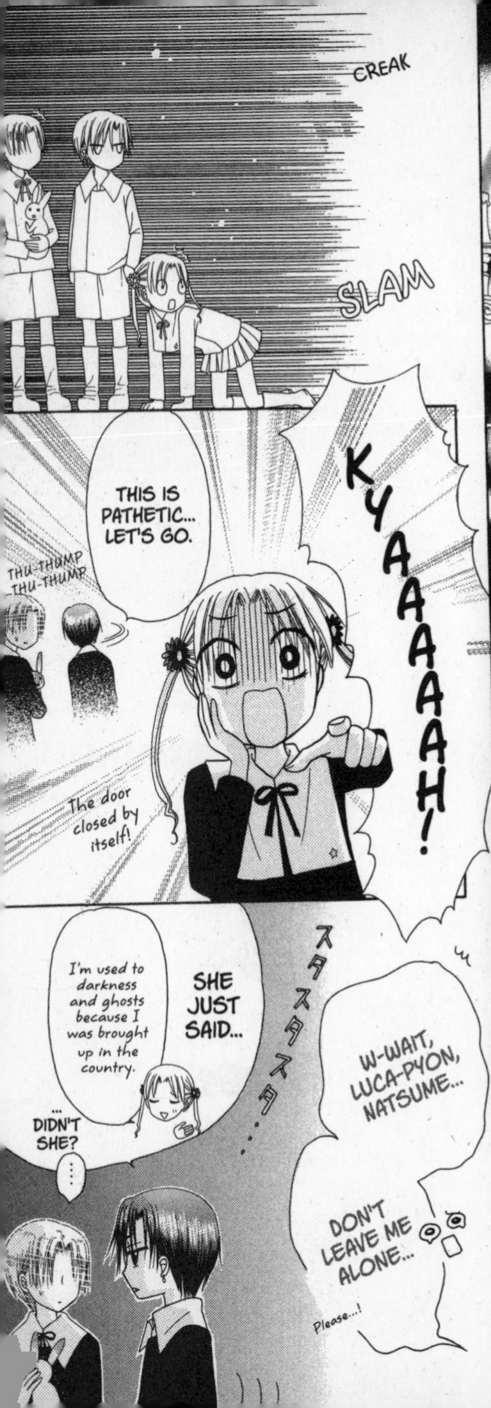
CREAK
SLAM
KYAAAAAAH!
THIS IS PATHETIC... LET'S GO.
THU-THUMP THU-THUMP
The door closed by itself!
W-WAIT, LUCA-PYON, NATSUME...
DON'T LEAVE ME ALONE...
Please...!
スタスタスタ...
SHE JUST SAID...
I'm used to darkness and ghosts because I was brought up in the country.
...DIDN'T SHE?
......

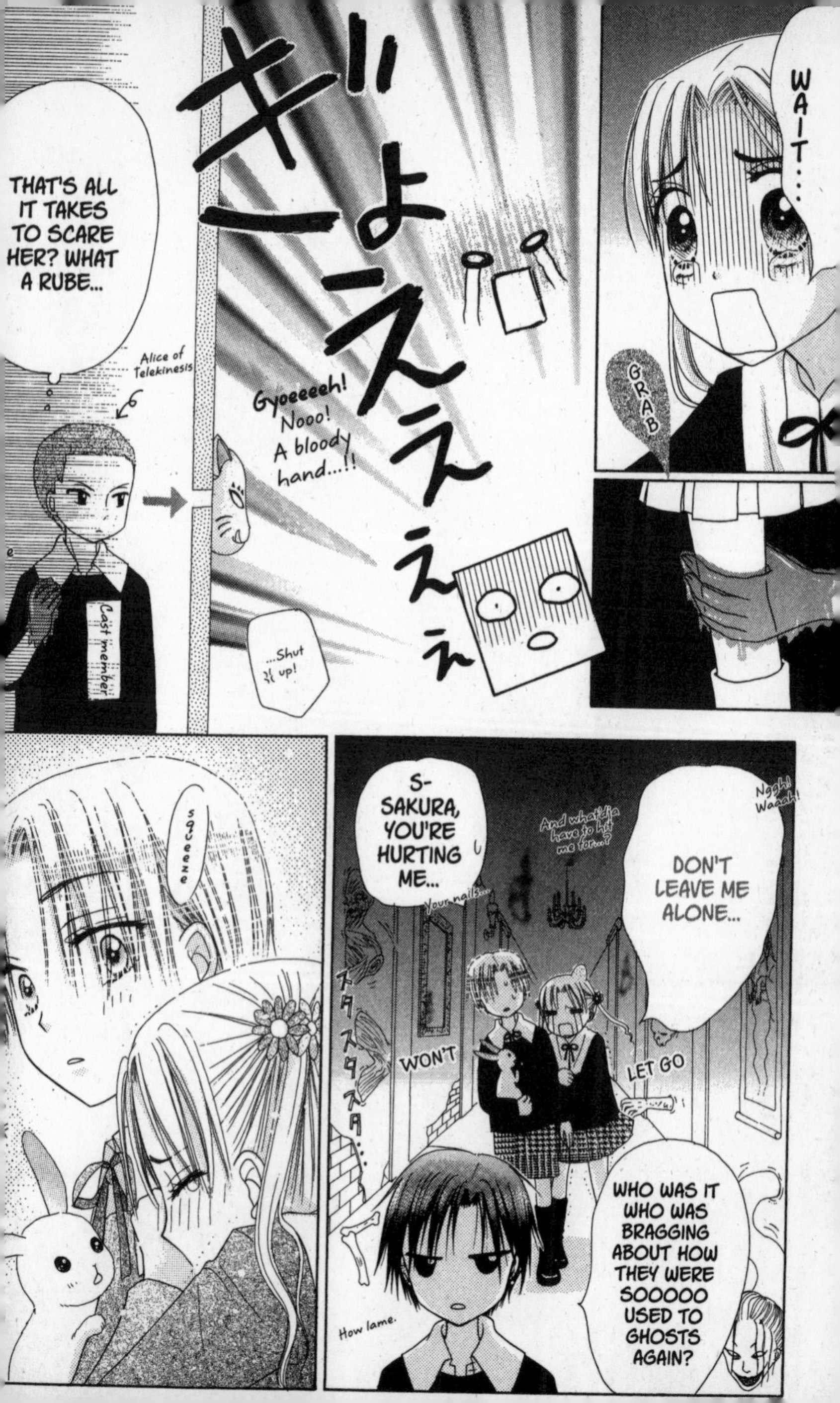
WAIT...
GRAB
ぎょーえええぇ
Gyoeeeeh! Nooo! A bloody hand...!!
...Shut up!
THAT'S ALL IT TAKES TO SCARE HER? WHAT A RUBE...
Alice of Telekinesis
Cast member
Nggh! Waaah!
DON'T LEAVE ME ALONE...
And what'd'ja have to hit me for...?
S-SAKURA, YOU'RE HURTING ME...
Your nails...
WON'T
LET GO
スタスタスタ…
WHO WAS IT WHO WAS BRAGGING ABOUT HOW THEY WERE SOOOOO USED TO GHOSTS AGAIN?
How lame.
squeeze

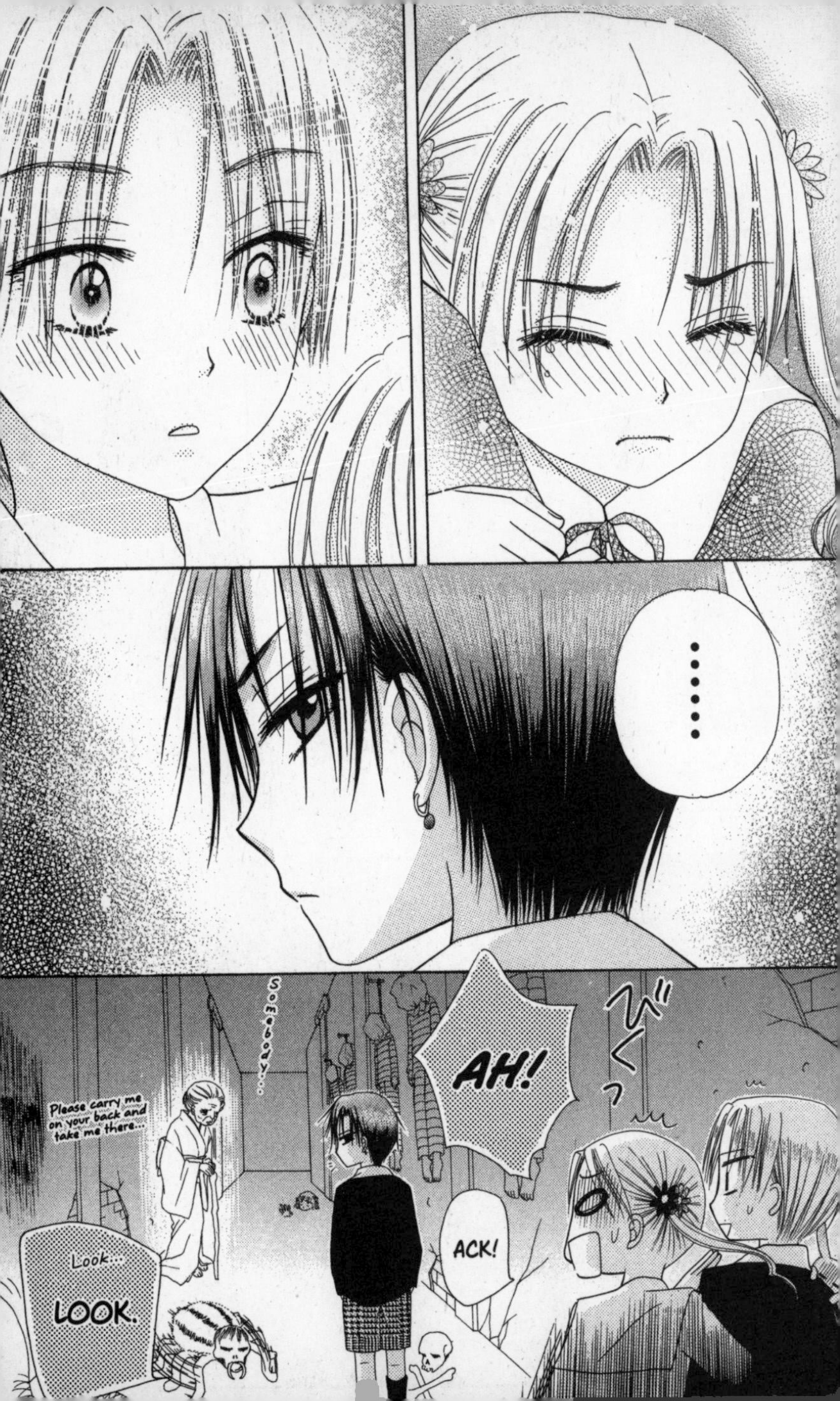

......
びくっ
AH!
Somebody...
ACK!
Please carry me on your back and take me there...
Look...
LOOK.

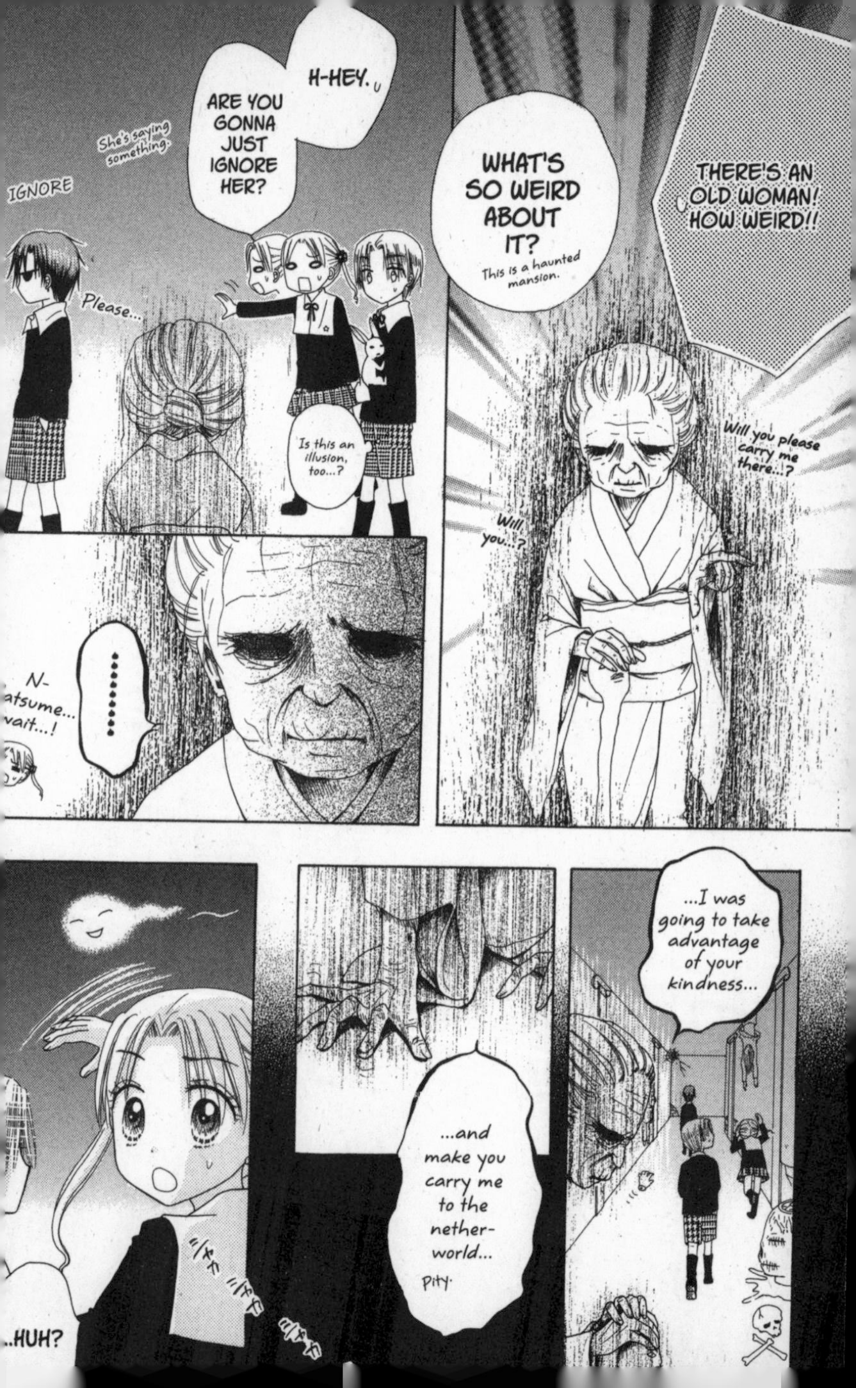
THERE'S AN OLD WOMAN! HOW WEIRD!!
WHAT'S SO WEIRD ABOUT IT?
This is a haunted mansion.
Will you please carry me there...?
Will you...?
H-HEY.
ARE YOU GONNA JUST IGNORE HER?
She's saying something.
IGNORE
Please...
Is this an illusion, too...?
....
N- atsume... vait...!
...I was going to take advantage of your kindness...
...and make you carry me to the nether-world...
Pity.
...HUH?
ニヤ
ニヤ
ニヤ

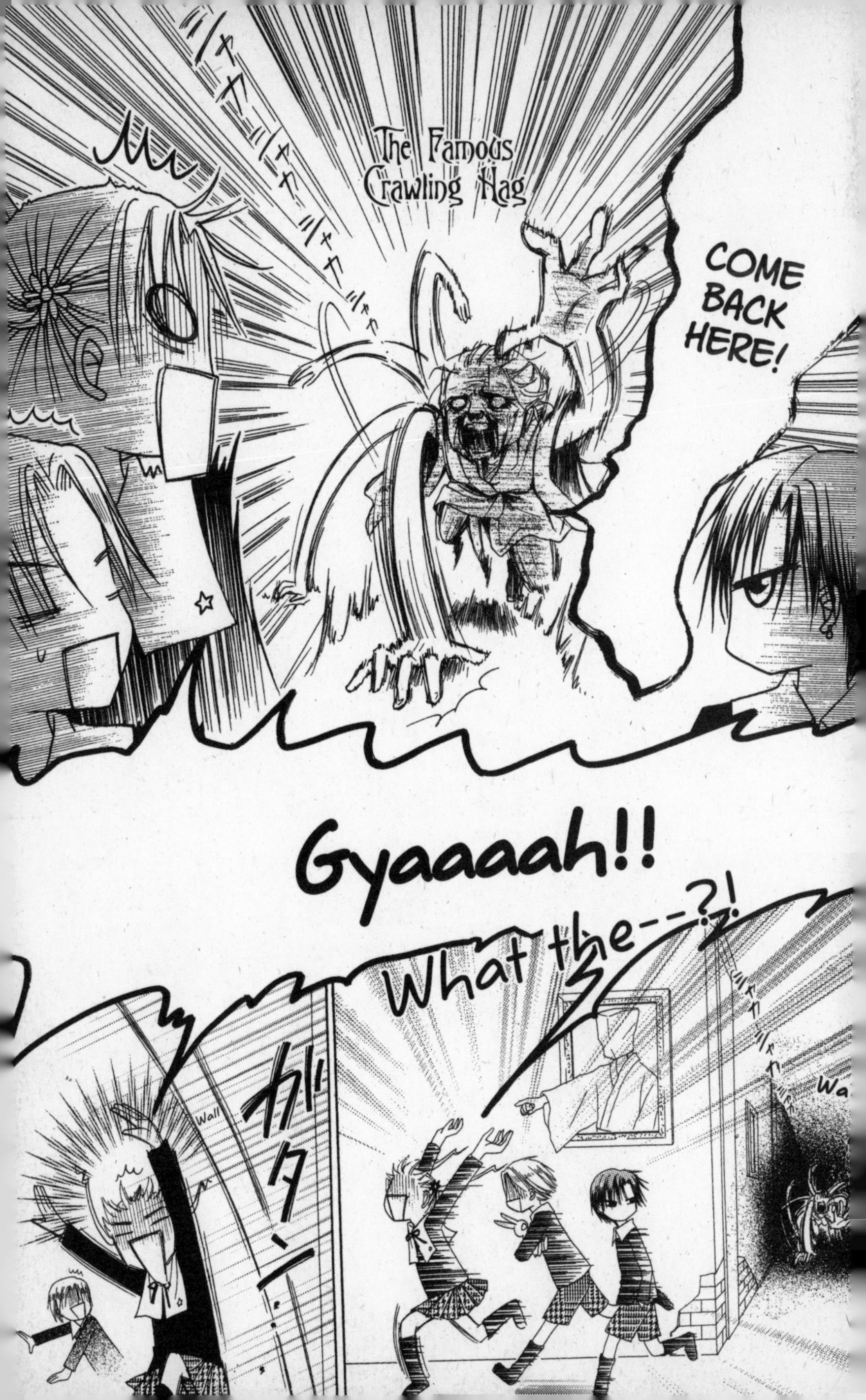
COME BACK HERE!
The Famous Crawling Hag
Mu
Gyaaaaah!!
What the--?!
Wall

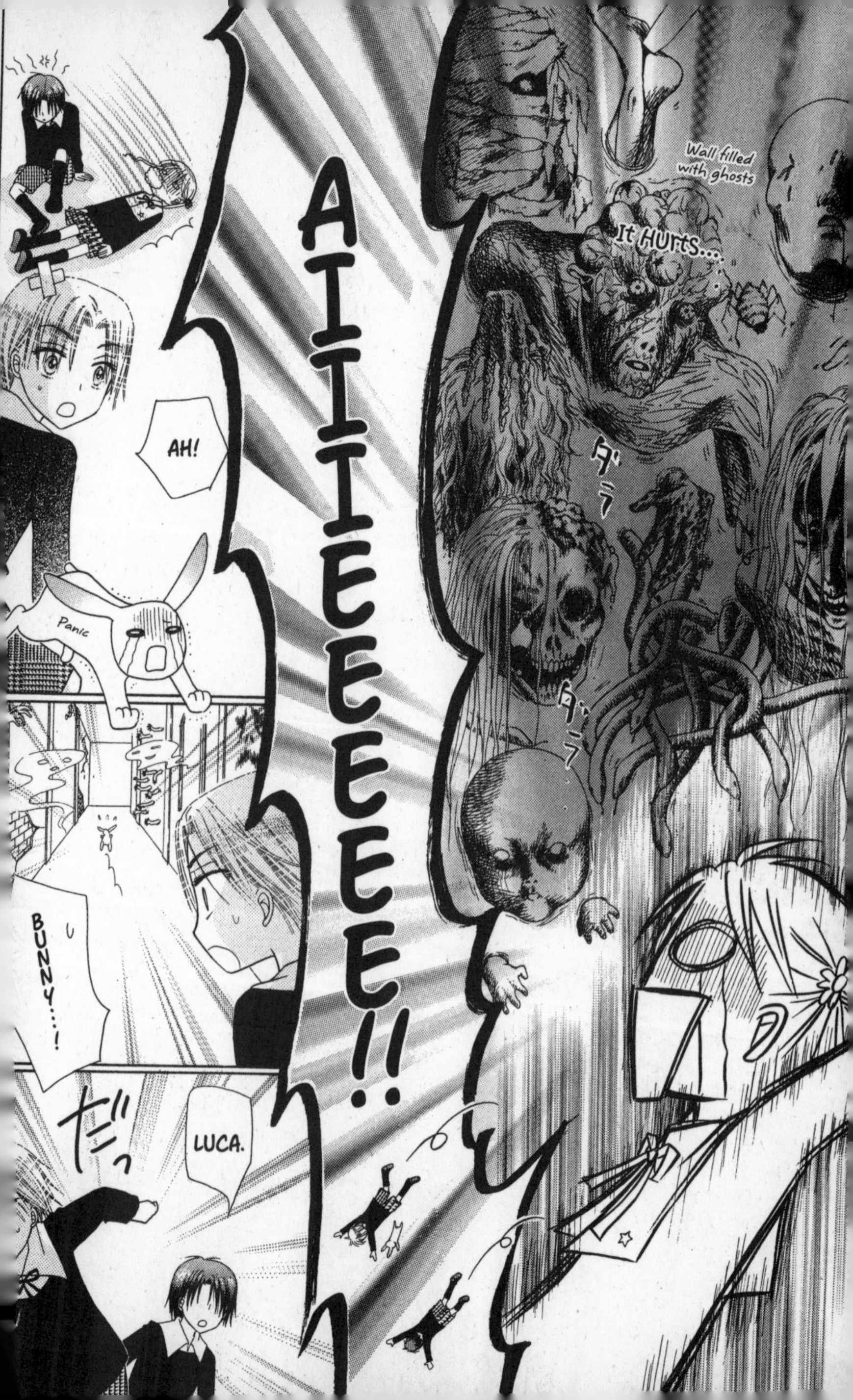

Wall filled with ghosts
It HURTS....
ダラ
ダラ
AIIIEEEE!!
AH!
Panic
BUNNY...!
LUCA.
ダッ

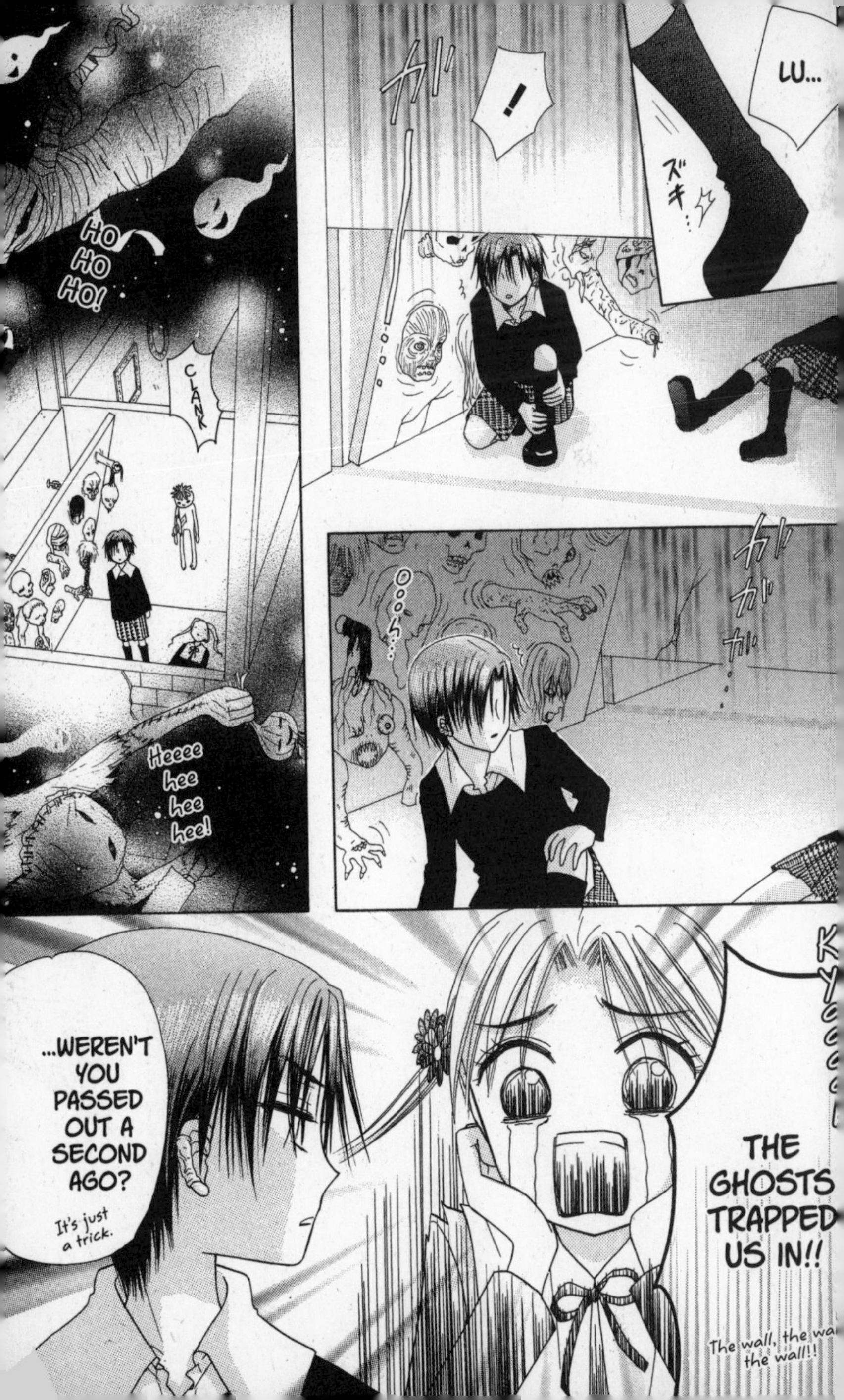

LU...
ズキ…
カッ
!
カッカッカッ
HO HO HO!
CLANK
Heeee hee hee hee!
KYOOOO
THE GHOSTS TRAPPED US IN!!
The wall, the wa
the wall!!
...WEREN'T YOU PASSED OUT A SECOND AGO?
It's just a trick.

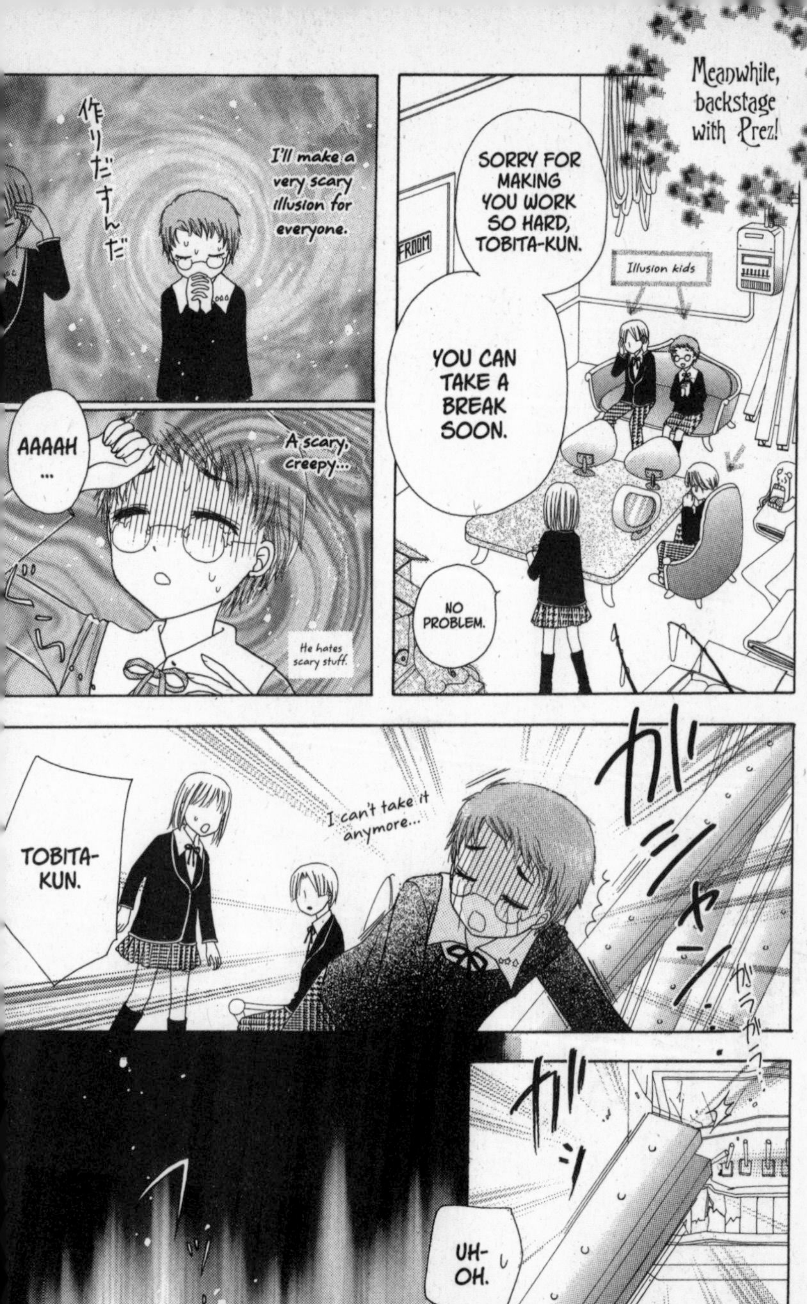
Meanwhile, backstage with Prez!
SORRY FOR MAKING YOU WORK SO HARD, TOBITA-KUN.
YOU CAN TAKE A BREAK SOON.
Illusion kids
NO PROBLEM.
作りだすんだ
I'll make a very scary illusion for everyone.
A scary, creepy...
AAAAH ...
He hates scary stuff.
ガシャーン
I can't take it anymore...
TOBITA-KUN.
ガッ
UH-OH.

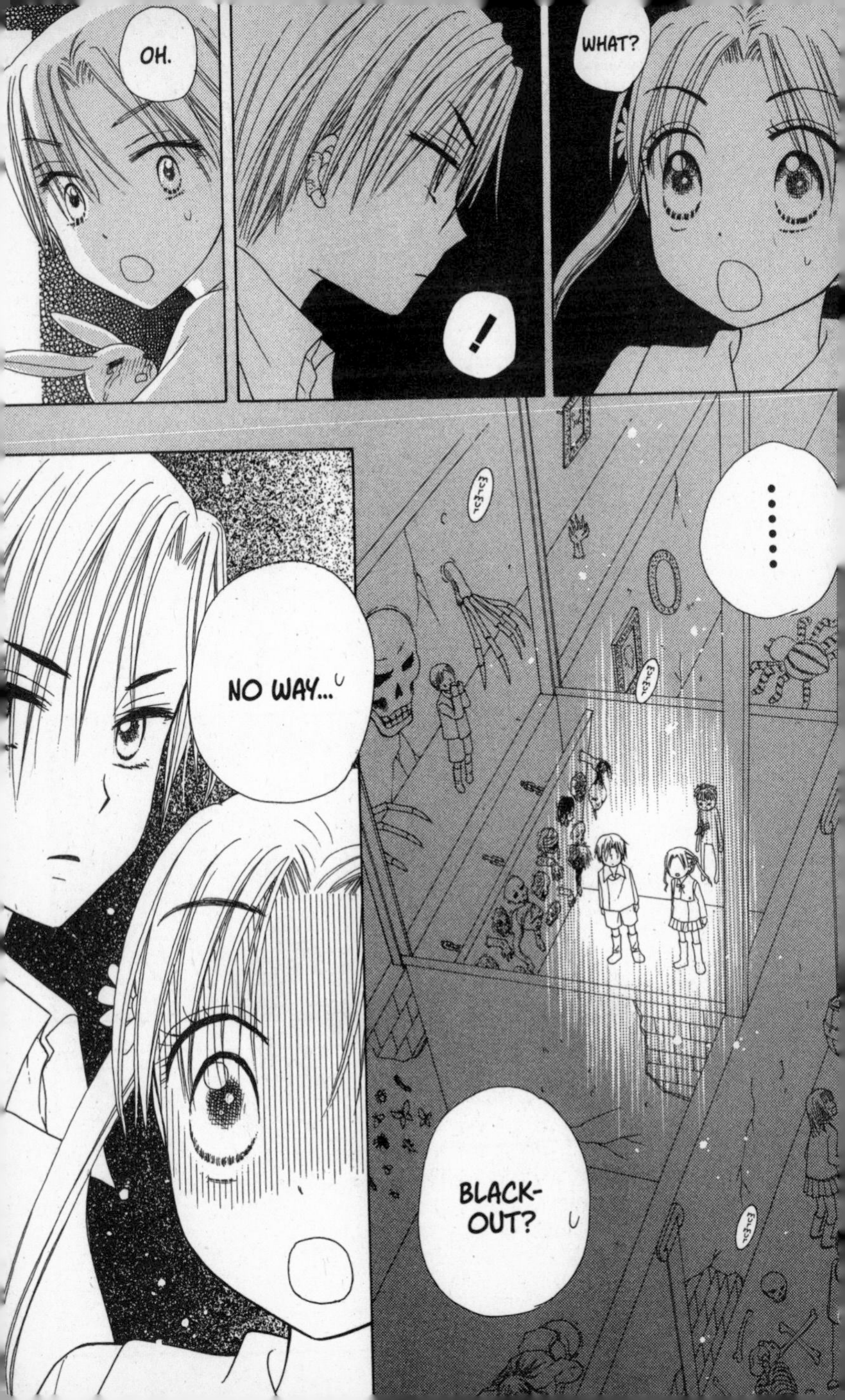
WHAT?
!
OH.
......
murmur
murmur
BLACK-OUT?
murmur
NO WAY...

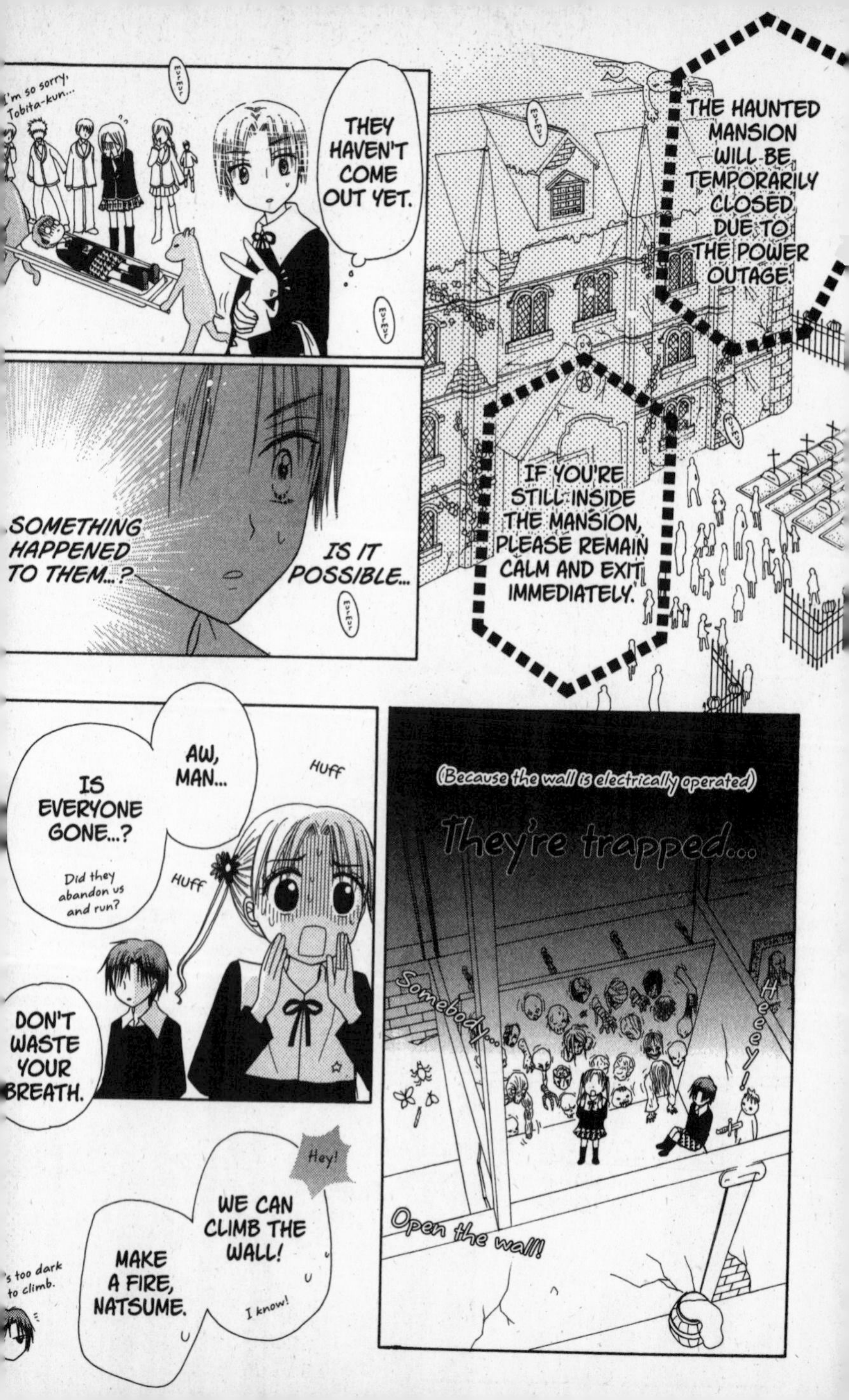
THE HAUNTED MANSION WILL BE TEMPORARILY CLOSED DUE TO THE POWER OUTAGE.
IF YOU'RE STILL INSIDE THE MANSION, PLEASE REMAIN CALM AND EXIT IMMEDIATELY.
THEY HAVEN'T COME OUT YET.
I'm so sorry, Tobita-kun...
IS IT POSSIBLE...
SOMETHING HAPPENED TO THEM...?
(Because the wall is electrically operated)
They're trapped...
Heeey!
Somebody...
Open the wall!
AW, MAN...
IS EVERYONE GONE...?
Did they abandon us and run?
HUFF
HUFF
DON'T WASTE YOUR BREATH.
Hey!
WE CAN CLIMB THE WALL!
MAKE A FIRE, NATSUME.
I know!
s too dark to climb.

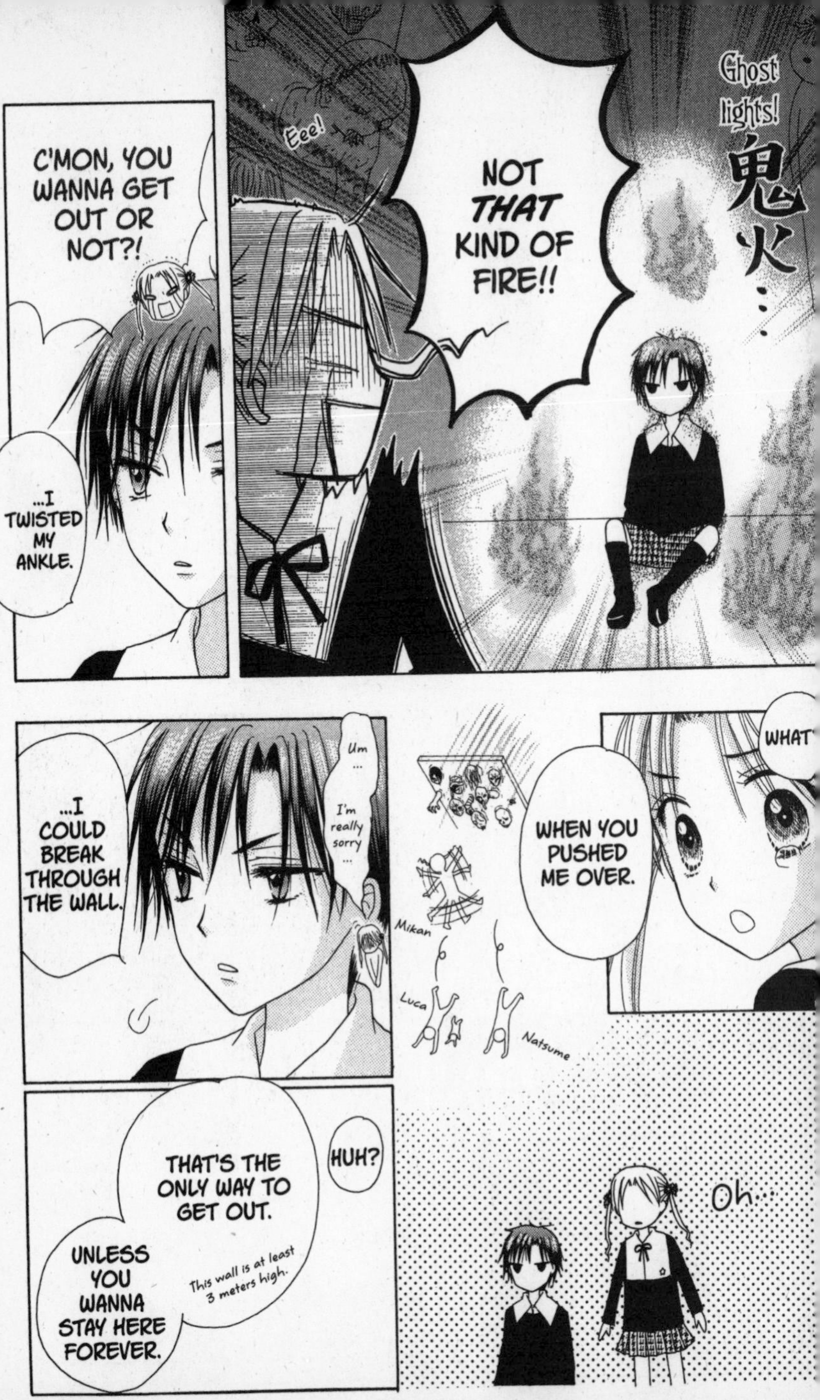
Ghost lights!
鬼火・・・
NOT THAT KIND OF FIRE!!
Eee!
C'MON, YOU WANNA GET OUT OR NOT?!
...I TWISTED MY ANKLE.
WHAT
WHEN YOU PUSHED ME OVER.
Mikan
Luca
Natsume
Um ...
I'm really sorry ...
...I COULD BREAK THROUGH THE WALL.
Oh...
HUH?
THAT'S THE ONLY WAY TO GET OUT.
UNLESS YOU WANNA STAY HERE FOREVER.
This wall is at least 3 meters high.

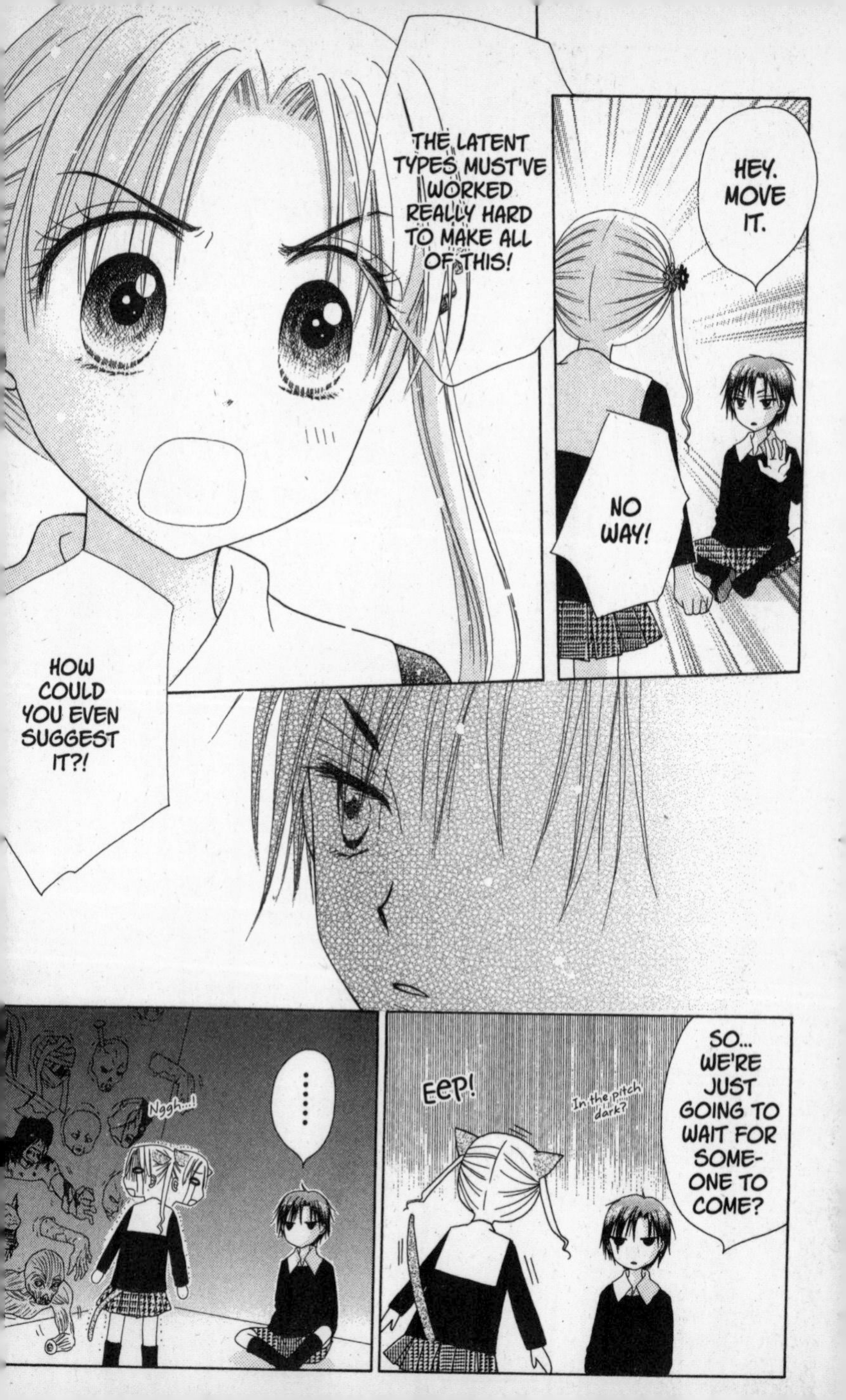
HEY. MOVE IT.
NO WAY!
THE LATENT TYPES MUST'VE WORKED REALLY HARD TO MAKE ALL OF THIS!
HOW COULD YOU EVEN SUGGEST IT?!
SO... WE'RE JUST GOING TO WAIT FOR SOME-ONE TO COME?
In the pitch dark?
Eep!
......
Nggh...!

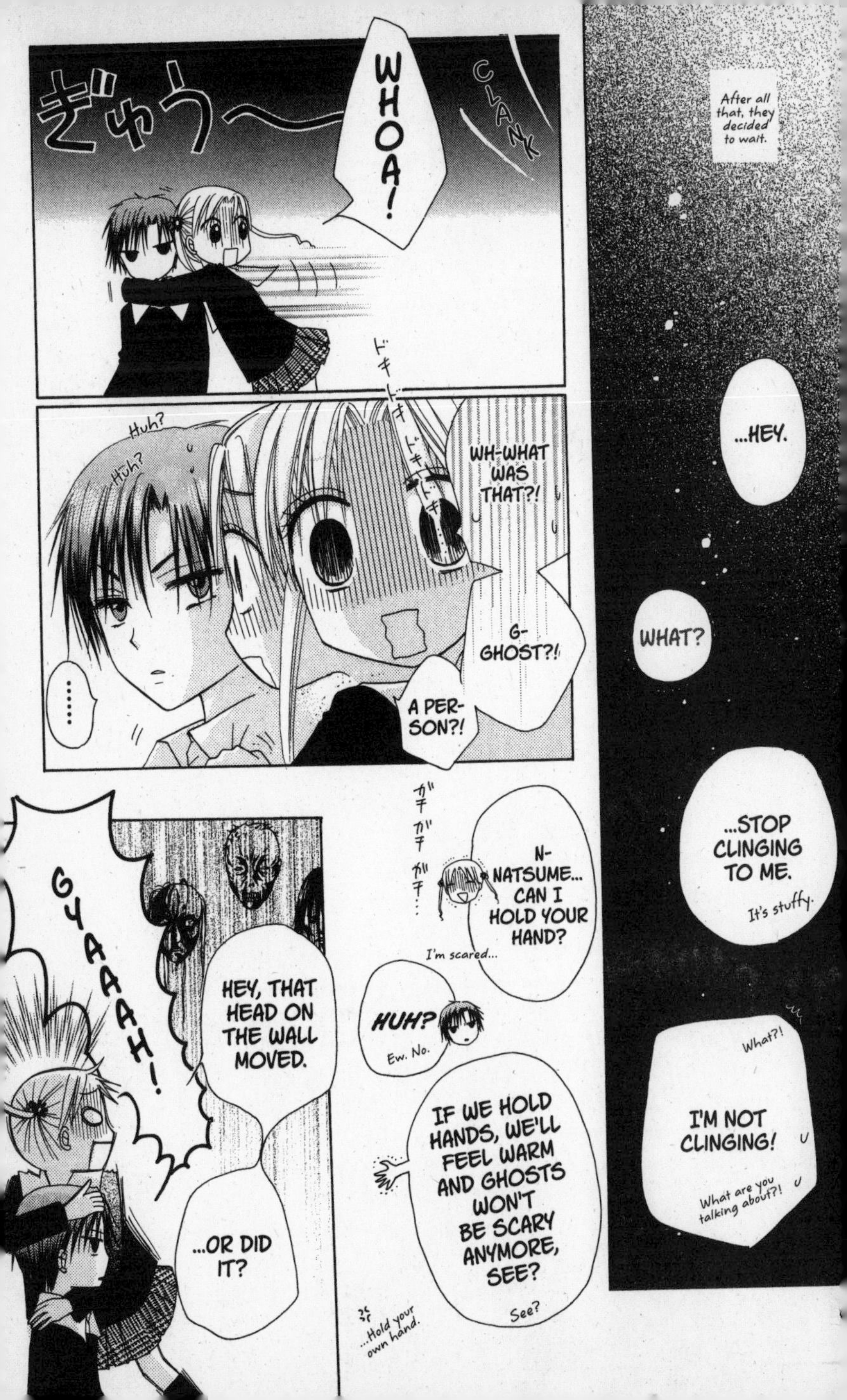
After all that, they decided to wait.
...HEY.
WHAT?
...STOP CLINGING TO ME.
It's stuffy.
What?!
I'M NOT CLINGING!
What are you talking about?!
WHOA!
CLANK
ぎゅう〜
ドキドキドキドキ
WH-WHAT WAS THAT?!
G-GHOST?!
A PER-SON?!
Huh?
Huh?
......
ガチガチガチ
N-NATSUME... CAN I HOLD YOUR HAND?
I'm scared...
HUH?
Ew. No.
IF WE HOLD HANDS, WE'LL FEEL WARM AND GHOSTS WON'T BE SCARY ANYMORE, SEE?
See?
...Hold your own hand.
HEY, THAT HEAD ON THE WALL MOVED.
...OR DID IT?
GYAAAAH!

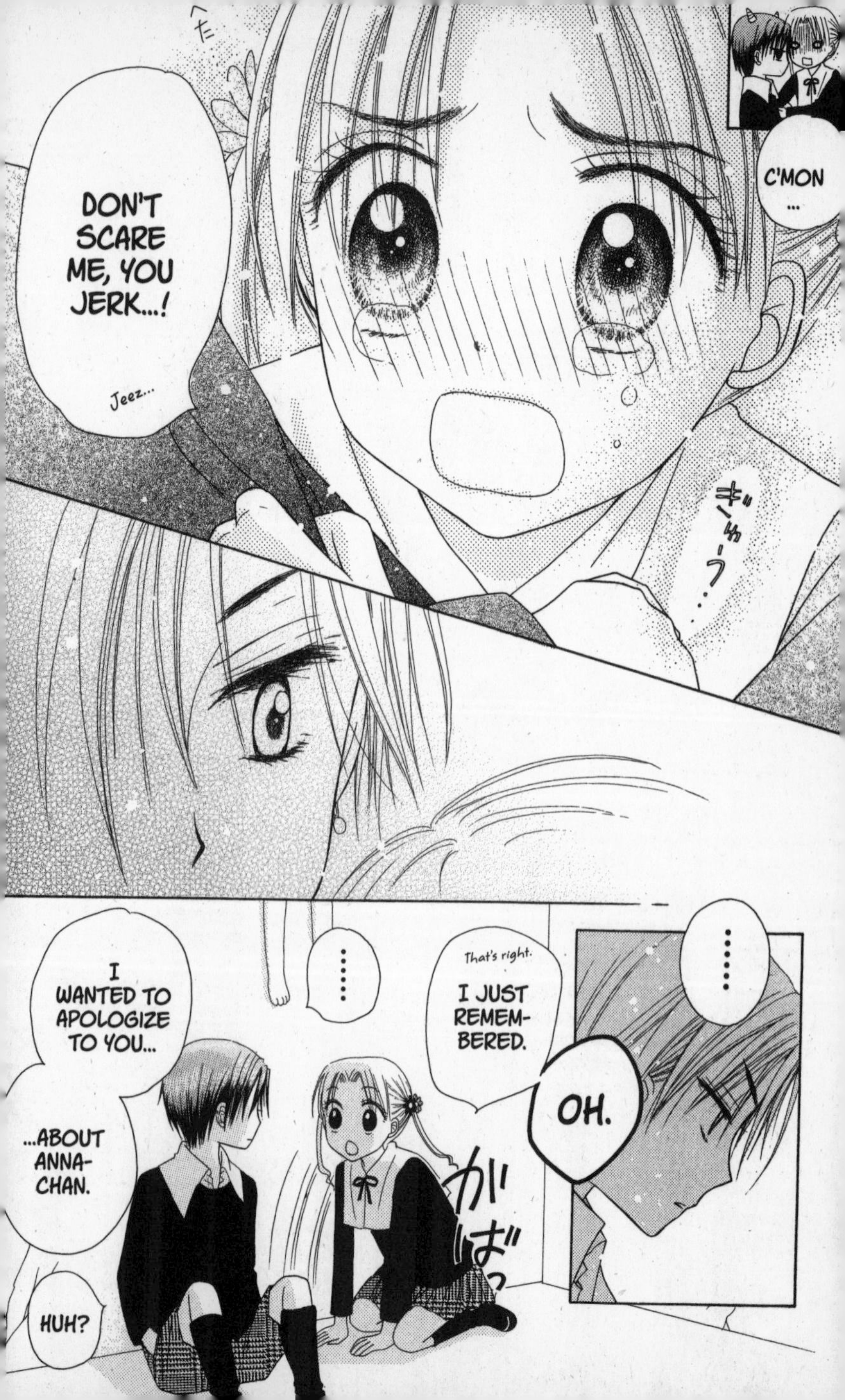
C'MON ...
ぎゅうっ...
DON'T SCARE ME, YOU JERK...!
Jeez...
へた
......
OH.
That's right.
I JUST REMEMBERED.
がばっ
......
I WANTED TO APOLOGIZE TO YOU...
...ABOUT ANNA-CHAN.
HUH?

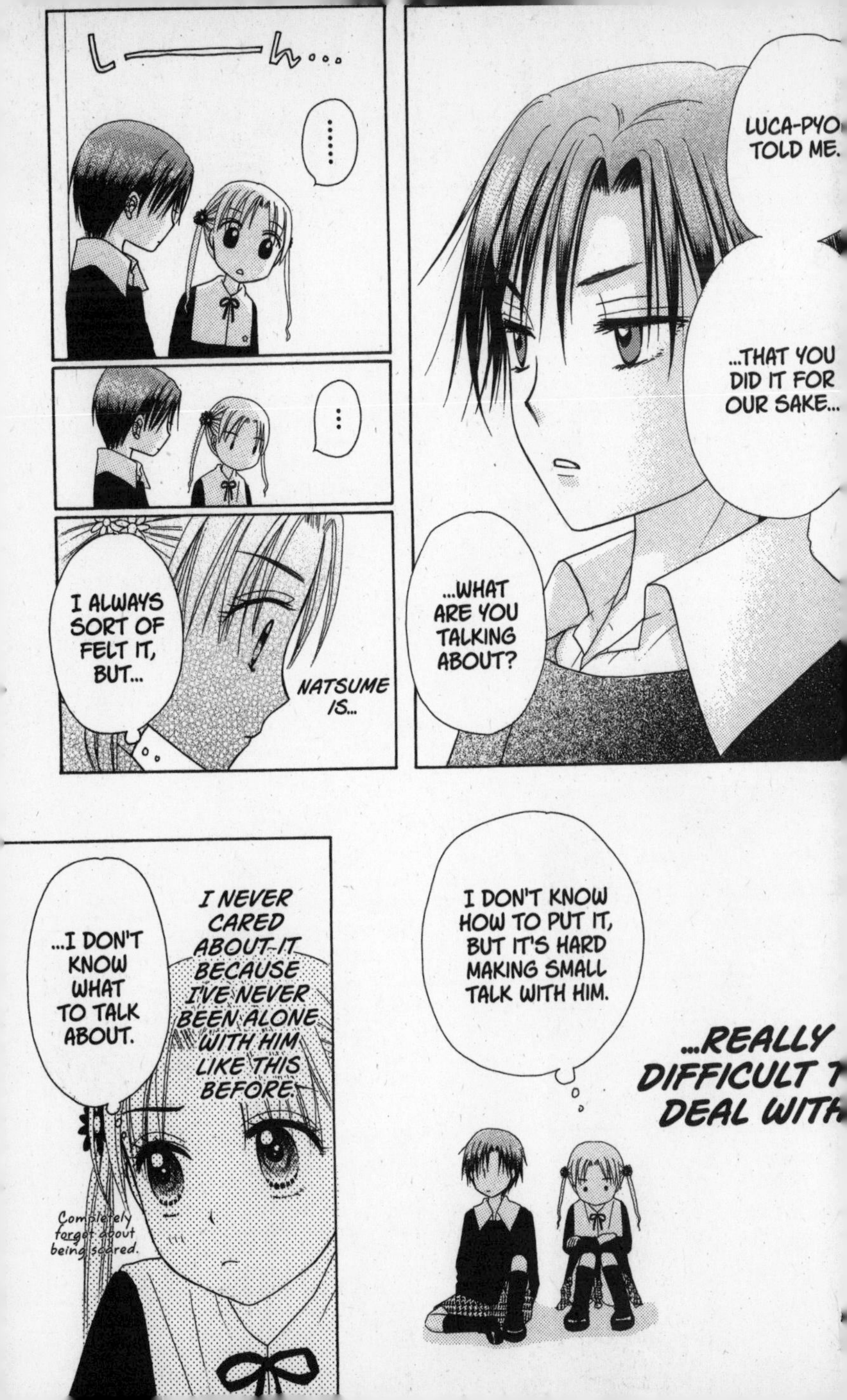
LUCA-PYO TOLD ME.
...THAT YOU DID IT FOR OUR SAKE...
...WHAT ARE YOU TALKING ABOUT?
し———ん...
......
...
I ALWAYS SORT OF FELT IT, BUT...
NATSUME IS...
...REALLY DIFFICULT T DEAL WITH
I DON'T KNOW HOW TO PUT IT, BUT IT'S HARD MAKING SMALL TALK WITH HIM.
I NEVER CARED ABOUT IT BECAUSE I'VE NEVER BEEN ALONE WITH HIM LIKE THIS BEFORE.
...I DON'T KNOW WHAT TO TALK ABOUT.
Completely forgot about being scared.

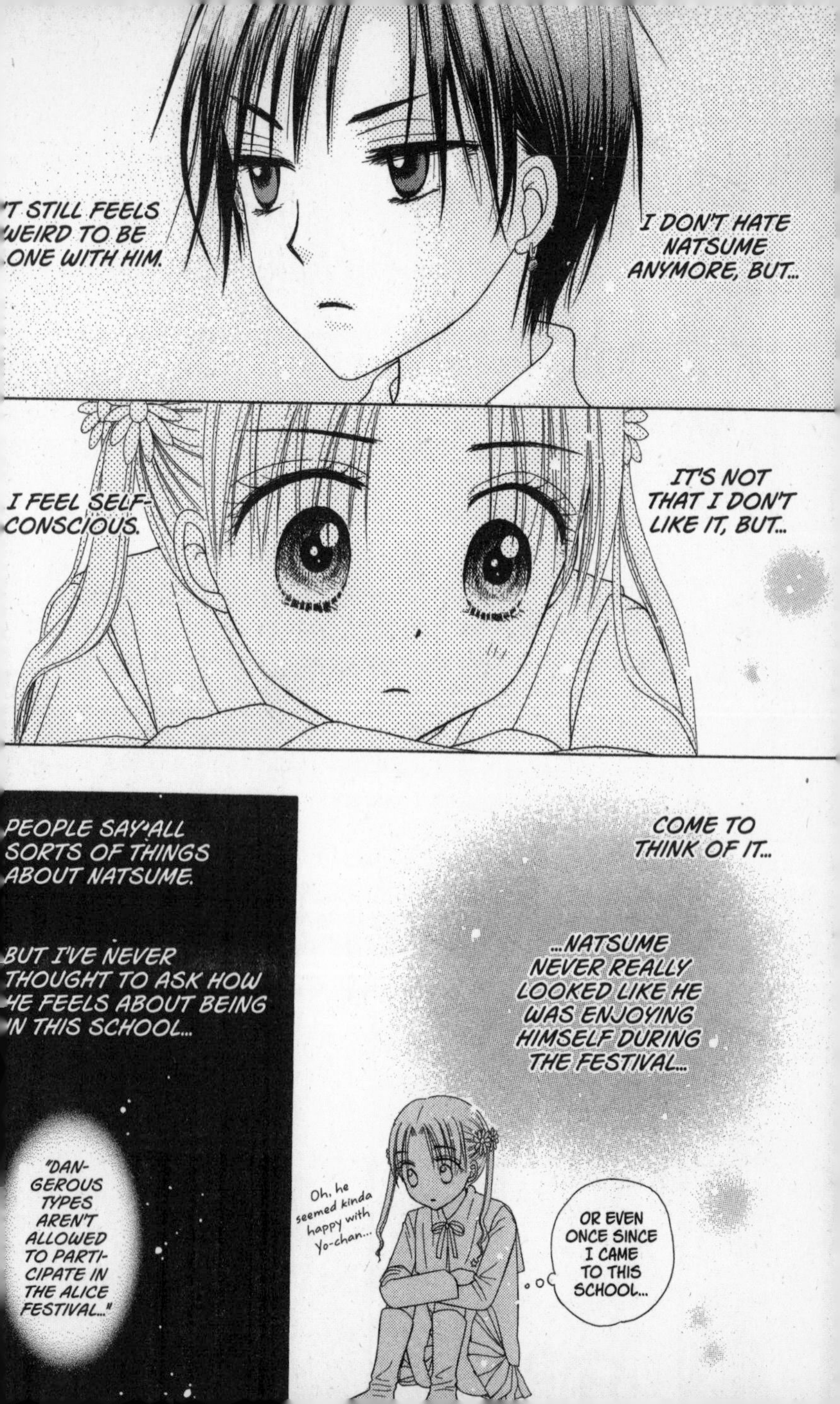
I DON'T HATE NATSUME ANYMORE, BUT...
'T STILL FEELS WEIRD TO BE ONE WITH HIM.
IT'S NOT THAT I DON'T LIKE IT, BUT...
I FEEL SELF-CONSCIOUS.
COME TO THINK OF IT...
...NATSUME NEVER REALLY LOOKED LIKE HE WAS ENJOYING HIMSELF DURING THE FESTIVAL...
OR EVEN ONCE SINCE I CAME TO THIS SCHOOL...
Oh, he seemed kinda happy with Yo-chan...
PEOPLE SAY ALL SORTS OF THINGS ABOUT NATSUME.
BUT I'VE NEVER THOUGHT TO ASK HOW HE FEELS ABOUT BEING IN THIS SCHOOL...
"DANGEROUS TYPES AREN'T ALLOWED TO PARTICIPATE IN THE ALICE FESTIVAL..."

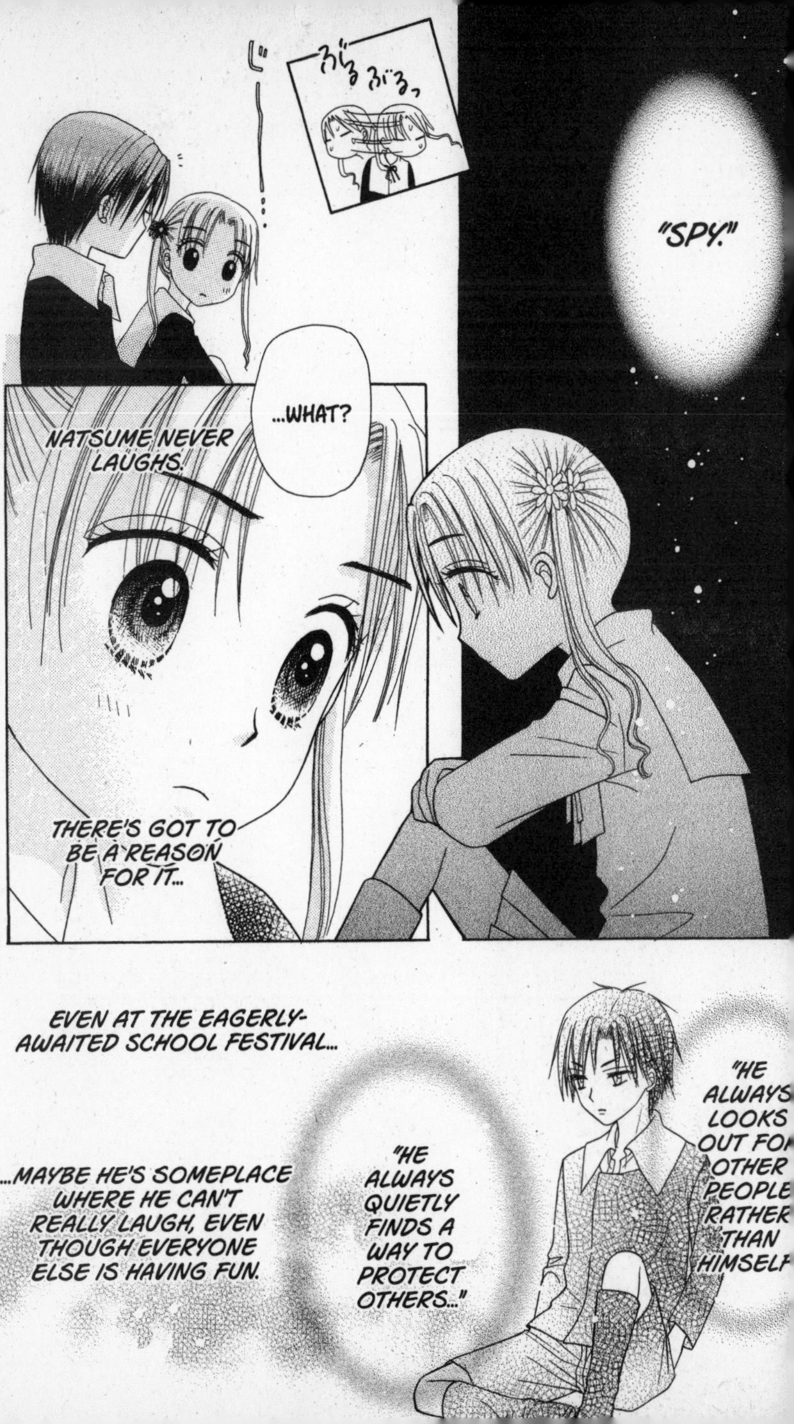

"SPY."
ぶるぶるっ
じー…
...WHAT?
NATSUME NEVER LAUGHS.
THERE'S GOT TO BE A REASON FOR IT...
"HE ALWAYS LOOKS OUT FO OTHER PEOPLE RATHER THAN HIMSELF
"HE ALWAYS QUIETLY FINDS A WAY TO PROTECT OTHERS..."
EVEN AT THE EAGERLY-AWAITED SCHOOL FESTIVAL...
...MAYBE HE'S SOMEPLACE WHERE HE CAN'T REALLY LAUGH, EVEN THOUGH EVERYONE ELSE IS HAVING FUN.

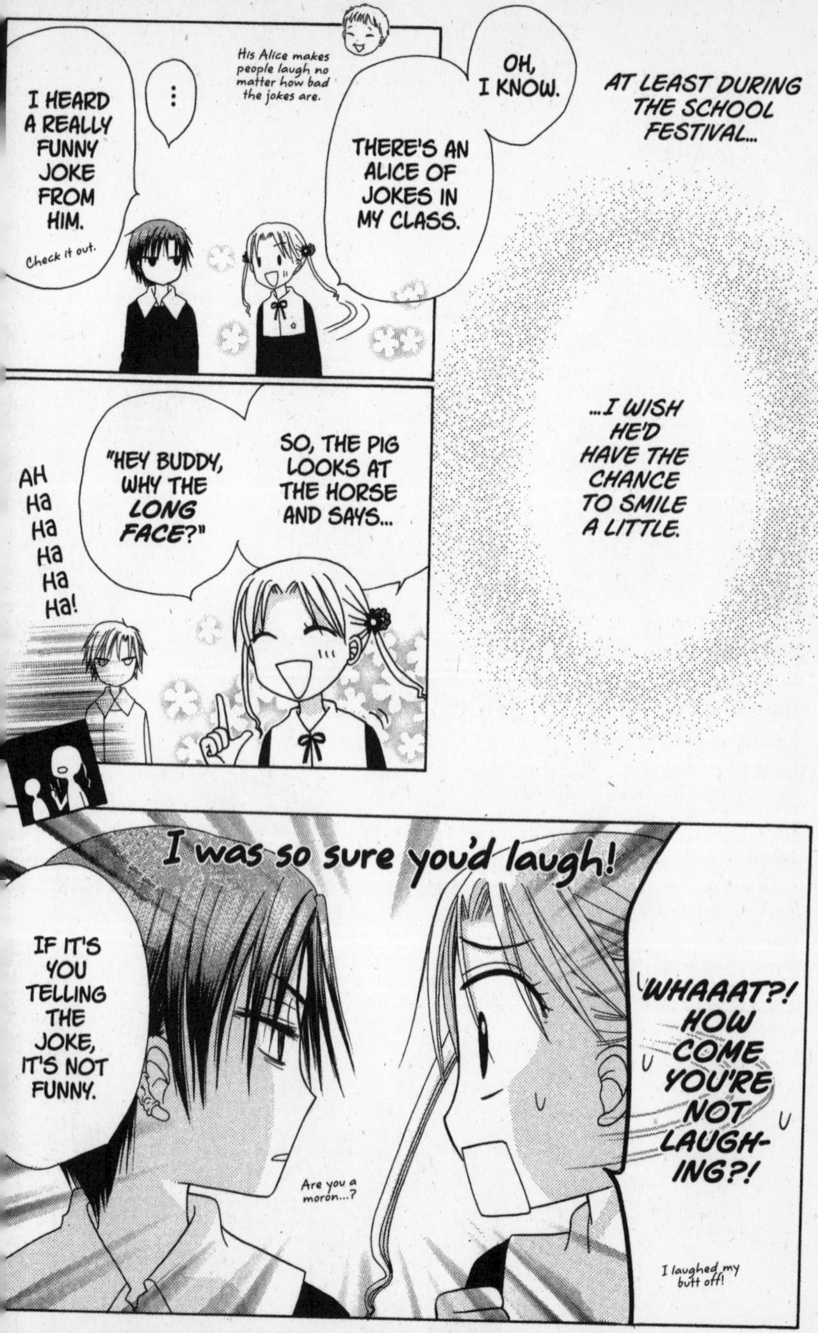
AT LEAST DURING THE SCHOOL FESTIVAL...
...I WISH HE'D HAVE THE CHANCE TO SMILE A LITTLE.
OH, I KNOW.
THERE'S AN ALICE OF JOKES IN MY CLASS.
His Alice makes people laugh no matter how bad the jokes are.
...
I HEARD A REALLY FUNNY JOKE FROM HIM.
Check it out.
SO, THE PIG LOOKS AT THE HORSE AND SAYS...
"HEY BUDDY, WHY THE LONG FACE?"
AH Ha Ha Ha Ha Ha!
I was so sure you'd laugh!
WHAAAT?! HOW COME YOU'RE NOT LAUGH-ING?!
I laughed my butt off!
Are you a moron...?
IF IT'S YOU TELLING THE JOKE, IT'S NOT FUNNY.

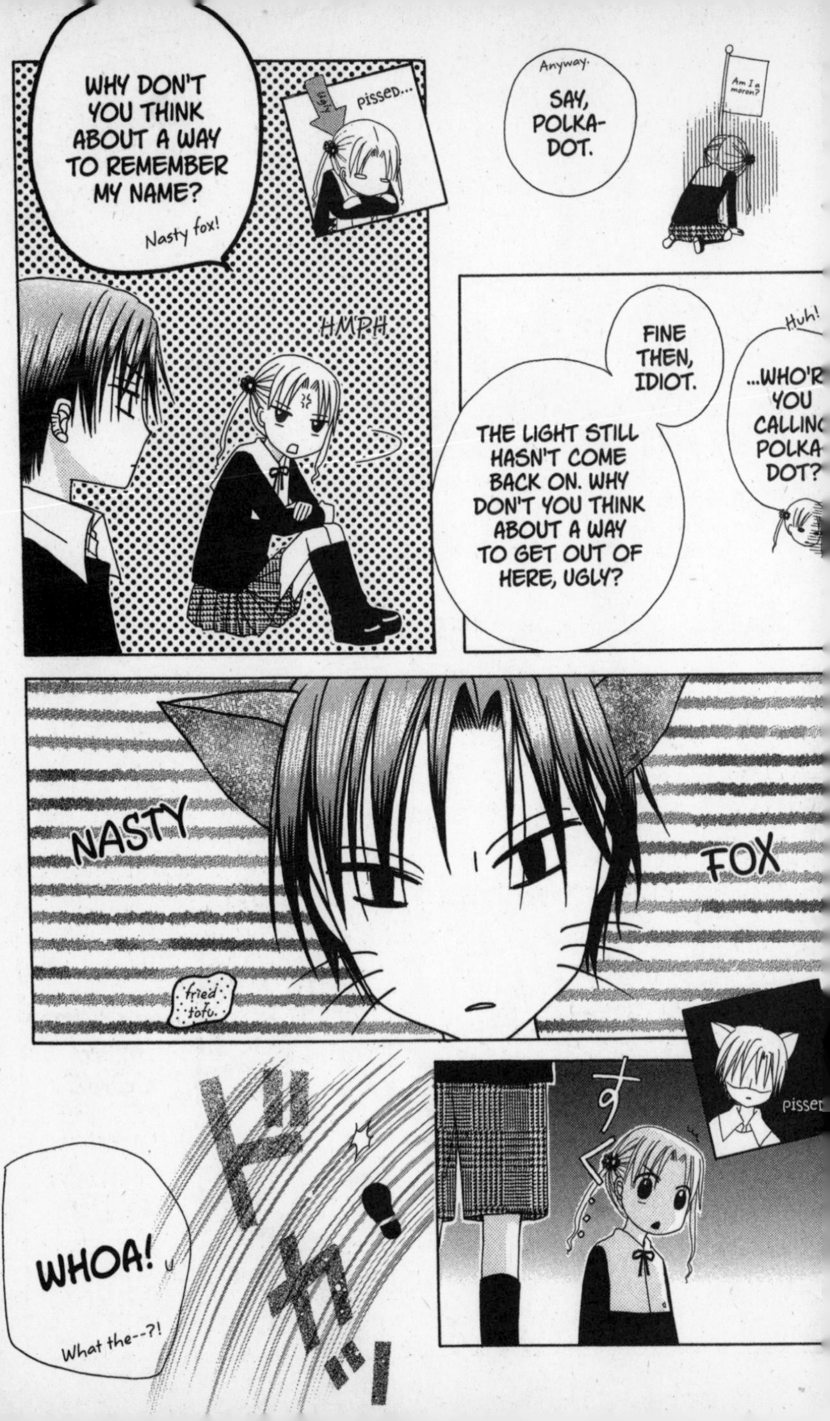
Anyway.
SAY, POLKA-DOT.
Am I a moron?
Huh!
...WHO'R YOU CALLIN POLKA DOT?
FINE THEN, IDIOT.
THE LIGHT STILL HASN'T COME BACK ON. WHY DON'T YOU THINK ABOUT A WAY TO GET OUT OF HERE, UGLY?
WHY DON'T YOU THINK ABOUT A WAY TO REMEMBER MY NAME?
Nasty fox!
pissed...
HMPH
NASTY FOX
fried tofu.
pisse
WHOA!
What the--?!

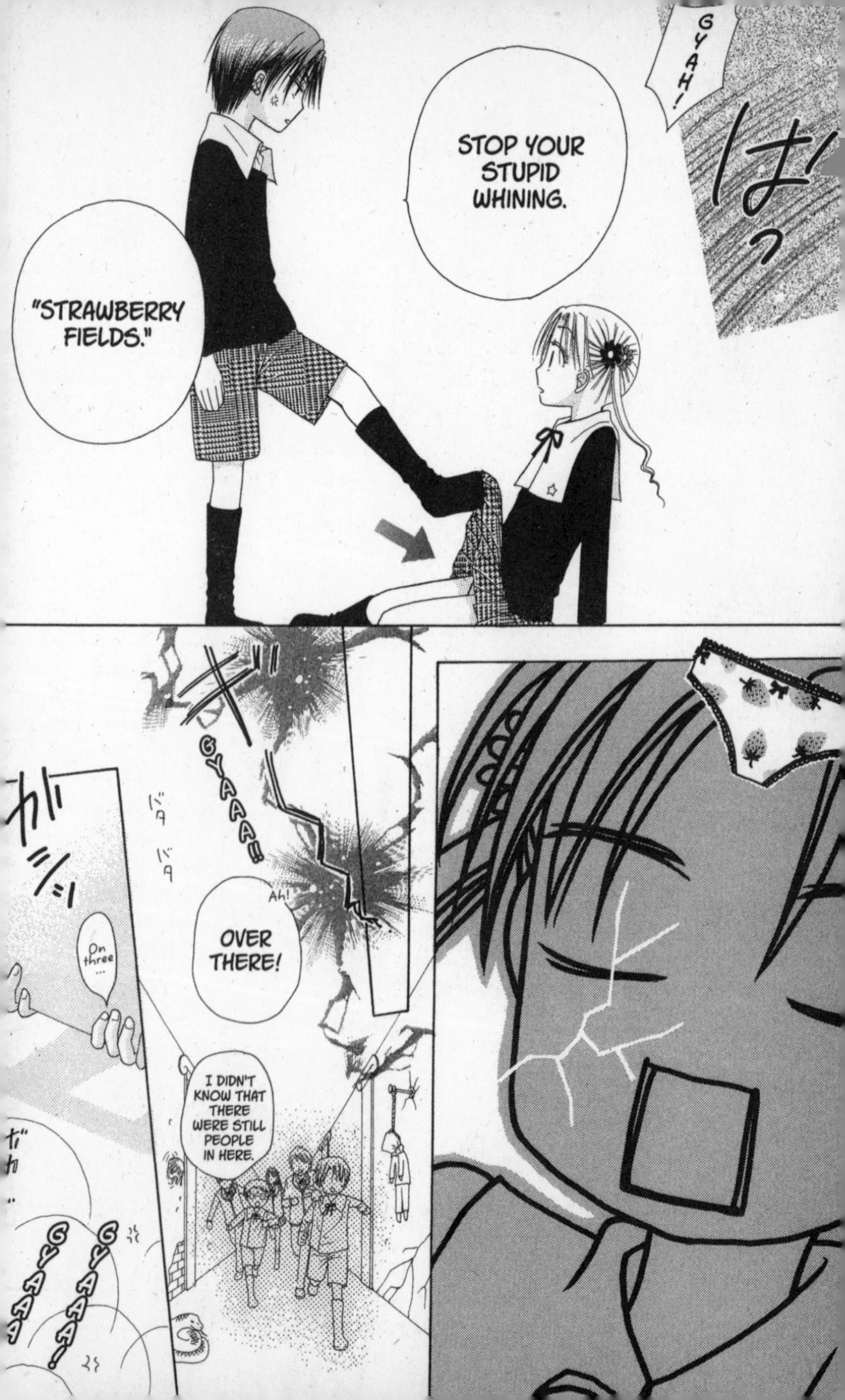
GYAH!
はっ
STOP YOUR STUPID WHINING.
"STRAWBERRY FIELDS."
GYAAAA!!
バタ バタ
Ah!
OVER THERE!
I DIDN'T KNOW THAT THERE WERE STILL PEOPLE IN HERE.
On three...
GYAAAA!
GYAAAA!

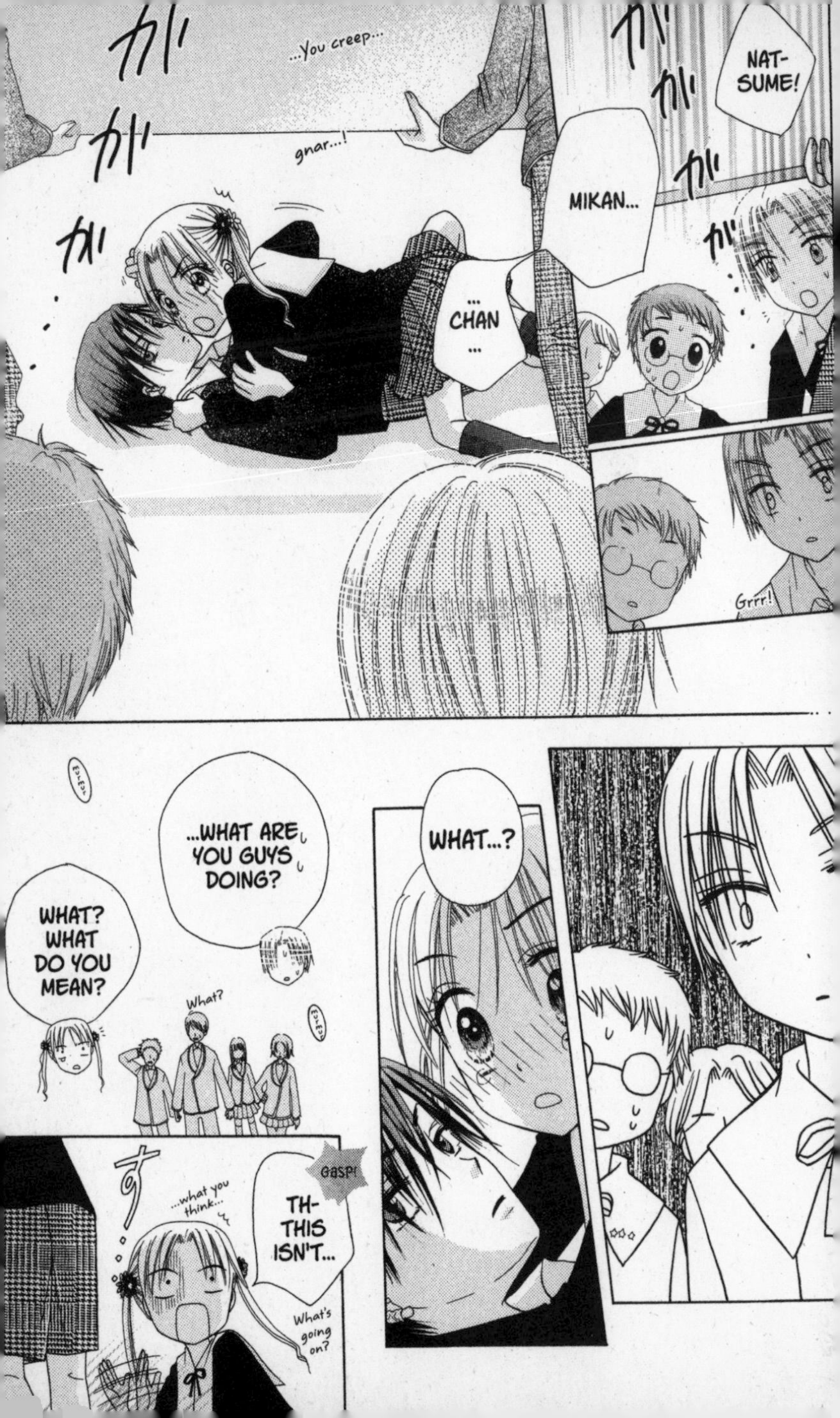
NAT-SUME!
MIKAN...
...CHAN...
Grrr!
...You creep...
gnar...!
WHAT...?
...WHAT ARE YOU GUYS DOING?
WHAT? WHAT DO YOU MEAN?
What?
GASP!
TH-THIS ISN'T...
...what you think...
What's going on?

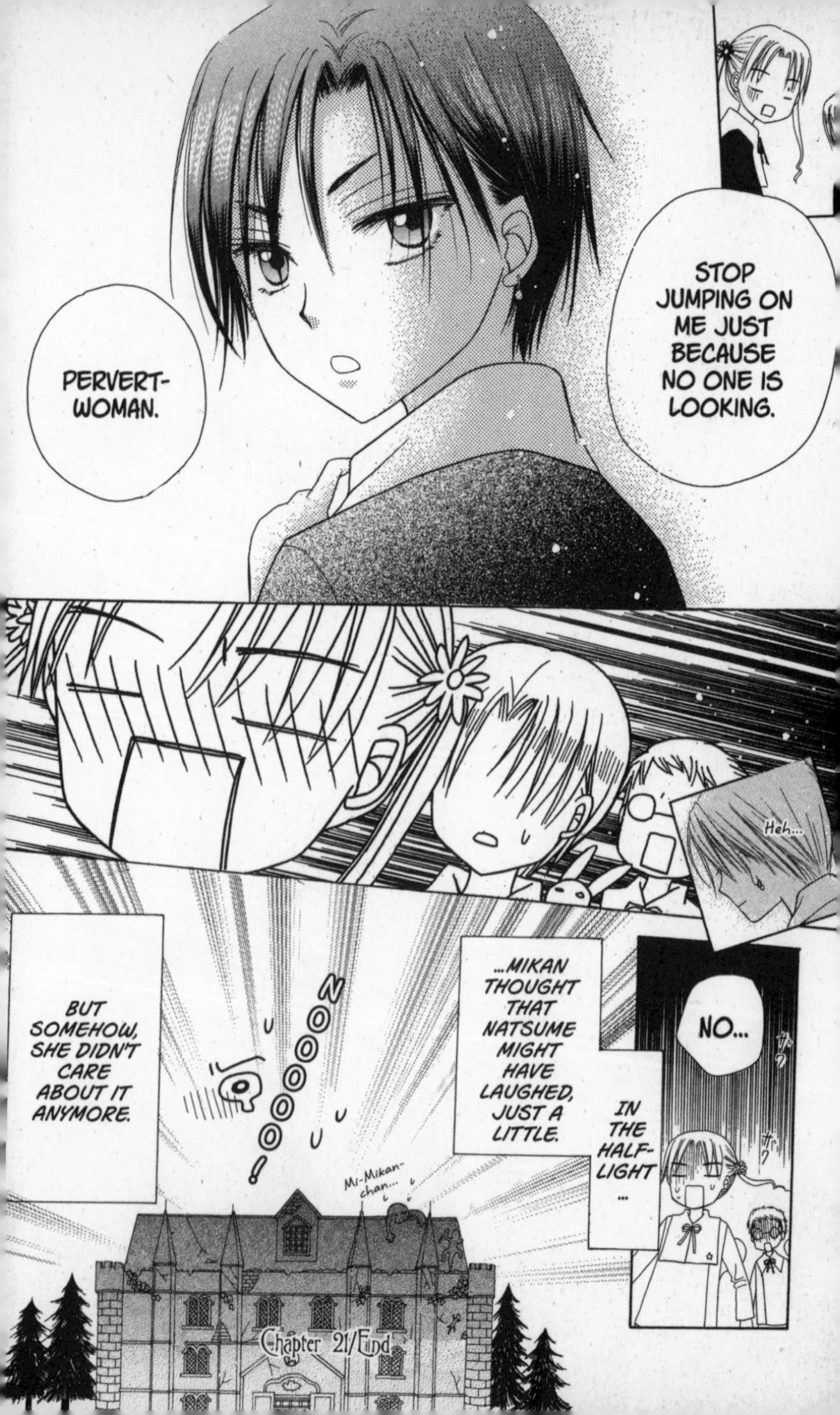
STOP JUMPING ON ME JUST BECAUSE NO ONE IS LOOKING.
PERVERT-WOMAN.
Heh...
NO...
IN THE HALF-LIGHT...
...MIKAN THOUGHT THAT NATSUME MIGHT HAVE LAUGHED, JUST A LITTLE.
BUT SOMEHOW, SHE DIDN'T CARE ABOUT IT ANYMORE.
NOOOOOOOO!
Mi-Mikan-chan...
Chapter 21/End

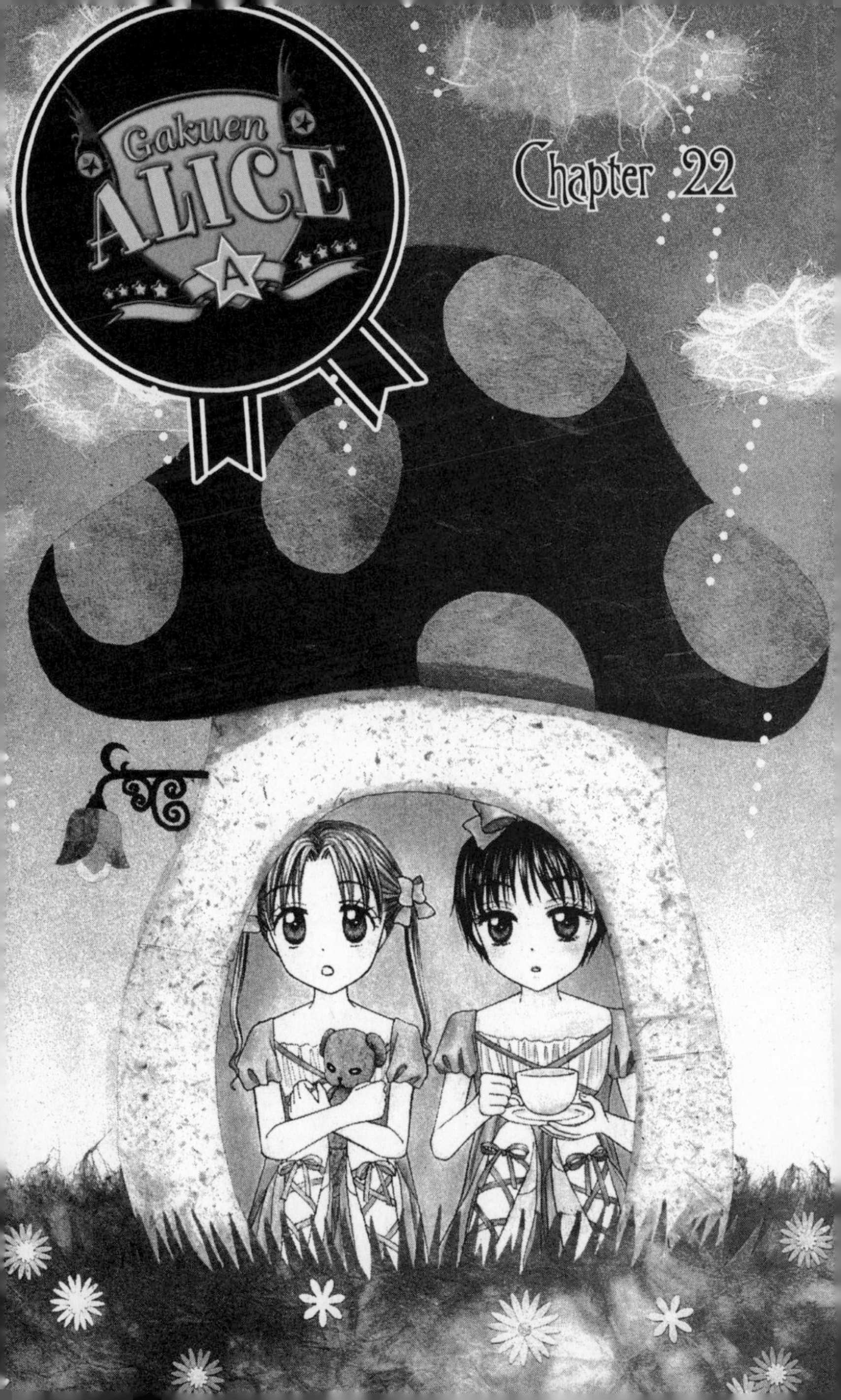

Gakuen ALICE
Chapter 22

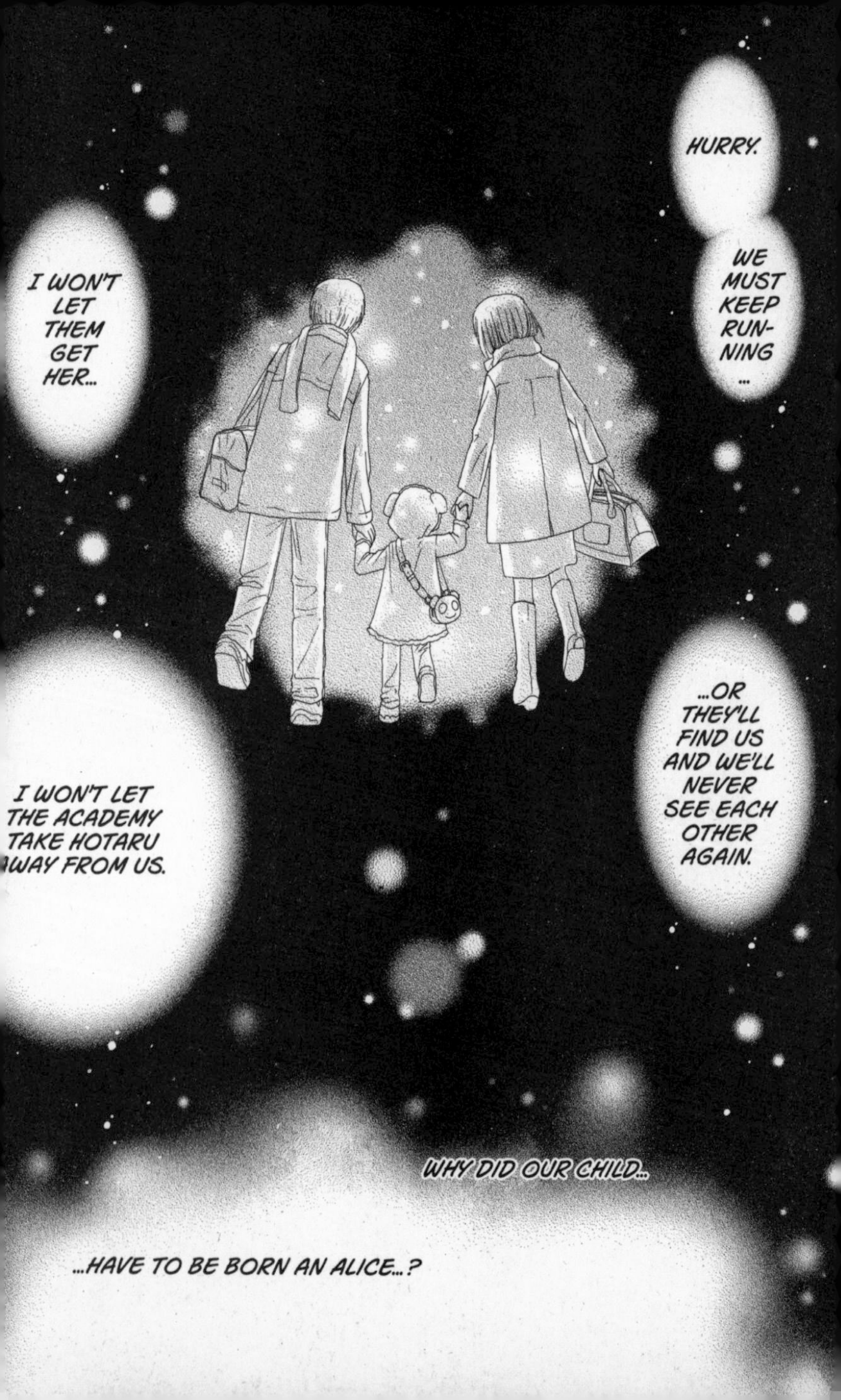
HURRY.
WE MUST KEEP RUNNING...
...OR THEY'LL FIND US AND WE'LL NEVER SEE EACH OTHER AGAIN.
I WON'T LET THEM GET HER...
I WON'T LET THE ACADEMY TAKE HOTARU AWAY FROM US.
WHY DID OUR CHILD...
...HAVE TO BE BORN AN ALICE...?

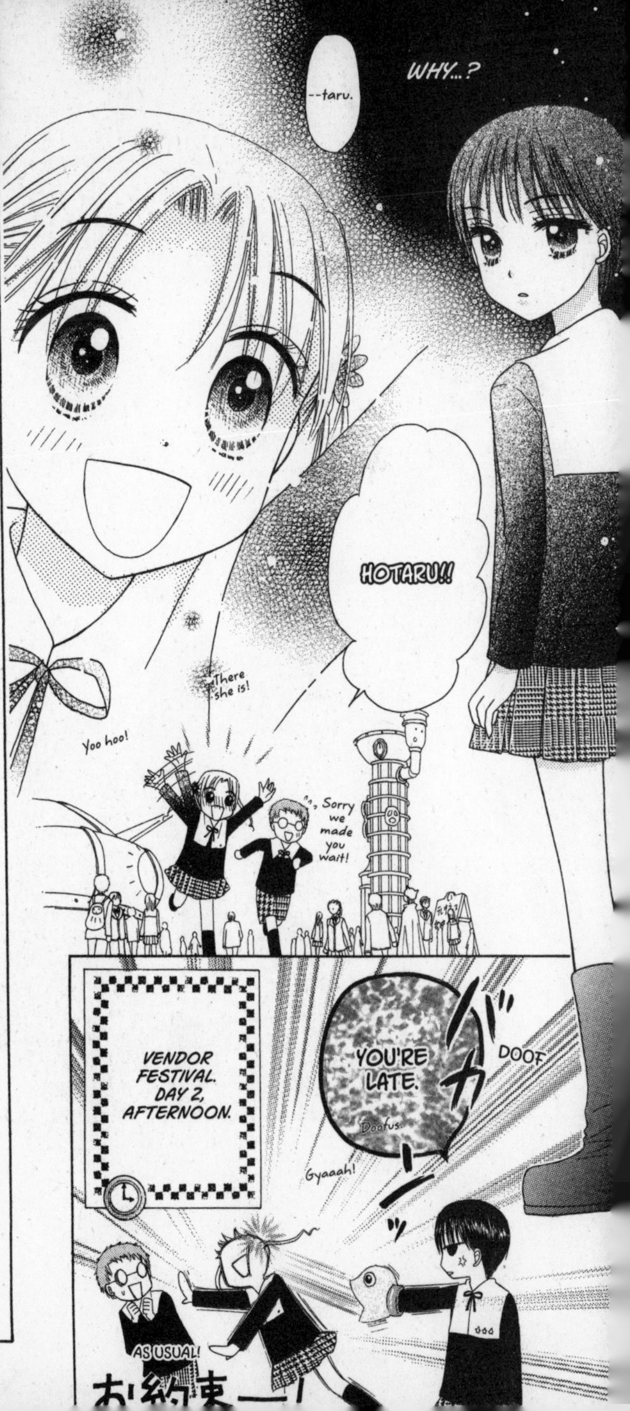
WHY...?
--taru.
HOTARU!!
There she is!
Yoo hoo!
Sorry we made you wait!
DOOF
YOU'RE LATE.
Doofus.
VENDOR FESTIVAL. DAY 2, AFTERNOON.
Gyaaah!
AS USUAL!
お約束ー!

Read at your own discretion.

Higuchi's Room 4

PROFILE 12

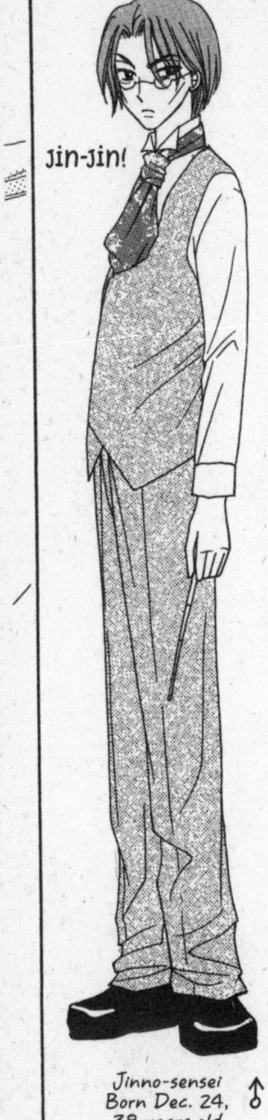
JIN-JIN!

Jinno-sensei ♂
Born Dec. 24,
38 years old
Capricorn,
Blood type AB

I wonder who would want to hear his profile, since so many readers hate him. But I like him. FYI, his hairstyle is modeled after Prime Minister Koizumi.

Theeeee end!

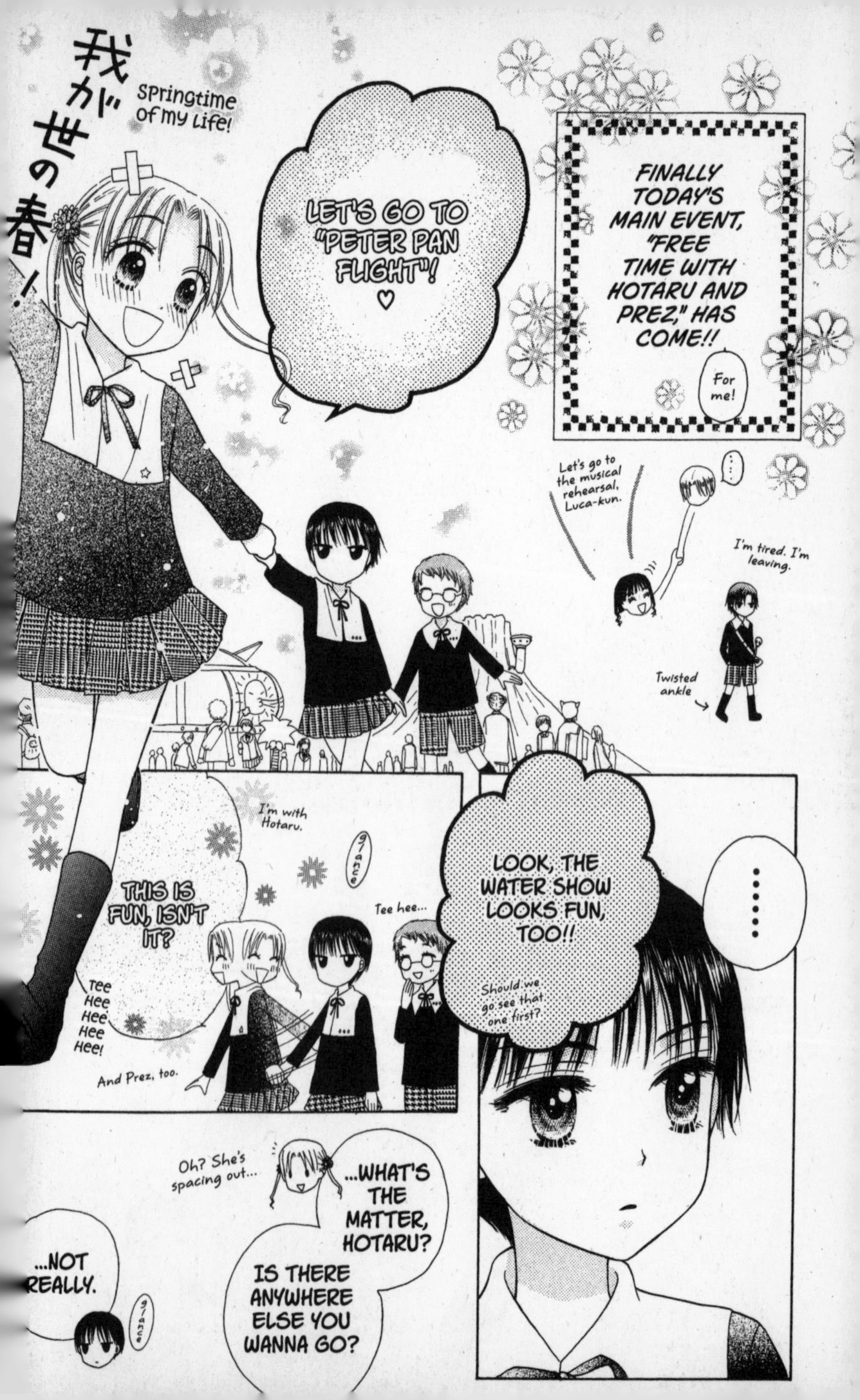
FINALLY TODAY'S MAIN EVENT, "FREE TIME WITH HOTARU AND PREZ," HAS COME!!
For me!
Let's go to the musical rehearsal, Luca-kun.
...
I'm tired. I'm leaving.
Twisted ankle
LET'S GO TO "PETER PAN FLIGHT"! ♡
Springtime of my life!
我が世の春！
LOOK, THE WATER SHOW LOOKS FUN, TOO!!
Should we go see that one first?
.....
I'm with Hotaru.
glance
Tee hee...
THIS IS FUN, ISN'T IT?
Tee hee hee hee hee!
And Prez, too.
Oh? She's spacing out...
...WHAT'S THE MATTER, HOTARU?
IS THERE ANYWHERE ELSE YOU WANNA GO?
...NOT REALLY.
glance

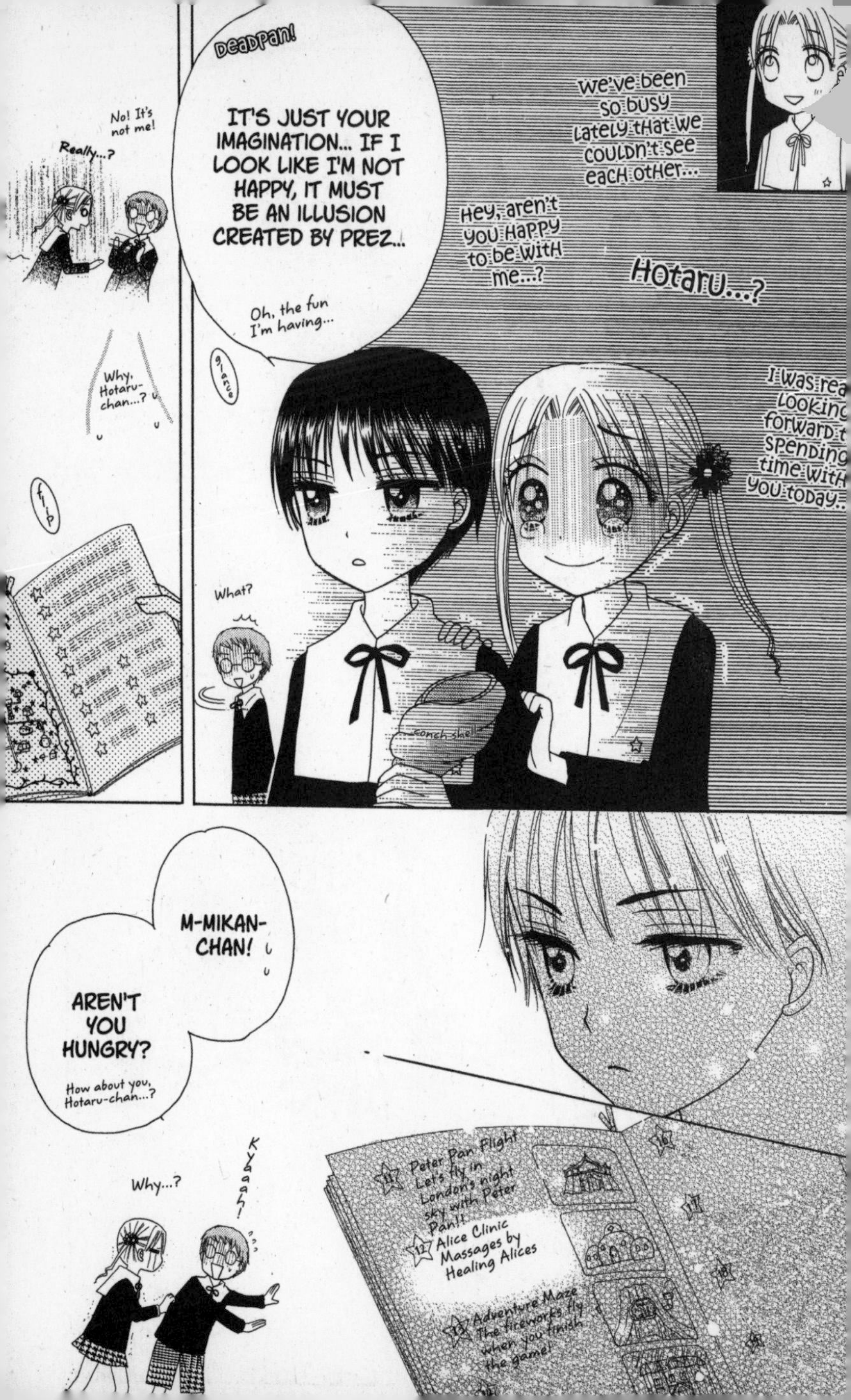

We've been so busy lately that we couldn't see each other...
Hey, aren't you happy to be with me...?
Hotaru...?
I was rea
looking
forward t
spending
time with
you today..
DEADPAN!
IT'S JUST YOUR IMAGINATION... IF I LOOK LIKE I'M NOT HAPPY, IT MUST BE AN ILLUSION CREATED BY PREZ...
Oh, the fun I'm having...
glance
What?
conch shell
No! It's not me!
Really...?
Why, Hotaru-chan...?
flip
M-MIKAN-CHAN!
AREN'T YOU HUNGRY?
How about you, Hotaru-chan...?
Kyaaah!
Why...?
11 Peter Pan Flight Let's fly in London's night sky with Peter Pan!
12 Alice Clinic Massages by Healing Alices
13 Adventure Maze The fireworks fly when you finish the game!
16
17
18

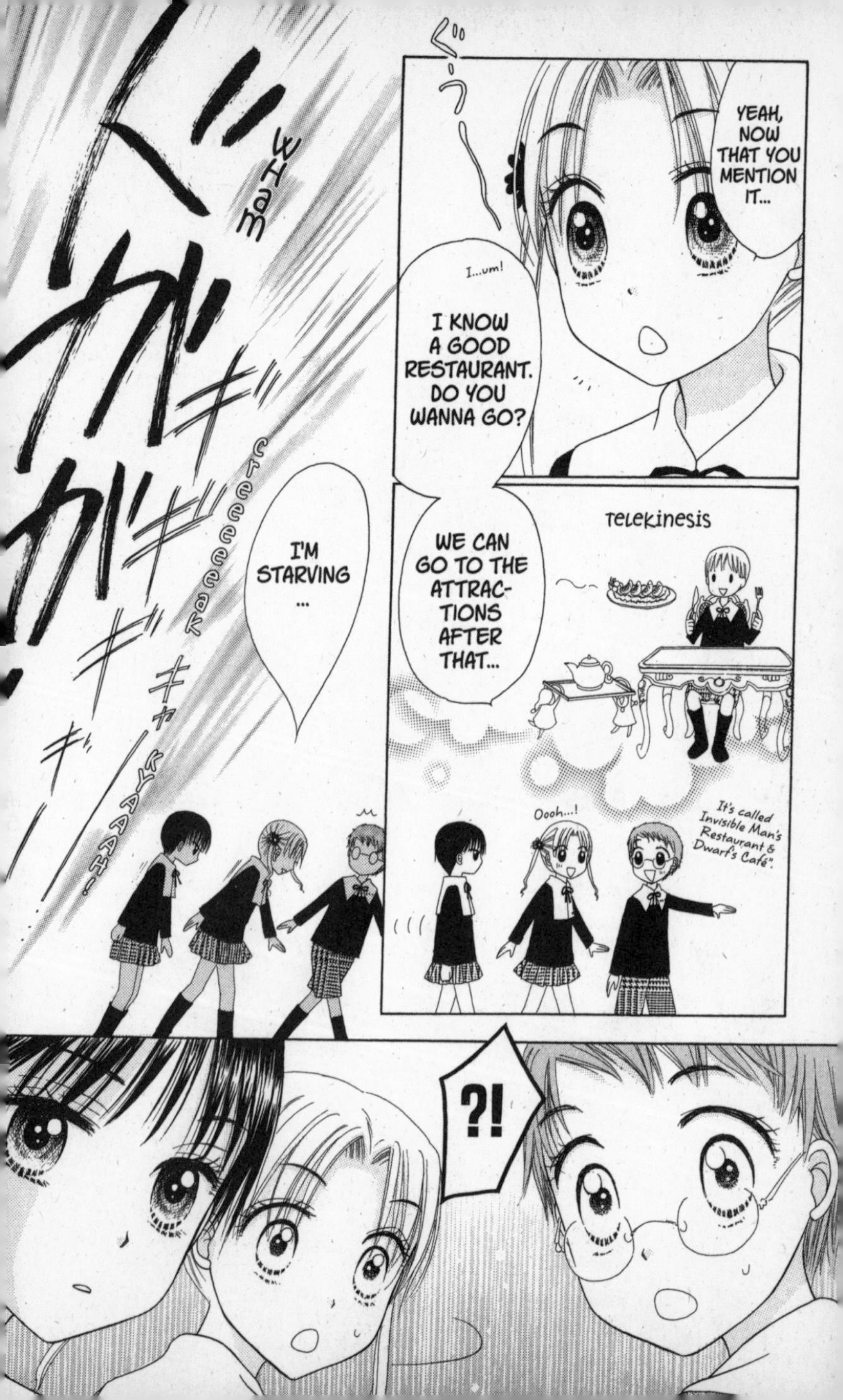

YEAH, NOW THAT YOU MENTION IT...
ぐう~
I...um!
I KNOW A GOOD RESTAURANT. DO YOU WANNA GO?
Telekinesis
It's called Invisible Man's Restaurant & Dwarf's Café".
Oooh...!
WE CAN GO TO THE ATTRACTIONS AFTER THAT...
I'M STARVING ...
WHAM
creeeeeeeak
キャー
KYAAAAH!
?!

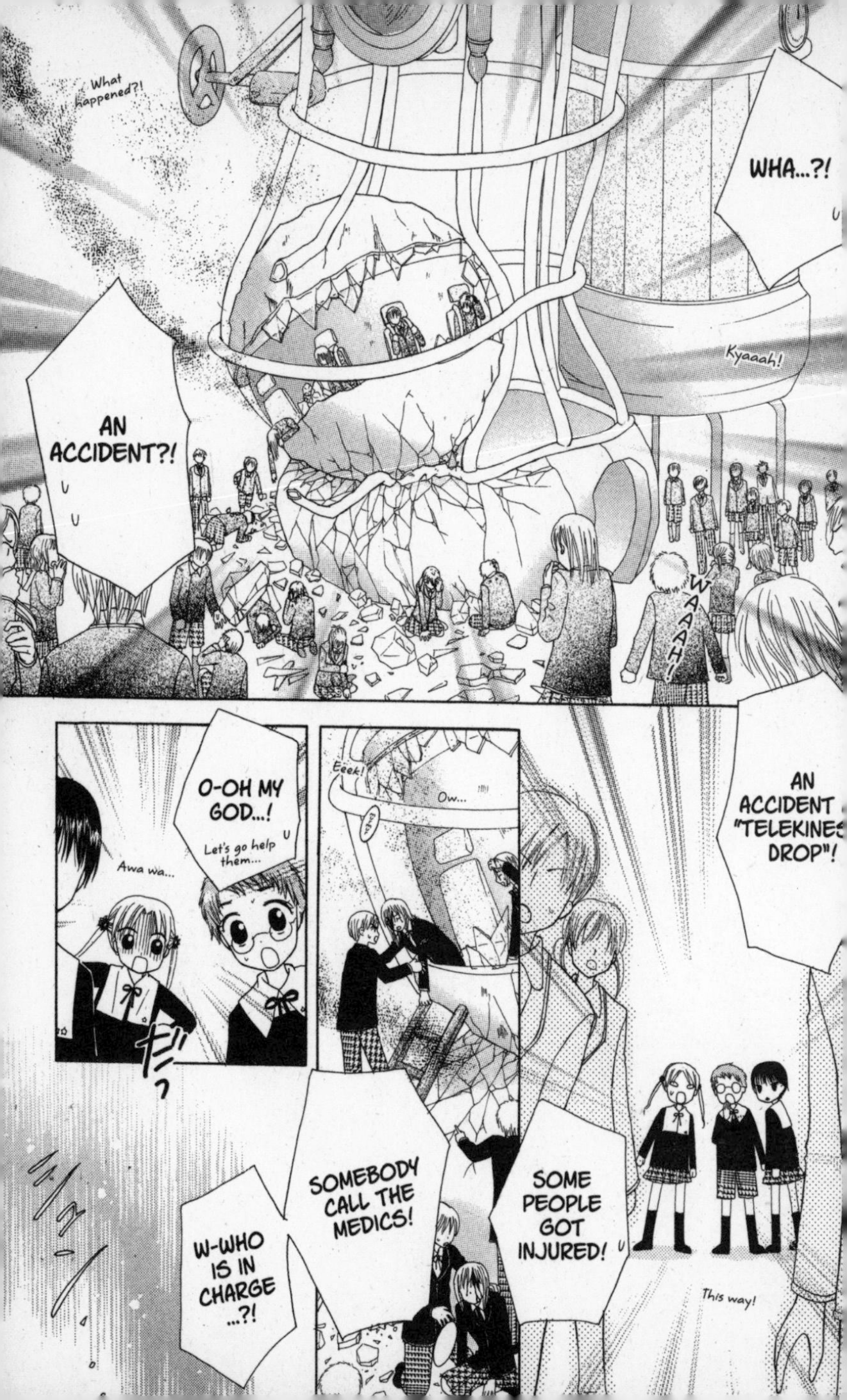
WHA...?!
What happened?!
Kyaaah!
AN ACCIDENT?!
WAAAAH!
AN ACCIDENT "TELEKINES DROP"!
Eeek!
Ow...
O-OH MY GOD...!
Let's go help them...
Awa wa...
This way!
SOME PEOPLE GOT INJURED!
SOMEBODY CALL THE MEDICS!
W-WHO IS IN CHARGE ...?!

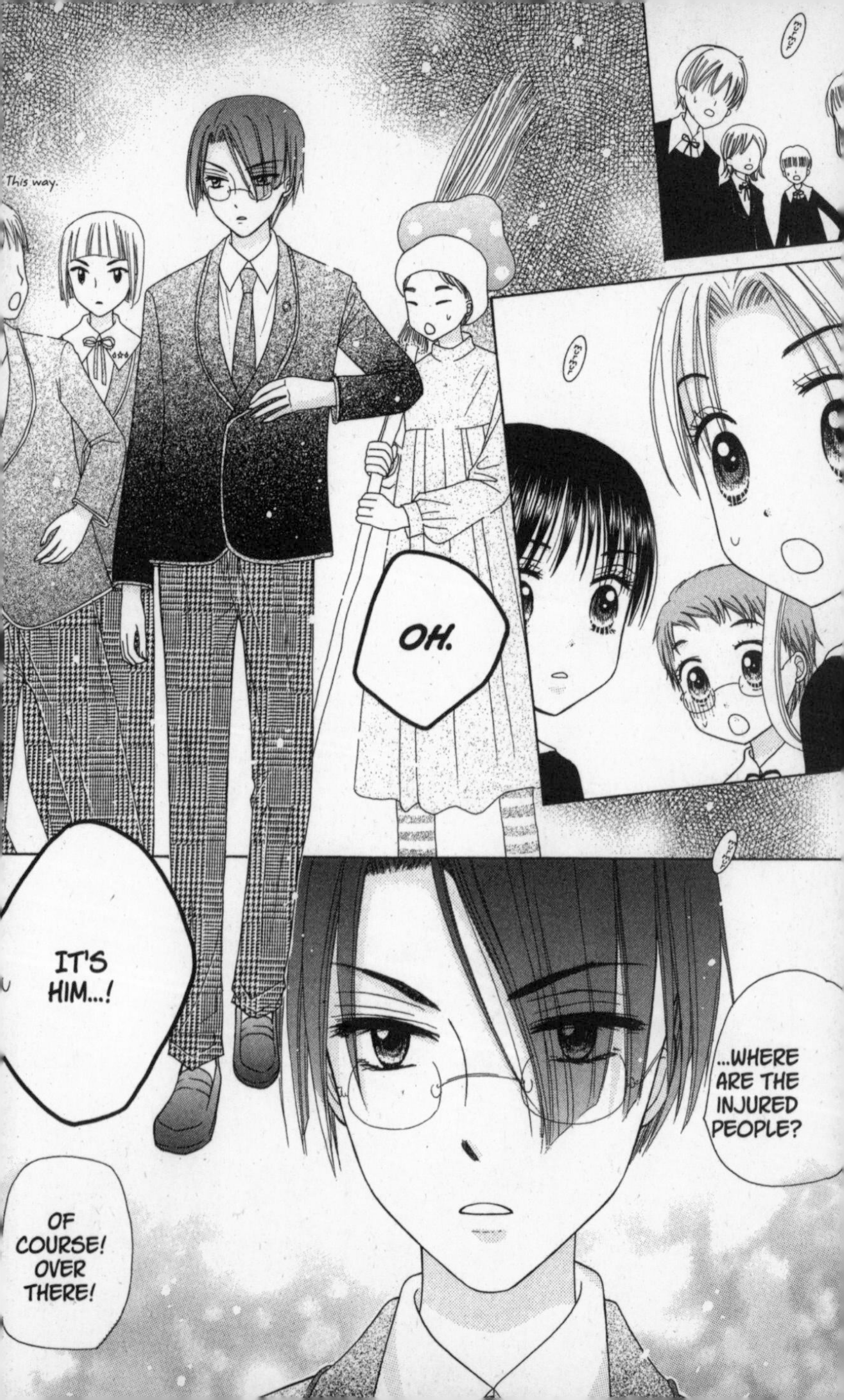
This way.
OH.
...WHERE ARE THE INJURED PEOPLE?
IT'S HIM...!
OF COURSE! OVER THERE!

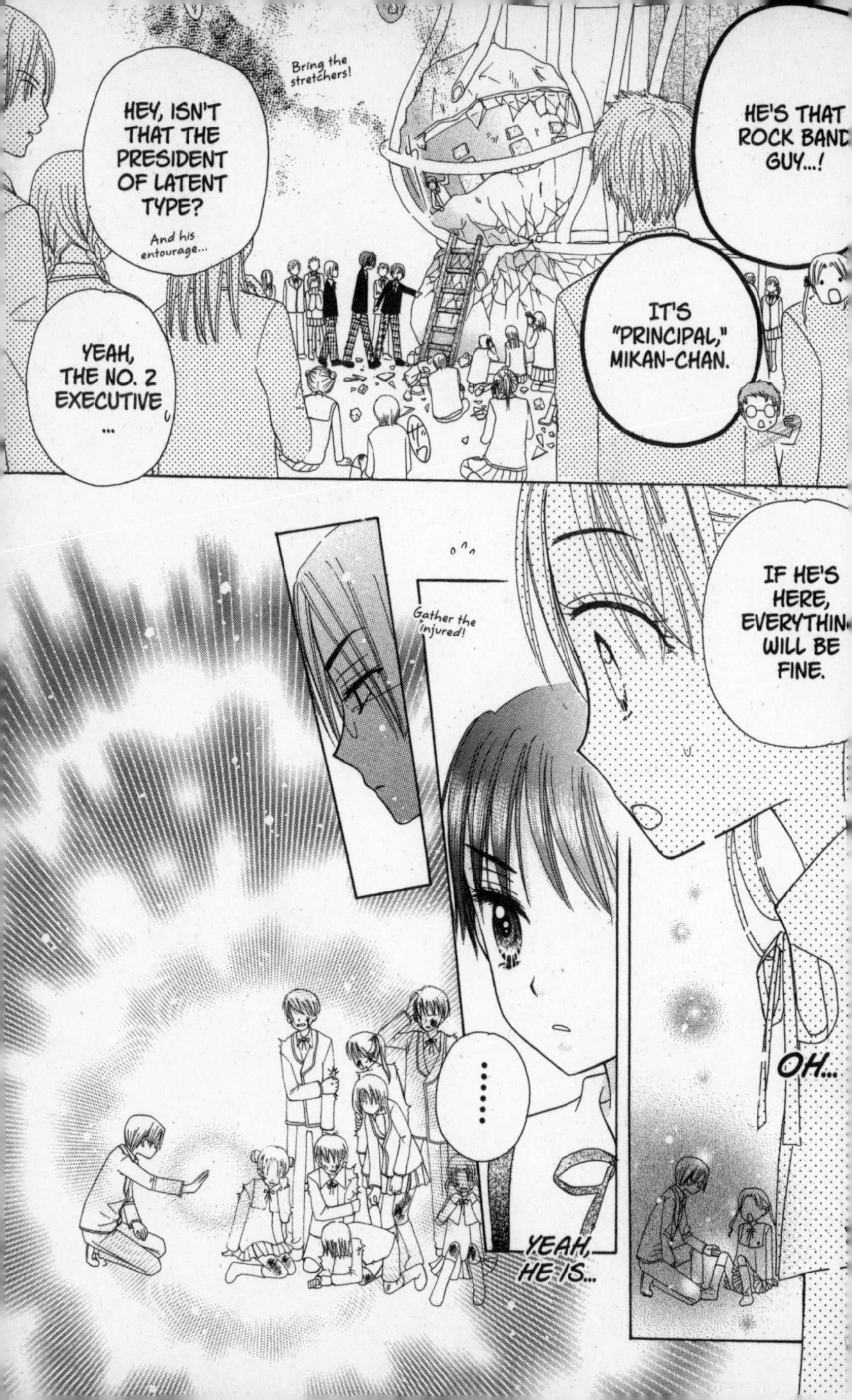
HE'S THAT ROCK BAND GUY...!
IT'S "PRINCIPAL," MIKAN-CHAN.
Bring the stretchers!
HEY, ISN'T THAT THE PRESIDENT OF LATENT TYPE?
And his entourage...
YEAH, THE NO. 2 EXECUTIVE ...
IF HE'S HERE, EVERYTHIN WILL BE FINE.
OH...
Gather the injured!
......
YEAH, HE IS...

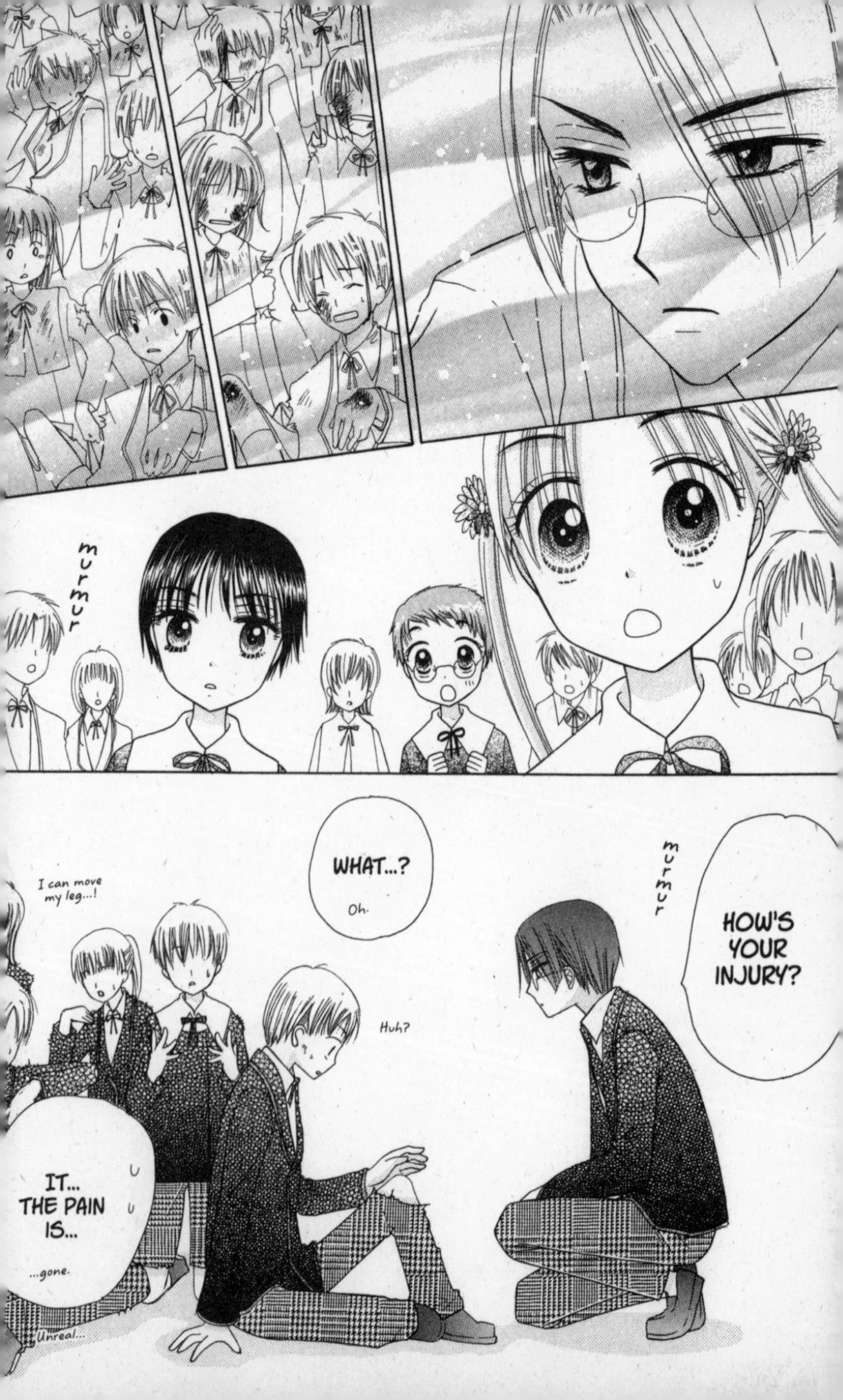
murmur
murmur
HOW'S YOUR INJURY?
WHAT...?
Oh.
Huh?
I can move my leg...!
IT... THE PAIN IS...
...gone.
Unreal...

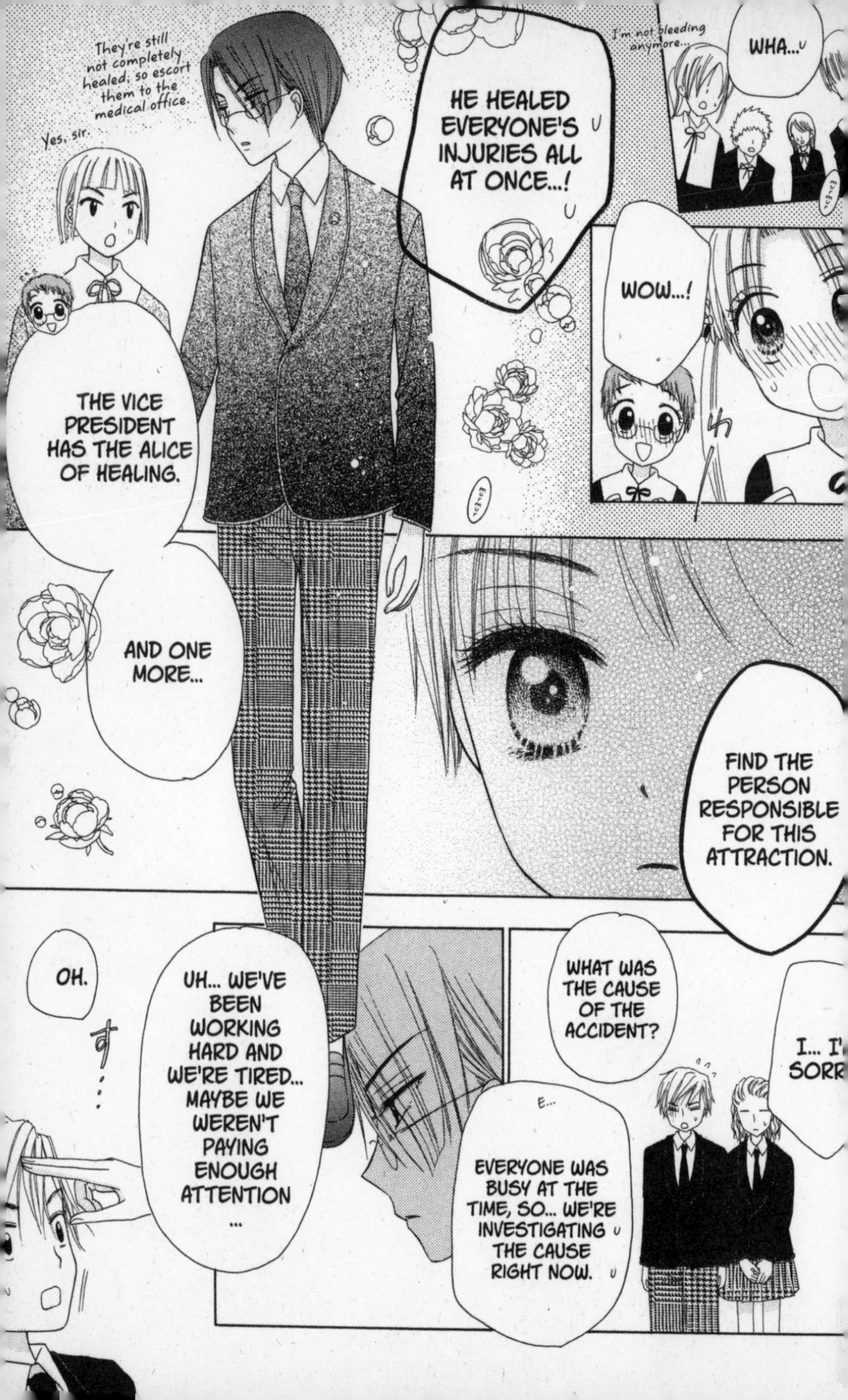

I'm not bleeding anymore...
WHA...
HE HEALED EVERYONE'S INJURIES ALL AT ONCE...!
WOW...!
They're still not completely healed, so escort them to the medical office.
Yes, sir.
THE VICE PRESIDENT HAS THE ALICE OF HEALING.
AND ONE MORE...
FIND THE PERSON RESPONSIBLE FOR THIS ATTRACTION.
I... I'M SORR
WHAT WAS THE CAUSE OF THE ACCIDENT?
E...
EVERYONE WAS BUSY AT THE TIME, SO... WE'RE INVESTIGATING THE CAUSE RIGHT NOW.
UH... WE'VE BEEN WORKING HARD AND WE'RE TIRED... MAYBE WE WEREN'T PAYING ENOUGH ATTENTION ...
OH.
す...

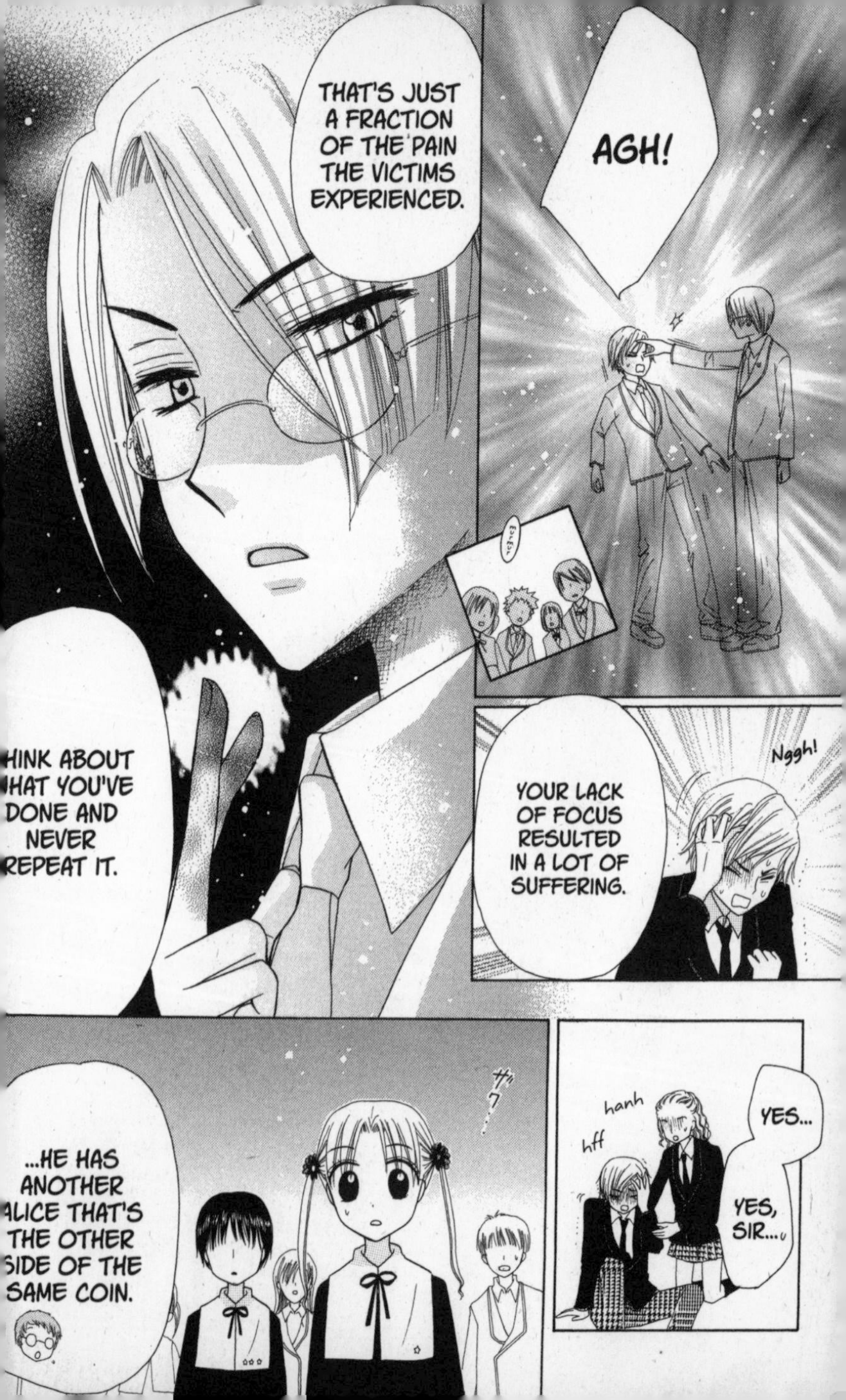
AGH!
Nggh!
YOUR LACK OF FOCUS RESULTED IN A LOT OF SUFFERING.
THAT'S JUST A FRACTION OF THE PAIN THE VICTIMS EXPERIENCED.
HINK ABOUT HAT YOU'VE DONE AND NEVER REPEAT IT.
YES...
YES, SIR...
hanh
hff
...HE HAS ANOTHER ALICE THAT'S THE OTHER SIDE OF THE SAME COIN.

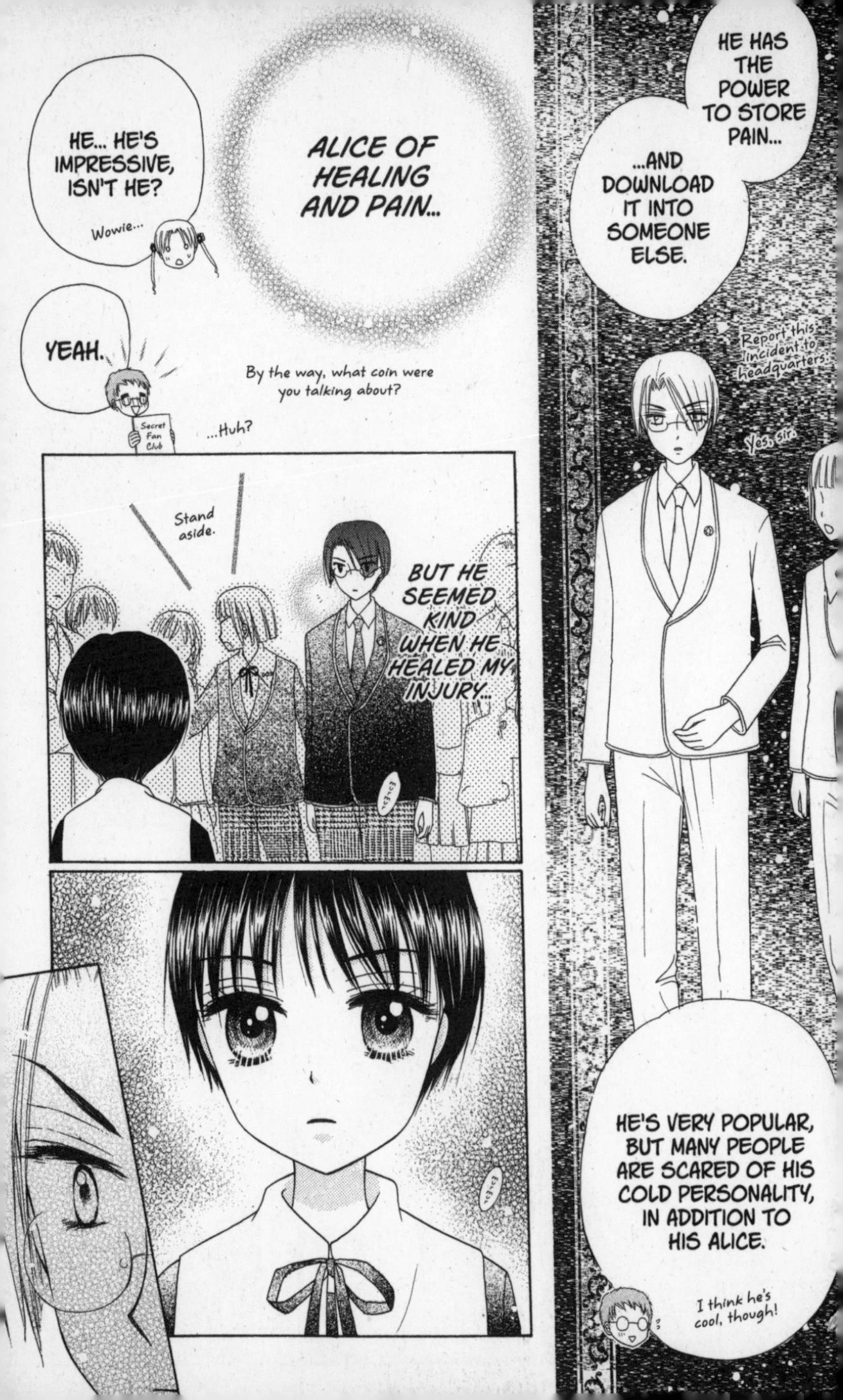
HE HAS THE POWER TO STORE PAIN...
...AND DOWNLOAD IT INTO SOMEONE ELSE.
Report this incident to headquarters.
Yes, sir.
HE'S VERY POPULAR, BUT MANY PEOPLE ARE SCARED OF HIS COLD PERSONALITY, IN ADDITION TO HIS ALICE.
I think he's cool, though!
ALICE OF HEALING AND PAIN...
HE... HE'S IMPRESSIVE, ISN'T HE?
Wowie...
YEAH.
Secret Fan Club
By the way, what coin were you talking about?
...Huh?
BUT HE SEEMED KIND WHEN HE HEALED MY INJURY...
Stand aside.

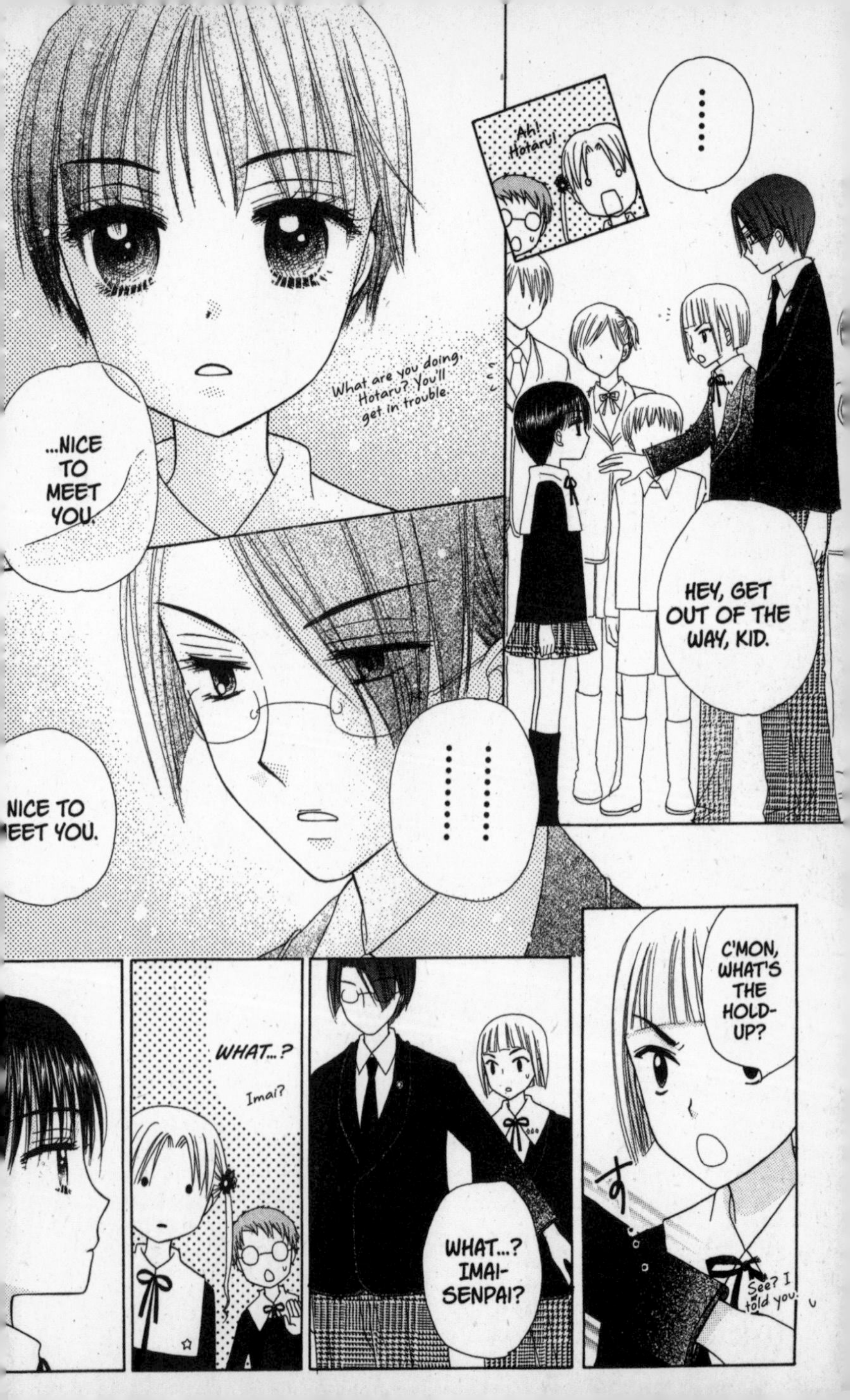
......
Ah! Hotaru!
HEY, GET OUT OF THE WAY, KID.
What are you doing, Hotaru? You'll get in trouble.
...NICE TO MEET YOU.
......
NICE TO EET YOU.
C'MON, WHAT'S THE HOLD-UP?
す
See? I told you.
WHAT...? IMAI-SENPAI?
WHAT...?
Imai?

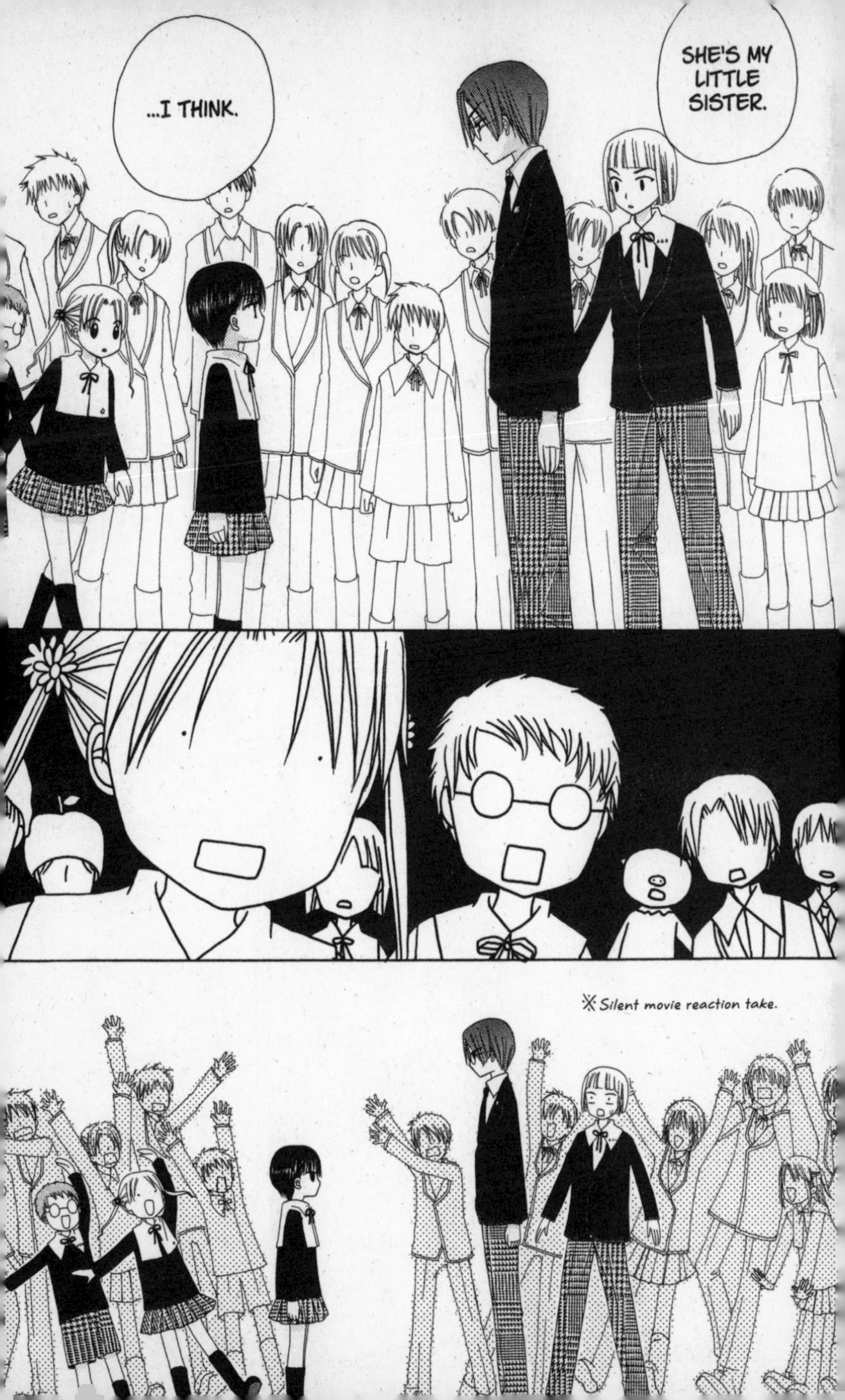
SHE'S MY LITTLE SISTER.
...I THINK.
※Silent movie reaction take.

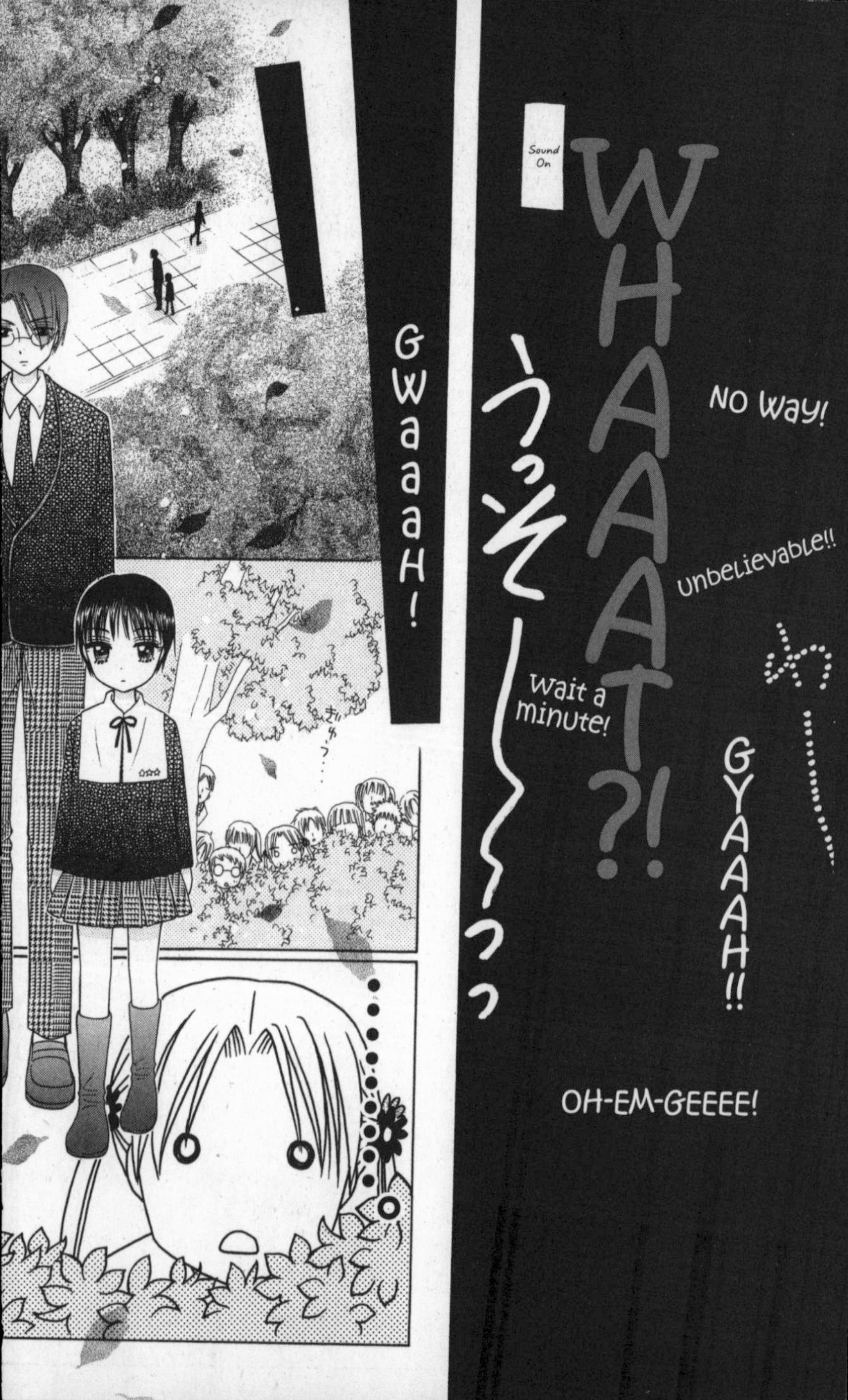
Sound On
WHAAAAT?!
NO WAY!
Unbelievable!!
Wait a minute!
GYAAAAH!!
OH-EM-GEEEE!
GWaaaaH!
....

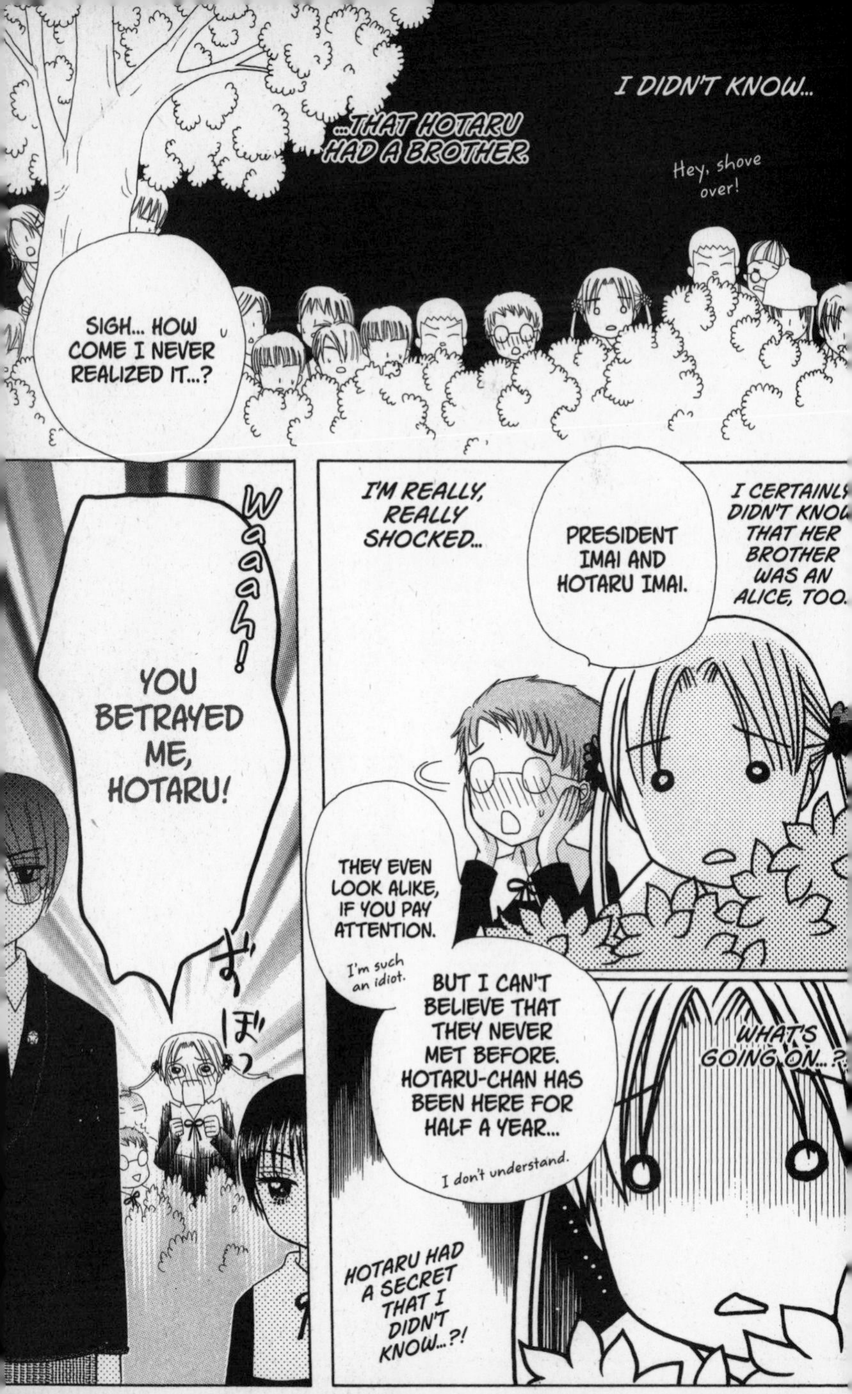
I DIDN'T KNOW...
...THAT HOTARU HAD A BROTHER.
Hey, shove over!
SIGH... HOW COME I NEVER REALIZED IT...?
I CERTAINLY DIDN'T KNOW THAT HER BROTHER WAS AN ALICE, TOO.
PRESIDENT IMAI AND HOTARU IMAI.
I'M REALLY, REALLY SHOCKED...
THEY EVEN LOOK ALIKE, IF YOU PAY ATTENTION.
I'm such an idiot.
WHAT'S GOING ON...?!
BUT I CAN'T BELIEVE THAT THEY NEVER MET BEFORE. HOTARU-CHAN HAS BEEN HERE FOR HALF A YEAR...
I don't understand.
HOTARU HAD A SECRET THAT I DIDN'T KNOW...?!
Waaah!
YOU BETRAYED ME, HOTARU!
ずぼっ

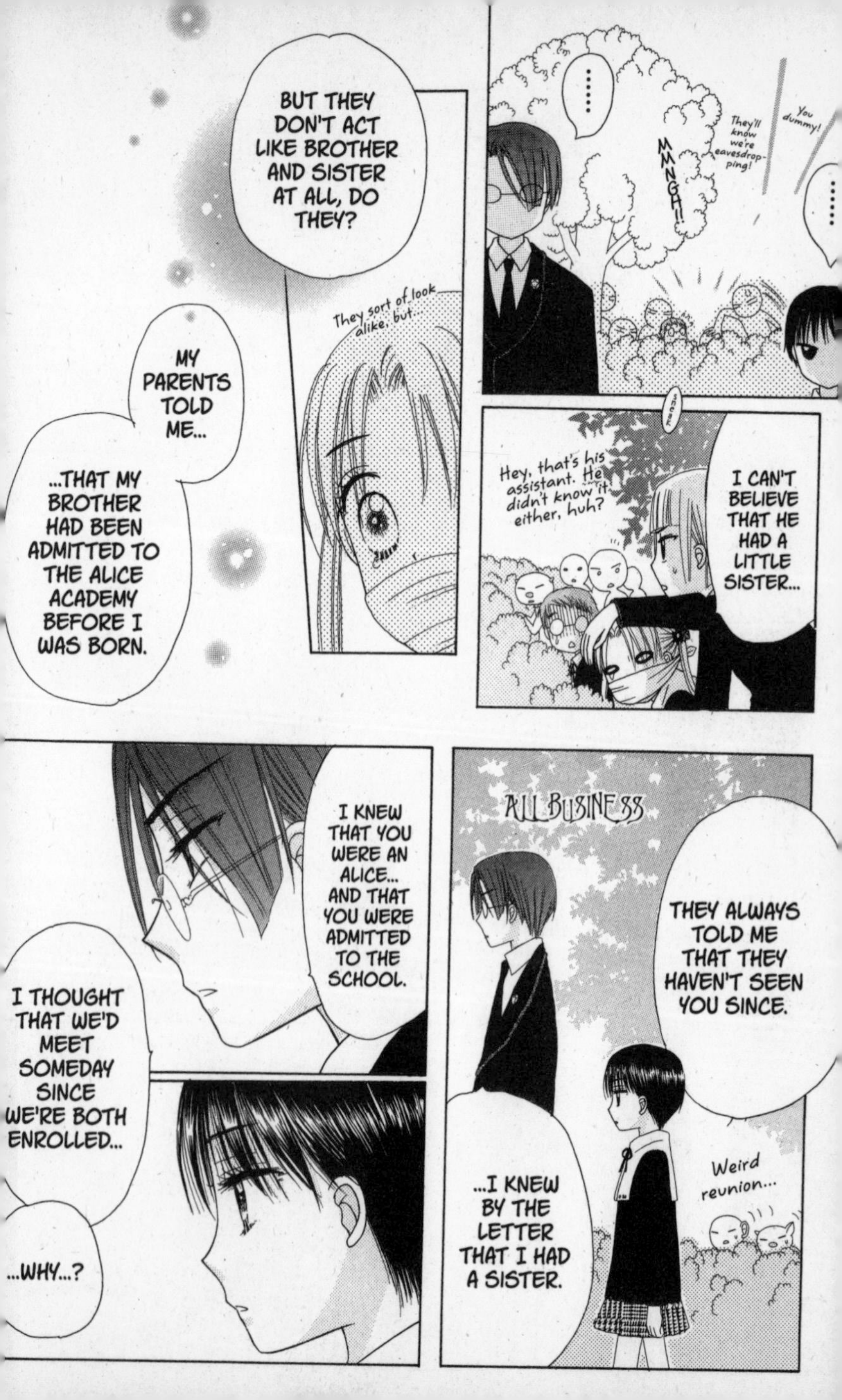

......
You dummy!
They'll know we're eavesdrop-ping!
MMNGH!!
......
sneak
I CAN'T BELIEVE THAT HE HAD A LITTLE SISTER...
Hey, that's his assistant. He didn't know it either, huh?
BUT THEY DON'T ACT LIKE BROTHER AND SISTER AT ALL, DO THEY?
They sort of look alike, but...
MY PARENTS TOLD ME...
...THAT MY BROTHER HAD BEEN ADMITTED TO THE ALICE ACADEMY BEFORE I WAS BORN.
ALL BUSINESS
THEY ALWAYS TOLD ME THAT THEY HAVEN'T SEEN YOU SINCE.
...I KNEW BY THE LETTER THAT I HAD A SISTER.
Weird reunion...
I KNEW THAT YOU WERE AN ALICE... AND THAT YOU WERE ADMITTED TO THE SCHOOL.
I THOUGHT THAT WE'D MEET SOMEDAY SINCE WE'RE BOTH ENROLLED...
...WHY...?

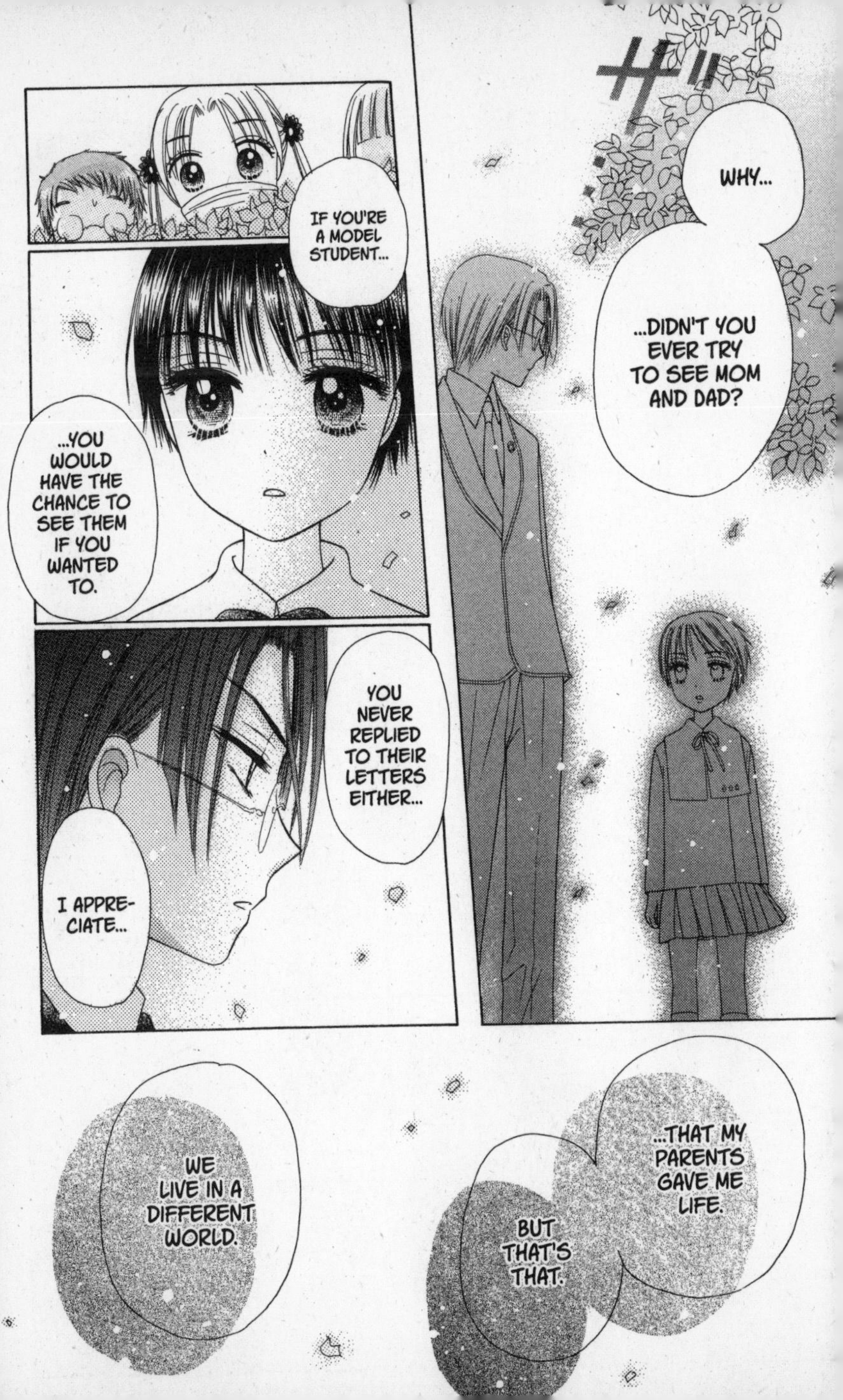
ザ
WHY...
...DIDN'T YOU EVER TRY TO SEE MOM AND DAD?
IF YOU'RE A MODEL STUDENT...
...YOU WOULD HAVE THE CHANCE TO SEE THEM IF YOU WANTED TO.
YOU NEVER REPLIED TO THEIR LETTERS EITHER...
I APPRE-CIATE...
...THAT MY PARENTS GAVE ME LIFE.
BUT THAT'S THAT.
WE LIVE IN A DIFFERENT WORLD.

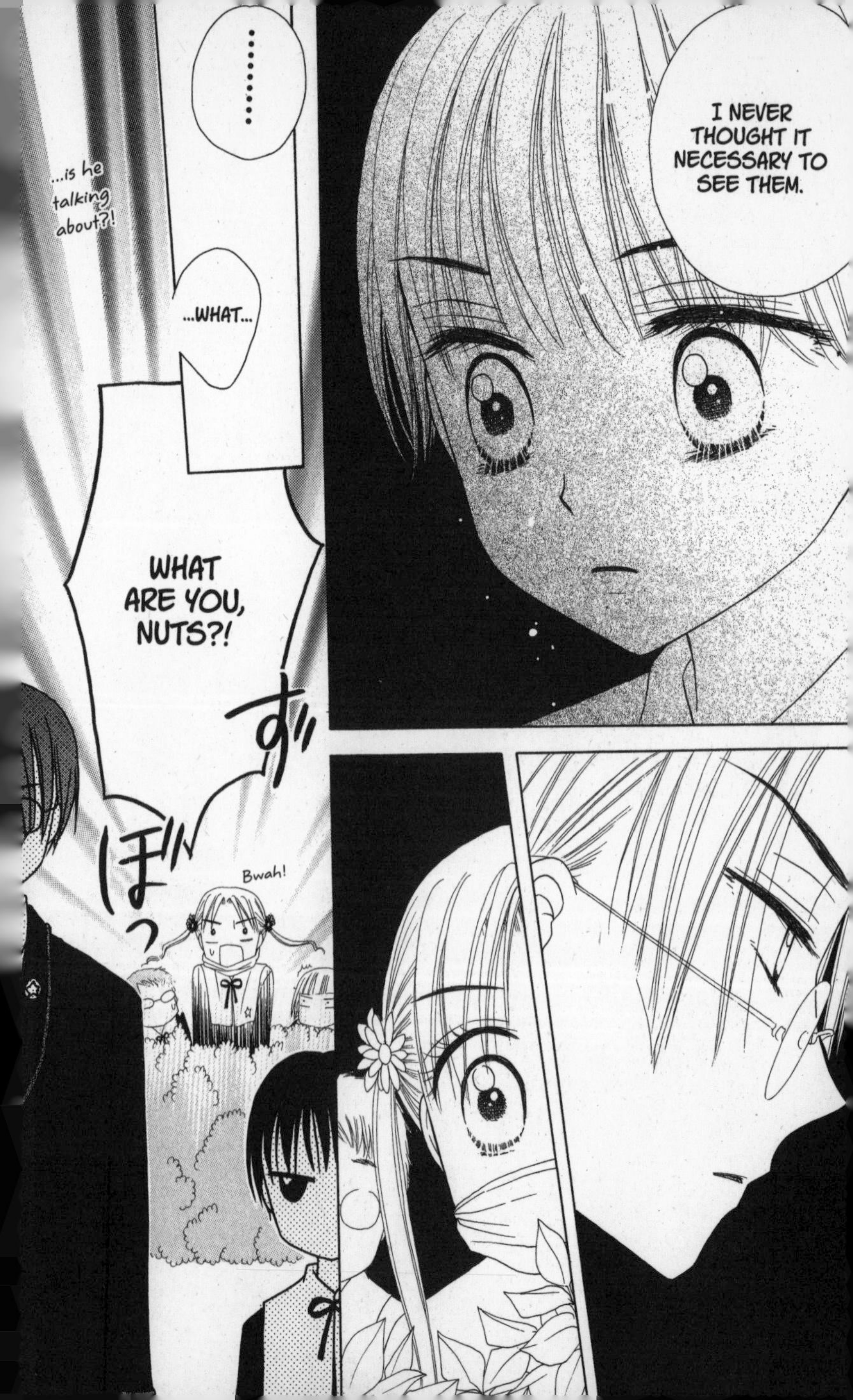
I NEVER THOUGHT IT NECESSARY TO SEE THEM.
......
...WHAT...
...is he talking about?!
WHAT ARE YOU, NUTS?!
ず
ぼっ
Bwah!

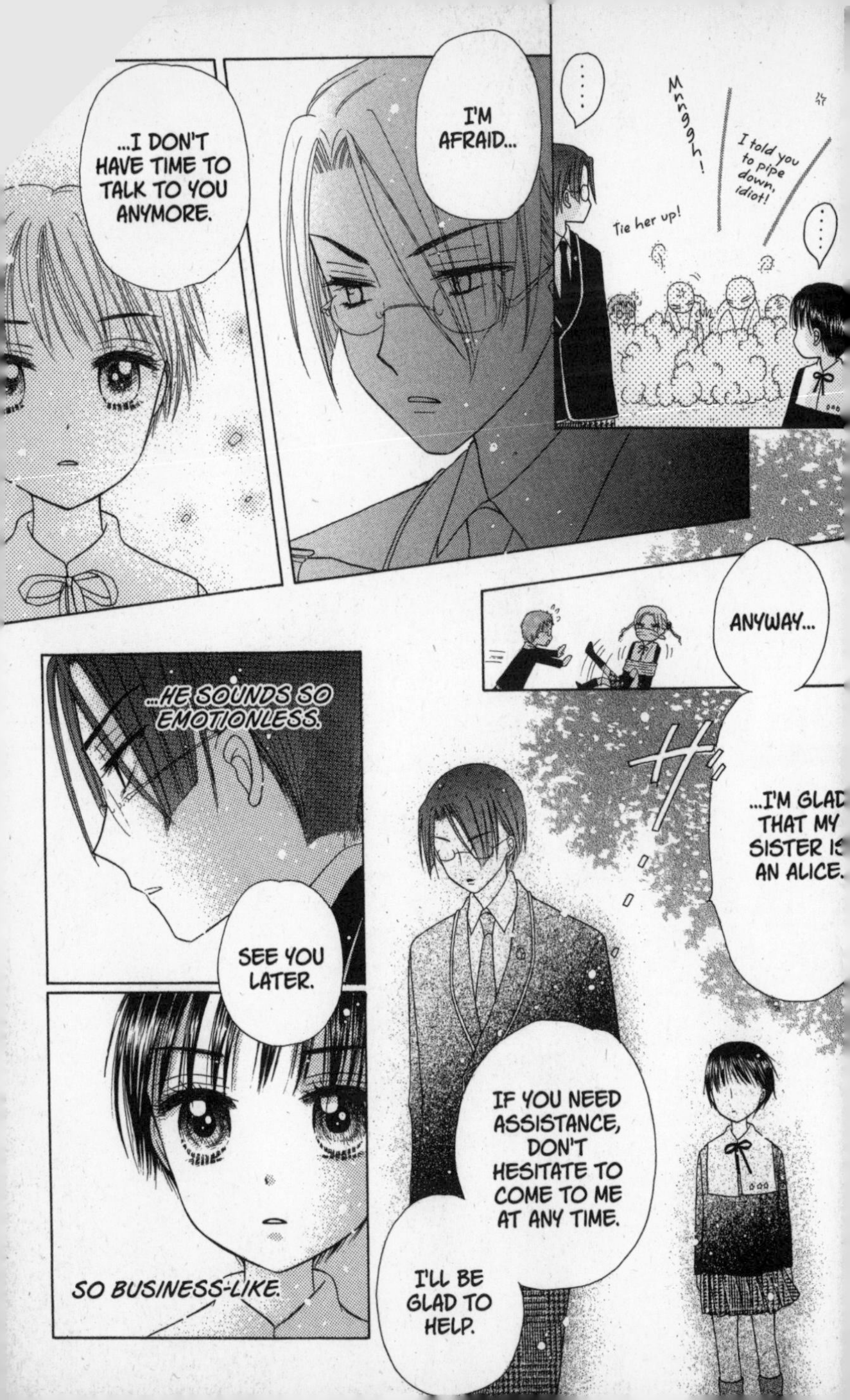
......
Mnnggh!
I told you to pipe down, idiot!
Tie her up!
......
I'M AFRAID...
...I DON'T HAVE TIME TO TALK TO YOU ANYMORE.
ANYWAY...
...I'M GLAD THAT MY SISTER IS AN ALICE.
IF YOU NEED ASSISTANCE, DON'T HESITATE TO COME TO ME AT ANY TIME.
I'LL BE GLAD TO HELP.
...HE SOUNDS SO EMOTIONLESS.
SEE YOU LATER.
SO BUSINESS-LIKE.

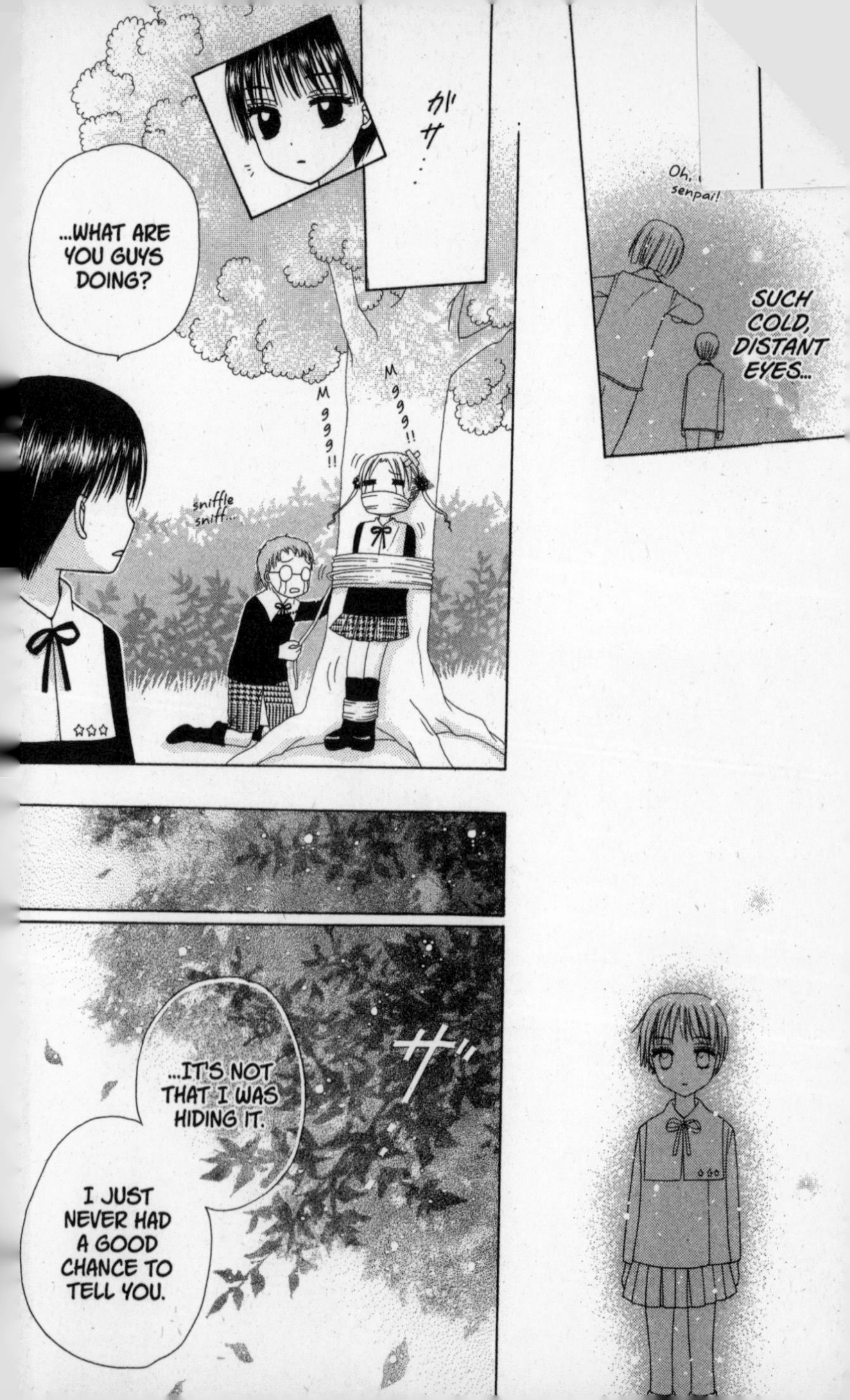
Oh,
senpai!
SUCH COLD, DISTANT EYES...
ガサ...
...WHAT ARE YOU GUYS DOING?
Mggg!!
Mggg!!
sniffle sniff...
ザッ
...IT'S NOT THAT I WAS HIDING IT.
I JUST NEVER HAD A GOOD CHANCE TO TELL YOU.

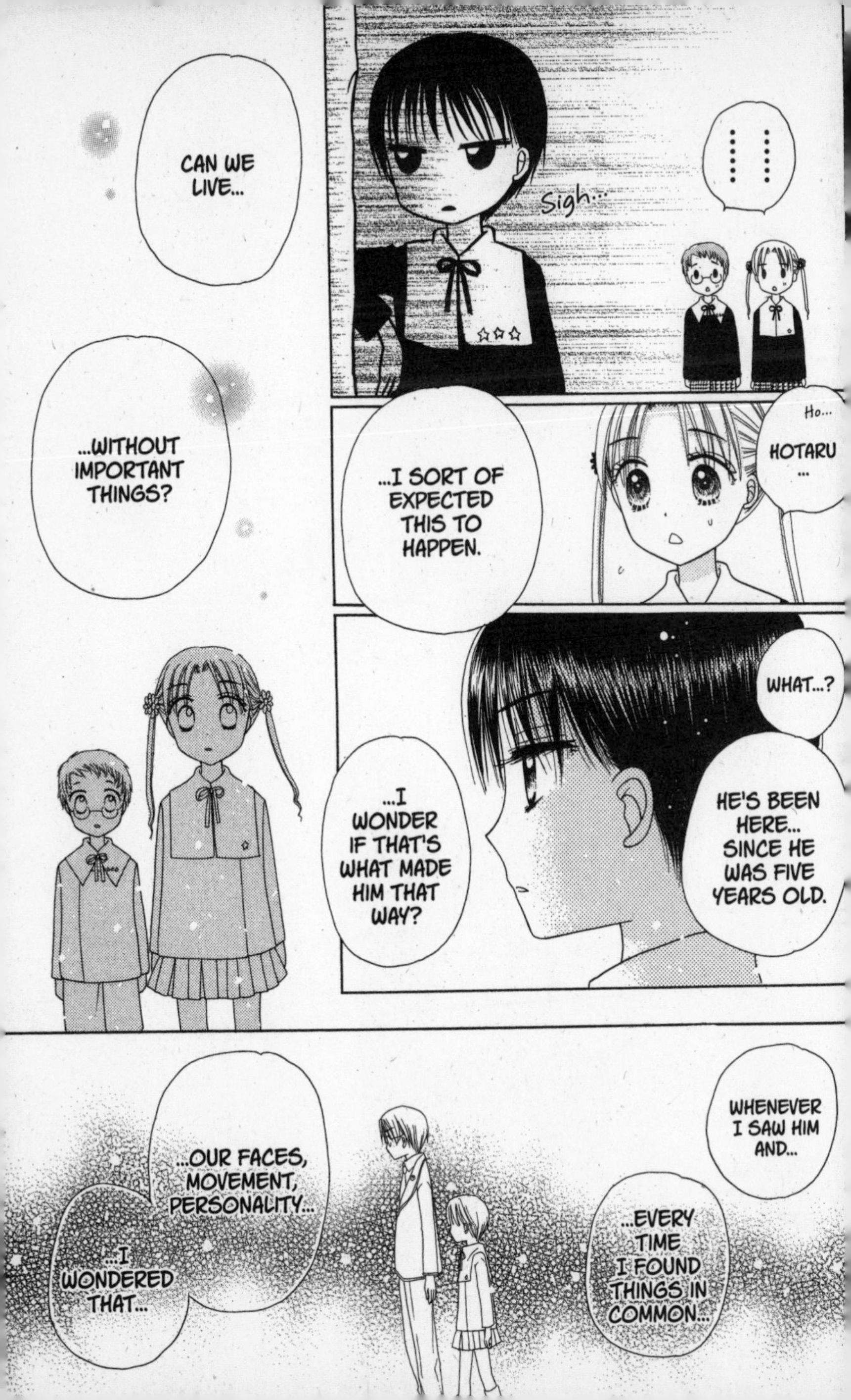
......
Sigh...
Ho... HOTARU...
...I SORT OF EXPECTED THIS TO HAPPEN.
WHAT...?
HE'S BEEN HERE... SINCE HE WAS FIVE YEARS OLD.
...I WONDER IF THAT'S WHAT MADE HIM THAT WAY?
CAN WE LIVE...
...WITHOUT IMPORTANT THINGS?
WHENEVER I SAW HIM AND...
...EVERY TIME I FOUND THINGS IN COMMON...
...OUR FACES, MOVEMENT, PERSONALITY...
...I WONDERED THAT...

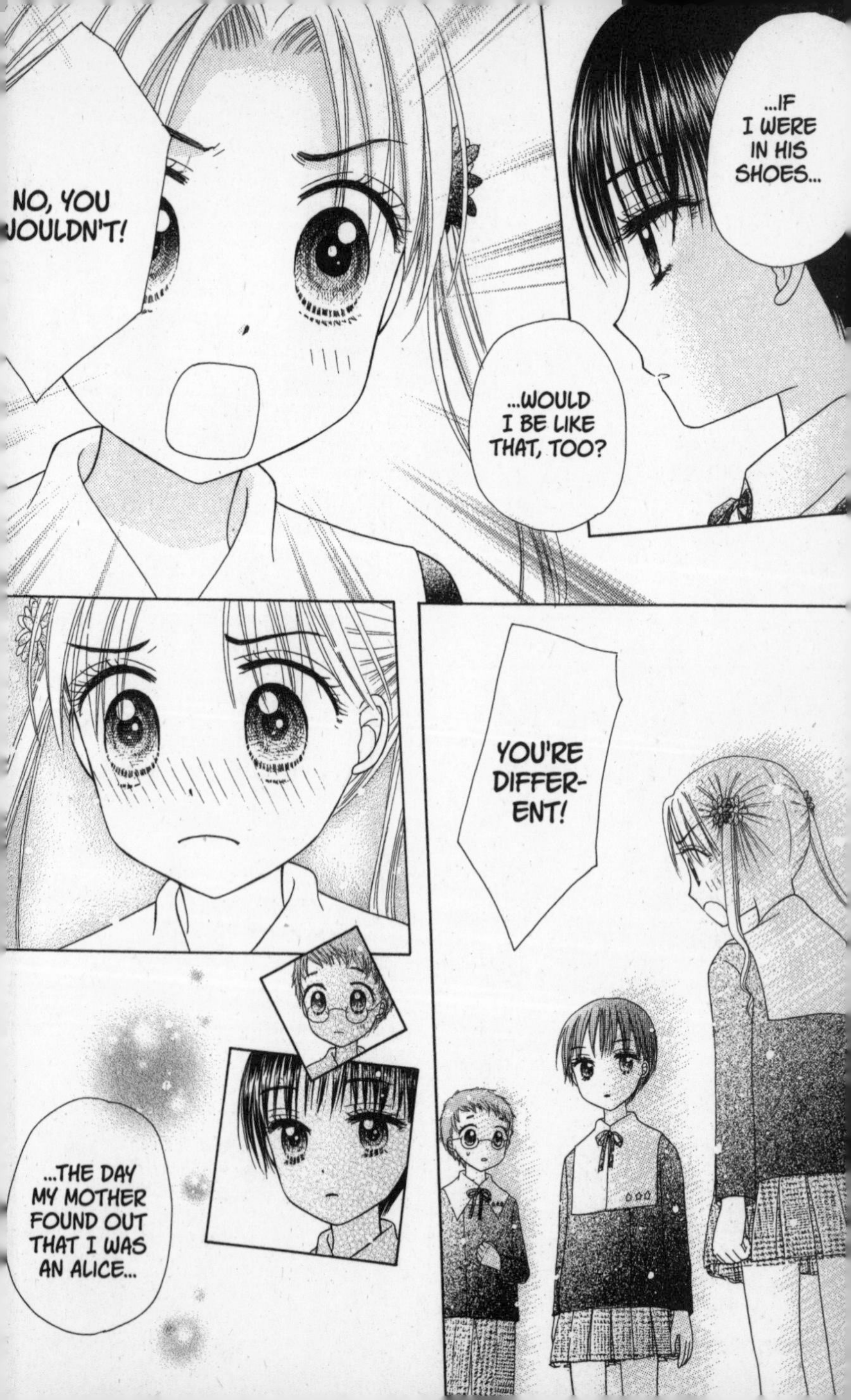
...IF I WERE IN HIS SHOES...
...WOULD I BE LIKE THAT, TOO?
NO, YOU WOULDN'T!
YOU'RE DIFFER-ENT!
...THE DAY MY MOTHER FOUND OUT THAT I WAS AN ALICE...

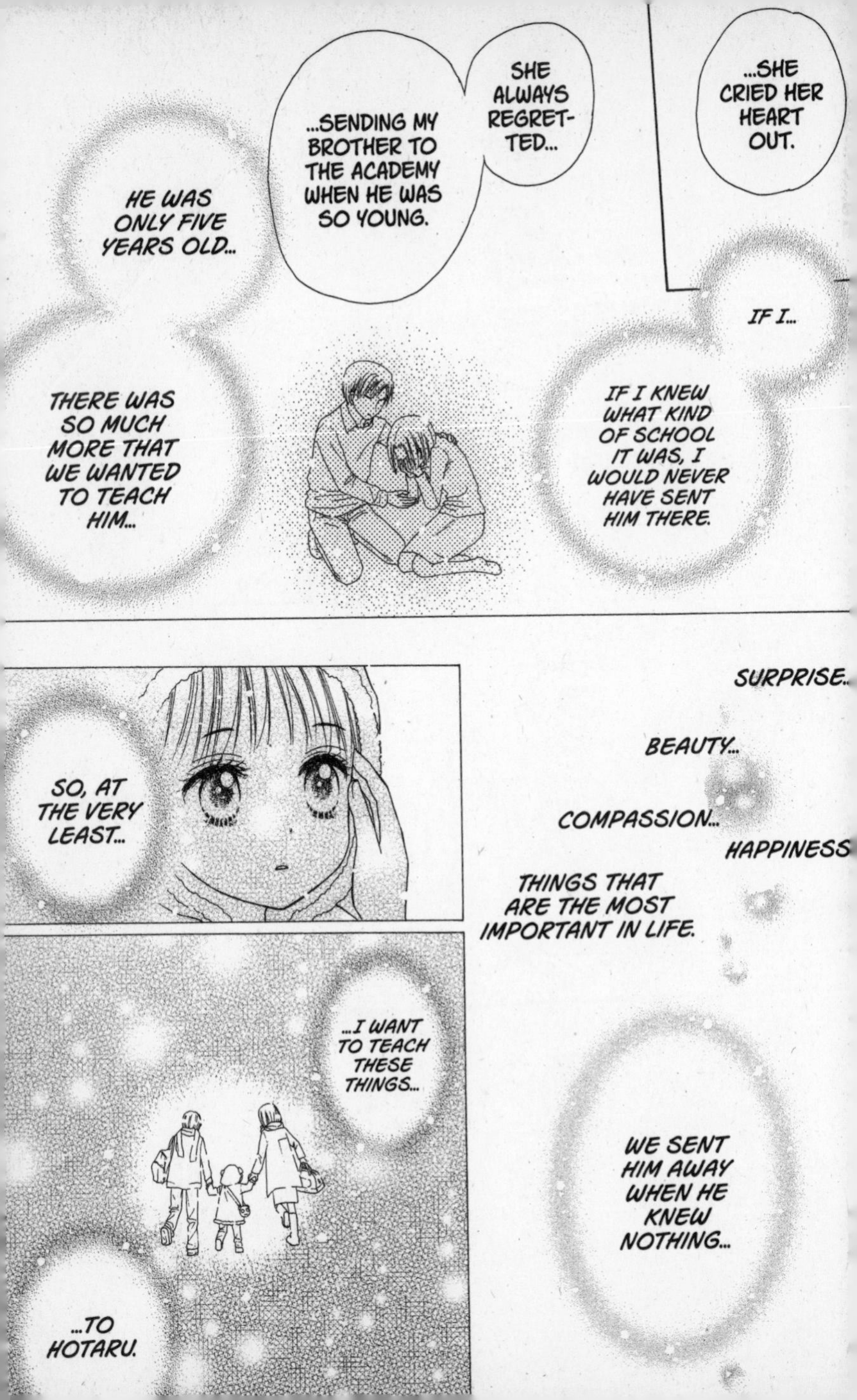
SHE ALWAYS REGRET-TED...
...SENDING MY BROTHER TO THE ACADEMY WHEN HE WAS SO YOUNG.
HE WAS ONLY FIVE YEARS OLD...
THERE WAS SO MUCH MORE THAT WE WANTED TO TEACH HIM...
IF I...
IF I KNEW WHAT KIND OF SCHOOL IT WAS, I WOULD NEVER HAVE SENT HIM THERE.
...SHE CRIED HER HEART OUT.
SURPRISE..
BEAUTY...
COMPASSION...
HAPPINESS
THINGS THAT ARE THE MOST IMPORTANT IN LIFE.
WE SENT HIM AWAY WHEN HE KNEW NOTHING...
SO, AT THE VERY LEAST...
...I WANT TO TEACH THESE THINGS...
...TO HOTARU.

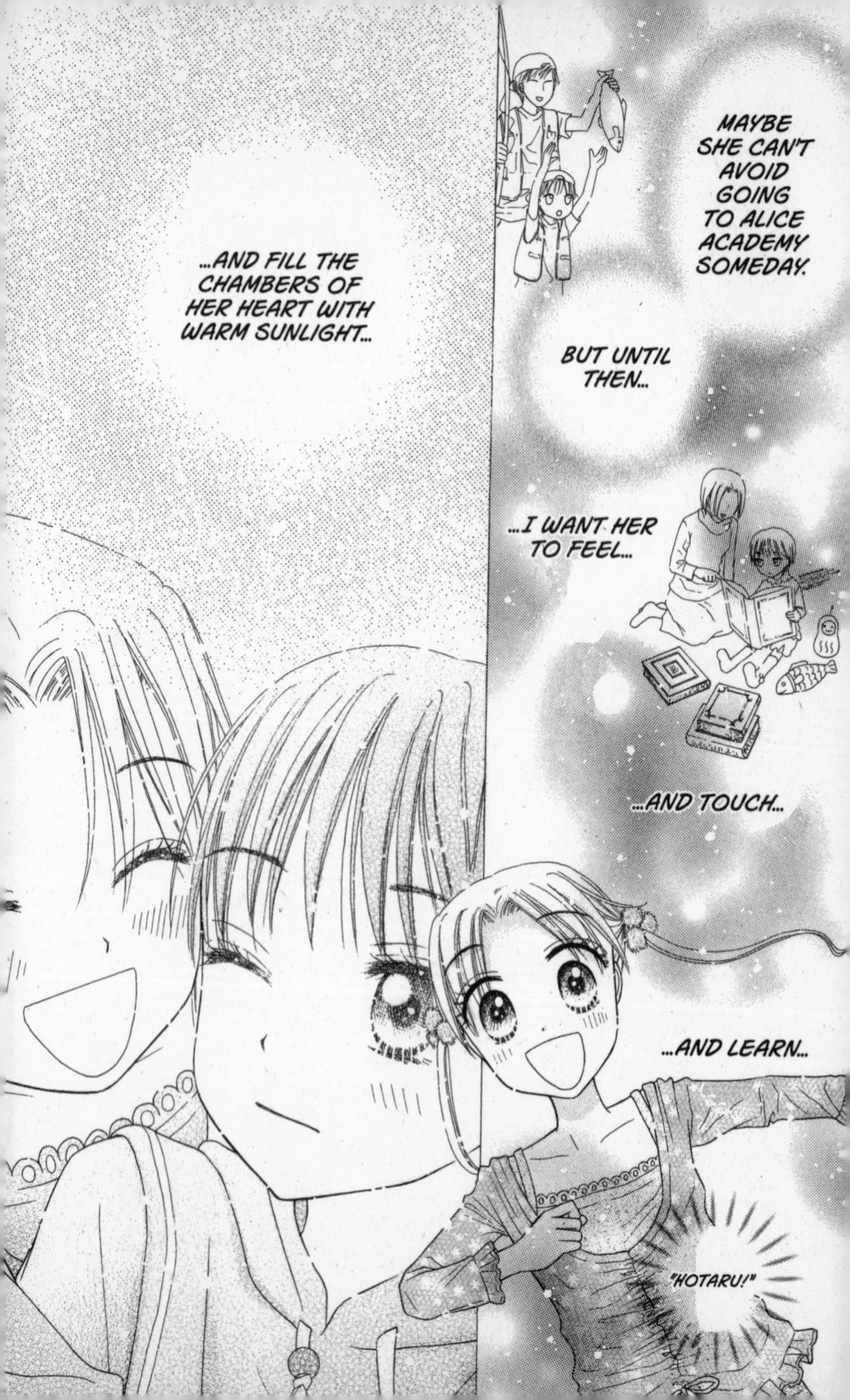
MAYBE SHE CAN'T AVOID GOING TO ALICE ACADEMY SOMEDAY.
BUT UNTIL THEN...
...I WANT HER TO FEEL...
...AND TOUCH...
...AND LEARN...
"HOTARU!"
...AND FILL THE CHAMBERS OF HER HEART WITH WARM SUNLIGHT...

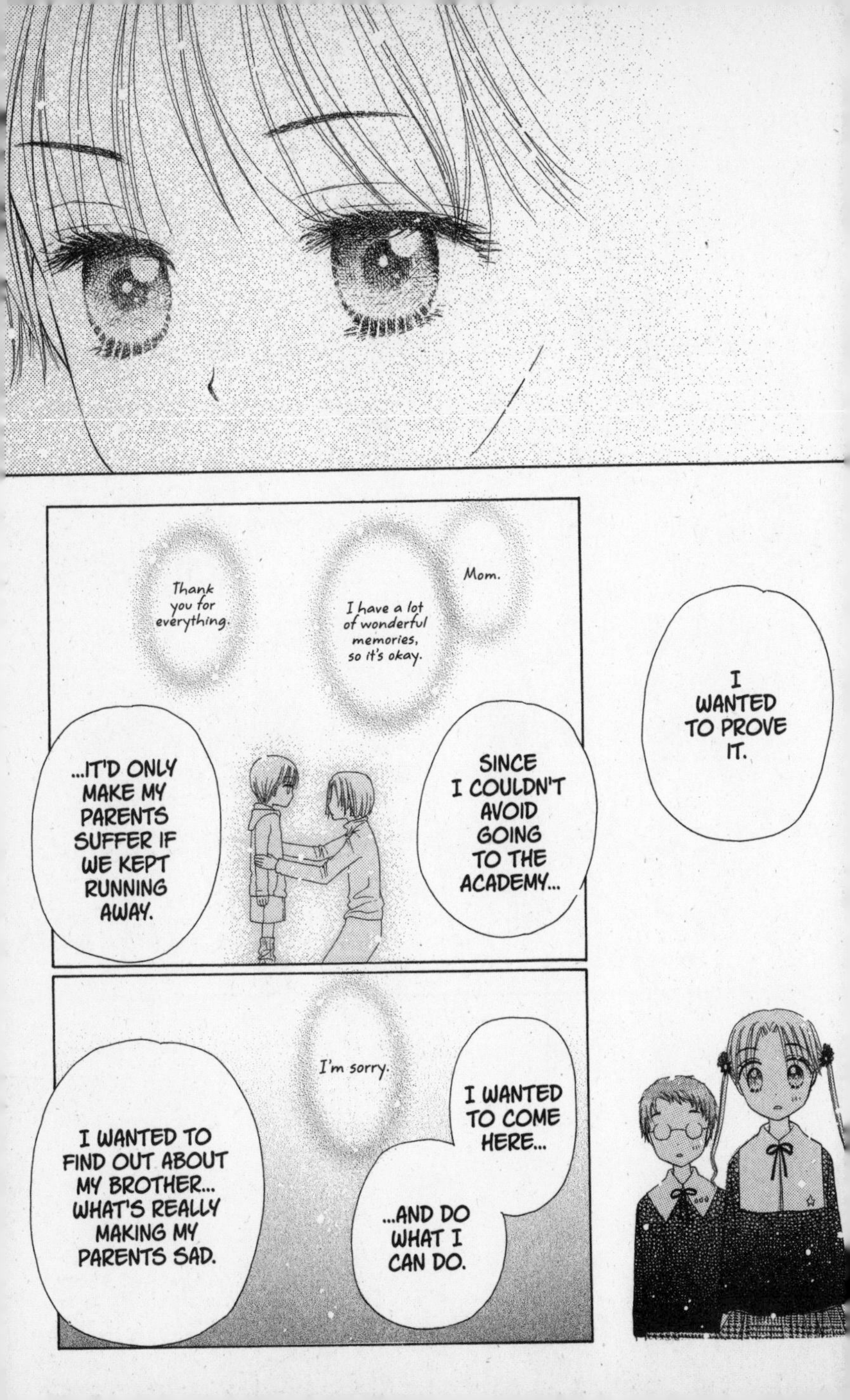
I WANTED TO PROVE IT.
Mom.
I have a lot of wonderful memories, so it's okay.
Thank you for everything.
SINCE I COULDN'T AVOID GOING TO THE ACADEMY...
...IT'D ONLY MAKE MY PARENTS SUFFER IF WE KEPT RUNNING AWAY.
I'm sorry.
I WANTED TO COME HERE...
...AND DO WHAT I CAN DO.
I WANTED TO FIND OUT ABOUT MY BROTHER... WHAT'S REALLY MAKING MY PARENTS SAD.

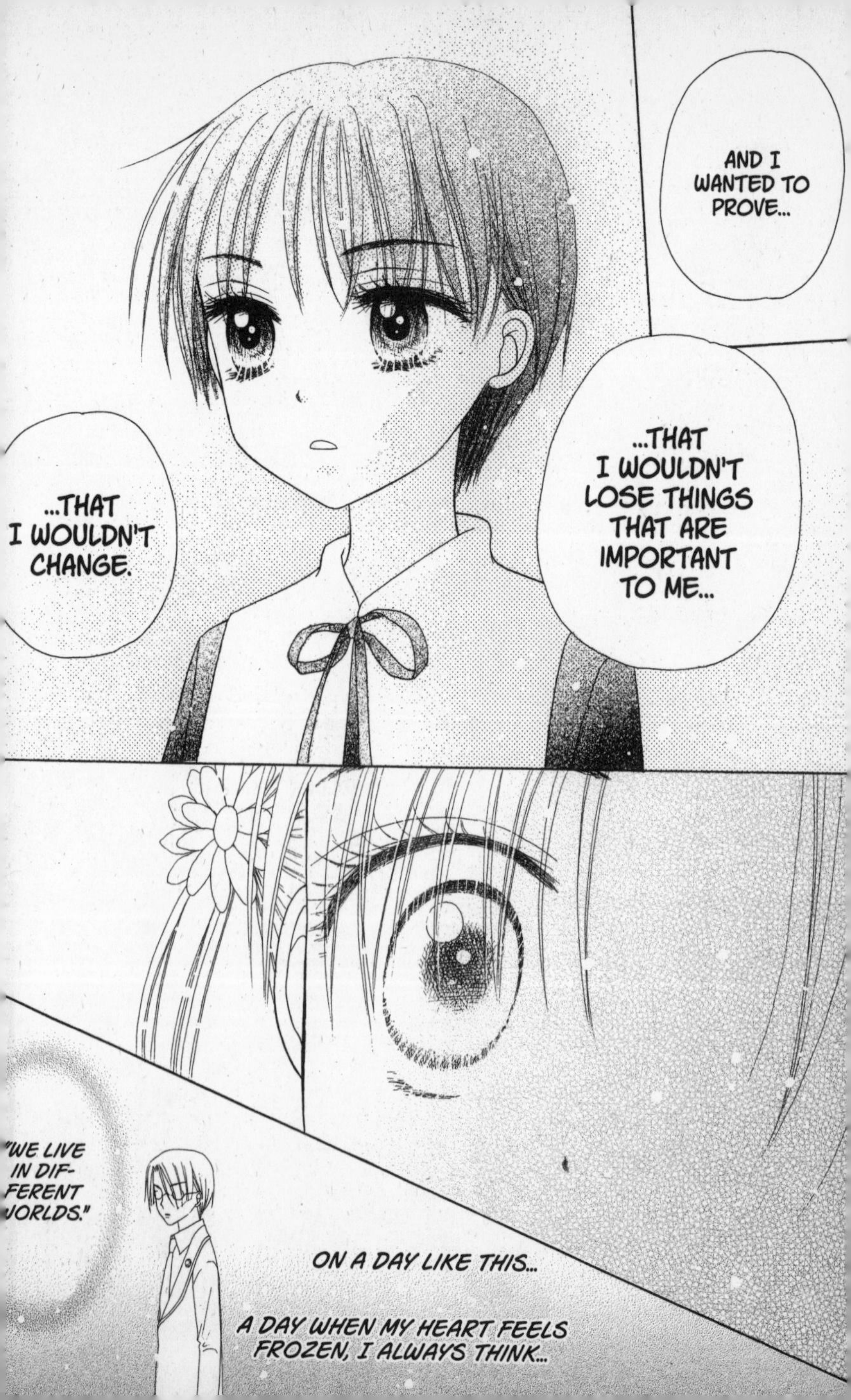
AND I WANTED TO PROVE...
...THAT I WOULDN'T LOSE THINGS THAT ARE IMPORTANT TO ME...
...THAT I WOULDN'T CHANGE.
ON A DAY LIKE THIS...
A DAY WHEN MY HEART FEELS FROZEN, I ALWAYS THINK...
"WE LIVE IN DIF-FERENT WORLDS."

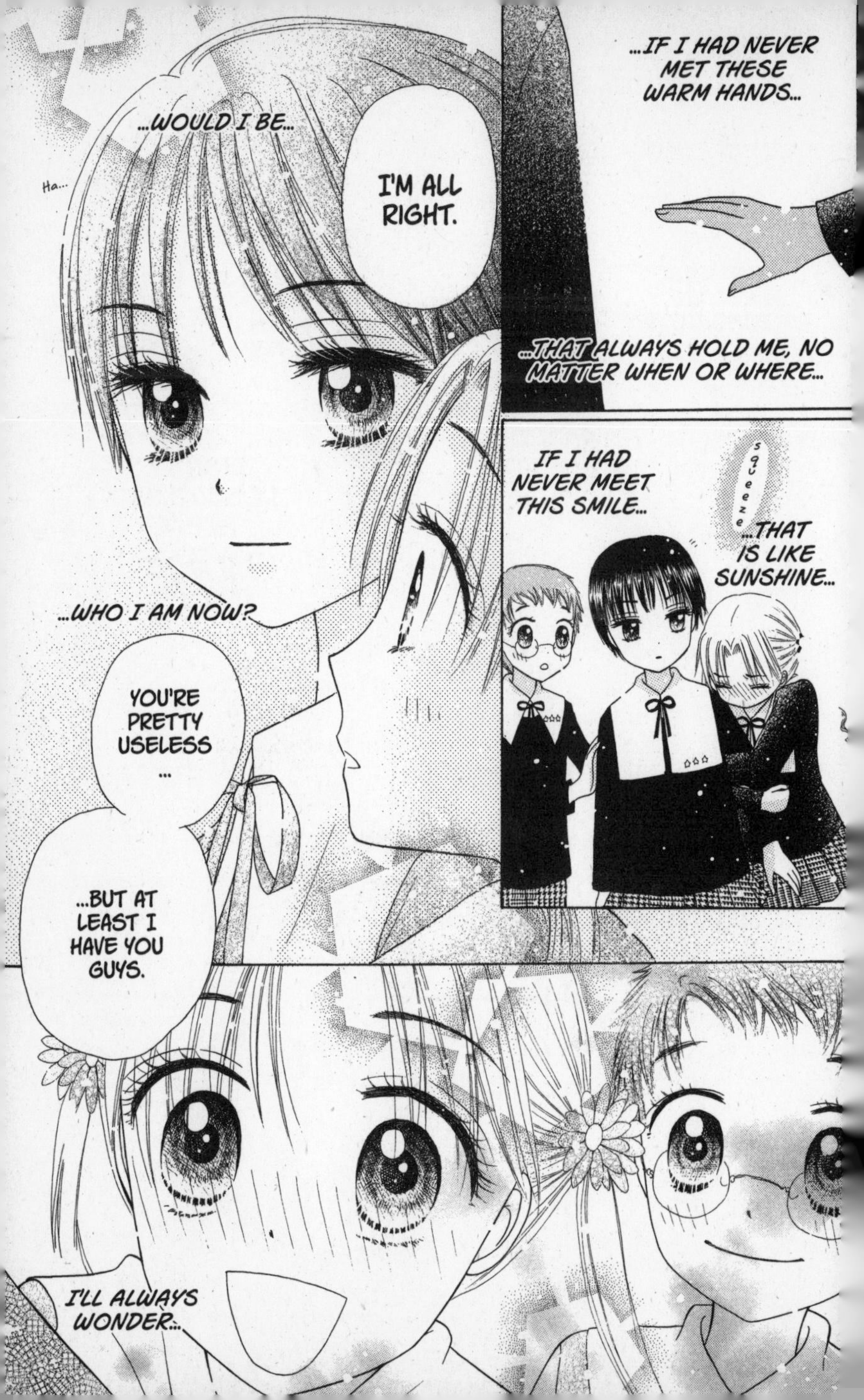
...IF I HAD NEVER MET THESE WARM HANDS...
...THAT ALWAYS HOLD ME, NO MATTER WHEN OR WHERE...
IF I HAD NEVER MEET THIS SMILE...
squeeze
...THAT IS LIKE SUNSHINE...
I'M ALL RIGHT.
...WOULD I BE...
Ha...
...WHO I AM NOW?
YOU'RE PRETTY USELESS ...
...BUT AT LEAST I HAVE YOU GUYS.
I'LL ALWAYS WONDER...

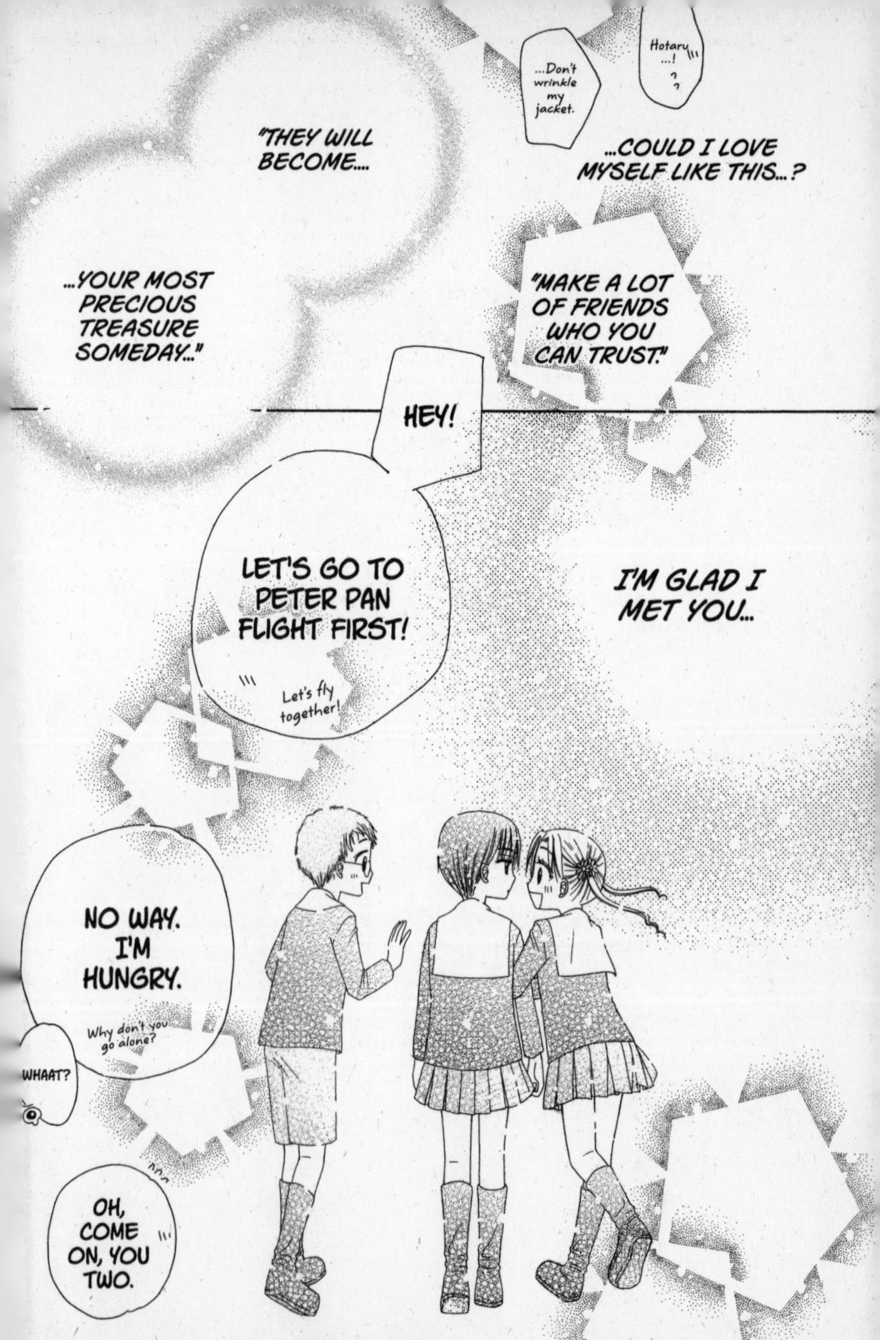
Hotaru...!
...Don't wrinkle my jacket.
...COULD I LOVE MYSELF LIKE THIS...?
"MAKE A LOT OF FRIENDS WHO YOU CAN TRUST."
"THEY WILL BECOME...
...YOUR MOST PRECIOUS TREASURE SOMEDAY..."
HEY!
I'M GLAD I MET YOU...
LET'S GO TO PETER PAN FLIGHT FIRST!
Let's fly together!
NO WAY. I'M HUNGRY.
Why don't you go alone?
WHAAT?
OH, COME ON, YOU TWO.

Chapter 22/End

Next time in

The Alice Festival is coming to a close, but the surprises aren't over for Mikan and her friends quite yet! Things get out of hand with Narumi's musical when an accident takes out some of the performers, and Mikan has to step in as the star of the show. But what will happen when she and Luca have to kiss on stage?! And as if that's not enough, as soon as the kids are back in class, it's time for exams, and Mikan is in for some bad news when the scores come back.

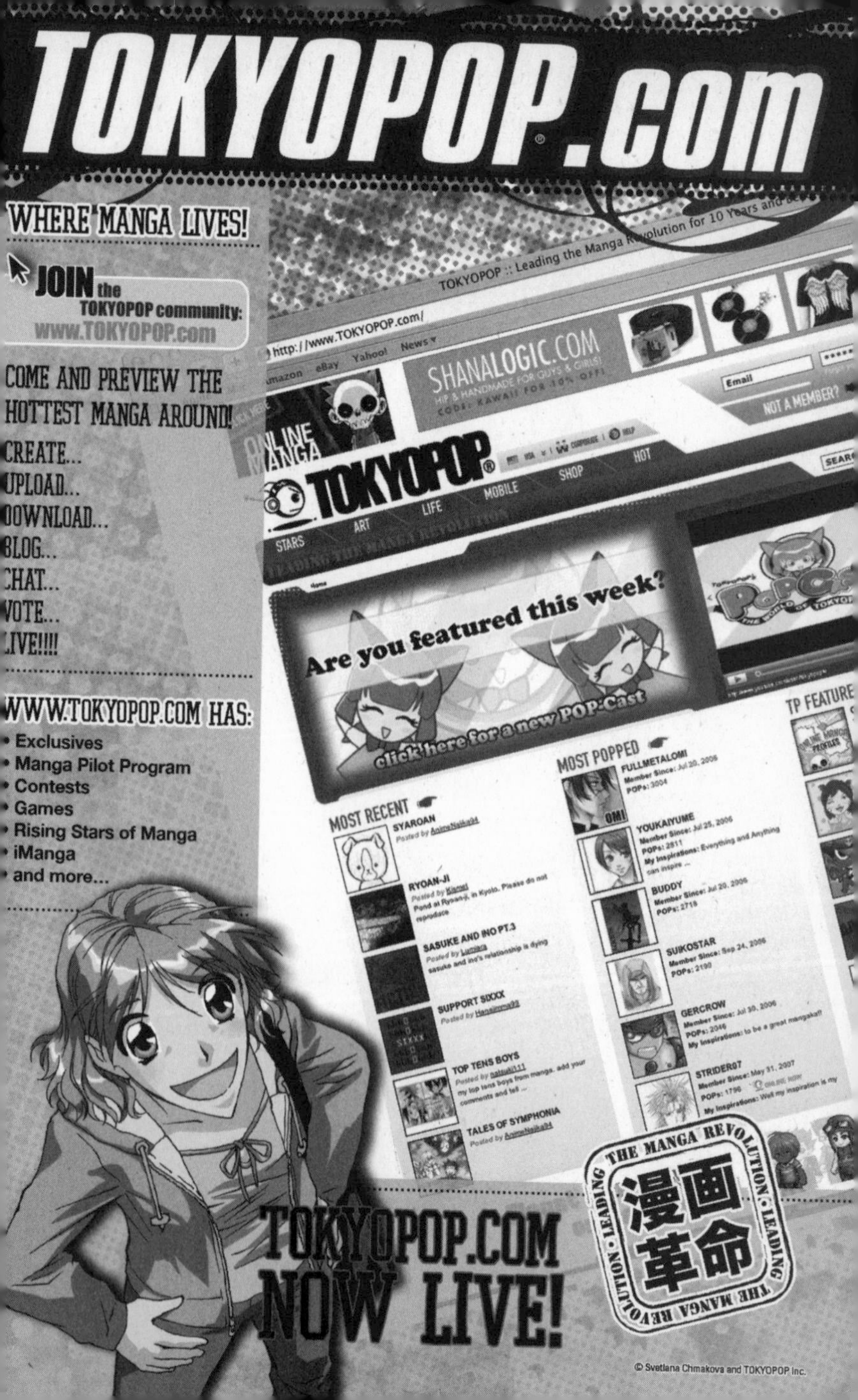
TOKYOPOP®.com
WHERE MANGA LIVES!
JOIN the TOKYOPOP community: www.TOKYOPOP.com
COME AND PREVIEW THE HOTTEST MANGA AROUND!
CREATE...
UPLOAD...
DOWNLOAD...
BLOG...
CHAT...
VOTE...
LIVE!!!!
WWW.TOKYOPOP.COM HAS:
• Exclusives
• Manga Pilot Program
• Contests
• Games
• Rising Stars of Manga
• iManga
• and more...
TOKYOPOP :: Leading the Manga Revolution for 10 Years and Beyond
http://www.TOKYOPOP.com/
SHANALOGIC.COM
HIP & HANDMADE FOR GUYS & GIRLS!
CODE: KAWAII FOR 10% OFF!
NOT A MEMBER?
ONLINE MANGA
TOKYOPOP®
STARS
ART
LIFE
MOBILE
SHOP
HOT
Are you featured this week?
click here for a new POP-Cast
MOST RECENT
SYAROAN
RYOAN-JI
SASUKE AND INO PT.3
SUPPORT SIXXX
TOP TENS BOYS
TALES OF SYMPHONIA
MOST POPPED
FULLMETALOMI
YOUKAIYUME
BUDDY
SUIKOSTAR
GERCROW
STRIDER07
TP FEATURES
TOKYOPOP.COM NOW LIVE!
LEADING THE MANGA REVOLUTION
漫画革命
© Svetlana Chmakova and TOKYOPOP Inc.

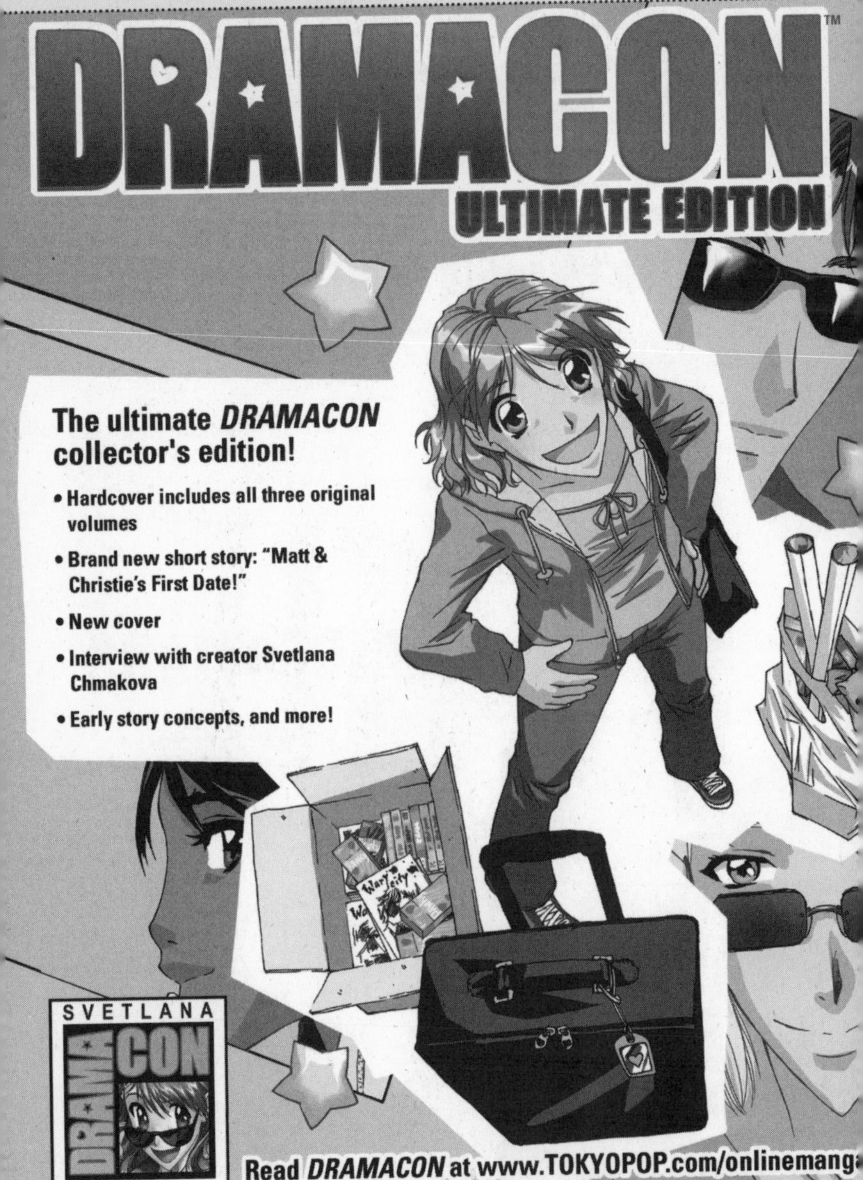
DRAMACON™
ULTIMATE EDITION
The ultimate DRAMACON collector's edition!
• Hardcover includes all three original volumes
• Brand new short story: "Matt & Christie's First Date!"
• New cover
• Interview with creator Svetlana Chmakova
• Early story concepts, and more!
SVETLANA
DRAMACON
CHMAKOVA
Read DRAMACON at www.TOKYOPOP.com/onlinemanga
© Svetlana Chmakova and TOKYOPOP Inc.

STOP!

This is the back of the book.
You wouldn't want to spoil a great ending!

This book is printed "manga-style," in the authentic Japanese right-to-left format. Since none of the artwork has been flipped or altered, readers get to experience the story just as the creator intended. You've been asking for it, so TOKYOPOP® delivered: authentic, hot-off-the-press, and far more fun!

DIRECTIONS

If this is your first time reading manga-style, here's a quick guide to help you understand how it works.

It's easy... just start in the top right panel and follow the numbers. Have fun, and look for more 100% authentic manga from TOKYOPOP®!